QUEER TRAFFIC

dissident acts

A series edited by
Macarena Gómez-Barris and Diana Taylor

Queer Traffic

Sex, Panic, Free Trade

JENNIFER TYBURCZY

DUKE UNIVERSITY PRESS
Durham and London
2025

Printed in the United States of America on acid-free paper ∞
Project Editor: Ihsan Taylor
Designed by A. Mattson Gallagher
Typeset in Minion Pro and Comma Base
by Westchester Publishing Services

Library of Congress Cataloging-in-Publication Data
Names: Tyburczy, Jennifer, author.
Title: Queer traffic : sex, panic, free trade / Jennifer Tyburczy.
Other titles: Dissident acts.
Description: Durham : Duke University Press, 2025. | Series:
Dissident acts | Includes bibliographical references and index.
Identifiers: LCCN 2025004879 (print)
LCCN 2025004880 (ebook)
ISBN 9781478032236 (paperback)
ISBN 9781478028963 (hardcover)
ISBN 9781478061182 (ebook)
Subjects: LCSH: Sex industry—Mexico. | Sex industry—United
States. | Sex work—Economic aspects—United States. | Sex
work—Economic aspects—Mexico. | Prostitution—Mexico. |
Prostitution—United States. | Queer theory. | Intersectionality
(Sociology) | Capitalism.
Classification: LCC HQ151.A5 T938 2025 (print) | LCC HQ151.A5
(ebook) | DDC 306.740972—dc23/eng/20250221
LC record available at https://lccn.loc.gov/2025004879
LC ebook record available at https://lccn.loc.gov/2025004880

ISBN 978148094524 (ebook other)

Cover art: Lechedevirgen Trimegisto, *México exhumado*.
Photo by Herani Enríquez HacHe. Courtesy of the artist.

This book is freely available in an open access edition thanks
to the generous support of the University of California
Libraries.

¡From Palestine to Mexico, all the walls have got to go!

CONTENTS

ILLUSTRATIONS

ABBREVIATIONS

BDSM	bondage and discipline, domination and submission, and sadomasochism
CBP	US Customs and Border Protection
CUSFTA	Canada-US Free Trade Agreement
CUSMA	Canada-US-Mexico Agreement (also known as USMCA and T-MEC)
EU	European Union
EZLN	Ejército Zapatista de Liberación Nacional (Zapatistas)
FBI	Federal Bureau of Investigation
FTA	free-trade agreement
GATT	General Agreement on Tariffs and Trade
IMF	International Monetary Fund
INEGI	Instituto Nacional de Estadística y Geografía (National Institute of Statistics and Geography)
INTERPOL	International Criminal Police Organization
IP	intellectual property
IPR	intellectual property rights

LGBTQ	lesbian, gay, bisexual, trans, queer
MERCOSUR	Mercado Común del Sur (Southern Common Market)
NAFTA	North American Free Trade Agreement
OECD	Organisation for Economic Co-operation and Development
PAN	Partido Acción Nacional (National Action Party)
PRD	Partido de la Revolución Democrática (Party of the Democratic Revolution)
PRI	Partido Revolucionario Institucional (Institutional Revolution Party)
PSA	public service announcement
TLCAN	Tratado de Libre Comercio de América del Norte (NAFTA)
T-MEC	Tratado entre México, Estados Unidos, y Canada (Treaty between Mexico, the United States, and Canada)
TRIPS	Trade-Related Aspects of Intellectual Property Rights
UNAM	Universidad Nacional Autónoma de México (National Autonomous University)
USMCA	US-Mexico-Canada Agreement (NAFTA 2.0)
USTR	US Trade Representative
WTO	World Trade Organization

NAFTA's Bottoms: An Opening

How you hold Hugo García Manríquez's poetry book determines who is on top and who is on the bottom. His bilingual translation of the North American Free Trade Agreement (NAFTA) (in English, *Anti-Humboldt: A Reading of the North American Free Trade Agreement*; in Castellano Spanish, *Anti-Humboldt: Una lectura del Tratado de Libre Comercio de América del Norte* [TLCAN]) uses a book design that assumes the position—top or bottom but never a switch (see figs. FM.1 and FM.2).[1] To produce this bilingual and bi-positional artifact, García Manríquez's 2014 poem works through the official English- and Spanish-language documents of the agreement (which are also the US and Mexican documents), with a title, "Anti-Humboldt," that refers to the nineteenth-century German explorer and naturalist Alexander von Humboldt, a symbol of colonial knowledge production against whom his poem performs its titular oppositional "anti." Through a poesis of disorganization and erasure, García Manríquez's poem unravels NAFTA and, with its seemingly anachronistic title, locates NAFTA's origins in the history of European expansion in wealth, knowledge, technologies, and commodities. The placing of the documents in vertical hierarchy, one inverted by the other, an inversion that highlights how language differences create conceptual ghosts and make some terms pregnant with meaning, performs the incommensurability of the two documents and how, in many ways, it thinks against itself, undoes itself in translation.

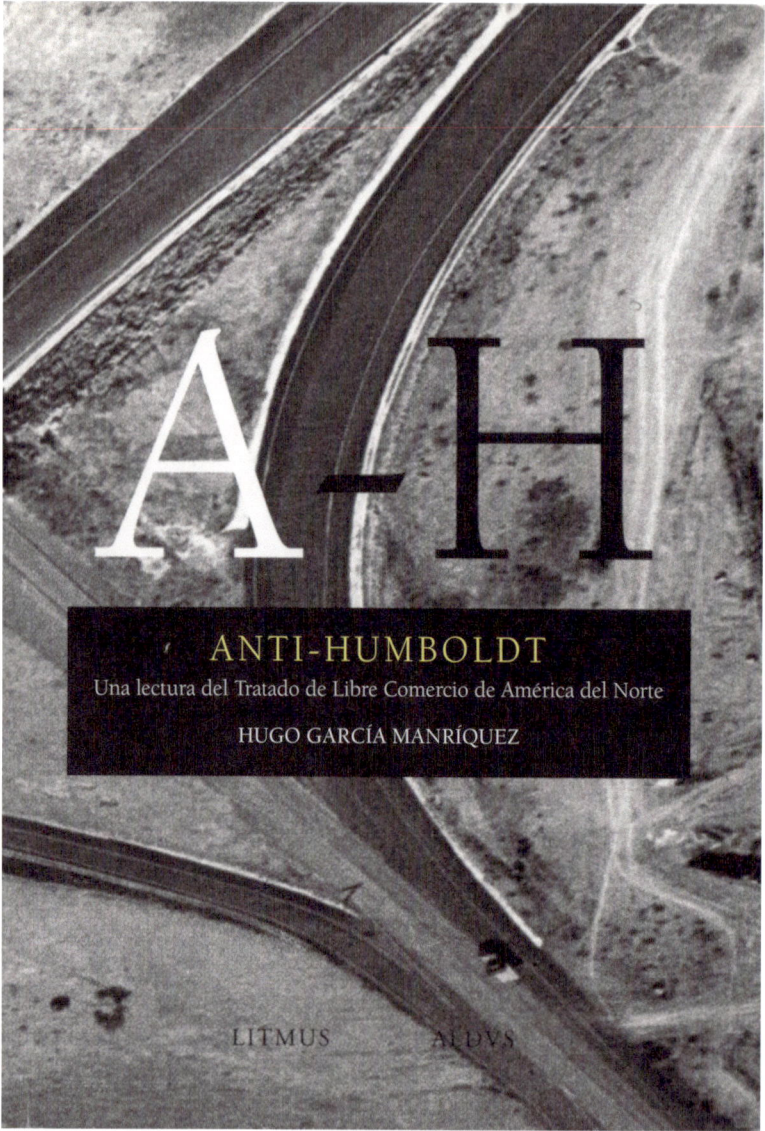

FM.1 Hugo García Manríquez, front cover of *Anti-Humboldt: Una lectura del Tratado de Libre Comercio de América del Norte* (Litmus Press, 2014).

Hugo García Manríquez, back cover of *Anti-Humboldt: A Reading of the North American Free Trade Agreement* (Litmus Press, 2014).

The performance of free trade depends on the claim, made in NAFTA itself, that "the English, French, and Spanish texts of this Agreement are equally authentic" (NAFTA, article 2206). This performance obfuscates the gaps in translation and the unequal power dynamics and colonial histories that always already dictated the terms of what was called, in the document's English name, "an agreement," and in its Spanish name, "*un tratado*," or treaty. Although "treaty" and "agreement" are collapsed as synonyms, and most international law experts do view the terms as interchangeable, *treaty* is a more specific term of legal binding between two or more states for a necessary or vital matter, while *agreement* is a more generalized term for a mutual agreement between parties. These terms and their nuanced yet ignored differences harken back to another pivotal moment in US-Mexico relations: the 1848 Treaty of Guadalupe Hidalgo, in which Mexico was forced to cede 55 percent of its territory to the United States. The collective memory of Guadalupe Hidalgo, often viewed by the transnational left as NAFTA's other imperialist bookend, oriented Mexico away from collaboration with the United States. Not even a century and a half later, however, then-President (and NAFTA signer) Carlos Salinas de Gortari embraced international trade and foreign investment, thereby sealing Mexico's asymmetrical "special relationship" with the United States. NAFTA kicked the door open to a new era during which Mexico would be coerced, through the ongoing accumulation of foreign debt, to participate in the hemispheric designs of the United States. The transnationalization of the ongoing War on Drugs and the Plan Mérida initiative, where, under the guise of combating drug trafficking, Mexico militarized its southern border with Guatemala to stem Central American migration, are two notable examples of the wide-reaching changes NAFTA provoked. Following García Manríquez's poem, I want to bracket these mismatched translations beyond their literal meaning to show how NAFTA and TLCAN perform as two intimately related yet frictive documents of the negotiations themselves and *as* performances that rehearse two overlapping and at the same time competing concepts of free trade (figs. FM.3 and FM.4).

The instantiation of NAFTA/TLCAN in 1994 might be viewed as a climax, the money shot of colonial and neoimperial capitalism whose linguistic and applied contradictions engendered an intimate slippage between the two documents, their interpretations, and applications. As García Manríquez's poem makes clear, NAFTA is not only one document and, despite its attempts to force harmonized sameness, there is no one way to read NAFTA. Embracing but also moving beyond an approach to such documents as texts, I propose that we view the translations of NAFTA/TLCAN as cultural artifacts of free trade. This view allows us to ask, what do we learn from cultural flows such as translations and, in the instance of NAFTA/TLCAN, willful *mistrans-lations*, as their terms of engagement shift and get adapted across borders? My hope is that this conceptual extension of what is considered the object and objective of free trade can help to make sense of a paradox in which the rhetoric of antiglobalization can be harnessed by, in one instance, the Zapatistas and left Chicana writers such as Cherríe Moraga, who described NAFTA as "the final surrender of the Mexican people's sovereign rights to land and livelihood" (1993, 229), and, in another instance, by Donald Trump, who in 2016 declared NAFTA "the worst trade deal maybe ever signed, anywhere" (Presidential debate, Hofstra University, September 26, 2016). NAFTA/TLCAN, as demonstrated through García Manríquez's placement of the two, one on top of the other, reveals the division of these translations into hierarchies of power, determined by their colonial histories, and the real-world violences that can emerge in the language gaps. At the same time, he gives his readers an opportunity to envision the queer potential of their intimate comingling. These gaps, made to appear and at other times dis-appear throughout the poem, are not just legal loopholes. Rather, they are openings within which to "dive from a harmonizing codification" (García Manríquez 2014, 75) and resist the fragmentation of our worlds, and all of us in them, into disposable commodities.

When it comes to conversations about global domination, broadly speak-ing but particularly in terms of the economy, Mexico is often cast as the bottom, what Octavio Paz has called *la chingada*, or the fucked. In attribut-ing to Mexico the state of being fucked, Paz would have us view Mexico as the sexually penetrated and denigrated other, owing to Mexico's entwined colonial history with Spain, France, England, and the United States. Paz's theory of *la chingada*, found in his iconic book *El laberinto de la soledad* (*The Labyrinth of Solitude*), describes a positionality for understanding Mexico's twentieth-century identity. One of the book's essays, "Los hijos de

FOLLOWING PAGES:

FM.3   Hugo García Manríquez, *Anti-Humboldt: Una lectura del Tratado de Libre Comercio de América del Norte*, NAFTA/TLCAN preámbulo (Litmus Press, 2014).

FM.4   Hugo García Manríquez, *Anti-Humboldt: A Reading of the North American Free Trade Agreement*, NAFTA/TLCAN preamble (Litmus Press, 2014).

PREÁMBULO

Los gobiernos de los Estados Unidos Mexicanos (México), de Canadá y de los Estados Unidos de América (Estado Unidos), decididos a:

REAFIRMAR los lazos especiales de amistad y cooperación entre sus naciones;

CONTRIBUIR al desarrollo armónico, a la expansión del comercio mundial y a ampliar l cooperación internacional;

CREAR un mercado más extenso y seguro para los bienes y los servicios producidos en su territorios; REDUCIR las distorsiones en el comercio;

ESTABLECER reglas claras y de beneficio mutuo para su intercambio comercial;

ASEGURAR un marco comercial previsible para la planeación de las actividades productivas y de la inversión;

DESARROLLAR sus respectivos derechos y obligaciones derivados del Acuerdo General sobre Aranceles Aduaneros y Comercio, así como de otros instrumentos bilaterales y multilaterales de cooperación;

FORTALECER la competitividad de sus empresas en los mercados mundiales;

ALENTAR la innovación y la creatividad y fomentar el comercio de bienes y servicios que esté protegidos por derechos de propiedad intelectual;

CREAR nuevas oportunidades de empleo, mejorar las condiciones laborales y los niveles de vid en sus respectivo territorios;

EMPRENDER todo lo anterior de manera congruente con la protección y la conservación de ambiente;

PRESERVAR su capacidad para salvaguardar el bienestar público; PROMOVER el desarrollo sostenible;

REFORZAR la elaboración y la aplicación de leyes y reglamentos en materia ambiental;

PROTEGER, fortalecer y hacer efectivos los derechos fundamentales de sus trabajadores;

HAN ACORDADO

PREÁMBULO

...gobiernos de los Estados Unidos Mexicanos, Gobierno de Canadá y de los ... ... de América, decididos a:

...FIRMAR los lazos especiales de amistad y cooperación entre sus naciones;

...NTRIBUIR al desarrollo armónico, a la expansión del comercio mundial y a ampliar la ...peración internacional;

...AR un mercado más extenso y seguro para los bienes y los servicios producidos en sus ...torios, REDUCIR las distorsiones ... en el comercio;

...ABLECER reglas claras y de beneficio mutuo para su intercambio comercial;

...GURAR un marco comercial previsible para la planeación de las actividades productivas y de ...versión;

...ARROLLAR ... de respectivos derechos y obligaciones derivados del Acuerdo General sobre ...nceles Aduaneros y Comercio, así como de otros instrumentos bilaterales y multilaterales de ...peración;

...RTALECER la competitividad de sus empresas en los mercados mundiales;

...NTAR la innovación y la creatividad y fomentar el comercio de bienes y servicios que estén ...egidos por derechos de propiedad intelectual;

...AR nuevas oportunidades de empleo, mejorar las condiciones laborales y los niveles de vida ...us respectivos territorios;

...PRENDER todo lo anterior de manera congruente con la protección y la conservación del ...iente;

...SERVAR su capacidad para salvaguardar el bienestar público, PROMOVER el desarrollo ...enible;

...ORZAR la elaboración y la aplicación de leyes y reglamentos en materia ambiental; y

...TEGER, fortalecer y hacer efectivos los derechos fundamentales de sus trabajadores;

...N ACORDADO:

13

PREAMBLE

The Government of Canada, the Government of the United Mexican States and the Government of the United States of America, resolved to:

STRENGTHEN the special bonds of friendship and cooperation among their nations;

CONTRIBUTE to the harmonious development and expansion of world trade and provide a catalyst to broader international cooperation;

CREATE an expanded and secure market for the goods and services produced in their territories;

REDUCE distortions to trade;

ESTABLISH clear and mutually advantageous rules governing their trade;

ENSURE a predictable commercial framework for business planning and investment;

BUILD on their respective rights and obligations under the General Agreement on Tariffs and Trade and other multilateral and bilateral instruments of cooperation;

ENHANCE the competitiveness of their firms in global markets;

FOSTER creativity and innovation, and promote trade in goods and services that are the subject of intellectual property rights;

CREATE new employment opportunities and improve working conditions an living standards in their respective territories;

UNDERTAKE each of the preceding in a manner consistent with environmental protection and conservation;

PRESERVE their flexibility to safeguard the public welfare;

PROMOTE sustainable development;

STRENGTHEN the development and enforcement of environmental laws and regulations; and

PROTECT, enhance and enforce basic workers' rights;

HAVE AGREED as follows:

PREAMBLE

The Government of Canada, the Government of the United Mexican States and the Government of the United States of America, **resolved to:**

STRENGTHEN the special bonds of friendship and cooperation among their nations;

CONTRIBUTE to **the harmonious** development **and expansion** of world trade and provide a catalyst to broader international cooperation;

CREATE an expanded and secure market for the goods and services produced in their territories;

REDUCE **distortions** to trade;

ESTABLISH clear **and mutually** advantageous rules governing their trade;

ENSURE a **predict**able commercial framework for business planning and investment;

BUILD on their respective rights and obligations under the General Agreement on Tariffs and Trade and other multilateral and bilateral instruments of cooperation;

ENHANCE the competitiveness of their firms in global markets;

FOSTER creativity and innovation, and promote trade in goods and services that are the subject of intellectual property rights;

CREATE new employment opportunities and improve working conditions and living standards in their respective territories;

UNDERTAKE **each of the preceding** in a manner consistent with environmental protection and conservation;

PRESERVE their flexibility to safeguard the public welfare;

PROMOTE sustainable development;

STRENGTHEN the development and enforcement of environmental laws and regulations; and

PROTECT, enhance and enforce basic workers' rights;

HAVE AGREED as follows:

la Malinche" (The children of Malinche), unpacks the bottom/top relationship between the Indigenous woman who came to be called Malinche (also known as Malintzín and Malinali, her Indigenous names; or Doña Mariana to the Christians) and the conquistador Hernán Cortés. In calling Malinche and her offspring *chingada*, Paz suggests that Indigenous peoples in Mexico (*los pueblos originarios*, the original peoples) literally got fucked by the arrival of the Spanish to the Americas. From this act of getting fucked emerged the fabled beginning of *mestizaje*, a racial mixture between *el chingón* (he who fucks, who is on top: in this instance, the white Spanish conquistador, Hernán Cortés) and she who is fucked or rendered bottom (Malinche as a stand-in for *los pueblos originarios*). Cast as the sometimes victim, sometimes hero, and sometimes traitor of Mexico for performing the roles of translator (slave?) and lover (survivor?), she is pitied, honored, and hated, even as the legendary roots of *Mexicanidad* and the racial politics of *mestizaje* rhetorically hinge on a history of sexual acts between Indigenous and Iberian bodies. The circulation of *mestizaje* as a concept and a performance of hybrid identity, as Licia Fiol-Matta has shown in *A Queer Mother for the Nation*, depended on the assimilation of Indigenous difference, the occlusion and erasure of Blackness, the adulation and celebration of Eurocentrism and whiteness, and "matrimonial eugenics" that policed sex, concentrating on those bodies with reproductive capabilities (2001, 82–83). Embedded within this mythic racialized identity story, *Mexicanidad*, while seen as the "bottom" in the free-trade threesome that NAFTA summons, contains a multitude of subject positions that go beyond the binary of *el chingón* and *la chingada*. As we shall see in the pages that follow, bottoms can be bratty, switchy, toppy, and full of (sexual) power.[2]

As one of the Americas' infamous power bottoms, Malinche remains a frequently cited figure in the Mexican cultural imaginary, but outside Chicana feminist reclamations of her as *chingona* (she who fucks; badass woman) (e.g., Alarcón 1983; Alcalá 2001), she is most often invoked in everyday and patriarchal speech as *malinchista*, a term that denounces those who seemingly prefer foreign cultural production to those objects *hecho en México* (made in Mexico). The message encoded in the term *malinchista*, a derivation of *malinchismo* or the traitorous attraction to the foreign to the detriment of the nation, points to the ongoing popular prevalence of seeing the Mexican condition as one of *la chingada*. Charges of *malinchista* (being like Malinche) and marking one's body with the signs of another culture gradually took on new contours in the years following NAFTA's passage, when more foreign goods, particularly from the United States (but not always made or assembled there), flowed through the formal market in monumental volume and with great speed. Mexico's pornographic proximity to the United States, conjuring Mexican autocrat Porfirio Díaz's oft-cited national lament "pobre México, tan lejos de dios y tan cerca de Estados Unidos" (poor Mexico, so far from god and so close to the United States),[3] is marked, then, not only by its geographic situation "below" or "under" Canada and the United States but also by NAFTA's rendering of it as the penetrated nation.

Mexico is portrayed as the penetrable exception to the ecstatic register within which the Anglo dominance of North America's impenetrable economic body is otherwise performed. In other words, the ecstatic register is the one where free trade is transcendent across three nations, even though only two (colonizing) nations benefit from it. Perhaps mirroring the gendered, raced, and sexed politics of *mestizaje* and its obscuring of certain racial histories of struggle, the arrival of free trade in the 1980s and 1990s among the formerly protectionist nations of the United States, Mexico, and Canada summoned a new regionality, the NAFTA-created expanse of "North America." For a time, this view of a collective North American region relegated the nationalist charge of *malinchista* to the pre-NAFTA past. Nation-states, if not always their people, embraced abstract claims to freedom and progress that could be embodied through the trappings of culture, but only in connection to the colonial conditions of cultural flows. When translated through the body politics of sartorial style and irreverent appropriation, drinking Coca-Cola or wearing a pair of Levi's jeans was no longer considered *malinchista*.

Rather than always already assuming the pathological penetrability of Mexico within the free-trade market, what J. K. Gibson-Graham problematizes as "the scene of abject submission" (2006, 94), I prefer to cast *malinchismo* as an embodiment of what Juana María Rodríguez calls "Latina longings" expressed "through a gesture of submission, a submission that engulfs, transforms, and redeploys that which sought to subjugate it" (2014, 93). Thus in this book, I don't seek to reclaim the *malinchista*; instead I want to wage a queer critique of the charge of *malinchismo*, a critique that thinks beyond the nostalgic return to a romanticized pre–free trade or pre-conquest world. Beyond the positing of her sole recuperative value in reproductive life as mother (to the nation or biological children), and in line with Chicana feminists who have explored the radical potentials of viewing *malinchismo* as an antipatriarchal interjection akin to lesbianism (Alarcón 1989; Moraga 1983), I too refuse Paz's depiction of her as "una figura que representa a las indias, fascinadas, violadas o seducidas por los españoles" (a figure that represents the Indigenous, fascinated, raped, or seduced by the Spanish) (1959, 78). Instead, I am interested in how Malinche, alongside other female, feminine, femme, and/or feminized figures who have been accused of being traitors to the nation under colonial and capitalist imperatives, uses sex and sexuality as tactics of subversive (mis)translation.[4] She does so not merely to survive but also to find, foment, and take pleasure through everyday practices that exceed resistance. Indeed, throughout the book, I look to explicit sex as a tactical means of perverting free trade's performative (and normative) desires. Following performance artist Jesusa Rodríguez, who enacted a wily and sexy version of Malinche as "the first cunnilingual translator of Mesoamerica" (2003, 232), the *malinchista* of free trade does not always and everywhere translate in service to the colonizer. Rather she uses the tongue to divert the course of colonialism's fantasies, one of which is free trade. As performance artist Carmelita Tropicana once cheekily said, "You've got to be multilingual. I am very good with the tongue" (in the film *Carmelita Tropicana: Your Kunst Is Your Waffen* [1994]).

In other words, Malinche is not Karl Marx's prostitute, what Marx held up as the quintessence of capitalist exploitation. She is more akin to Roderick Ferguson's revision of Marx's "whore" as the "black drag-queen prostitute" (2003, 1), strutting her stuff along the Christopher Street pier in Marlon Riggs's film *Tongues Untied* (1989). She is pushed to the dangerous margins of the city by so-called urban renewal projects engineered by Rudolph Giuliani, first in New York and then exported through his hired consultancy in Latin American cities such as Rio de Janeiro and Mexico City (Davis 2013; Mountz and Curran 2009). Since the time of Marx and the inception of capitalist critique, then, the view that sex work is "only a specific expression of the general prostitution of the laborer" (Marx and Engels 1988, 100) sets the expressly sexual woman, whether she be queer, cisgender (cis), straight, or transgender (trans), vulnerable to the charges of dupe, slut, predator, parasite, failure, and victim.[5] The long history of erotophobic discourses that manufacture sex panics around sexual labor and commerce can be traced throughout the Malinche archive: hegemonically, she can only ever be cast and remembered as a betrayer to the *pueblos originarios*.

But talk that conflates all sex work with the ultimate form of capitalist labor exploitation is more well traveled than the women it claims to care about. Sex and trade, then, share a particular kind of relationship to power, one that cannot be sufficiently analyzed using the same tools that other NAFTA scholars such as Alyshia Gálvez (2018) have honed when examining the cultural influences of, in the instance of her study, the dumping of US government–subsidized corn into Mexico; nor can sex and trade be examined solely through the scholarship on illicit flows (e.g., drugs, guns, animals) that constitute both the underworld and the byproduct of trade liberalization. In this body of literature, the circulation of sexual goods and labor is either overlooked or evacuated from conversations on the licit flow of banal items such as car parts, dairy, or corn or else it is lethally reduced to yet another criminal flow. *Queer Traffic* seeks to build on the literature of free-trade flows to bring to light the sex of seemingly nonsexual trade, while also showing how the particularities of sex on the move require a queer performance studies lens that attends to the materiality of the body and that values pleasure, sexual deviance, and gender dissidence as indispensable nodes in the global struggle for race, class, and disability justice.

In her elegant treatise *The Intimacies of Four Continents* (2015), Lisa Lowe details how trade is one phenomenon that can show us how the intimate bringing together of nations (or in her study continents) along the axis of what is assumed to be an almost Maussian gift-exchange exercise in international friendship belies the asymmetrical power relations that trade both reflects and produces. While Lowe and other scholars have seized on "intimacy" as both a subject and a heuristic for understanding how global economic relations influence contexts of human relatedness, this book uses sex—the explicit, raw, and messy kind—to rethink the concept of free trade. In keeping with queer and feminist scholarship on intimacy "that undo[es] familiar connotations about 'private' life by emphasizing its historical and social situation" (Wilson 2012, 32), I take the work on sexuality and globalization to a fleshier level of inquiry to embrace the potential desire for such imagined and embodied "bottomness."

This is not just any bottomhood. Queer scholars and artists have thoroughly reclaimed bottomhood as a site of power and pleasure that recycles shame and abjection (Fung 1991; Nguyen 2014; Scott 2010; Stockton 2006), refuses the absolute link between masochism and the abdication of control (Musser 2014), expands notions of receptivity for femme lesbian and queer sexuality (Cvetkovich 1995; the film *Untitled Fucking* [2013]), and positions anality as a productive model for thinking about sexual subject formation in Latin America (Calderón/Flandes 2016; Falconí Trávez 2021; PachaQueer 2016; Pelúcio 2014; Pierce 2018; Sáez and Carrascosa 2011). Xiomara Verenice Cervantes-Gómez (2020, 2024) has even resituated Paz's essay to think about the ways in which homosex, the sexual binary *pasivo/activo*, and the cis-centric logic of *lo chingado* (the sexual bottom, the fucked) and *el chingón* (the sexual top, the fucker) determine the contours of the Mexican nation-building project and the vertical hierarchy of world domination. NAFTA's bottoms are certainly penetrated—a receptivity pertinent to all three NAFTA nations—but they are not, necessarily, topped or dominated.

Stories about nation-states as tops or bottoms, as dominant or submissive, obscure how free trade's tentacles suction and squeeze everyday people both within and across national boundaries. These stories cover over the catastrophic abuses of power enacted by the United States and Canada against Mexico, as well as the intranational atrocities waged against embodied difference across and within the three NAFTA-signing nations. They reveal the transnational and subnational collaborations to exact such abuses under the banner of "friendship," a rhetorical flourish that greases the wheels of free trade and its fetish for market-led foreign policy and multinational corporations. In other words, "a view from the bottom" (Nguyen 2014) is a slippery vantage point but one necessary to traverse new terrain outside normative top/down argumentation waged both for and against NAFTA. It propels me to examine other objects, people, and their circulations already disqualified as inconsequential market actors or enemies of free-trade capitalism. I do so as a queer performance studies scholar to ask, how is NAFTA performed, and what does NAFTA want? How does NAFTA move culture, and how is NAFTA itself a cultural form that moves? I raise these questions both within the NAFTA document itself and through its adjacent policies with a particular focus on the performance of NAFTA and its myriad influences on sexual subjectivity and practice.

Certainly, the style of free trade promulgated during the 1980s and 1990s spread the proverbial legs of North America to all kinds of cultural flows in this trinational ménage à trois. In this book, I hope to add to the queer conversation on power and positionality to reveal how sex informs the coloniality of free trade from the 1980s to the present and how ideas about class, race, sexuality, disability, and gender often determine which kinds of embodied differences are regulated to *malinchista* status and thus propelled into highly precarious realms dictated by surveillance, criminalization, and death. Throughout, I celebrate those who have ingeniously repurposed, *rasquache*-style, the coloniality of free trade to forge nonnormative circuits of art and sexual exchange.[6]

Queer Traffic is thus aligned with those who break from the normative flows that free-trade infrastructures sanction as valuable and worthy of movement, even as it tracks the often-violent acts that are crucial performances of NAFTA-style free trade. I write this book for the *mayates* and the *chacales*, for the *maquilocas*, the lesbian transfeminists, the *maricas*, and the Two Spirit; for the sex workers, the pornographers, and the erotic performers; for trans women, such as Alexandra R. DeRuiz, crossing the border in high heels (2023), and Roxana Hernández, who struggled to survive (and lost that struggle) in the hole at the Cibola County Correctional Center; for the traffickers in life-giving drugs; for the pill dividers and stockpilers; and even, in some instances, for *los coyotes* or *los polleros* (coyotes, chicken herders), slang terms for what the human security regime calls "human traffickers" and "people smugglers."[7] Following Cathy Cohen, I want to turn my attention to practices of deviance to act as a "witness to the power of those at the bottom, whose everyday life decisions challenge, or at least counter, the basic normative assumptions of a society intent on protecting structural and social inequalities under the guise of some normal and natural order to life" (2004, 33). While the United States, Canada, and Mexico rhetorically compete for who is most *chingada* by NAFTA, thereby weaponizing bottomness, I transcend this discourse to track a regional voice of dissidence and dissent across the imaginary coordinates of North America. I do so to uncover the fallaciousness of arguments made by the toxic white masculinity of the trinational and transnational capitalist class and to move beyond the essentialized gender constructs of Paz's essay to find pleasure, resistance, and solidarity in and with illegible, illicit, and illegal flows. As I write this in the fall of 2020 amid the COVID-19 pandemic, and the unflow that is global vaccine and therapeutics distribution, I invite a rethinking of the myth of global connectivity that NAFTA discourse sells. To follow the traces of NAFTA's sexual traffic unravels a queer tale, one that repurposes abjection into a radical and unruly otherwise to the cosmopolitan illusion of harmonized markets and transnational friendships under free trade.

This book went to press in the immediate aftermath of the 2024 presidential election. In the coming years, we will hear incessant talk about using tariffs as coercive foreign policy sticks to punish other nations, including Mexico and Canada. Panics over sex work, drugs (including abortion pills and gender-affirming-care), reproductive rights, and migration will be created and fortified. Rhetorically, these panics will be referred to as sex trafficking, drug trafficking, abortion trafficking, and human trafficking. They will consistently be invoked and framed as indisputable reasons to shut down the border, to build walls, to deport undocumented people, and to indict and incarcerate those who circulate life-giving and life-affirming medications and medical services. Trade experts may declare that unfettered free trade has come to an end. NAFTA (now the USMCA) may or may not be abandoned, obliterated, or renegotiated, as it was in 2020. What won't change is the use of trade as a border regulatory schema to surveil and demonize the movement of people and goods considered anathema to the normative values of an increasingly fascist world. As this book revisits the struggles of people who forged rich sexual social lives amid contexts of violence and criminalization in the lead-up to this moment, the tactical and deviant practices you'll read about will, I hope, inspire us to collectively pursue a different and queerer future.

Introduction

SEX ON THE MOVE

I was genuinely surprised when the Mexico City office of the Secretaría de Economía (Secretary of Economy) responded to my email asking about the flows of sexual goods across the Mexico-US border. It was 2012, eighteen years after the North American Free Trade Agreement, or NAFTA, went into effect (1994). These men, most likely US-trained neoclassical economists, responded that my questions intrigued them and requested I meet with them at their offices in la Colonia Condesa.[1] I entered the towering glass and concrete building, had my bag scanned, and received a lanyard that marked me as *visitante* (visitor). After ascending to the designated floor, I was greeted by a room full of suited Mexican businessmen gathered around a desk too small for all of us to sit comfortably. Ignoring the discomfort, I restated my questions: how can we begin to map the circuits, quantify the volume, and review the styles and brands for, say, dildos imported into Mexico from the United States? After giving my inquiry some thought, they explained that it would be impossible. They told me that, unlike in the free-trade agreement (FTA) between the United States and Colombia, there is no "adult novelty" or "erotic sector" designation in NAFTA.[2] NAFTA, they explained, organizes objects by material. Thus, if we wanted to track the importation to Mexico of largely China-made, US-distributed dildos, we would have to wade through the glass, silicone, metal, VixSkin, and any of the other materials that go into producing dildos in the twenty-first century. Dildos as such are never discussed in NAFTA. As a particular kind of sexual good, they become lost in thousands of different material descriptors. They exist in the shadows of NAFTA.

In 2020, eight years after meeting with these businessmen, I came across a 2010 US *Customs Bulletin and Decisions* document that reviewed the singular case of the "Finger Vibrator." In this document, officials of the US Customs and Border Protection (CBP)—one Gail A. Hamill on behalf of Myles B. Harmon, director of the Commercial and Trade Facilitation Division of the CBP—address Sylvia Perreira of Eagle Global Logistics, a subsidiary of the global supply management company CEVA Freight, LLC. The letter's objective was to inform "Ms. Perreira" that there had been a ruling where the tariff classification for this "Finger Vibrator" had changed from "heading 8543, Harmonized Tariff Schedule of the United States ('HTSUS'), as 'Electrical machines and apparatus, having individual functions, not specified or included elsewhere in [chapter 85]'" (4) to "heading 9019, HTSUS, specifically in subheading 9019.10.20 as 'Massage apparatus'" (6). Unlike anything else I had read in, on, or about free trade, this ruling gets explicit. It defines the Finger Vibrator not only physically but also in regard to its corporeal use-value:

> The article concerned is the Finger Vibrator. The product measures approximately 2 inches long x .75 inches wide. It consists of a soft, silicone plastic, finger-shaped housing. The back of the device incorporates a ring shaped band which is placed over the user's finger. Within the housing is a battery-operated, electric vibrator mechanism. The Finger Vibrator is activated by pressing a button located on the bottom of the device. . . . [T]he Finger Vibrator's function is to provide a massage for "intimate personal pleasure." (US Customs and Border Protection 2010, 4)

The letter goes on to cite the *Oxford English Dictionary*'s definitions of "massage" as "the rubbing, kneading, or percussion of the muscles and joints of the body with the hands, usually performed by one person on another, esp. to relieve tension or pain" (5) and of "apparatus" as "the things collectively in which this preparation consists, and by which its processes are maintained; equipments, material, mechanism, machinery; material appendages or arrangements" (8). The CBP official even assigns body parts to which this "massage apparatus" can be applied, explicitly listing the "abdomen, feet, legs, back, arms, hands, face, etc." (5). Of course, "etc." is not an explicit identification so much as it is an implication of what cannot be spoken—the genitalia, nipples, anuses, and perinea against which the Finger Vibrator would most likely be applied for such "intimate personal pleasure."

Hamill went on to explain that the CBP's 2010 designation change and its attendant general rate of duty as "free" were reached after a series of Harmonized System (HS) Code attributions and revocations, which spanned the presidencies of Bill Clinton and George W. Bush. The CBP letter goes on to state that, despite CBP's "reasonable efforts" to find related rulings in their existing databases, "no further rulings have been found" (2) and that the duty-free rate and its HTSUS designation "are provided for convenience only and are subject to change" (6). In other words, sex toys like the Finger Vibrator are never fully or permanently integrated into the harmonization system through which free trade adjudicates whether an object is deemed intelligible and therefore legitimate and legal within free-trade infrastructure. This case therefore illuminates one way in which sexual goods inhabit the liminal space between the licit and the illicit and remain vulnerable to the whims of the CBP and other administrative gatekeepers that decide what and how goods, ideas, and services flow under NAFTA.

Depending on your geopolitical orientation, when you think about NAFTA you might think about supply management and the dairy industry, Ross Perot and his "giant sucking sound" to describe US jobs heading south to Mexico, Trump and Justin Trudeau at the Group of 7 (G7) in 2018; or NAFTA's chapter 19 and antidumping, or the sunset clause. First Nations' rights might come to mind, or you might focus on *maquilas* at the Mexico-US border, Subcomandante Marcos and the Zapatistas, cultures of extractivism and Canadian mines in Mexico, labor rights, the accumulation of capital, and a living wage. You might think about borders, deportations and US Immigration and Customs Enforcement (ICE), and people from other parts of the hemisphere migrating from conditions of great precarity or in search of the fictional "American (or Canadian or Mexican) dream." You might even look at your own body at this very moment, the clothes you're wearing, the brand of your shoes, the cellphone in your hands that you might glance at if you find this paragraph boring. Or perhaps you'll recall what you see (and don't see) at the grocery, the retail store, or that television series you've been pining away for but that's only available on Netflix USA.

To talk about NAFTA you don't, on the face of things at least, need to talk about sex. This book proposes, however, that paying attention to sex promotes a deeper understanding of NAFTA, the trade agreement's mundane iterations, and its broader significance. An FTA in effect since 1994, NAFTA has had the capacity to create an intimacy between objects and bodies, closing the geographic gap between what was once a distant object to become a domestic mainstay in the home, the retail space, the workspace, the play space, dungeon, or sex club. At the same time, it keeps certain morally proscribed objects at a distance, holding them out as exemptions to the "free-trade" rule of a borderless world but only for the exchange of certain goods and services. In what follows, I wage a queer analysis of NAFTA to expose how free trade can build new borders and modes of surveillance, a moral moat of administrative law to erect a patriarchal and paternalistic security regime wherein the state takes on the feigned benevolent role of protector of the people. It does so in the name of "national security" and the "war on terror" to create exemptions to the free-trade ideology of unregulated trade. NAFTA's unaccounted-for, criminal, and disposable flows and exchanges provide a glimpse into what qualified as "treasonous," "seditious," and "terroristic" in a world before the events of September 11, 2001. NAFTA weaponized border politics and surveillance in new and controlling ways. With the policies and politics activated under NAFTA, sexual outlaws— their cultures, ideas, and objects—became collateral damage. Throughout the book, I take a performance studies approach to show how NAFTA positions sexual culture as a threat to free trade, even as the diverse cultural and social performances I analyze invent informal and renegade pathways to life-giving and pleasure-enhancing scenarios.

Historic associations between sex and the highly racialized and classed categories of the criminal propel sex toward an embedded and often-frictive intersecting circuit with illicit flows of exchange (as in the drug and arms trade), cultural movements driven by panic (as in the anti–sex trafficking "rescue industry"), and the "gray" and "black market" (as in practices of smuggling pornography and piracy). In contradistinction to the literature on illicit flows that often reiterates the binary of licit and illicit, I acknowledge their co-constitution. I therefore distinguish sex on the move as a particular kind of exchange, which is distinct from and yet related to the irregularity and unpredictability of global flows writ large. I don't employ this procedural tactic to recuperate sexual flows considered to be obscene, illicit, or illegal—on the contrary, I revel in the outlaw status of these sexual flows. Rather, I want to uncover how charges of the criminal foisted onto the movement of sexual culture serve to distract from the shadow economies most responsible for the misery that free-trade ideologies, and their attendant capitalisms, impose.[3]

I began this chapter with the vignette in Mexico City and my analysis of the CBP document on the Finger Vibrator to bring together the unlikely but peculiarly revelatory pairing of "sex" and "free trade." This pairing, I argue, exposes sexual culture on the move as a pivotal site of struggle in the era of late racial capitalisms, or, as it is most often referred to, neoliberalism(s). I use "neoliberalism" to indicate the multiple forms of capitalism that free trade promotes and polices across the 1980s, 1990s, and into the twenty-first century, even as my analysis is specific to transnational and subnational encounters within the three countries—Mexico, Canada, and the United States—that NAFTA attempts to "harmonize." Negotiating a variety of unexpected directions, I never assume neoliberalism to be a monolith or a totalizing phenomenon to explain all things. Instead, I use NAFTA to springboard into the wide range of influences that free trade, as an ideology, praxis, and policy, can have on flattening or outright destroying cultural formations of sexual difference.

The mid-1990s battles to get NAFTA ratified both by the three nations and by the US Congress innovated the concept of "harmonization." It is an international process of capital investment and accumulation that attempts to align, make similar, or make identical the regulatory requirements and governmental policies of differing geographies (Leebron 1996, 43; Nakagawa 2001, 1) while also defining "normative viewpoints about the world [that] must be brought into alignment" (Duina 2006, 5). When it comes to regulating sexual culture on the move, the harmonization process attempts to render sweet and pleasing those aspects of queer culture that can be made to sing with late racial capitalism's obsession with forms of pleasure and enjoyment that exclude disabled, genderqueer, Black, Brown, Indigenous, poor, and working-class subjects. That which cannot be harmonized is unintelligible to free trade under NAFTA. In this book, I show how free-trade policies have vast and enduring effects over the higher cultural, social, and economic value assigned to some bodies, body parts, and sex acts over others and how the very terms that dominate NAFTA's imaginary—harmonization, for example—are potent sites of meaning. I highlight how the alignment of certain body parts as joining together harmoniously reflects the sexual normativity of free trade as invested not only in able-bodied penis-in-vagina sex (and not other forms of sex or body parts, or the "etc.") but also in normative assumptions about what constitutes "good sex" (vanilla, coupled, in private, hetero) and "bad sex" (homo, trans, for money, solo or group, in public).

By "sex," I refer to the communicative, corporeal, and transactional activities of fucking and to certain embodied performances of intimacy and eroticism that both uphold neoliberalism and overflow it. That is, these activities can be convivial with diverse neoliberalisms and their varied calls to pleasure-seeking subjects, but they can also traffic in unruly libidinal desires that escape even neoliberalism's wily and highly adaptive ideologies of white supremacy, settler colonialism, patriarchal heteronormativity, erotophobia, and the twenty-first-century embrace of certain gay and lesbian issues into what queer scholars have called "homonormativity" (Duggan 2004), "homocapitalism" (Rao 2015), and, in relationship to the so-called war on terror, "homonationalism" (Puar 2007). I want to bring close to this study modes of queerness that have come to be considered hostile to homonormative politics of pride and to the neutered spaces of bourgeois respectability that mainstream culture begrudgingly affords to "LGBT" experience. "Sex," Juana María Rodríguez argues, "whether in overt commercial exchanges, casual anonymous encounters, or intimate relations structured around love and care, continues to function as a kind of trade" (2014, 61). *Queer Traffic* tracks and traces collective forms of dissident living as non-NAFTA forms of trade and refuses to turn away from sexual practice as political, pivotal, and powerful, especially for those who love "bad objects" outside the charmed circles (Rubin 2011a) of hetero- and homonormativity. For this reason, and to dislodge bodies from categories that would assume a knowledge about them, I intentionally focus on sexual practices and performances and not categories of sexuality. As a praxis, sex goes beyond a categorical understanding of identity or even a set of orientations, geographically and phenomenologically understood, to focus on acts performed by bodies in contexts that are always already oriented toward, around, or in juxtaposition to objects as they relate to pleasure and desire. Sex can make that connection not just between the macro and the micro but also between the rhetoricity of official free-trade language and the fleshiness of the body. In its perceived excess, sex shows how FTAS are not policies far recessed from the structures and systems of everyday life. Rather, the spectacular surveillance technologies that arise to protect normative trade from deviant sexual culture are often packaged in a brand of theatricality performed in the service of sex panics. These panics scapegoat what Jeffrey Weeks, writing amid the sex panics of the early 1980s, called "Folk Devils" (1981, 14).[4] NAFTA, as I argue throughout the book, is a critical juncture in the long history of inventing sexual scapegoats and mobilizing fears and anxieties about cultural and social mobility that divert attention away from the actual problems of global flows and toward easily targeted social groups who are cast as immoral, degenerate, or predatory.

Queer is not synonymous with sex. This book, however, focuses on components of queerness that are explicitly sexual. It does so to illuminate how corporate/state collaborations fuel free-trade infrastructures that are fiercely rejected by labor, Indigenous, and environmental activists. It examines these infrastructures for how they selectively criminalize certain sexual acts toward punitive ends, even as it reserves the possibility for sex as a fount for what Macarena Gómez-Barris refers to as "submerged perspectives" (2017), or dissident acts of refusal to the violent order of extractivism and racial capital. The point is not only to queerly read NAFTA as a crucial moment in sexual cultural life but also to unravel and unsettle the performance of free trade at the sites of its many contradictions and loopholes.

Queer, I admit, is a vexed term for this book. I view the act of grappling with the applicability and functionality of *queer* in the Americas as a performance of irreverent refusal to the directives of neoliberalism and the historical tendency to apply Anglo-specific forms of queer theory to incommensurable contexts in Latin America. Going beyond a politics of disruption and discomfort, I join Mexican scholars such as Rodrigo Parrini, Siobhan Guerrero Mc Manus, and Alba Pons when they argue that "lo *queer* es una estrategia práctica y una manera de producir modos de existencia y formas de vida" (queerness is a practical strategy and a way to produce modes of existence and forms of life) (2021, 1). The use of queer (and *cuir* or *kuir* as phonetic and reformulated translations of the word in Spanish) must then morph and change according to the subnational micropolitics enacted by bodies on the ground and the circuits of exchange that connect them. Like other scholars grappling with *queer* across the Americas (Córdoba García, Sáez, and Vidarte 2005; Domínguez-Ruvalcaba 2016; Epps 2008; Falconí Trávez, Castellanos, and Viteri 2014; Pierce et al. 2021, 321–327; Russo Garrido 2020, 6–7), I pay attention to materiality and affect, mobilizing "queer" beyond a project of reading, to delve into how "the promise of a queer engagement is thus," citing Deborah Cowen, "in its potential for transforming relations of rule through the desire and occupation of those relations differently" (2014, 223). The challenge in doing a queer analysis of free trade is to balance the convivialities of queer with networks of power, to acknowledge the trade-offs, risks, and rules of engagement, and still revel in the ingenious ways that even those squashed by harmonization, the paranoid smoothing of the global flow, disturb, twist, and make strange the wide-reaching tentacles of free trade.

By "free trade," I specify the political and economic ideology intended to level transnational economies in allegiance to national markets, foreign investment, and global exchange. This ideology reaches well beyond economic matters, or even the countries who sign on. Any form of capitalism comes into being through the performativity of economic dogma—the citation and repetition of market imperatives by powerful corporate and government actors, no doubt, but also through local and everyday performances of desire for certain forms of production, consumption, exchange, and circulation. In this book, I refuse the reification of mapped coordinates and dominant vertical hierarchies of scale, eschewing allegiance to the "nation," the national, and the seduction of the universalizing global to opt instead, following sexual geographers and queer diasporic scholars, for a regional, subnational, and transnational approach to tracing and tracking how sex moves across borders. Indeed, when I employ the terms *nation* or *nation-state* I use them as shorthand for settler-colonized entities bound by borders won through war, genocide, deterritorialization, dispossession, and histories of debt managed by international entities such as the World Bank and International Monetary Fund (IMF).

To be sure, I sometimes write about the nation-state, and Mexico certainly serves as an anchor for my discussions; however, I do so only to contextualize the micropolitics of the subnational, a kind of *polygeography* that uncouples or dethrouples the hegemonic regionalities that FTAs summon into existence (e.g., North America). Rather than reify the trade blocs of free-trade geographies such as NAFTA, MERCOSUR (the Southern Common Market), BRICS (Brazil, Russia, India, China, South Africa, and, as of January 1, 2024, Egypt, Ethiopia, Iran, and the United Arab Emirates), or the EU (European Union), I favor other lovers, such as the intimate relations between Mexico and Guatemala, Honduras, and El Salvador (particularly in chapter 4). In other instances, I explore how sex and trade have more in common with other nonnational or nontransnational sexual geographies (particularly in chapter 1). This scalar multidirectional approach moves promiscuously, outside and inside, up, over, and through, from the top and from the bottom and back again, to upend colonial cartographies and formal capitalist economies by rejecting the normative hemispheric logic of privileging *el norte*.

NAFTA's fictive trinational union of "North America" represents one crucial moment in the scramble to divide up the world into those included and excluded from FTAs with Anglo-dominant countries in North America and Europe. The 1994 agreement made history as the first of its kind to bring into its rhetorical embrace a so-called developing nation, Mexico. In fact, some scholars of NAFTA claim that the FTA was always primarily about

Mexico.[5] In *Understanding NAFTA* (1996), William Orme explains that what NAFTA, the document, most wanted was to open Mexico to foreign investment. Although Mexico became indebted to the United States and other global institutions such as the IMF, the World Trade Organization (WTO), and the World Bank prior to the period I cover, I focus on free-trade practices in Mexico over the course of the last two Institutional Revolutionary Party (PRI) presidencies, under Miguel de la Madrid (1982–1988) and Carlos Salinas de Gortari (1988–1994), and subsequent instantiations of free-trade harmonization into the twenty-first century across the National Action Party (PAN), the Party of the Democratic Revolution (PRD), and the National Regeneration Movement (MORENA). However, even these processes cannot be easily separated out, as Amy Sara Carroll shows in her epic book *REMEX: Toward an Art History of the NAFTA Era*. For Carroll, "the NAFTA era" can be traced from Canada's and the United States' post-1960s restructuring and through "the transnational economic crises of the 1980s; the duration of NAFTA's negotiation beginning in the early 1990s; its protracted enactment from January 1, 1994 to January 1, 2008; and its post-2008 fallout effects, including extreme narco-violence and economic free fall worldwide" (2017, 8). As the 2018–2020 fireworks for the NAFTA 2.0 renegotiation alerted us, there is no "post" to what Carroll calls "NAFTAification" (8).

In the 1990s, NAFTA was only one of many FTAs that comprised an "almost craze in the sedate world of economics, springing up here, and there and everywhere" (Urata 2002, 21). While volatile and intense debate preceded and followed the signing of NAFTA, as well as the NAFTA 2.0 version (the US-Mexico-Canada Agreement, or USMCA), NAFTA was one of thirty-three new FTAs formed between 1990 and 1994 to be followed, between 1995 and 2001, by another one hundred FTAs (Duina 2006, 3). For its geographic breadth, NAFTA has been singled out as "undoubtedly the most impressive free trade area in place" (Duina 2006, 22). NAFTA's impressiveness, however, can also be measured by its reiterative citationality for any number of FTAs, the WTO, and their mechanisms that followed. Undeniably, NAFTA stands out for forging a global model that aggressively harmonized the notion of desirability and exchange value across vastly different geopolitical contexts and across drastically disparate cultures.

Thus on January 1, 1994, when NAFTA went into effect under Mexican President Carlos Salinas de Gortari, some truly believed his proclamation that free trade would catapult Mexico into the so-called first world. Those in opposition, most notably the Ejército Zapatista de Liberación Nacional (EZLN), along with the trinational coalition of labor and environmental activists that anti-NAFTA sentiment historically brought into being, resisted the abstract promises of freedom that covered over what for them was NAFTA's situatedness in the "coloniality of power" (Quijano 2000). True, the North American Agreement on Labor Cooperation (NAALC) and the Commission on Environmental Cooperation (CEC), diminutively known as NAFTA's "side agreements," represent the meaningful consequence of the collaboration between labor, Indigenous, and environmental activists across the US-Mexico-Canada borderlands. They forged, at least in the global imaginary, a direct connection between labor, land rights, the environment, and international trade, topics formerly considered to have little if nothing to do with one another (Kay and Evans 2018). These side agreements held the potential for "a queerer approach to trade-related decision making" (O'Hara 2022, 36). Yet these side agreements have no legal teeth and therefore cannot be enforced.

In the United States and Canada, preferential FTAs became a priority in the 1980s and 1990s, though debates about free trade had been ongoing for over a century. As an FTA, NAFTA, arguably much more than the 1989 Canada-US Free Trade Agreement (CUSFTA) that expanded to include Mexico, can be viewed more as a "free investment agreement" than an FTA. It is no coincidence, then, that NAFTA becomes notable as much for what it leaves out as for its sheer breadth as a value-laden catalog of things, millions and millions of things, fragmented within a tome of a twenty–two-chapter document whose labyrinthian legalese leaves one awash in the compartmentalization of nearly every facet of everyday objecthood into bits and parts. Putting aside the weak, unenforceable, and unenforced NAFTA side agreements on labor and the environment, NAFTA is more accurately viewed as obfuscating the actual movement of bodies, objects, and ideas across borders, papering over issues of labor, immigration, the environment, racial justice, Indigenous populations and their lands, histories of slavery and colonialism, and disability, gender, and sexual inequalities.

Instead, NAFTA proceeds as though all three nations came to the table on equal grounds, as if centuries of land grabs, border militarization, security regimes, austerity measures, and land extraction had no bearing on how the document should be written, how the parties should enter such an agreement considering these pasts and presents, and what NAFTA would spell for the future. In this way, while NAFTA enters the historical stage during a time of new conceptions and applications of globalization as a term and of "free trade" as a performative political economic practice that creates certain pathways for people, objects, and ideas, its particular brand of racial capitalism belies its historical ties to older forms of trade, such as the transatlantic slave trade and the pillaging of the Americas by European colonialists since the sixteenth century.[6] The almost simultaneous domestic gutting of social welfare by the Clinton administration, the revocation of the Glass-Steagall Act, and Operation Gatekeeper (Operación Guardián), whereby the Tijuana–San Diego border was militarized to stem migration and appease anti-immigrant sentiment in the United States (Nevins 2002), only begin to reveal NAFTA, and all of the trade-related policies it inspired globally, as a neoimperial and racist tool across the Americas and the planet. "Free trade is not about deregulation," says NAFTA expert Roger de la Garde, "but regulation of another kind" (as cited in Jones 1996, 348). This regulation, I argue, is certainly about the transnational movement of commodities and capital, but it is also about the movement of people both within and between the imaginary coordinates that bind the fiction of the nation-state and the racist and classist panics that can be fomented as people move across borders and boundaries of all kinds.

My conversations with the Mexico City businessmen and the CBP document on the Finger Vibrator thus unravel a variety of often disaggregated and occluded nodes about sex, culture, and free trade on which this book hinges. First, they both unfolded during a historical period where a new form of globalization—one marked by trade liberalization as the order of the day—took hold, globally speaking, but specifically in relationship to an agreement that conjures into existence a new regionality, the imagined community that we have come to know as "North America." NAFTA, with its fetish for offloading production and building up consumption, did not mark the beginning of free trade. Indeed, as Rosemary Hennessy and Martha Ojeda show, the road to NAFTA was driven by a much longer history in which Mexico incurred a tremendous amount of debt owing to "uneven economic growth generated by the history of colonialism" (2006, 1).[7] What they call "the first generation of free trade policies" in the mid-nineteenth century saw British and US goods flooding Mexican markets, exacerbating deficits and debts on the heels of the Treaty of Guadalupe Hidalgo and the loss of more than half of Mexico's territory to the United States. The signing of NAFTA in the 1990s marked a critical juncture in what Jodi Kim has so aptly called "debt imperialism" (2018) and ushered in the second generation of free-trade policies marked by a frenzy of countless other FTAs in the 1980s and 1990s.

My experiences with the Mexico City businessmen and the CBP document equally reveal how government bodies and nonstate capital entities, such as transnational corporations (TNCs), conspire in their (e)valuation and circulation of cultural goods and the subsequent creation of political and economic infrastructures through which some goods, but not all, can "freely" flow. Infrastructure simply names that which is required for everyday activities to function (Wilson 2016, 249). Paradoxically, it is the very ubiquity of infrastructure that renders it invisible, a priori rather than created and maintained by abstract powers—such as free trade—that prioritize certain life activities and the movement of certain people, goods, and ideas over others. I root out the "embedded strangeness" of free trade (Star 1999, 379), its erotic investment in sexual normativity rendered invisible through its ubiquity, and the pleasures and desires of dissident sexuality that cannot be contained by such a system or that the free-trade infrastructural network unwittingly spawns.

The queerness of free trade is precisely that it isn't free, but rather an unstable "capital fiction" (Beckman 2012) that depends on the now-prevailing ideological fantasy that the market benefits everyone. Free trade regards some objects, but not all, as assimilable into global capitalism and therefore "legal" for importation and consumption. Sex serves as my primary heuristic to expose the lie that free trade is interested in the embodied experience of "freedom." It roundly refuses the model of freedom that is allegedly secured through global markets. Looking through the lens of sex is one way of exposing the myth of the "free" in free trade and its role in exporting a rhetoric of freedom that purports to be Western-originating, secular, and universal but that traffics in notions of liberal subjectivity based on a highly classed, raced, gendered, and able-bodied experience of white bourgeois cis-masculinity.

In the chapters that follow, I explain how NAFTA disciplines the movement of capitalism's indigestible objects with charges of "obscenity," "terrorism," and "trafficking," thereby creating new categories of "illegal" objecthood. Tracing NAFTA's sexual history uncovers yet another function of free trade: how the rhetoric of romance and friendship sold NAFTA as an obligatory and reciprocal circuit of both giving and receiving that damages the groups and people to whom objects marked as "obscene" are most pertinent. Ultimately as a free-trade performance, NAFTA capitalizes on human suffering, often caused by macroeconomic policies such as the Washington Consensus, as a profit-generating enterprise. Throughout the book, I show how flows under NAFTA invent new categories of "obscene" objecthood and "illegal" personhood by not only normativizing the separation of sex and the economy into discrete categories but also juxtaposing NAFTA's "bad objects" with more acknowledged ones such as avocados, car parts, and dairy products. Vibrators and dildos, unlike these other more assimilable though not seamlessly celebrated NAFTA goods, simply move differently, existing on the edge of those new political infrastructures that free trade formalizes (not necessarily creates) after it is rhetorically and theatrically invoked.

So, even as the CBP ruling for the Finger Vibrator casts embodied eroticism as its "etc.," and even though, statistically speaking, it is "impossible" to track sexual commerce across borders ("not specified or included elsewhere"), sex on the move is, nevertheless, always suspect. It must be ratified by dominant institutions and provided a formal infrastructure to flow; even then, the changing mores of a particular time and place can reverse its course, erecting barriers to create blockages. Free trade has become one such infrastructure within which certain forms of normative sex can flow. At the same time, its attendant erotophobic roadblocks surveil and police any form of sex considered abhorrent to the morality of free trade at every checkpoint along the way in its journey through the gatekeepers of (sexual) commerce.

In the circuits through which culture travels, sex consistently emerges as a deviant and irreverent flow, the *queer traffic* of free trade. In conversing with actors ranging from bureaucrats to pornographers and in studying choreographies, social movements, and street vocabularies that crisscross the interdisciplinary textures of analysis indicative of a performance studies lens, the often disaggregated and unaccounted dialectical relationship between sex and free trade becomes demystified. From this interdisciplinary stance, sex on the move reveals its potential to illuminate the "disorganized capitalism" (Lash and Urry 1987) of all global flows *and* the movement of sexual culture as its own kind of flow, one that can disrupt market logics through practices performed in excess of resistance. In this paradigm, the presumed diversifying function of unregulated capitalism creates the contexts within which precarious subjects find themselves under attack, physically and culturally, or else, as in the case of sex workers, co-opted for transnational projects of "perverse humanitarianism" (Hoang 2016) that block and curtail movement across borders, nationally and normatively speaking. Thus, rather than impose an epistemological divide between capital and culture, I use sex to unsettle the performance of free trade and to expose NAFTA's investments in sexual normativity and how these investments have profoundly restructured sex and sexuality in the Americas, just as they have provoked alternative acts of dissent to a uniform sexual, social, and economic world.

The figures I discuss for the remainder of the introduction are strategically chosen to unravel the contradictions, complexities, and multiple temporalities of free-trade capitalism on the materiality of lived and imagined experience. My aim is to debunk what Jodi Dean has rightly named the "consumer/criminal doublet" of free trade (2009, 63) and to concretize the urgency and politics of queer traffic as a project about life and death, about the murderous results of the kinds of extractive toxic masculinity that define US-Mexico relations of dominance.

NAFTA's "Winners"

NAFTA's impact on everyday life is informed by one's class, race, and gender position. The populations I designate as NAFTA's "winners" intimately feel the effects of NAFTA with regard to their accumulated wealth, but they rarely recognize (or admit) NAFTA's role in this accumulation. To flesh out a segment of those whose lives ostensibly benefited from NAFTA, I turn to Daniela Rossell's controversial photography project *Untitled (Ricas y famosas: Mexico 1994–2001)* (The rich and famous) to study the ways in which her series provides otherwise unattainable access to how elite Mexican women blend conservative, progressive, and globalized narratives of consumption in their highly guarded domestic spaces. For this specific class of women in Mexico City, what it means to be heterosexual is a transnational concept, one in which women are expected to perform imported ideas about modern sexuality while maintaining some vague connection to the varying ideas about what constitutes traditional Mexican values. Rossell's series captures how privileged Mexican women perform sexual cosmopolitanism through neoliberal ideology in the insular and highly guarded space of the home. The series shows how conservative notions of gender and race continue to dominate the limited social identity of classed female heterosexuality in twenty-first-century Mexico City, often viewed as the beacon of both neoliberal modernization and politically progressive thought in the republic.

Speaking from her experience as the daughter of Mexican political and cultural elites, Rossell says of the subjects in her photography series, "Wealthy women in Mexico are prisoners of their houses, style and excess. Most of them live in the salon. They really want to look American, like what you see on TV, and they go to a lot of work to accomplish that. It's a kind of hell" (as cited in Centre for Contemporary Culture Strozzina 2010, 118). The homes of rich Mexican women are virtually inaccessible to outsiders. *Untitled (Ricas y famosas)* goes inside the formidable iron gates and past the heavily armed security guards to show how elite Mexican women furnished their homes and fashioned their bodies with imported luxury goods within the first seven years after NAFTA went into effect. Her series visualizes the contradictory effects of neoliberal capitalism on elite women's sexuality and blurs the backstage/frontstage performance binary, to draw from Erving Goffman's work (1959), through the presentation of everyday privileged Mexican life in private, interior spaces. These displays occurred without an audience, but these women obviously knew they were being watched, and they set the scene and seized on recognizable conventions to perform a twenty-first-century version of Mexican female heterosexuality.

Rossell's subjects—often friends or relatives of her own affluent and powerful PRI family who had volunteered to be photographed—carefully chose how to present themselves to the camera. Coupling society portraiture and performance, in these photos Rossell's sitters unabashedly embrace their lavish domestic surroundings, signaling their nouveau riche status. Their ornate and overprotective environments, which often resemble children's rooms, fairy-tale scenarios, or natural history museums, suggest that the ways in which these women stylize their self-presentation risk fashioning them into objects of desire: just another garish house decoration or an expensive luxury good to be bought, traded, and sold, or, in the case of Mexico City's culture of *secuestro exprés* (express kidnapping), ransomed.

Consider, for instance, the two untitled photos referenced as *Inge and Her Mother Ema in Living Room* and *Medusa* (see figs. I.1 and I.2). In both images, women assume the space of their homes and are surrounded by what have become the stock decorations of the wealthy Mexican household: in one, the racist anti-Black figurines that circulate within the US antique market; in the other, the commodification of rural and collective identity–based Indigenous cultures as suitable for home décor but incompatible with neoliberalism's emphasis on the individual. In both these photos, sexualized femininity and the feminized space of the home are portrayed as something that does not necessarily belong to these women; rather, the photos show how their intimate and erotic lives have also become explicitly commodified, assigned value, advertised, commercialized, packaged, and consumed. More importantly, they reveal how racialized heterosexuality has been central to neoliberalism's transnational project. The long history of racism against Indigenous peoples and the long-standing refusal of Blackness in the imaginary of who is included in nationalist myths of *mexicanidad* (Mexicanness) and *mestizaje* recede to the background to become mere foils to the white beauty aesthetics of Rossell's sitters. The depiction of local racist populism with elite agendas stands out in the visual rhetoric of the photographs, which when displayed in a series do not simply evidence the primacy of race in the economy of female pleasure but through repetition produce the

I.1   Daniela Rossell, *Untitled (Ricas y famosas)*, 2000, C-print, 50 × 60 inches. Courtesy of the artist and Greene Naftali Gallery.

very effects that they name and describe. Perhaps the performative effect of these photographs when viewed together by art gallery spectators elicited such strong responses from the portrait sitters, some of whom threatened Rossell with lawsuits and violence after viewing them.[8]

When photographing her subjects, it seemed to Rossell "they had meticulously studied and memorized these roles . . . that say in detail what they were expected to do, how they were expected to stand, and to perform for a camera. And they seemed to be roles that were already written by someone else and for no one in particular. There was a feeling of 'this is going on, whether I'm here or not.'"[9] What "is going on" is the embodiment of the aesthetic and sexualized values of consumer culture and how those values depend on the construction of a feminine sexualized identity and the stereotype of racially inferior others, and vice versa; how the work is to be received by the viewer, however, is ultimately unclear. *(Untitled) Ricas y*

I.2　Daniela Rossell, *Untitled (Ricas y famosas)*, 2000, C-print, 50 × 60 inches. Courtesy of the artist and Greene Naftali Gallery.

famosas shows how the culturally specific gender and race performances enacted by these women intersect with class-based performances that depend on localized consumption and dominant narratives of Mexican culture as well as globalized consumer culture and its idealized projections of sexualized femininity; but Rossell's photos can also be viewed as comments on Mexican sociopolitical conditions and the fetishization of wealthy women as objects of the male gaze, or as camped-up performances where the women take pleasure in citing the well-known tropes of commodified femininity.

The women who participated in *Untitled (Ricas y famosas)* embody the neoliberalized condition of sexuality for upper-middle- and upper-class women in Mexico City. They typify the emergence of a new stratum of female consumers defined through economic circumstances, transnational media, and the accrual of imported material things. Specifically, *(Untitled) Ricas y famosas* chronicles the influence of neoliberal economic policies on the forging of a feminine Mexican elite and how the signing of NAFTA simultaneously redefined Mexico's relationship with economic, beauty, and sexuality models from the United States. Based on racialized stereotypes, these models pit light-skinned Mexican women as aesthetic ideals against Indigenous-inspired dolls and Black figurines. These decorations act as temporal contrasts: the sitter is marked as cosmopolitan only through a juxtaposition with the pastoral depictions of indigeneity and antique Black figurines of "Americana" memorabilia positioned to indicate a denial of co-evalness to the subjects referenced by these decorations.

The racialized dynamic depicted in the photographs highlights the danger of neoliberalism's paradoxical expansion and contraction of pleasure. Looking at the influence of NAFTA through the performance of portraiture and the furnishing of interior space illuminates the multiple and multivalent contradictions of free trade in Mexico and the transnational inequalities and differences that arise from new forms of globalization. Sex can certainly be subversive of capitalism—as a transformative desire that incites new economic forms and social experiences—but for the elite women in Rossell's photographs, this is rarely the case. They show how, in the NAFTA era, bourgeois class aspirations and white privilege create the context for feminine sexual pleasure. The market may create conditions within which Rossell's sitters can claim great cultural and financial capital, but that same market destabilizes and unmakes their erotic capital, leaving them only a small space among foreign models of sexual liberation, domestic structures of patriarchal heterosexuality, and global capitalist exploitation to enact and enjoy a commercialized version of sexual pleasure.

Trade has always been a queer affair. Any conversation about sex and free trade must therefore engage a conversation on the varied working-class, nominally male persons who constitute a set of erotic actors gathered under the label "trade." The sexual moniker "trade" can be traced to the seventeenth-century slang of female sex workers (Chauncey 1995, 69). In queer studies, it has become a quintessential term for illuminating the contradictions and complexities of sex versus sexuality, since it references sexual practices that don't line up with assumed normative identity categories. Depending on the time period in question, trade can denote heterosexual-identifying men who have sex with men for money, gifts, companionship, and/or for pleasure and who may (but not exclusively) play a penetrative role in sexual encounters, male hustlers or sex workers, or the men who pay for such encounters (Chauncey 1995, 70; Montez 2020, 66). In other words, "trade" signifies an ever-shifting array of people who exchange sex and sexual labor to negotiate their race, ethnicity, gender, and class status through informal economies of sexual commerce.

The connection between trade, as in free trade and international commerce, and trade, as in a play on gay terminology that encompasses a set of sexual subjectivities and practices, spins on the axis of a libidinal but asymmetrical power dynamic that "makes visible an exchange, a scene in which power differentials (of race and economic position particularly) operate but do so unstably" (Montez 2020, 65). This power dynamic has been explored for what it can tell us about queer desire, the hypermasculinity of US imperialism, and the consolidation of the nation-state (H. Pérez 2015, 2–3, 6); about artistic exchanges that both conform to and resist the classed and racialized normativity of the art market (Montez 2020, 61–82); and about the panic surrounding disruptions of commercial shipping and formal sanctioned infrastructures of global merchandising flows (Cowen 2014, 129–162, 197–232). I too regard trade queerly: it refers to market exchange and equally to the attractions and desires for lower-class, allegedly "straight" male sex partners. The performance of the hustle so indispensable to living under and after NAFTA and the contradictions and convivialities of queer desire with free-trade capitalism direct my attention to an expressly working-class subset of trade known as "rough trade" and even more specifically to the Mexican figure of the *chacal*.

The long queer history of the *chacal* dates to the sixteenth century, when, according to *chacalógos* (*chacal* scholars), he was described as a cruel and even carnivorous predator.[10] According to Miguel Alonso Hernández Victoria, the literal meaning of the word, translated into Castellano Spanish from Turkish, Persian, and French, is "jackal" or "accomplice." Hernández traces the queer history of the *chacal* to the paranoia for racial purity via the *casta* system and New Spain's Inquisition, where certain people were labeled as sodomites and put on trial for their racial and class differences as well as for their nonconformity with colonial conceptions of sex and gender.[11] As a Mexico-specific "rough trade" character rooted in a long history of racialized desire, the *chacal* stereotypically describes a member of Black, Brown, and Indigenous populations who is poor or working class.[12] He embodies a kind of masculinity that is at once distinct from the stereotype of the capital-bearing, gym-chiseled gay man and indicative of another kind of "natural" beauty that has become eroticized and in many cases commercialized by gay men with cultural and financial capital within Mexico and the transnational circuits of sex tourism.[13] Today, the *chacal* has become a motivator for hailing the pink dollar in urban Mexican locales, with some gay bars in Mexico City and Tijuana, for example, inviting gay patrons to enter their space by promising queued-up bargoers ¡*Ven por tu chacal!* (Come for your *chacal!*)

NAFTA certainly didn't invent the *chacal*. Indeed, Luis Zapata energized the desire for lower-class male hustlers as early as 1979 with the publication of *El vampiro de la colonia Roma*, often regarded as the first gay novel in Mexican literature. However, the *chacal* takes on new resonances as a commodity in the NAFTA era, a phenomenon at least partially inspired by the reentrenchment of Mexican nationalism in leftist artistic expression, as in the work of Nahum Zenil and Julio Gálan. The *chacal* became a fetish for neomexicanist artists at the same time that neoliberalism and NAFTA began to co-opt and sell sexual dissidence under the guise of acceptability, tolerance, and First World discourse. In other words, gay visual and literary interest in the *chacal* as an eroticized figure in Mexico collides with the exoticized circulation of this figure across the polygeographies of the subnational and transnational marketplace. In this marketplace, the *chacal* is both consumed and criminalized as he takes up a class position attractive to gay discourses and representations of desire and the class- and race-based xenophobia that structures free-trade capitalism, particularly in relationship to migration. The *chacal* is one of many figures caught in the snares of the consumer/criminal binary of free trade, both a fount of queer pleasure and a racialized thief who steals market pleasures from others, owing to the perception of his needy class status.

NAFTA has had a devastating impact on the lives and livelihoods of many Mexican people, and the *chacal* characterizes one subject that has explicitly and intimately felt the financial violence of the FTA. According to a 2013 report from Mexico's National Institute of Statistics and Geography (Instituto Nacional de Estadística y Geografía, or INEGI), 1.7 percent of the country's inhabitants (1,340,000 people) make up Mexico's elite class.[14] Between 1992 and 2000, with the implementation of NAFTA, the 1994 tequila crisis (*el error de diciembre*), and multiple recessions, most Mexican households saw their incomes stagnate or fall, but Mexico's privileged elite, such as Rossell's photographic subjects, experienced income growth in the double digits.[15] In 2011, the Organisation for Economic Co-operation and Development (OECD) reported that, since the 1990s and for all its member countries, the Gini coefficient, a standard measure of income inequality, had steadily risen, meaning that the household incomes of the top 10 percent grew faster than those of the poorest 10 percent; during this time period, the ratio for Mexico, at 27 to 1, was the highest of any OECD country (as a benchmark, the ratio in the United States was 14 to 1).[16] For rural and agricultural populations, in particular, the reform of the Mexican Constitution's Article 27 opened the land for investment and led to the decimation of the national farming industry in favor of Canadian mining, tourism, and transnational gentrification projects that ultimately transformed locations such as Cancún, Cabo San Lucas, and San Miguel de Allende into Anglo-residential and tourist enclaves. This reform was one of many chips offered by Salinas de Gortari to President George H. W. Bush in the lead-up to the signing of NAFTA in 1992.

In a 2013 interview with Hernández in Mexico City, I asked him whether and, if so, how NAFTA influenced gay culture in Mexico City. He went immediately to the *chacal* to answer my question. Here he talks about how the desire for the *chacal* can be seen as a market interrupter when it comes to what he calls "la óptica gay comercial" (the gay commercial point of view):

> ¿Y el chacal qué es? Es el hombre que sabe a tierra mojada, es el albañil, es el indígena; es el ranchero, es el proletario. Son todos aquellos cuerpos construidos a partir del hambre y la miseria, que simbolizan o se ven como algo bello: las facciones toscas del indígena, las facciones toscas del mestizo, los cuerpos que no son atléticos. Es el enamorarte y el volver a reinterpretar una belleza que existe, y esa es la propuesta, por ejemplo, de estos grupos de cazadores de chacales. Y es que a nosotros no nos gustan ni los güeritos, ni los bonitos, ni

los altos, ni los delicados. Nos gustan los rudos, los fuertes, lo que no es considerado desde la óptica gay commercial.

(And what is a *chacal?* He's a man who tastes like wet earth, the construction worker, the Indigenous man, the rancher, the proletarian. All those bodies built out of hunger and destitution, who come to symbolize or to be seen as something beautiful: the rough features of Indigenous men, the rough features of mestizo men, bodies that are not athletic. It's how you fall in love and once again how you reinterpret a beauty that does exist there, and that's the idea, for example, that drives these groups of *chacal* hunters. And the thing is we don't even like *güeritos* [light-skinned] or pretty boys or tall men or delicate flowers. We like tough guys, strong men, everything that is not valued through the commercial gay lens.)

One of many contradictions in the imaginary of the *chacal* is precisely this fetishization of that which a NAFTA world has demoralized and decimated. In many ways, then, this *chacal* moment harkens back to the persecution of those described in colonial times as "indios," "negros," "mulatos," and "moriscos" (Moors) (Gruzinski 1985). The *chacal* of the past and the *chacal* of today are both persecuted and marginalized. With NAFTA, Mexican foreign policy decisions and the US domination of formerly nationalized Mexican industries that had sustained laborers worsen the suffering of rural, Indigenous, and working-class people; at the same time, the *chacal* becomes a commodity within the global flows of gay desire and gay capital.

On the one hand, then, there's the well-heeled middle-class Mexican or the global sex tourist on the hunt for the *chacal,* and on the other are the Black, Brown, and/or Indigenous laborers who are the objects of desire, the temporary lovers or hustlers making ends meet in a NAFTA-devastated economy. In the mix and indispensable to a book that finds hope in sex practice and desire, Hernández's argument cannot be discounted: the desire for the *chacal* can and sometimes does interrupt the Anglo-dominant politics of beauty aesthetics and their many circuits of exchange; moreover, the desire for the *chacal* can destabilize the cultural and economic market logic of the pink dollar and the solidification of gay capital accumulating in popular Pride flag–waving bars, such as those in the Zona Rosa in Mexico City. The *chacal* won't be found in these bars but rather in the underground alternative economies of dilapidated cinemas, public parks, and working-class cantinas like those in the fierce nightlife cultures of Garibaldi.

Lebanon-born and Mexico City–based photographer Pedro Slim captures these contradictions of desire and capital flows in his 1997 series *De la calle al estudio* (From the street to the studio).[17] In the series, young Black, Brown, and Indigenous men pose for the camera. All of them are shirtless (except for "Rogelio," who also holds a lit cigarette), and many of them are completely naked. Their facial expressions vary from intimidating or withdrawn, to jovial, coquettish, and enticing, to melancholic or resigned. One looks away from the camera entirely. They are thin, with their low-hanging jeans ready to fall from their narrow hips. Some are scarred; many are tattooed; others are pockmarked. One model ("Domingo") has vitiligo and a large surgical bandage over his stomach, suggesting an open wound underneath (see fig. I.3). Shirtless, barefoot, in jeans and plaid boxers, he has his hands on his hips, with a strong stance as he looks to the side, offering only his profile to the camera. In this photograph, Slim frames what Robert McRuer has aptly called "crip times" (2018), or the ways in which local and transnational policies such as austerity measures cause displacements that produce disability, precarity, and unpredictability. It points to the ways in which neoliberalism creates contexts of precarity and how disability must be central to our understanding of the uneven economic development wrought under NAFTA. Even so, the model's stance connects to how disabled people reclaim and reconfigure the term *crip*, historically a derogatory slur that derives from the word "cripple." As McRuer states, crip "has functioned for many as a marker of an in-your-face, or out-and-proud, cultural mode of disability" (2018, 19). Viewed through McRuer's nuanced theory of crip times, a theory that confronts both neoliberal austerity and foregrounds resistance to its economic and medical models, Slim's photograph eroticizes not merely the body of his subject but also that subject's "flamboyant defiance" (19) to the capture of a medicalizing, pitying, or subjugating gaze.

In other photos, however, Slim's emphasis leans more on a version of aesthetics aimed at recuperating his beleaguered subjects into commodities saleable on the transnational art market. Art critic and curator Olivier Debroise described Slim's method as "'recoge' en las calles de la ciudad de México y sus alrededores, a 'tipos populares' masculinos y los instala en el escenario sombrío de su estudio" ("collecting" masculine "working-class guys" from the streets of Mexico City and its surroundings, and he places them into the somber setting of his studio) (1997). In some of these black-and-white photos, Slim positions his models standing or sitting atop raised pedestals, bending over to touch their toes or crouching over their crossed legs, their backs and buttocks to the camera (see fig. I.4). Reminiscent

I.3   Pedro Slim, "Domingo," *De la calle al estudio*, © 1994, gelatin silver print.
Courtesy of the artist and CLAMP, New York.

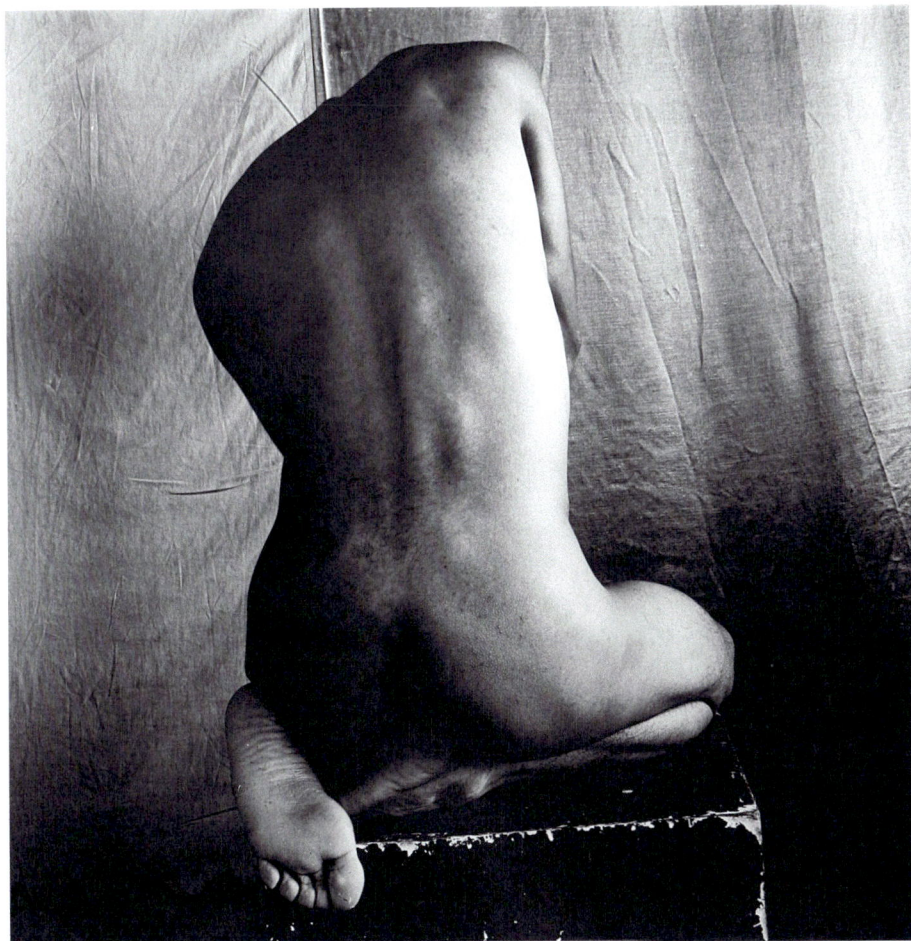

I.4   Pedro Slim, "Untitled," *De la calle al estudio*, © 2006, gelatin silver print.
Courtesy of the artist and CLAMP, New York.

of Robert Mapplethorpe's *The Black Book*, though with noticeable differences (e.g., the inclusion of body hair), Slim's photos depict an ethically
fraught sculptural style for photographing race, class, and disabled difference. Akin to how Kobena Mercer's analysis of Mapplethorpe's *The Black
Book* advanced the idea of an ambivalent critical stance (1994, 171–220), I
look to Slim's series to both acknowledge the deep roots of racial fetishism
in its visual iconography and to recognize its potential to discomfort and
disarm the homophobic viewer, personified for Mercer in 1994 by Senator
Jesse Helms. While the discomfort of Slim's subjects is visible in some of the

photographs, the crux, Debroise argues, is "la perturbación del espectador, poco acostumbrado a que se la interpele de manera tan sútil y violenta a la vez" (the disturbance of the spectator, unaccustomed to being questioned in such a simultaneously subtle and violent way) (1997). As Mercer argues for the Black men whom Mapplethorpe photographed, men Mercer describes as "a distinct collective subject in the late-capitalist underclass," Slim's use of raised platforms might similarly be viewed as positioning his subjects "onto the pedestal of the transcendental Western aesthetic ideal" and "a deconstructive move [that] begins to undermine the foundational [white supremacist] myths of the pedestal itself" (200). *De la calle al estudio* certainly disrupts the expectations of heteronormative viewership and the exclusion of lower-class Mexican men from white-dominant conceptions of beauty; yet, at the same time, in placing his nudes, his disrobed *chacales*, on raised platforms he uses a common museum-display technology that objectifies for sale on the transnational art market.

Scholars such as Laura G. Gutiérrez have rightly claimed that "sexual permissiveness in cultural representation and in public discourse has found a sort of ally in neoliberalism in the context of Mexico" (2010, 7). Without attempting to recuperate Slim's series for some social justice cause, I instead position Slim's photographs as quintessential to the times of NAFTA. His photos give the viewer an opportunity to think with and through the contradictions of gay capital in NAFTA's wake. Slim's photos ultimately reveal the intimate connection between sex and trade and the ways in which sexual desires for nonnormative subjects such as the *chacal* can become complicit with capitalist imperialism and a turn toward the nationalistic, even if these desires grew out of subcultural, deviant, or underground histories of cultural consumption.

Today, if one considers how Trump leveraged NAFTA to catapult himself to the presidency in 2016, the radical potential of desiring those most devastated under NAFTA becomes more complicated. After descending the Trump Tower escalator to announce his candidacy, Trump reiterated his long-standing criticism of NAFTA, stating his "intention to renegotiate NAFTA or withdraw from the deal under Article 2205."[18] With this threat, he rewrote histories of power as they relate to the three NAFTA trade partners. He seized on a right-wing version of what Wendy Brown has called a "sense of woundedness" (1995), in which "American" identity is understood to be screwed by NAFTA and particularly by Mexico, embodied in Trump's much-maligned cast of caricatures, such as opportunistic *maquila* workers and "bad hombres." In doing so, he played into long-standing and growing xenophobic misconceptions about an "invasion" at the US southern border and into false claims that migrating peoples play central roles in smuggling drugs and guns into the United States and in depleting public services while committing violent (sexual) crimes.[19] Trump recruited the well-worn tool of charging certain social groups with sexual deviance to distract from his and his cronies' nefarious economic activities. He also played into the broad disappointment with NAFTA, across the political aisle, to use race, sex, binary conceptions of gender, and a predatorial depiction of Brown working-class masculinity to foment a panic about a plethora of illicit cultural flows, arousing the ethnonationalist frenzy that catapulted his presidential campaign to victory in 2016.

What with their sagging pants, their tattoos, their dark skin, and visible indigence, Slim's *chacales* could be made to visually match the ethnonationalist stereotype of "bad hombres." When Trump fabricated his "bad hombres" and "rapists," his words caught fire not because he was inventing these ideas, but because sex, cast in racist and antipoor terms, is ingrained in racial capital's approach to adjudicating the encroachment of foreign investment. Trump sold his "bad hombres" to the electorate to continue to fuel the very lucrative project of blocking the movement of men who look just like Slim's subjects. A strategy as old as the slave trade itself, Trump's positing of migrating men of color as sexual predators, as threats to the purity of the nation and white womanhood, demonstrated his ongoing interest in stoking sexual panic for marshalling political and economic power.[20]

Sexual panics emerge to do something for the politics of the moment, such as fuel the NAFTA surveillance state. They are not a product of but are activated by free-trade discourse and policies. The specific surveillance apparatus that NAFTA 1.0 (1994) innovated, and NAFTA 2.0 (2020) extended, shields those most integral to the process—the governments, lawmakers, and criminal punishment enforcers—from being surveilled themselves. It enlists the participation of everyday people to do the surveillance work of the state by teaching them how to identify certain visual markers of difference considered worthless to global trade. The surveillance infrastructure redirects our attention away from its architects and toward contrived figures such as "bad hombres," or Trump's rough trade. NAFTA led to an uptake in all kinds of surveillance directed at stemming the flow of certain goods and bodies. It created illicit forms of capital and cultural flows and "illegal" categories of people that came to be viewed and treated not as trade, but as traffic(k).

One of this book's primary aims is to unravel and undo the criminalizing technologies that arise from ethnonationalist rhetoric. I join "queer" with "traffic," rather than "trade," to explicitly crisscross scholarship that does the indispensable diagnostic work of uncovering past and current structural violences with studies that focus on resistances and refusals. I transit, dare I say traffic(k), in the gaps between extreme forms of violence enacted through neoliberal appeals to individual freedom and responsibility and the richness and dexterity of sexual subjects who escape the snares of the "special bonds / *lazos especiales*" that the NAFTA preamble announces.[21] Refusing to push away that which free-trade ideology has labeled "criminal," "terrorist," and "obscene," *Queer Traffic* analyzes the sexual panics that implicitly and at times explicitly fuel the surveillance of sexual subjects and objects on the move.[22] It revels simultaneously in the boldness, and at times raunchiness, of the sexual material culture in question as well as in the illicit performances of production, consumption, and circulation that guide its path.

The disaggregation and ideological displacement of sex from transnational policies such as FTAS function as a weapon for the radical right (sometimes in collusion with the left) to create sexual panics that imbricate carceral and market infrastructures. Discourses that accompany sex on the move are mobilized and deployed to create surveillance policies on pornography, homosex, sex work, migration, medications for sexually transmitted infections (STIS), to list only a few of the topics I discuss in this book. These paternalistic, colonial, and carceral policies purport to save but only control and further exploit labor through optics that target vulnerable populations such as sex workers. Ultimately, they diminish the possibilities for nonlucrative pleasures that are not marketable or saleable through international trade. These discourses go beyond language to congeal in actual domestic and transnational policies that do all kinds of surveillance and policing work to divert attention away from the structural violences that NAFTA has wrought on Indigenous, working-class, poor, female, femme, trans, and Black and Brown peoples across the polygeographies of the NAFTA borderlands. Throughout the book I emphatically attend to the friction of sex on the move with formally criminalized flows—not to further criminalize the latter flows but to trouble the ways in which sex can be employed to invent new remunerative categories of criminal practices and identities that can be integrated into the surveillance infrastructures that NAFTA innovated. I thus apply *queer traffic* to a multiplicity of actors and actions to show how sex panics invent criminal targets charged with being the enemies of free trade, and thus of every normative consumer. I also apply it to the unsanctioned cultural movements of goods, bodies, and ideas that resist, transform, or refuse the consumer/criminal binary that free-trade capitalism requires to seduce us into participation.

Queer Traffic

The etymological history of the word *traffic* reveals the suppleness with which it has been applied across articulations of capital ideology, from the beginning of the slave trade to the White Slavery panic of the twentieth century to what anti–sex trafficking activists call "modern slavery." I look to the genealogy of *traffic*, its applications and circulations, to track different articulations of capitalism and their noncapitalist modes so as to uncover the ways in which the term persists in creating binary distinctions between licit and illicit flows. The *Oxford English Dictionary* defines the term, as used in sixteenth-century Europe, as "the commercial transportation of goods or commodities on a large scale from one nation or community to another for the purpose of buying and selling; commerce," or more generally, "the buying and selling or exchange of goods and commodities for profit; trade, business." Less than a century later, *traffic* was directly applied to sex workers, not coincidentally during a time of urban panics that inordinately connected contagion and disease to prostitution. The *Oxford English Dictionary* then found that regional nineteenth-century usages of the term indicated something considered "worthless or insignificant stuff; rubbish, trash" and certain populations as "worthless or disreputable people; rabble."[23] This book embraces these different definitions, which show how the term has been used to reflect and solidify binarized categories of morality. In other words, *traffic* always already encapsulated burgeoning taxonomies of objects and bodies into categories of deviant or normal, licit or illicit, criminal or citizen, taxonomies always fluctuating with the ever-evolving and globalizing reach of racial capitalism and the settler colonial state.

By bringing close, rather than pushing away, other criminalized pathways, queer traffic is a mode of circulatory performance that unsettles panics about the circuits through which sex travels. The criminal of free-trade binary thinking is an ample and ever-cunning category that contains anyone or anything deemed useless to participation in the pleasures of the global market. As Jodi Dean explained, "The criminal figures the ever present threat of loss, the losing that the fantasy of free trade disavows" (2009, 68). These subjects and their objects, their spaces, and their desires can never be harmonized into free-trade markets and therefore must be expelled for fear that the neoliberal fantasy of free trade be revealed as such. The imposition of the criminal onto licit and legal circuits of sexual culture, and onto those bodies who engage in production and consumption practices considered to be illicit and illegal, rubs against cultural expressions on the ground. In these spaces, racial, class, and gender power dynamics are forged not only within the frame of the object in question or in practices of consumption that surround that object but also in the very circuitry that characterizes its movement, not from one place to another but through the "nexus of cultural production that defines the things, places, and practices within its loops" (Novak 2013, 18). It is the underground, alternative, and stigmatized routes through which these objects and bodies travel that render them queer traffic as opposed to trade.

Queer traffic(k) rubs up against these other pathways to analyze the panics that implicitly and at times explicitly fuel the surveillance of sexual subjects and objects on the move.[24] I flirt with the addition of the "k" in the gerund traffic(k)ing to signal the ways in which a theory on queer traffic requires some deep play with illicit categories of (sexual) criminality. I do so to push back against the ever-proliferating use of "trafficking" as a term that often does more to incarcerate the same subjects it purports to "rescue." Historians Julia Laite and Philippa Hetherington rightly question trafficking as a "moving signifier that hides as much as it reveals" (2021, 7). Similar to them, I employ *queer traffic* to investigate "trafficking" as a term with "little useful explanatory power, other than the way it reveals the socio-political contexts in which it was deployed" (8). Throughout the book, I am critical of the discourse of anti–sex trafficking and its policing and criminalizing uses against sex work(ers), migrating people, and the movement of sexual culture. This is not to say that involuntary prostitution and sexual exploitation do not occur, but rather to highlight how the malleability and imprecision of what I call "sex trafficking talk," and its sedimentation in national and transnational policies, flattens colonial and neocolonial histories and covers over the damaging influences of free trade (Tyburczy 2019).

One such actor often discussed in connection to the precarity-inducing influences of NAFTA is the female *maquila* (factory) worker. Feminist scholars have long made convincing arguments about why gender is crucial to conversations of free trade, particularly for females working in free-trade zones on the Mexico-US border (Gaspar de Alba and Guzmán 2010; Ojeda and Hennessy 2006; Salzinger 2003; Wright 2006). Apart from the noteworthy example of Rosemary Hennessy's book *Fires on the Border* (2013), which discusses erotic relationships among women workers as some of the affective fuel of labor organizing (what she calls "passionate politics"), these studies largely avoid talk about sex, as it has so often been used as a tool to silence and blame *maquila* workers, at work and upon death. While border towns such as Juarez and Tijuana became free-trade zones in the 1980s, nearly a decade before NAFTA, the murders and disappearances of *maquila* workers reached a crescendo after NAFTA and the almost simultaneous Operación Guardián (Operation Gatekeeper). In 2006, under the transnationalization of the War on Drugs, which exacerbated what Rossana Reguillo (2011) has called the "narco-machine," or an infrastructure of violence that she likens to Nazi prison camps, these numbers again grew.[25] While the countless Mexican feminist scholars have tirelessly and bravely studied *feminicidios* on the border and throughout Mexico, "there has been no systematic accounting of victims or accountability by the authorities, which results in only more confusion, more impunity for the perpetrators, and less chance of resolution" (Gaspar de Alba and Guzmán 2010, 10). This lack of accounting for these lives, and cultural narratives about women's pathologies, creates and sustains normative social relations that assume the incompetence of poor, female, and Indigenous subjects as economic actors. Sayak Valencia (2010) has aptly named this scenario *capitalismo gore* (gore capitalism), or the specificities of precarity in Mexico as they intersect with the performance of toxic masculinities. In her now widely translated book, Valencia demonstrates how the normalization of epistemic violence in Mexico has shaped subcultures, such as *narco* cultures, that seize on the spectacularity of death as a quintessential practice of economic motivation dependent on deregulation, entrepreneurship, and the neoliberal promise of economic success. In this context, *narcos* become the quintessential neoliberal capitalists and *maquila* workers the ultimate in disposable surplus populations. For Valencia, NAFTA, particularly with regard to how the agreement reconfigured labor, reaffirmed the violences of the heteropatriarchal system and steered Mexico down a "sinuous road that led to Mexico's descent into gore capitalism" (2015, 131).

Deceased *maquila* workers came to be regarded as *maquilocas*, a term invented to disparage murdered *maquila* workers, some of whom are young, Brown, Indigenous, and originally from the south of Mexico and therefore have no familial network (other than other *maquila* workers). The *maquiloca* is a fictive subject created by the white heteropatriarchy that undergirds free-trade capitalism and by the infrastructural pathways of the violently imposed process of smoothing over disparate economies. Her sin is movement, the audacity to migrate to the north, to seek a life and a livelihood. Murdered or disappeared *maquila* workers in places such as Juarez and Tijuana are, upon their death, described as sexually licentious women with uncontrollable desires or as sex workers who, the logic of the *maquiloca* demands, put themselves in the position of being murdered, raped, or disappeared. According to Alicia Gaspar de Alba and Georgina Gúzman, while still alive, victims are cast as "*'las inditas del sur,'* the little Indian girls from the south of Mexico—poor, dark-skinned, and indigenous-looking" (2010, 1). In death, they are described as a "few dead prostitutes" (2). The adjudication for her death is sex, and pathological desire in general. She was driven mad by the *maquila*, the story goes. Morally insane and made sex-crazed by the lascivious urban lifestyle on the border, she relinquished her traditional values and their classed, raced, and gendered roles. Her money only goes toward vices. She drinks too much. She wears the wrong things, articles of clothing that "ask for it." She walks down alleys that are too dark, too late at night. She dares to live a life where she is read as alone, disposable, without community. The charge of *maquiloca* encourages the act of not accounting for these deaths: seduced by the neoliberal tenet of personal responsibility, the dead paid the price for their own failures, heeding the multinational demand for cheap labor in the *maquiladora* industry. An assemblage of state and nonstate actors commits these acts of gender, race, and class violence; however, it is the privileging of investment under NAFTA's policies and across a wide range of border economies that forges the context of murder, rape, and death. Writing about a NAFTA context of *feminicidios* and how they are staged in theater, Patricia A. Ybarra rightly asserts that "neoliberalism is a serial killer" (2018, 105).

I want to divert *maquiloca* discourse, rerouting the antisex, antimigration, and anti-Indigenous interpretation of the *maquila* worker as the pathological *maquiloca* to ruminate on the queer crip potentials of *la loca* and her positionality at the edge of free-trade capitalism. *Maquiloca* is coded language for prostitute, and *loca*, which means "crazy" or "madwoman," points toward the risks associated with women's independence and freedom. It also connotes sexual deviance and a perspective on sex as a "disreputable disability" (Mollow 2012) that attaches itself to anyone read as female, femme, or feminine presenting. As Lawrence La Fountain-Stokes shows in his monumental book *Translocas*, the reinvention of that which has been used as an insult has a long feminist and *cuir* history in the Americas (2021, 28–44). La Fountain-Stokes's use of the term transloca resignifies *loca* to admiringly refer to "insane women, effeminate homosexuals, drag performers, or transgender subjects" who "tread a dangerous ground . . . make and break allegiances, and . . . redefine meanings and sensibilities" (2, 18). Historically, *maquiloca* labels those cis women who dared to migrate alone for work at the border. Conceptually it means to pathologize all female, femme, and feminine-presenting people and their desires to move as madness, as foolish dalliances with deadly forms of sexual danger. The use of *loca*, or the madwoman, in *maquiloca* has never been repurposed for its proximity to queerness, but in this book, I want to put some pressure on feminist accounts that have too quickly aligned sex work and pornography with the narco-machine and sex trafficking to recast the figure of the *maquiloca* as an actor who desires the freedom to move, sexually or otherwise. In fact, movement and circulation is what free-trade discourse promises but rarely delivers for the sexual subjects that this book holds most dear.

To save the *maquiloca* from the madness she embodies and invites, both the political left and the right collaborate in fomenting sex panics, such as the global anti–sex trafficking panic, which result in national and transnational policies that actually stunt her movement and her activities. To do this, she must remain a pitiable subject, one who is sexually innocent and nonsexual and whose sole recuperative value is to be interpreted as mother and nurturer, rather than human being and sexual subject. What if the *maquila* worker were living *la vida loca*? What if she engaged in sex work to supplement her earnings? What if she is also trans and immediately clocked as "sex worker," regardless of how she earns her money? What if she embodied all these risks and was killed? Does that adjudicate her killing? By playing into free-trade capitalism's binary system of licit/illicit, legal/illegal, criminal/consumer, feminist scholars who immediately align pornographers, sex workers, pimps, and consumers of sexual materials with "human trafficking" actually work against the desires of the potential *maquila* worker to migrate, to work, and to be a full and dignified sexual subject, no matter how raunchy, audacious, or flagrant her sexual practices might be to an academic or activist audience.

By ceding sex to free-trade capitalism and its long-standing tool of "public morality" and "obscenity" exceptions, such analysis plays into the neoliberal fantasy of deserving and undeserving victims and reiterates the free-trade paradigm of success as mere survival and sexual and erotic cultures as frivolities for which there is no time, energy, or resources. These frivolities become opportunities to amplify already-existent structures of criminalization based in racialized gender inequities and the embodiment of difference. The blurriness of "trafficking" provides easy and always available leverage to criminalize a whole host of legal activities such as migration and sex work. Subjects such as the *maquiloca* became the refuse of licit and legal trade between nations, the disposable rabble who could not be organized, neither by the slave traders and the conquistadores nor by government-co-opted labor unions such as the Federation of Mexican Labor (CTM), which divided poor laborers from the middle-class sector and acquiesced to NAFTA's local and transnational policies and practices. Chased by panics about insatiable appetites out of control, the *maquiloca* represents one free trade–invented figure fictionalized through the same heterocispatriarchal and racist norms that militarize the infrastructures through which queer and trans bodies, objects, and ideas are smuggled in or blocked from moving across borders.[26]

Following the cue of the disparate band of sexual and gender outlaws who make up *Queer Traffic*'s interlocutors, I look to the gaps and margins of the NAFTA documents, their mistranslations, and their potential loopholes to focus on those who attempt to evade free-trade infrastructures and forge different pathways for sexual culture on the move. Focusing on sex reveals free trade's fault lines and invites me to track and trace unaccounted-for flows of cultural production at the edge of neoliberalism's seemingly all-encompassing reach. To do so requires an alignment with sex workers, pornographers, and others deemed sexual deviants who live, breathe, produce, consume, and circulate disruptive forms of sexual culture well beyond the confines of the homonormative or the pleasingly queer. I traverse underground sex cultures that may on their face seem disconnected from other queer lives and cultures. At other times I recount experiences with sexual subjects who have been claimed as "victims" so as to foment sex panics, which hijack the struggles of the subjects they claim to care about and instead discipline unruly bodies and their movements across borders. I therefore trace queer flows of sex and culture through the shaping of trade law, particularly NAFTA as a site for the invention of new categories of obscenity and "illegal" personhood through the classed and raced designation of the "criminal." In these practices of abjection I find the contradictions of late racial capitalism and the pleasures and perils of *queer traffic*.

Queer traffic refers not only to things, people, and practices but also to the pace and velocity of free trade, or what I call *NAFTA time*. This concept attends to movement across space as well as to the tempo of movement through time. Indeed, queer traffic is a method for simultaneously negotiating multiple temporalities and polygeographies to reflect the nonlinearity of sex on the move and its varied circuits. It extends queer scholarship on time to alight on moments of sexual and temporal dissidence that make a mess of the free-trade policies and infrastructures that control global flows. Queer traffic, then, is both a theoretical and a methodological tool with which we can "recognize how erotic relations and the bodily acts that sustain them gum up the works of normative structures we call family and nation, gender, race, class, and sexuality identity, by changing tempos, by mixing memory and desire, and recapturing excess" (Freeman 2010, 173).[27] It provides a flexible mode for following sexual trade, for moving erratically across the NAFTA years, in both the lead-up to and the ongoing aftermath of 1994.

If there are two temporal poles that bracket the tempo of NAFTA time, they are the disorienting breakneck speed of the whirring *maquila* conveyor belt and the tedious and exhausting wait of the Central American migrant for their asylum petition number to be called.[28] In this book, the erotic pleasures experienced while dancing, flirting, and sometimes just smoking a cigarette are diversions from exploitation. They disrupt NAFTA time, adjusting its pace and tempo, but not (always) for political or activist reasons. Using sex to alter the pace with which trade travels is not necessarily productive; on the contrary, it can be a relief from the pressure to always and everywhere resist.

To become attuned to the pace and rhythm of these pathologized practices of exchange and consumption, my methodology had to remain supple, flexible, and multimodal. To study the imbrication of sex and trade economies, I employed mixed methods from both the humanities and the humanistic social sciences. Over the course of ten years, I conducted participant observation and community-based participatory research and more than one hundred interviews with leading academics, activists, and artists who specialize in the diverse cultures of sex, labor, trade, the economy, performance, and visual art across Mexico City, Tijuana, Toronto, and Vancouver. Qualitative research and auto-ethnographic reflections are complemented by archival research conducted at el Centro de Investigaciones sobre América del Norte (CISAN), the Centro de Documentación y Archivo Histórico Lésbico, and the Museo Universitario Arte Contemporáneo (all in Mexico City); the Sexual Representation Collection at the Bonham Centre for Sexual Diversity Studies (University of Toronto); The ArQuives: Canada's LGBTQ2+ Archives in Toronto; the Archivo de el Colegio de la Frontera Norte (Tijuana); and the Mexico-US Business Committee (MEXUS) collections at the Dolph Briscoe Center for American History and the Nettie Lee Benson Latin American Collection (Austin, Texas).

Throughout the book, I cast a wide net to uncover the relationships among free trade, sex panic, and NAFTA. At times direct, at others indirect, the unfettered connections I make between sex and NAFTA, both preceding and following the implementation of the agreement in 1994, can more faithfully be seen as ripples and dispersions in the waters of free trade, rather than one-to-one causal relationships. To do so, I juxtapose scenarios such as the Finger Vibrator and my interactions with the Mexican businessmen that began this introduction with practices of smuggling, piracy, pill dividing and stockpiling, "overeating" the colonizer's food, and the harboring of migrant peoples at the edges of the vertiginous flows of free trade. I analyze these queer traffic practices engaged by my interlocutors, and sometimes by myself, as performances of access to the material goods and lived experiences that they/we desire. I follow crossborder and intranational circuits of cultural production, which range from audiovisual, print, and digital pornography; US-imported food stuffs; HIV/AIDS drugs and treatments; and sex toys and other erotic accoutrement. I draw inspiration from labor, environmental, and Indigenous rights advocates to present a story of how an international trade agreement nominally about the movement of goods and capital has had and continues to have such a profound material influence on the level of the body. The stories I tell can be found nowhere else. They bring together two objects of study—free trade and sex—that have been purposefully disaggregated from each other in the name of security and in the anticipation of a normative consumer who is assumed to be uninterested in, disgusted by, or too easily corruptible to enjoy in the production, consumption, and circulation of dissident (sexual) acts and the objects that pertain to them.

Queer Traffic: A Twisted Route

Each chapter celebrates a queer traffic praxis, one in which actors negotiate the limits of free-trade capitalism in relation to questions of access, pleasure, mobility, and embodiment. To highlight the distortions of history through the nonlinearity and multidirectionality of NAFTA time, my chapters are intentionally out of chronological order. The book begins in 2012–2013 (when I began my research); works backward through the 1980s, 1990s, and early 2000s to cover the lead-up and immediate aftermath to the CUSFTA and NAFTA; and then jumps to 2015–2018, the years that set the stage for the NAFTA renegotiations that began in 2018. In chapter 1, "Porn Pirates," I examine how illicit reproductions—pirated and pornographic media—get swept up in panics of theft, terrorism, and sex trafficking. NAFTA innovated the now-global parameters for what constitutes intellectual property (IP) law infringement, and I zoom in from this transnational regime of regulation to focus on a non-NAFTA form of exchange at the Tepito market in Mexico City. The "porn pirates" are the men who sell pirated pornography at their booths in Tepito, a "tough neighborhood" point of sale that has contributed to pornography's false reputation in Mexico as illegal contraband. These porn pirates intervene in transnational and subnational panics around explicit sexual media in two ways: they render accessible pornographic productions that are either too expensive or too taboo for working-class peoples to buy and consume; they also eroticize an aesthetic of female embodiment within the films that disrupts the circuit of a dominant US-porn industry based in California and obsessed with thinness and whiteness. The close of the chapter extrapolates the lessons learned from the display of the pornographic archive at Tepito and the myths about pornography as a vehicle for sex trafficking and addiction.

Chapter 2, "Importing Degradation," travels to Toronto and Vancouver to examine how, in the lead-up to and aftermath of the CUSFTA in 1989 and NAFTA in 1994, the Canadian government enabled Canada Customs to search, seize, and in many instances destroy queer, trans, and Black print material destined for gay, feminist, and leftist bookshops. It shows that NAFTA's opening of borders to the "free" flow of goods actually operationalized and weaponized existing local and domestic governance (i.e., the Butler Law, the Customs Tariff Act, and the Criminal Code) to regulate and render "obscene" sexual cultural production that failed to match rhetorical and normative claims to national (Canadian) citizenship. I argue that Canada's anxieties over the cultural dominance of the United States reached a crescendo in the CUSFTA/NAFTA years and inordinately focused on queer cultural materials. I combine interviews with sexual radicals on the ground fighting Canada Customs in the 1980s and 1990s with archival research conducted at The ArQuives and the Sexual Representation Collection at the Bonham Centre for Sexual Diversity Studies at the University of Toronto, all of which attest to the surveillance and panic cultivated to stem the tide of queer materials into Canada.

In chapter 3, "Sex, Drugs, and Intellectual Property Law," I reexamine the influence of NAFTA's chapter 17, the agreement's IP provision, on the fiction of pharmaceutical scarcity of antiretrovirals in the years following NAFTA's signing. The pharmaceutical invention of antiretrovirals occurred synchronically with the implementation of policies regarding IP law in NAFTA. This IP law, developed by NAFTA architects, was then taken up by the WTO and exported globally. In other words, the fight for HIV+ sexual health in the 1990s spurred multinational pharmaceutical corporations to

innovate IP law, using NAFTA as a testing ground. These laws and policies became instruments of death, killing countless HIV+ peoples across the NAFTA
borderlands and beyond. Queer and trans sex are scapegoated as the cause
of disease and contamination, while NAFTA creates and imposes scarcity
onto the circuits through which antiretrovirals and other drugs could flow.
I diagnose NAFTA as a necropolitical infrastructure of sex and death and
transit through Tijuana and Mexico City, where I met groups of activists
and artists creating informal networks of care and aesthetics to counter the
scapegoating of queer sex as the cause of illness and death.

The several months I spent alongside lesbian, gay, bisexual, trans, and
queer (LGBTQ) migrants traveling to and through Tijuana, many with the
hopes of gaining asylum in the United States or forging a life in Tijuana,
are the topic of chapter 4, "Dancing *Punta* on NAFTA Time." This chapter
expands what we think of as activism and attends to the granular details
of LGBTQ migrants passing NAFTA time. From birthday parties, to smoking cigarettes, and especially to dancing the Afro-Latinx, Afro-Indigenous,
Garifuna dance form *punta*, these everyday practices arose as sexy and potent ways to deeply play with their often-interminable waits at the Mexico-
US border. NAFTA's violent influences on border security regimes and the
landscape of the border contextualize the many dangers of pausing in Tijuana to wait but also uncover the commitment of queer and trans migrants
to create moments of pleasure despite growing ethnonationalist sentiment
about and attacks on their persons. In so doing, migrating LGBTQ people
fashion their own terms of their waiting through ephemeral performances
of pleasure that steal from NAFTA time.

The frictions, overlaps, and divergences of the social performances I
explore in these chapters defragment how everyday actors marshal the
power of aesthetics to interrupt transnational, subnational, and regional
free-trade policies. Just as social performers aesthetically respond to NAFTA,
Canadian and Mexican cultural performers also directly and indirectly take
up the topic of NAFTA to rehearse other forms of living. NAFTA's cultural
performances uncover free trade's sexual proclivities and its connections to
the social performances of consumption, production, and the circulation
of certain normative forms of embodied sexualities.

To reflect on the activation of queer traffic aesthetics throughout
the book, and to disorder my own pace, tempo, and destination, a brief
performance art *desviación* (deviation) follows each chapter.[29] This focus
on anti-NAFTA and NAFTA-adjacent performance art and my contextual-
ization of these performances in relation to NAFTA as a policy and ideology

further illuminate the non-NAFTA aesthetics of the social performances discussed throughout the book. These cultural performances, directly related to NAFTA, or that I read in connection to NAFTA, show how aesthetics cohere objects of analysis typically considered discrete.

Collectively, the performances speak to the ongoing relevance of NAFTA to contemporary Mexican and Canadian performance artists and the ways in which the FTA invents normativities as they relate to indigeneity, (dis)ability, gender, race, and body size. They attend to the slippages and mistranslations of NAFTA and now the USMCA and look to embodied performance to overcome language's limitations for analyzing (and understanding) NAFTA. The performances I discuss in these deviations—including those by César Martínez Silva and collaborator Orgy punk; by Erika Bülle Hernández; by Lechedevirgen Trimegisto; and by Montreal-based 2boys.tv in collaboration with performance artist Alexis O'Hara (Montréal) and Richard Moszka (Mexico City)—employ aesthetic choices for bringing into action regional queer/*cuir*/*kuir* and anarchist cultures in the ongoing wreckage of neoliberal projects throughout the Americas. From chains and masks to nipple rings, bondage collars, erotic piercings, and rubber fetishes enacted through the kink persona of the gimp, these performances all use sex and sexual play to perform in close proximity to but not in step with the horrors and abuses of NAFTA time. While all the performances employ kink attire or practices to wage a political critique of the fantasy of free trade, many of them also have something to say about rehearsing life differently during the "crip times" of NAFTA. Though aesthetically and methodologically distinct, these crip performances question free trade's tendency to flatten or harmonize difference. They talk across debility and disability, its connections and divides, to propose and walk audiences through tactics for disrupting market logics in everyday life. The point is to show not how neoliberalism disables but rather that neoliberalism's debilitating forces produce disabilities by making precarious populations available for injury (Puar 2017). They acknowledge the NAFTA borderlands as sites of violence, surveillance, and panic while also embracing how sexual subjects endeavor to carve out contexts of pleasure.

From porn pirates in Tepito to obscenity smugglers at the Canada-US border, underground circulators of hormones and antiretrovirals, and queer and trans migrants dancing *punta*, *Queer Traffic* honors those who have creatively negotiated the formal pathways of surveillance and panic that characterize free-trade policies. Throughout the book, I highlight what NAFTA does alongside the embodied possibilities that people carve out in the times and spaces of NAFTA. The social and cultural performances this book covers offer a multifaceted set of queer traffic tactics that interrupt the politics and policies of free trade. The stakes of these everyday performances, overtly or implicitly, are the very power over embodied life that NAFTA, as an instantiation of capital's colonial history, enacts and extracts. To meet that power, from top to bottom, to bottom up and back again, the people I met in doing this research taught me, shared with me, the methods they employed in these scenarios. These queer traffic methods show how an aesthetics of the body apply well beyond the stage, the gallery, the museum, and the art market to spill out across these different arenas and encounters.

At its most optimistic, this book hedges a kind of hope for queer culture and aesthetics to dream of other forms of living that go beyond mere survival, despite the destruction and devastation of late racial capitalism and the ongoing horrors of colonial decimation. The belief that life could be lived otherwise emerges from my encounters with people on the ground who reroute the pathways through which they can engage in sexual economies of exchange. I follow these pathways that evade the surveillance apparatus of the state and center those communities and individuals who assume some of the biggest risks in negotiating the sexual and affective contracts and policies implicit in free-trade ideology.

1

Porn Pirates

The two of us—one *gringa* and one *mexicana* (I'll call her Fabiola)—wound our way through the enormous eighty-block, open-air *tianguis* (from the Nahuatl word *tianquiztli* for market) in Tepito, Mexico City. We chatted as we licked the thick, viscous tamarind syrup from the sides of our *micheladas* while reggaetón music blared from various speakers. Fabiola was looking for a particular stall that sold delicious *pambazos* and another one that sold a certain kind of knock-off sneaker.[1] I was on the hunt for pornography, Mexican pornography in DVD format to be exact, and Tepito (meaning "small thing" in Nahuatl) was the primary market in Mexico City to buy pirated DVDs. Fabiola had insisted that she accompany me, warning me that it was unsafe for me to go alone to this particular *tianguis*. As we neared the pirated-film stalls, she gestured toward the black-tarped tents where thousands of pirated DVDs were meticulously organized in boxed, categorized rows and impeccably protected within their individualized, paper-thin plastic casing, a prophylactic if there ever was one. As I moved from booth to booth, she stood outside waiting for me. I greeted the stall attendant with a *buenas tardes* and began to dig into this incredible pornographic archive. After much searching at various booths, I still hadn't found any Mexican pornography. Much of the porn available was pirated copies from the United States and Italy. I asked one attendant if he had any Mexican pornography.

He shook his head to say no but also asked one of his nearby colleagues to see if he had any at his stall.

No more than fifteen minutes had passed, and I had developed a reputation: the *gringa* in search of Mexican pornography, though most stall attendants addressed me by the classed and raced designation *güera*.[2] When I asked several consecutive stand attendants for any DVDs of Mexican-produced pornography, the men (always men) running the booths began to yell to their nearby colleagues, "Oye, esta güera está buscando pornografía mexicana" (Hey, this *güera* is looking for Mexican pornography). Admittedly I blushed and chuckled as I entered the nearby booths, acknowledging the dissonance between the stigma of the object I was in search of and the honorific *güera* used to describe me. As I moved from stall to stall, I also knew that I was able to circumnavigate the Tepito pirated-porn booths precisely because I was not read as a Mexican woman. My skin color, my gender expression, my perceived nationality (though sometimes I was read as *española* or *chilena*), and the recognition of my classed status as *güera* all afforded me the luxury of not being harassed while vocally and visibly searching for Mexican pornography.

Attendants of such informal yet highly organized points of purchase as the booths in Tepito comprise a specific classed and raced labor force. Sometimes referred to as *los ambulantes* (itinerant salespeople), more than twenty thousand vendors make up this vast culturally legitimized market that is nonetheless considered dangerous and cheap by the middle-class Mexican imaginary. These vendors, who forge non-NAFTA routes for the circulation of explicit sexual media, are just a fraction of those who work in the immense informal economy in Mexico. In 2014, only a year after I visited Tepito, the International Labour Organization (ILO), drawing from the work of INEGI, estimated that the informal economy makes up nearly 60 percent of all employment in Mexico (ILO 2014, 1, 5). In this chapter on explicit sexual media and those who produce, circulate, and perform in it, queer traffic describes the non-NAFTA pathways, what I will call *pornways*, through which pornography moves through the informal market. Working outside the state's normative definitions of corruption and organized crime, the informal circulation of audiovisual pornography in Mexico is a performance of consumption in the underground, not the criminal underworld, of free trade. Largely inaccessible for poor and working-class people, save for pirated reproductions in Mexico City, pornography is often cast as traveling in the same or interrelated illegal circuits as drug smuggling and sex trafficking.

After its implementation in 1994, NAFTA marked a major structural adjustment of the informal pirated-media market (Lobato and Thomas 2012, 449). It became the first FTA to include obligations to protect intellectual property rights (IPR) in its chapter 17 (Terry, Ederer, and Orange 2005) and served as a model for the WTO's Trade Related Aspects of Intellectual Property Rights (TRIPS) agreement that was debated toward the end of the Uruguay round of the General Agreement on Tariffs and Trade (GATT). After NAFTA, IPR trade policies—inclusive of copyright, patents, trademarks, and trade secrets—became key features of FTAs and served as the global model for the implementation of future IP laws in other nations. As José Carlos G. Aguiar has shown, "Copyright infringement has been integrated into Mexico's security agenda and become a federal crime; unauthorized reproduction and retail of protected material is perceived as a form of organized crime; as a result, sellers are defined as criminals" (2013, 250).[3] The infringement on copyright, as anyone who has ever tried to fast-forward through the threat of fines and prison confinement that opens nearly every DVD would know, was always regarded as theft. NAFTA revolutionized IP law transnationally, and subsequently the WTO fashioned its IP law and its charges of criminality for violating such laws based on NAFTA's 1990s innovations in this area of transnational (il)legality. This IPR regime, with its "racial investments in whiteness and continuing implications for racial (in)equality" (Vats and Keller 2018, 742), criminalizes the practices of exchange that operate at the edge of the transnational porn industry.

After September 11, 2001, media pirates came to be viewed not only as criminals but as terrorists. The expansive weaponization of the "war on terror" included infringements of NAFTA-engineered IPR laws. As Bhaskar Sarkar points out, piracy and terrorism have been linked since the 1980s, but the post-9/11 era inspired "a new sense of purpose" (2016, 346).[4] NAFTA's innovations in IP law contributed to this "new sense of purpose" in criminalizing media piracy and linked those who produce, consume, or circulate pornography to organized crime, narco-traffic, and sex trafficking. I highlight the stakes for those who participate in Mexico's pornways, while examining some of the most controversial pornographic productions, to contemplate the stakes of embodiment for the men who sell and make it and for the women who perform in this audiovisual form of explicit sexual media. Porn piracy is one form of queer traffic, of non-NAFTA trade, that actively evades the IPR regime of the trade agreement to create contexts of unaccounted-for reproductions and consumptions in Mexico's informal market. The pirated copy, as Iván A. Ramos contends while writing about punk subcultures and bootlegs in Mexico, "enables a queer reading practice that resists the State's longing for order" (2022, 243). The untamed anarchism of the Tepito pirated-porn booths disrupts free-trade markets and security logics via person-to-person interaction in a context of consumerism marked by teeming excess.

Free trade is nominally all about the consumer, and yet, when it comes to what I'm playfully calling "porn pirates," certain forms of consumption and their related consumers come to be labeled as excessive, pathological, and criminal. Pirates are often cast as mutinous and sea-bound and yet another enemy of free trade, as they are also terrestrial disrupters of formalized trade flows.[5] By engaging in the production and consumption of nonformalized pornways, porn pirates create illicit reproductions as acts of access to the consumption and circulation of pornography. I begin by giving a brief history of Mexico's relationship to pornways, which illustrates how all porn in Mexico can be viewed as queer traffic. I then examine how the panic over sexual flows specific to the NAFTA years is played out on, first, the bodies of pornographers and *fayuceros*, or those that sell what is considered to be cheap, knock-off contraband, sexual or otherwise, and, second, the bodies of the women who perform in low-budget hotel or homegrown pornography, especially those women who are curvy and full-figured. The term *pornways* makes explicit this connection between pornographic circulation and women facing off against the US porn industry and its privileging of Anglo-based body ideals in pornographic film. I embrace the frictive relationship of porn to criminal flows but refuse the erotophobic stance, both inside and outside of pornography circuits, that aligns piracy with terrorism and porn consumption with addiction and pathology. This chapter irreverently takes up the caricature of the "pirate" invented by the international IPR regime and argues against the use of IPR as a NAFTA-inspired and war on terror–extended infrastructure to surveil and punish the men who sell porn at markets such as Tepito.

Mexico's Pornways

The history of porn in Mexico has always been about the market and trade. Pornographic productions in Mexico trace back to the silent cinema era, and the circulation of postcards, among other media, and pornography has existed in Mexico since the advent of reproduction technologies such as film and photography. Indeed, Zeb Tortorici's groundbreaking archival research (2018, 2023) shows how sexual artifacts, from sixteenth-century criminal and Inquisition records to the pornographic antique treasures he finds at

Mexico City's outdoor market La Lagunilla, have traveled through popular and institutional spaces of regulation and consumption since the colonial period.[6] In vintage markets and *tianguis* such as Tepito, pornography has been a material commodity of exchange since at least the 1970s when *fayuca*, or foreign goods smuggled into Mexico, largely from the United States at the time, became a highly organized and successful informal business enterprise in the cosmos of street trade (Cruz Hernández and Hernández 2015, 170). It wasn't until the 1980s and 1990s, with NAFTA and new technologies such as the VCR and the DVD player, that *piratería* (pirated reproductions) became a common market item for sale alongside other second-hand and free trade–sanctioned and nonsanctioned goods (Konove 2018, 173–174).

In the 1980s, pornographic films such as *Behind the Green Door*, *Taboo*, *The Devil in Miss Jones*, and even more experimental films like Rinse Dream's *Café Flesh* (entitled *El café del futuro* in Mexico) arrived in VHS and Beta format, mostly through the underground circuits of cinema clubs, or for those individuals fortunate to own a VHS or Beta player for private home viewing. It wasn't until 1994, the year NAFTA was implemented, however, that Gerard Damiano's cult porn classic, *Deep Throat*, arrived in Mexico City with great fanfare. In a 2013 interview in Mexico City with underground cinema expert Jorge Grajales, he recalled the marquees reading "las grandes del porno por primera vez en México" (the greatest porn films in Mexico for the first time).[7] Porn in the 1970s, especially parodic porn films such as *Deep Throat* and *Flesh Gordon* (entitled *El sexonauta* in Mexico), could finally be shown on the big screen. In fact, porn offered the Mexico City–based cinemas of Mexico's former Golden Age, such as the Cine Teresa, the Río, and the Venus, a gasping last breath. Describing all cinema houses in Mexico in the 1980s as *cines piojo* (lice-ridden theaters), in our interview, Grajales recalled their poor sound and dilapidated spaces:

> Cines piojo porque eran ya muy descuidados. Los resortes salían de los sillones. Habían ratas. Los pisos estaban descuidados, pegajosos y así, lo mismo que los grindhouse en los Estados Unidos. Muchos de estos cines aquí en México, que eran pues los grandes templos cinematográficos del esplendor de nuestra industria en los años 40's y 50's, pues terminaron siendo así. Y cuando estos cines estaban a punto de cerrar, la única opción que tuvieron fue proyectar cine pornográfico.
>
> (Lice-ridden theaters, because by then they were really neglected. The springs came out of the chairs. There were rats. The floors were

filthy, sticky and stuff, just like grindhouse theaters in the United States. Many of the movie theaters here in Mexico City, previously the grand temples of cinematic splendor of our film industry in the 1940s and 1950s, well, they ended up in this state. And when these theaters were on the verge of closing, the only option they had was to show porn.)

These cinemas, with their vanished grandeur, have, of course, their own stories of decline, but, as geographer Felipe Zúñiga explained to me one afternoon in 2013 outside his office in the Centro Histórico (historic center), the waning lives of these once great cinemas coincided with the first major neoliberal crisis, the country's bankruptcy, and the debt crisis of 1982. "Y luego viene el temblor, el 85," Zúñiga explained, "entonces crisis y temblor, al Centro Histórico y su vida nocturna pues la lleva a un desgaste muy fuerte" (And then came the 1985 earthquake, so the economic crisis and the earthquake lead to a really intense deterioration of the historic downtown area and its nightlife). Owing at least partially to its association with these *cines piojo* of the Centro Histórico and their proximity to famed *zona ruda* (coarse zone) Garibaldi and the *barrio bravo* (tough neighborhood) Tepito, pornographic film came to be associated with the real and imagined dangers of these locales. After NAFTA, the popular imaginary linked porn both with dangerous spaces and a transnational paradigm that solidified pornography's reputation as criminal traffic.

The late 1980s and the cinema privatization programs of the Carlos Salinas de Gortari administration, as Ignacio M. Sánchez Prado has shown in *Screening Neoliberalism* (2014), also precipitated the advent of cinema multiplexes in Mexico City in the lead-up to NAFTA. Sánchez Prado details how the popularity of "American-style romantic comedies" (63), middle-class aesthetics, and the class stratification of these Mexican cineplexes matched the neoliberal rhetoric of economic *apertura* (opening) that Miguel de la Madrid began in the 1980s and Salinas de Gortari cemented in the 1990s (62–104). These high-end multiplexes, where affluent urban and professional middle-class audiences could afford the hefty ticket price, stood in stark distinction to the *cines piojo* that Grajales and Zúñiga described. Perhaps it is no surprise then that the resurgence of the Mexican film industry, supported by that of cinema multiplexes, in the 1990s did not coincide with the birth of a Mexican pornography industry. In fact, the elite cinema multiplexes further marginalized the circulation and consumption of pornography in Mexico by seemingly confirming pornography's illegality and its association with the criminal. Other forms of sexual cinema such as *sexicomedias* (sex comedies), films about *ficheras* (cabaret women, sex workers), and the genre known as *los nudie-cuties* (*cinema de desnudas*, or nude cinema) had been popular to working-class Mexican society since the mid-1970s and continued to be widely available in pirated form, not only in Tepito, but at the DVD stands one can find at some metro transit hubs.[8]

And yet whether pornographic film was ever illegal and, if so, when it became legal is more folklore than fact. Censorship of sexual content in Mexico's mass media, particularly after the 1940s, operates more on the level of rumor (Anne Rubenstein, personal email, 2020). Ernesto Román Pérez even goes so far as to say that "no es gratuito que la casi totalidad de la historia del cine pornográfico realizado en México pueda estar más cerca de la leyenda que de la historia propiamente dicha" (it is not without reason that almost the entire history of pornographic cinema made in Mexico may be closer to legend than to history itself) (2006, 61), even as he states that the film authorities of Salinas's government "autorizan el material pornográfico" (authorized pornographic material) (28). To explain porn's reputation in Mexico, and the persistent stigma of approximating the body to sexual media, I therefore look neither to Catholic sermons nor conservative politicians' speeches on the corruptive qualities of pornography, though these surely exist in abundance; nor do I cite the phenomenon of *doble moral* (the double standard of convenient and selectively applied morality), mentioned in nearly every interview I conducted in Mexico from 2012 to 2013. These factors certainly help to explain how pornography and its sites of consumption and circulation came to be viewed as *suciedad* (filth). Drawing from Deborah R. Vargas's theory of "*lo sucio* as a Latino queer analytic," I locate the charge that pornography is filth as a set of "racialized discourses of difference" in intimate relationship to "neoliberal projects that disappear the most vulnerable and disenfranchised by cleaning up spaces and populations deemed dirty and wasteful" (2014, 716, 715). What rendered pornography into dirt and filth was its perceived effect on the urban landscape of Mexico City, a city desperately trying to show the world that it was "safe" and "open for business" for the transnational capitalist class, particularly in the lead-up to NAFTA and especially under the guidance of the Lebanese-Mexican telecommunications tycoon Carlos Slim.

As one of NAFTA's biggest beneficiaries, Slim and his global conglomerate Grupo Carso, with the support of then-leftist Mexico City mayor Andrés Manuel López Obrador, hired the Giuliani Partners Group to "clean up" Mexico City, much like Rudy Giuliani had purportedly done through zero-tolerance policing in Times Square. That which is considered the filth of free trade shares an inextricable link to bodily sensations in this hemispheric history of disciplinary urban design. So too, as Samuel R. Delany has shown, does the circulation of capital curtail the pleasures of what he terms "interclass contact" (2001, 111–193). Pornography, considered a low-class "body genre" (Williams 1991) in its incitement of bodily reaction and the arousal, emission, and exchange of fluids, possesses all the requisite attributes of that which requires cleaning—so much so, that any audiovisual material containing nude women, from the nudie-cuties to the erotic masked wrestler or *luchador* films, and even uncensored versions of the *fichera* films, were always made to be shown in foreign markets. For example, Grajales told me about the inaccessibility of the 1955 film *La fuerza del deseo*, directed by Miguel M. Delgado and starring Ana Luisa Peluffo:

> No se consigue en México, ni en el formato de video. No existe en dvd. De hecho nunca llegó al formato de cintas Beta, vhs, mucho menos ahora dvd ni Blu-ray. La tiene Televisa, usualmente la pasa a través de sus canales, pero en la versión cortada que es la que todos los mexicanos conocemos. Nunca hemos visto, por lo menos gente de mi generación y anteriores.

> (It's not available in Mexico, not even as a video. It isn't available as a DVD. In fact, it never arrived as a Beta or VHS tape, let alone now in DVD or Blu-ray. Televisa has a copy. They usually show it on their channels, but in the shortened version, which is the one all of us know in Mexico. We've never seen the original, at least people from my generation and previous ones.)

If one wasn't fortunate enough to see this film in *cines piojo* in the 1980s and 1990s, one site in a long gendered history of male sexual spectatorship in movie theaters (Rubenstein 2020), one would never again be able to see the uncensored version in Mexico. Within Mexico, then, the circulation of all sexually explicit material can be considered queer traffic, not only for its frictive relationship with illegality and illicit consumption but also for breaking with its perceived unidirectional flow northward and its (albeit male-driven) movement through underground *cines piojo*.

Perhaps owing to its visual presence in the underground circuits of the informal market, the belief that the production, circulation, and consumption of pornography, pirated or otherwise, remains illegal is not uncommon. Thus, while Mexican pornways might largely but not solely contain normative performances of hetero and cis sex, and while piracy is viewed as illicit yet socially legitimized in Mexico, the purchase of any audiovisual form of pornography is still widely regarded as a criminal act. Underground yet highly visible markets for pirated goods, such as Tepito, play a key role in filling the gap in affordable sexual media for the working classes after the near disappearance of *cines piojo* in the twenty-first century. Some of these cinemas have since become sex shops. Within some of these shops exist viewing booths where one can watch some of the pornographic film that they sell on their shelves for an often unaffordable formal market price with the value-added NAFTA tax. What could be considered Mexico's porn industry, then, largely exists within the confines of informal market vendors such as those in Tepito, or the more precarious street vendors such as those in La Merced, a red-light district that has been less successful in thwarting police raids. In comparison to the thousands of multicolored tarps that populate the Tepito streets every day of the week, save Tuesday (the vendors' day off), many merchants in La Merced display their wares on blankets that can be quickly gathered to avoid police fines, bribes, arrests, or violence. Still, vendors in the Tepito *tianguis*, while socially legitimized, occupy a precarious labor sector that can be shut down at the whim of the zero-tolerance state and police force.

What ultimately became the *tianguis* in Tepito has a long, embattled, yet successful history of resistance to authorial control since the colonial period (Cross 1998, 87). Indeed, Tepito's reputation as a market of stolen or illegal goods became destiny when the three-hundred-year-old market, the Baratillo (from *barato*, or cheap) moved to the neighborhood in 1902 (Konove 2018, 2). Ultimately the name Baratillo fell out of favor, and by the mid-twentieth century the market came to be known by the name of the neighborhood itself (171). Today, Tepito is infamous for specializing in the socially legitimized sale and consumption of goods that travel outside the licensed boundaries of NAFTA circuits of exchange. These goods, *fayuca*, are known to be cheap "contraband" sold on the "black market" and *hecho in China* (made in China). These *fayuca* flows have been forged by a secretive and locally powerful collective of vendors known as *los ambulantes*, which, particularly after the inclusion of China into the WTO in 2001, include Mexican, Chinese, and Korean traders and importers and exporters (Alba and Braig 2022, 202–203; Gillespie and McBride 2013). While based in a longer history of trade that dates to the Mexica (Aztec) empire, *los ambulantes* retain their relationship to itinerant movement but are codified at the edge of the late racial capitalist state not necessarily in resistance to its neoliberal practices, but definitely in refusal of its infrastructures. While technically illegal, most informal market vendors, as John C. Cross has shown, sell their products owing to "irregular agreements" with certain city officials. "Under a neo-liberal model inspired partly by the desire to 'modernize' the city after the passage of NAFTA," Cross explains, street vending became a target of "pressure from more formal merchants who were themselves being pulled into the tax structure of the state as part of the rationalization of the fiscal system required by Salinas' neo-liberal policies" (1998, 187). While other markets throughout Mexico sell *fayuca*, Tepito is unique for its history not only as a *barrio bravo* but also as a site where talented young pugilists hope to train their way out of poverty, many inhabitants worship Santa Muerte (Saint Death), and *los ambulantes* engage in (in)famous stand-offs with the state or police control. Abandoned by the Mexican state, Tepito, with its relationship to death, poverty, and Indigenous struggle, is marked too in its homage to its patron god, Xipe Totec, the flayed Mexica deity of commerce (Cruz Hernández and Hernández 2015, 172), a figure who will reappear in a *desviación* (deviation) that follows this chapter.

In the Office of the USTR's global list of "notorious markets for counterfeiting and piracy," Tepito always makes the cut (2022, 48). If you're looking for pirated pornographic audio and/or visual recordings, then Tepito is the market in Mexico City to find such illicit reproductions. Bringing the body close to Tepito and its pirated wares, while socially legitimized, is a gendered, raced, and classed performance with the illicit, one that incorporates an unspoken-for fascination with longer racialized histories of Indigenous economies that operate outside of or in contradistinction to the market economy, with the elision of "Black" with contraband, and the estimation of goods from China as inferior to those goods traveling from Mexico's official trading partners. In line with the Indigenous roots of *los ambulantes*, those who traffic in *piratería* divert the NAFTA-choreographed supply chain, circulating illicit reproductions in the underground of the Mexican informal market. In general, then, piracy acts as a socially legitimate performance of repetition that occurs in a wide array of markets and guerrilla points of purchase wherein those left out of NAFTA can work in the informal sector that makes up most of Mexico's economy.

In Mexico, piracy as a method of queer traffic circumvents NAFTA as the arbiter of free-trade interactions across North America. Writing specifically about Tepito, Ramon Lobato (2012) proposes that piracy be viewed as a method of access to high-cost goods otherwise unreachable to poor and working-class peoples. While "copyright infringement is not always directly linked to the interrogation of power structures," Lobato admits, in the case of Tepito, piracy does describe "a mundane and unremarkable activity in which almost everybody engages in order to partake in film culture" (85, 87). Outside the logic of the global copyright regime, porn pirates insert themselves into the networks of the global economy they are usually excluded from to engage in what Lucas Hilderbrand, writing about bootleg analog videotape, calls an "aesthetics of access" (2009, 6, 34). In so doing, they deliver on the desire for sexual film culture by forging alternative yet highly organized and politicized pornways through which sexual culture can flow to Mexico City viewers.

Hotel Garage, Huilas Mexicanas

In the end, my search for pornography in Tepito yielded mostly pirated-porn films from Japan, the United States, and Italy. The only Mexican pornographic productions I could find were those filmed in motels. These low-tech, low-cost productions are advertised as nonconsensually shot with *cámaras escondidas* (hidden cameras) and constitute an entire genre of Mexican pornography known as *Hotel Garage, huilas mexicanas* (Hotel Garage, Mexican whores) (see figs. 1.1 and 1.2). Hotel Garage refers to rent-by-the-hour motels where your car is concealed behind a thick black PVC curtain to evade the shame with which being seen or recognized in one of these locales might entail. As I watched the films, I immediately noted that the female actors in the films—brown, curvy, with natural breasts and un-shorn pubic hair—differed greatly from the thin, white bodies heavily made up and shaved, and often with synthetic breast implants that dominate US porn. In this dynamic, the unruly circulations of pornography throughout Mexico, from pirated porn to the *Hotel Garage, huilas mexicanas* enterprise, face off with the hegemonic body ideals manufactured in Porn Valley (San Fernando Valley in Southern California) and the digital circuits of Montréal as the global home of Mind Geek, the Luxembourg-registered and Canadian-based company that owns and operates online porn sites such as Pornhub, RedTube, and YouPorn (Alilunas 2021).

The *Hotel Garage, huilas mexicanas* films are billed as including three to five different women, but sometimes seemingly show the same woman in various vignettes. Throughout these films, the presence of the handheld camera is apparent, suggesting that *cámaras escondidas* is a marketing ploy that capitalizes on the eroticization of secret surveillance. In *Hotel Garage, huilas*

1.1   *Hotel Garage, huilas mexicanas,* film cover of vol. 4 (2012). Personal collection of Jennifer Tyburczy.

1.2   *Hotel Garage, huilas mexicanas*, film cover of vol. 5 (2012). Personal collection of Jennifer Tyburczy.

mexicanas, cámaras escondidas, Paulina, Paola, Gabriela (vol. 4), upbeat music greets the viewer as the male actor says "estás helada" (you're freezing) before they both laugh as she warms up her hands before jerking him off, all the while keeping her socks on. Laughter, particularly from the women performers, is consistent throughout these films. As per most of these films, the male performer's face is hidden, off camera, or, in other instances, partially concealed by an errant gray dot that doesn't always accomplish the job. In this film, the footage is grainy, the lighting so dim you can hardly see where flesh meets flesh. Sound comes in echoey waves, distant, and it's not always clear who is speaking. Along the bottom of the screen throughout many of these films, the viewer can see the timing of the camera tape. Back onscreen, the male protagonist gets pedagogical, educating her on how to suck his cock, asking if she likes it, to which she nonchalantly responds "sí." In another film, *Hotel Garage, huilas mexicanas, cámaras escondidas, 100% reales, Abril, La Chacha, Brenda y Roxxana, Mexicana caliente* (vol. 3), Abril is nervous at first, but begins to relax, laughing hysterically as a man hands her a huge black double dildo that never gets used.

Narrative is rarely a part of these films. Thus *Hotel Garage, huilas mexicanas* (vol. 5), particularly the segment with "Camila," becomes a notable case as it begins outside a motel and not during or right before the sexual act as most others do. Riding in the passenger seat of a car, Camila is headed toward the motel with two men, who ask her, insinuating that she is indeed cheating on her boyfriend, "Does he check your cellphone?" The phone rings, and all seem genuinely startled, but it's only her alarm and not her boyfriend. They all laugh, relieved. Volume 5 is also unique insofar as we see the male actor's face, at least from the side. As opposed to my viewings of other motel porn, which I found to be humorous and yet cold, more like strangers awkwardly fucking, volume 5 performs passion and sensuality. One male actor moves slowly, spending a lot of time on her buttocks and breasts, the camera worshipping her body. He doesn't penetrate her until minute 7:16, an event we can barely make out. In pornographic film, lighting and the zoom capabilities of the camera determine the fleshy details of sex acts and organs. In the case of *Hotel Garage, huilas mexicanas*, the lack of available and affordable technology to produce pornography impedes the hardcore, even as it might allow for other kinds of scenes. This too is a free-trade phenomenon: NAFTA destroyed the *fayuca* market in such electronics as video equipment, as imports appeared in formal market retail spaces (Aguiar 2013, 256). What we see (and can't see) in the homegrown porn genre of *Hotel Garage, huilas mexicanas* reflects this phenomenon.

There is a widely held belief that all *Hotel Garage, huilas mexicanas* films are merely endless reproductions of the same vignettes, women, and sex acts. I did encounter one of these films named *Hoteles de México: Putas en el hotel* (Whores in the hotel, 2011). This film's carefully xeroxed cover and plastic casing (the same for all pirated porn at Tepito and other locations) bills itself as part of the *Hotel Garage, huilas mexicanas* porn enterprise but is actually a compilation of pirated-porn materials, with all white actors. Indeed, in one interview with a Mexico City–based homegrown pornographer, he told me that the women interested in starring in his productions often claim, "I've been in a motel porn video." "Impossible!" he exclaimed during our interview and in rhetorical response to this would-be porn actor. Impossible, he exclaimed, because according to his belief, they are all pirated compilations of the same scenes. "And if you were in one," he followed up, using me as a stand-in for the motel porn actor, "I am sending an official state complaint to that hotel." Thus, even some of the few pornographers in Mexico also circulate the idea that motel porn is nonconsensually filmed and illegal. They play into the *Hotel Garage, huilas mexicanas* marketing ploy that makes the claim of hidden cameras on their covers. This rhetorical performance of distance from pirated porn, whether sincerely believed or not, intensified in Mexico City after the 2012 sex-trafficking laws. These laws followed a decades-long collaboration between the United States and Mexico, formally beginning with Bill Clinton's Trafficking Victims Protection Act (TVPA) in 2000, Barack Obama's adoption of the Act, and George W. Bush's expansion of antitrafficking legislation through his Bridge Project, a joint venture between Bush and politically powerful evangelical leaders and antitrafficking celebrity activists in Mexico, such as Rosie Orozco.[9] Often elided with sex traffickers, pornographers must consistently and directly, both on film and surrounding the production of that film, disavow any connection to the ever-growing sex panic that Laura Agustín (2007) calls the anti–sex trafficking "rescue industry."

Fed up with the "dumping" of all-white, all-English (or Italian) speaking casts, in endless compilations, some filmmakers interested in making pornography in Mexico have endeavored to do so, though without commercial success. NAFTA promised potential pornographers access to the technological equipment they desired to compete with foreign pornography and its portrayal of the hardcore, literally close-up shots of genitals, sexual acts, and body fluids, and historically the elusive scopophilic search for the sexual truth about female pleasure (Williams 1999). While that same industry may have held some hope of stocking what was in the 1990s the nascent sex-store phenomenon in Mexico City, the flooding of the pornographic landscape with pirated-porn reproductions largely from the United States suggests a pornographic form of *malinchismo*: an imposed preference for the beauty aesthetics of Anglo cultures (body size, skin color, breast and butt size, relative absence of hair). *Hotel Garage, huilas mexicanas*, while highly criticized, fetishizes a beauty standard predicated on the twenty-first-century *mexicana* body. While pornographers like the one I quoted earlier disparage hotel porn for its reputation as an illegally produced and circulated object, they nevertheless create homegrown pornography that serves the domestic market with all Mexican and Spanish-speaking casts. I now turn my attention to one such homegrown pornography company, one of only a handful in Mexico City and throughout the republic: Matlarock Films.

"100% Amateur Mexicano" Pornways

While there is no formal porn industry to speak of in Mexico, in 2012, I met a few small-scale pornographic film producers, one of which was Matlarock Tlahuicole Films.[10] Matlarock, headed by two men, Matla and Héctor Reyes, viewed the deluge of US-originating porn as akin to "dumping," a free-trade term most often heard in connection to the sale of subsidized corn from the United States in Mexico (or dairy products in Canada) and that describes the phenomenon of a country selling an exported good for less than the good's domestic fair-market value in the importing country. Thus, Matlarock sought to evade these formal pathways and focused instead on creating a kind of pornographic (sub)nationalism that traded in imagery that they describe as *100% amateur mexicano*. With the aim to forge a pornway that eroticizes *mexicanidad*, Matlarock created an archive of desires that thwarts the normative flows of NAFTA. The genre they work in, according to Héctor Daniel Guillén Rauda (2016), is definitively commercial amateur porn, though they pay the men who perform in their films nothing; the few women interested in performing receive between 1,500 and 3,000 pesos per shoot at a 2012 exchange rate between Mexico and the United States of 12 to 1. At the time of my visit to their studio, Matlarock sold each DVD for 30 pesos. They were also promoting a deal on three videos for 50 pesos. A little scrap of paper inside the plastic casing of one of their videos reads: "Oferta de 3 videos amateur / Editorial Matlarock / Piensa en tu economía / $50 pesos" (Deal on three amateur videos / Matlarock Films / Stick to your budget / $50 pesos). In creating commercial amateur porn, Reyes and Matla also seek to push back against the normative body aesthetics of the pornography industry, though unlike in *Hotel Garage, huilas mexicanas*, actors are expected to follow a loosely scripted narrative.

On two occasions I took a *pesero* south down Calle Nuevo León to visit Matla and Reyes at their filming studio, a one-bedroom apartment in a tall concrete high-rise. Both times Reyes jovially greeted me at the door as I caught my breath from going up the five flights of stairs. He showed me the studio and the equipment he used to film the scenes. I took note of a framed print of Hieronymus Bosch's *The Garden of Earthly Delights* that hung above the plaid blue loveseat that sees so much sexual action in their films. He offered me a beer as we sat down at a small wooden table off the kitchenette. When we began our chat, Reyes alone participated, while Matla just listened. Soon, though, Matla joined in; it seemed he was interested in expressing his views on the intersection of NAFTA and Mexican pornways and particularly the difficulties of making porn in Mexico. The first visit consisted of a two-hour interview with Reyes and Matla, a tour of the apartment studio, an invitation to return to witness a shoot, and their gift to me of DVD copies of three of their twenty-six films, one of which I will discuss below. The second visit was more unplanned as the shoot did not occur while I was visiting, though one of their actors, whom I will refer to as Sandra, offered to speak with me about her experience performing in their films and the pressures of Anglo body aesthetics on Mexican women interested in porn performance.

What began as the hobby of two self-proclaimed *cachondos* (horny men) became Matlarock Tlahuicole Films after their first couple of DVDs met with interest at kiosk distribution sites. If they were selling another kind of product, Reyes humorously told me in an interview in 2013, "Pues las puedo vender en la papelería, la tlapalería y en Aurrerá, por ejemplo, en un supermercado, en Walmart o donde quieras" (Well, I could sell them at the stationary store, the hardware store, Aurrerá, for example, in a supermarket, at Walmart or wherever) but with his product, pornographic films, "su mercado es muy reducido" (your market is really limited). At the time of the interview they were attempting to sell in sex shops, such as Erotika, a gay-owned "sex boutique" empire and the largest grossing sexual product chain in Mexico. However, in our interview, Reyes told me that Erotika "es un rollo ya bien americanizado" (is a really Americanized kind of thing). Matla added,

> La gente joven ve nuestro material y no le gusta . . . porque volvemos con los prototipos, con los prototipos de la mujer, como dice Héctor, americana. Yo diría norteamericana porque hay que recordar que también somos americanos aquí. Yo diría norteamericanas, o sea

los senos prominentes, los miembros masculinos pues muy grandes, no? Y nosotros no hacemos eso porque lo que queremos retratar es México, la ciudad de México, y su entorno.

(Young people see our materials, and they don't like it . . . because we end up with the same stereotypical images, with the same images of women, like Héctor said, who are American. I would say North American because we have to remember that Mexicans are also Americans. So I would say North American women, that is, with big breasts, really big penises, right? And we don't do that because what we want to portray is Mexico, Mexico City, and its surroundings.)

Here Matla makes a political statement about the transnational porn industry, just as much as he criticizes the arrogance of the United States referring to itself as "America" when it is merely just a part of the larger hemispheric region of the Americas. This geopolitical hubris, Matla reasons, is deeply connected to the normative body aesthetics desired by Erotika. For these reasons, Matla explained they had not yet pursued the internet as a digital infrastructure for their films.[11] "Porque la mayoría de la gente que va al internet son chavos precisamente, dieciocho, veinte años. Son chavos que no los interesan nuestros productos" (Because the majority of people who go to the internet are young men, primarily eighteen to twenty years old. They're young men who aren't interested in our products). To render the 100% amateur *mexicano* they instead focus on three areas: location (Mexico City), race and ethnicity (Brown and mestiza), and language (Spanish but more specifically Mexico City slang, or *chilango* slang). In focusing on this "homegrown" recipe for their porn films, Matlarock aims to avoid the export/import dynamics of NAFTA, not only as it pertains to goods but as it pertains to their female actors' embodied presence. In so doing, they give new sexual meaning to the saying "buy local."

Working within the constraints of NAFTA trade, Erotika's owners, Fernando Macías and Uriel Valdez, intentionally call their stores sex boutiques, arguing that the term *sex shop* is no longer in style, as it references an illicit period in the transnational history of such stores. With twenty-seven locations, all decorated in the same three shades of pink, Erotika reflects what Lawrence Herzog (1992) has described as the impact of free trade on the built urban environment as a global cultural landscape. As a NAFTA-stocked sexual space, the sex boutique chain participates in forging a globalized class of cosmopolitan sexual subjects, in particular the previously neglected niche markets of women and gay men, and it uses NAFTA-authorized sexual trade to create feelings of belonging to transnational scenes of sexual First Worldness (Tyburczy 2016b). However, even while Erotika monopolized the import market in items such as sex toys, in our 2013 interview Macías lamented the importation taxes imposed by NAFTA and the complicated paperwork and bureaucracy required to run their business in the NAFTA era. Erotika therefore reflects another complicated story of what I referred to as NAFTA's "winners" in the introduction, but this time as it pertains to the businesses of gay men.

In contrast to Matlarock, Mecos Films, a gay porn company financed by Erotika and their adjacent distributor WHAM! Pictures, had a wildly different experience in the national and transnational market. Mecos, which in this instance means "semen" or "gizz," works only with men and sells their films at Erotika stores for a prohibitively expensive sticker price.[12] Backed by Erotika and available for viewing in Erotika stores' porn-viewing booths, Mecos's films have a high production value and therefore the capability to provide viewers with a hefty dose of the hardcore. Moreover, Mecos successfully moved their films through the international gay film festival circuit and the global arthouse porn network, winning awards that interrupted the massive US-dominated gay porn industry. Their ludic films, some of which draw out the sexual components of *lucha libre* wrestling and Aztec semiotics, thus created an alternative aesthetic to free-trade flows, one that values the presence of *mexicanidad* in pornographic film festivals. Mecos therefore eroticizes *mexicanidad* to create an archive of desires and sex acts that forges a different gay thematic and aesthetic within the formal circulation of porn and its performances. As Gustavo Subero has shown, some Mecos films "challenge stereotypical representations of Latin(o) homosexuality as they commonly circulate in the West" (2010, 232). The films Subero concentrates on, the *lucha libre*–inspired films *La putiza* and its sequel *La verganza*, incorporate music, narrative, and symbols familiar to Mexican nationals and the diaspora, but they also employ actors who are largely thin, muscular, and not exclusively but frequently hung. Likewise, both films play on Mexican national themes that match some of the reentrenchment of Mexican nationalism in leftist artistic expression that sexually explicit neomexicanist art did for gay sexuality in the 1990s. Even so, as Subero shows, these films do circulate stories and scenes that depart from the well-worn tropes of exoticized ethnicity that many Western pornographic films fetishize.

In contrast, the film *Corrupción mexicana* (Mexican corruption), by director El Diablo, reaches toward another bodily aesthetic. As Xiomara

Verenice Cervantes-Gómez asserts of the film, "Some of the men are balding, one has very untidy dreadlocks, beards are unkempt, sixpack abs are not featured, there are major height discrepancies, and most of the men have fully grown, ungroomed pubic hair" (2024, 129). Furthermore, the film revels in some of the more dangerous elements of the Mexican landscape during NAFTA times, eroticizing contexts such as police surveillance and narco-violence. Indeed, the back cover of the DVD case declares: "Una audaz producción que nos lleva a un viaje por el país a través de sus calientes y corruptos habitantes. Cuatro historias revelan la cachonda realidad de México: secuestros, soborno, violencia, sexo rudo, humiliación, drogas, y engaños . . . Cualquier coincidencia con la vida real, no es casualidad . . . es pura calentura!" (A daring production that will take us on a journey through the country by way of its hot and corrupt inhabitants. Four stories reveal the horny reality of Mexico: kidnappings, bribes, violence, rough sex, humiliation, drugs, and deceptions. . . . Any similarity to real life is not coincidental . . . it's purely hotness!). At times, then, Mecos films eroticize the violent masculinities of *narco culturas* and the aesthetics of *narco moda* (narco fashion). At others, they render sexy working-class men, for example, the porn pirates that one might encounter at Tepito or the figure of the *chacal*. The film does so in ways that cater to the global obsession with "rough trade" that dominates the gay elite sex tourism circuit. However, when Mecos films travel across borders, they tend to flow toward the Anglo-dominant countries that host such porn festivals, for example the Toronto Gay Film Festival, though Mecos's online store can only be accessed in Mexico (Smith 2017, 8).

While as a marginalized straight/swinger porn company Matlarock needs to take extreme care with what their actors do and what they say onscreen, Mecos sexes up what can be the everyday horrors of living during NAFTA time. Mecos and Matlarock profoundly differ then in terms of creating pornography for the everyday working-class Mexican and the parameters for what actors can verbally and physically perform. Indeed, Mecos has not attracted the attention of the censors or the anti–sex trafficking rescue industry in the same ways that Matlarock has. On the contrary, the Mexican state "even allowed them to officially name their company 'La Verga Parada' (The Erect Cock) for tax purposes" (López 2009, as referenced in Smith 2017, 27).

At one point in our interview, Reyes and Matla spoke to the particularities of what they viewed as the *malinchismo* of the sex-shop industry that financially supported pornmakers such as Mecos: "Yo voy a una sex shop aquí en México y les digo mira tengo este producto, y la gente busca algo mexicano. Es mexicano. Está en español. Entonces lo ven y dicen 'no, es que están bien gordas, están bien feas,' no de *Playboy*. Nos vemos. Y dicen 'mira cuando tengas chavas como estas [en *Playboy*], tráeme tus videos'" (I go to a sex shop here in Mexico City, and I say, hey, look, I have this product, and people are looking for something Mexican. It's Mexican. It's in Spanish. So, they see it and they say, "No, the thing is, they're too fat, and they're really ugly. They're not *Playboy* material. See you later." And they say, "Look, when you have girls like this [in *Playboy*], come back with your videos"). The porn actor I'll refer to as Sandra, a curvy Mexican actor who was recruited to perform by Matla through his porn-specific talent agency Latin Agent, agreed with this sentiment and told me so during my second visit to the Matlarock studio:

> Sandra Sí veo que estamos bajo la sombra de Estados Unidos, de las actrices de Estados Unidos. Entonces sentimos que debemos mejorar nuestro cuerpo, ponernos así bien buenas como las de Estados Unidos, y actuar igual que las de allá porque no tenemos otra referencia. En el porno que encontramos en Internet todo es de Estados Unidos, o la gran mayoría. Encontrar de otros lados es muy raro, y es muy casero. Entonces no tenemos otro ejemplo. Es lo que conocemos y tenemos que adecuarnos a eso si queremos tener éxito. Hay unas chicas que tienen en mente llegar a Los Ángeles, y ya internacionalizarse desde Estados Unidos. Entonces lo que tienen que hacer es acoplarse a lo que ellos quieren.

> JT Y qué es lo que ellos quieren, en tu opinión?

> Sandra Pues mujeres altas, delgadas, como con muchas tetas, muchas nalgas, y que sobreactúen tanto, así. Como lo tenemos nosotros, aunque aquí es más flexible, porque como no hay muchas mujeres comunes así, como las de allá. Pues a casi cualquier chica que se vea bien, puede ser aceptada.

> (Sandra I do think that we are in the shadow of the United States, of the actresses in the United States. So, we feel that we should improve our bodies, work to be as hot as the women in the United States, and act like the women from there because we don't have any other reference point. In the porn that we find on the internet, it's all from the United States, or the vast majority of it. Finding porn from other

places is very rare, and it's very homemade. So we don't have any other examples. It's what we know and we have to adapt to that if we want to be successful. There are some girls who are thinking about moving to Los Angeles, and to enter the international stage from there. So what they have to do is fit into what they want in the United States.

JT And what do they want, in your opinion?

Sandra Well, women who are tall, thin, like with big tits, lots of butt, and who overact a lot, like that. Like what we have, even though here it's more flexible, because since there aren't many ordinary women like that, like the girls over there. And so, almost any girl who looks good, she can be accepted in.)

In our chat, Sandra spoke to the ways in which female Mexican porn actors feel extreme pressure to copy the beauty ideals of *gringa* porn and thus adapt their bodies to fit a particular aesthetic that is thin, normatively fit (thus the muscular *muchas nalgas*), and white. The domination of certain female corporealities over others is not only based in a fat/thin binary but also points to the global supremacy of whiteness in the global sex industry. Citing Kamala Kempadoo's assertion that "white sexual labor is most valued within the global sex industry" (1998, 11), Mireille Miller-Young argues that this "racial politics of beauty" dominates US pornways (2014, 241). This visual economy keeps Black women, especially voluptuous Black women, from being cast or else it typecasts Black women who are "seen as less attractive and more fitting for low-budget film work in ghetto porn and related subgenres of Black and interracial porn" (Miller-Young 2014, 243). Unlike in the United States, however, where the BBW (Big Beautiful Women) subgenre has gained in prominence and popularity, Mexico has no comparable industry and thus no subgenres to speak of. Within Mexican pornways in 2013, pornmakers could only name one transnational female Mexican porn star, Melodie Petite, whose name precisely signals her small frame. Unintentionally, Matlarock and some *Hotel Garage, huilas mexicanas* films put full-figured women at the center of their pleasurescapes. They eroticize the curvaceous Brown body that has otherwise been pathologized by the "obesity epidemic," a panic inspired by the legitimate environmental problems wrought by the transnational circulation of cheap foodstuffs and a topic to which I return in the second performance deviation with Erika Bülle Hernández's performance art piece, *A las niñas gordas nadie las quiere* (No one likes fat girls). In doing so, Matlarock films carve out a space for the casting of the curvy female porn actor between the *morbo* (morbid curiosity) of the US fat-porn genre and the relative occlusion of voluptuous people from the hemispheric form of sexual and gender dissidence known as "postpornography" (Bülle 2020, 35–36).

As a straight, swinger-oriented pornmaker with the objective to create porn "100% *mexicana*," Matlarock confronts the "dumping" of US pornography, with its sleek production value and its fetishizing of certain bodies, beauty standards, and sex acts; yet Matlarock struggles to find women to perform in their films and locales that will carry their merchandise. After the passing of the 2012 Ley General Para Prevenir, Sancionar y Erradicar los Delitos en Materia de Trata de Personas (General Law to Prevent, Sanction, and Eradicate Crimes Related to Trafficking), many sex and entertainment expositions were forced to close, perhaps most significantly the sex expo Sex & Entertainment. Amid the sex-trafficking panic and the surveillance pressure of the state-run agency of Radio, Televisión y Cinematografía (Radio, Television, and Cinematography, or RTC), Matlarock must use great care with what words are used by actors while performing. For example, they told me that the word *nena* (little girl) would, under the RTC's watchful eye, place the film in the category of child pornography. Actors must now perform verbal consent onscreen before any eroticism is initiated, and most of their films begin with public service announcements (PSAS) such as "Se unen en contra de la trata" (United against trafficking) or "Manifestación en contra la pedofilia" (Protest against pedophilia). While there are queues of men interested in creating porn with them, Matla told me, women are reluctant to perform in pornography. After the 2012 law, he says women more often vocalize a fear of being kidnapped by what he referred to as "*tratantes de blancas*" (sex traffickers, though literally translating as sex traffickers of white women) if they collaborate with pornographers or seek out opportunities to perform in pornography.[13] One consequence of these formalized panics is that it is nearly impossible to find women to perform in pornographic film. If working-class Mexican porn pirates are cast as free-trade traitors for violating the sanctity of IP law, then the homegrown pornographer, simply in the act of making explicit sexual media, is viewed as a sex trafficker.

When women do perform in Matlarock films, they often conceal their identities. Let's consider the Matlarock film *El vendedor* (The salesman), in which the female protagonist, who goes by the name of "Dany" in the film, wears sunglasses and a baseball cap (see fig. 1.3). Before we see anyone onscreen, however, the viewer encounters the declaration "Apoyamos a Igualdad de Género para una mejor convivencia unete" (We support gender equality for better coexistence. Join us), a more coded antitrafficking message intended to evade the state and transnational surveillance apparatus of the US-created Trafficking in Persons (TIP) report and the tremendous operational reach of Mexico's anti–sex trafficking laws.[14] Following this PSA, the first scene opens with Dany making a phone call while seated on the same blue plaid loveseat with the *Garden of Earthly Delights* hanging above it that I saw in the studio. We soon realize that Dany is responding to the personal ads saying, "Espero que respondan para poder cogerme" (I hope they answer so I can get fucked). She keeps calling people from the ads, but no one answers. Suddenly there's a knock on the door. She goes to answer it, and upon opening the door she encounters male actor J. Ventura, a regular in Matlarock films. As per the title of the scene, Ventura is a *vendedor*. He shows Dany the books and DVDs he's holding to see if she's interested in buying them, the figure of the entrepreneur, yet another NAFTA-inspired character. She immediately comes on to him as she examines one of the DVDs. Of course, it's a Matlarock film, the first volume of their first year clearly printed on the hardcover copy of the DVD. The presence of the DVD hardcover is a small but important detail. Encasing the DVD as such gives it a formal appearance, differentiating the DVD from the cheaper plastic casing of the pirated porn sold at Tepito.[15] Dany is successful in her seduction, and they begin to engage in some heavy frottage. Somewhat disguised, Dany wears sunglasses and a baseball cap along with her gray leggings, a white tank top, and white kitten heels. Ventura is dressed in unremarkable street clothes with nothing masking his face. Clothes begin to come off as she sucks his cock. Leaving her sunglasses and baseball cap on, but otherwise completely naked, Dany breaks the fourth wall to show her backside and breasts to the camera, swaying back and forth as she reveals a full bush of hair on her pubis. After this act of exhibitionism, they manually put on the condom, a moment of explicitly and intentionally eroticizing safe sex. Putting on the condom thus becomes yet another sex act in the performance.[16] She mounts him, fucking him on the couch for a while until they switch positions, him getting behind her. He pulls out to cum near her mouth. She eats some of it and rubs the rest on her breasts as her still-sunglassed face looks into the camera.

If you look inside the printed paper sleeve that also encases the DVD, you'll find another common feature of Matlarock films, a short *entrevista amateur* (amateur interview) with the female lead of the film (see fig. 1.4). In the interview, Dany claims to have always wanted to be a porn actor. Upon being asked by an unnamed interviewer referred to as "Mr." about why she never performed in other films, Dany responds, "No me seleccionaban por

1.3   Cover for *El vendedor*, Matlarock Films, year 1, vol. 3.

LA ENTREVISTA AMATEUR

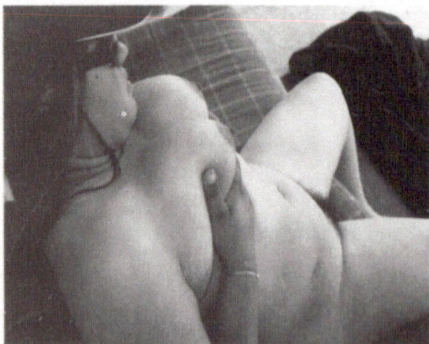

NOMBRE : DANY
EDAD : ALGUNOS
OCUPACION: PROD. LACTEOS
MR. QUE TE MOTIVO A HACER
ESTE VIDEO
D. SIEMPRE HE QUERIDO SER
ACTRIZ PORNO
MR. Y POR QUE NO
D. NO ME SELECCIONABAN POR
MI CUERPO HASTA QUE EN-
CONTRE A MATLAROCK Y ME
SENTÍ MUY BIEN
MR. AHORA ENTIENDO POR
QUE TRABAJAS EN LACTEOS
PUES TE GUSTA LA LECHE EN
DEMACIA
D. SI ME ENCANTA LA LECHE
EN SU ENVASE ORIGINAL ESPE-
RO QUE PARA LA SEGUNDA
TEMPORADA DE GENTE SW
ME DEN LA OPORTUNIDAD DE
RECIBIR LA LECHE DE MAS DE

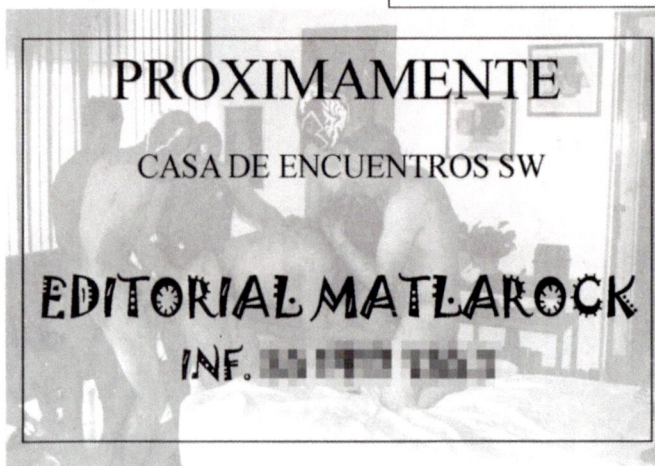

CONTACTOS SW DENTRO DEL CD
Y ESPECIAL DE LA EXPOSEXO 09

PROXIMAMENTE

CASA DE ENCUENTROS SW

EDITORIAL MATLAROCK

INF.

1.4   "Dany: La entrevista amateur," Matlarock Films.

mi cuerpo hasta que encontré a Matlarock y me sentí muy bien" (They didn't pick me because of my body until I found Matlarock, and I felt really good). I cite the "Dany" and "Mr." of this interview not as evidence of some deep-seated truth for would-be female porn actors in Mexico. Nor am I claiming that Dany, or any of the female actors for that matter, enjoys herself in the film previously described. I am arguing, however, that Matlarock films display an appreciation and desire for the curvy female actor within a national context riddled by two of many panics: the enormous reach of Mexican anti–sex trafficking law (that can criminalize all forms of public sexual culture) and the national and transnational pressure on women's bodies in the name of the "obesity epidemic." Matlarock films might not result in social justice for women in Mexican society; however, they do offer an archive of instances where a question posed by self-identified fat performance artist and theorist Erika Bülle Hernández, "En realidad, ¿un cuerpo gordo puede ser deseable?" (In reality, can a fat body be desirable?) (2018, 60), is answered in the affirmative. Matlarock certainly embraces the casting of full-figured females, without labeling the films as "BBW," and eroticizes a corporeality that has come under attack in dominant discourse across the Americas. I want to make clear, however, that the onscreen performance is not necessarily dissident, especially when it comes to who is performing what kinds of sexual acts and in what ways. Matlarock films constitute one form of queer traffic not necessarily for what is displayed in the mise-en-scène of the film itself, but rather when considered within the larger transnational free-trade practices that dictate what sorts of pornography move to where and in what quantities, and how some bodies are regarded as self-destructively abject in public discourse and therefore undesirable to porn consumers other than as a niche fetish.[17]

Only Certain Consumers

. . . You know, with the success they've had in selling this [NAFTA] discourse, it's as if you or I wake up in the morning and feel freer as human beings because there's 25 brands of toothpaste. Nowadays, it's as if . . . the discourse itself has been so successful . . . it's often sold in the sense that there's no other way. This is our world, and you either jump on the bandwagon, or you get run over.
Laura Carlsen, director of the Americas Program, interview, 2013

In one of only a few pro-NAFTA PSAs available for viewing today, el Consejo Nacional de la Publicidad under the administration of NAFTA signer Carlos Salinas de Gortari put out a TV spot in 1992 wherein thin, white-haired, and middle- and upper-class *abuelas* (grandmas) sit around a table in what is supposed to be a cookie commercial.[18] They get distracted, however, by the porcelain cups containing their coffee or tea, extolling the "beauty" and "quality" of the cup and saucer. Their scripted admiration for these functional objects, the likes of which they've supposedly never seen before, is staged to interrupt the commercial. One of the women demurely apologizes to the commercial's cameraman and crew, explaining that they just can't help but marvel at the porcelain plateware, which will be exported to Canada and the United States. With el Tratado de Libre Comercio de América del Norte (TLCAN/NAFTA), she reasons out loud, the quality of Mexican products has risen and, with the increase and desire for Mexican things and all the money that portends, "podíamos vivir mejor" (we could live better). Performatively repeating the claim of Salinas that NAFTA would usher Mexico into the so-called First World, these *abuelitas* promote the export of licit traffic—the cups and saucers—all the while performing appropriate consumption practices for women. NAFTA interrupts their cookie-eating as they shift their attention to the crockery as a symbol of free trade's likely success and its undeniable benefit to consumers in all three NAFTA-signing nations, but especially in Mexico. Like the Carlsen interview excerpt I began this final section with, the commercial theatricalizes how promises of unlimited consumer choice can hail all of us into compliance with free trade while also implicitly showing the viewer how to appropriately consume (crockery over cookies).

When it comes to sex, like cookies its consumption tends toward the "too much," toward its supposed dangers and ripeness for addiction. Sex, disability studies scholar Anna Mollow explains, is often figured "as the pathology of a disabled minority" and "made to signify a sexualized disreputability" applied "to those termed 'promiscuous,' 'addicted,' 'compulsive,' or 'queer,' who are blamed for 'spreading AIDS'; the 'obese' or 'overweight,' who supposedly can't get enough of the food they are said to substitute for sex" (2012, 304).[19] In a post-internet world, the sexual panic known as "porn addiction" even has its own pathological diagnosis: PPU, or problematic pornography use. It's an addictive practice said solely to affect men, thus reinscribing femme, feminine, and female subjects as only performers and not consumers or producers of pornography. As certain antisex forms of radical feminism from the 1980s and 1990s have been institutionalized into transnational law and policy, as in the panic around sex work, "porn addiction" is regarded as a "disease" that directly translates to violence against women. "Pornography is the theory, and rape is the practice," as radical feminist Robin Morgan proclaimed (1980, 139). When racialized, the transnational embrace of PPU can serve to bolster racist ethnonationalist assertions of Black and Brown men, particularly if they are poor or working-class, as "predators" of "women and girls" (implied to be white) if they consume, produce, or circulate porn.

Bush Jr.'s Operation Predator is a case in point. Under the newly formed ICE, Bush began this initiative in 2003 and used administrative law at the border to track and trace not necessarily physical forms of child pornography, but rather those suspected of being pedophiles as they moved across national lines. Operation Predator involved a collaboration between ICE, the US Postal Inspection Service, the Federal Bureau of Investigation (FBI), the International Criminal Police Organization (Interpol), the Department of Justice, and the Secret Service, among other agencies. In the 2004 house hearing, "Alien Removals under Operation Predator," John Walsh, chairman of the National Advisory Board of the National Center for Missing and Exploited Children and former host of the television show *America's Most Wanted: America Fights Back*, vociferously demanded that Mexico sign an extradition treaty as a condition for staying in NAFTA. "Force them to sign that treaty when you give them that NAFTA money," he claimed to have said to Bill Clinton. In an unmistakable tell about the reach of NAFTA to intervene in Mexican sovereignty, he went on, as if speaking directly to Mexican state leaders, "You can say, 'You want to keep the relationships? You want the free-trade zones? You want to be our good neighbor? Well, send those dirtbags back, and let us go down and get your criminals, too, and try them under American law.'"[20] Just as the Mann Act, also known as the White Slave Traffic Act of 1910, has played an ongoing role in policing the movement of sex workers crossing state lines, Operation Predator, which Bush developed two years before he started collaborating with antitrafficking evangelical activists in Mexico, offered ICE yet another tool to track and trace Black, Brown, poor, and Indigenous peoples and their transnational movement as well as any form of pornography on the move.

Néstor García Canclini argues that all consumption is normatively "associated with useless expenditures and irrational compulsions," moralistic conceptions of what is really "the ensemble of sociocultural practices in which the appropriation and use of products takes place" (2001, 37, 38). Sexual consumption, as Rodrigo Parrini and Ana Amuchástegui (2012) have argued, is a related "signifying practice," the articulation of which engenders a kind of bourgeois subject enamored with the discourse of sexual freedom bound within the contours of what they call "normalised transgressions." Charges of excessive consumption, regardless of its normative investments, get attached to working-class populations as failed economic actors who should be purchasing their basic needs instead of porn. Within this context, porn pirates become criminals producing and circulating endless illicit reproductions of low-tech porn, both foreign and domestic, and thereby catering to the supposed insatiable lasciviousness and sexual desires of Mexican males. IP law, invented by the writers of NAFTA and endlessly reproduced globally through the WTO, criminalizes porn piracy as tantamount to terrorism. These laws restrict access to pornography and work in tandem with NAFTA-adjacent initiatives, such as Operation Predator, to control the flow of sexually explicit material and the movement of those suspected of transporting that material across borders. NAFTA plays an important role in connecting all these scenarios and policies. In the first instance, it creates a context wherein US-made pornography is both everywhere and at the same time inaccessible other than through the pirated copies found in markets such as Tepito. The high cost, the English-speaking dominance, and the desire for different corporealities led to the underground porn markets of the *Hotel Garage, huilas mexicanas* enterprise and homegrown pornographers such as Matlarock. The latter, and to a certain degree the former, center the full-figured female body as an object of desire outside the niche markets of BBW porn. Free-trade capitalism valorizes consumption, but only certain forms that are decided not unilaterally by multinational corporations but by an "interactive sociopolitical rationality" that depends just as much on the administration of capital as it does on activities that "participate in an arena of competing claims for what society produces and the ways of using it" (García Canclini 2001, 39). Indeed, the connections between porn actors Dany and Sandra and porn pirates and sellers at Tepito were never imagined by NAFTA proponents. They exist on the margins of free-trade capitalism and free trade's obsessions with profit, capital, and the precarity of labor options in the late twentieth and twenty-first centuries.

The Free Eating Agreement

In *Xipe Totec Punk*, Mexican artist César Martínez Silva pulls along a gro-
tesque creature, the mythic Indigenous god Xipe Totec, here performed by
Martínez's collaborator, Orgy punk. Orgy punk's costume is a full bodysuit
of Gran Reserva *jamón serrano* (prosciutto) with a *salchicha caliente* (hot
sausage) dangling between his legs, bright green high heels, and a match-
ing green mohawk. Dressed in a black chef's uniform (one that doubles as
a priest's garb), Martínez alternates Canadian and American flag masks
over his mouth, at once a symbol of being silenced or overcome by Anglo
dominance and a precocious harbinger of the ongoing COVID-19 pandemic
(see fig. 1a.1).[1]

After Martínez leads the chained being into the gallery, the assembled
crowd gathers and ultimately eats, with glee, delight, and desire, the ham
pieces hanging from Orgy punk's body. The public gathered at this gallery,
the PHI Centre for the Arts in Montréal, plays along with the performance's
game. They literalize how neoliberal globalization trades in flesh across the
Americas. In so doing, Martínez and Orgy punk use performance as an "act
of transfer," to quote Diana Taylor. In this act of transfer, the performance
"take[s] us beyond the colonizing and restrictive epistemic grids that some of
our Eurocentric disciplines and practices impose on us" (2020, xi), pushing
us to travel back and forth through time to analyze colonial strategies of the
past and their permutations in the present and future. *Xipe Totec Punk* is one

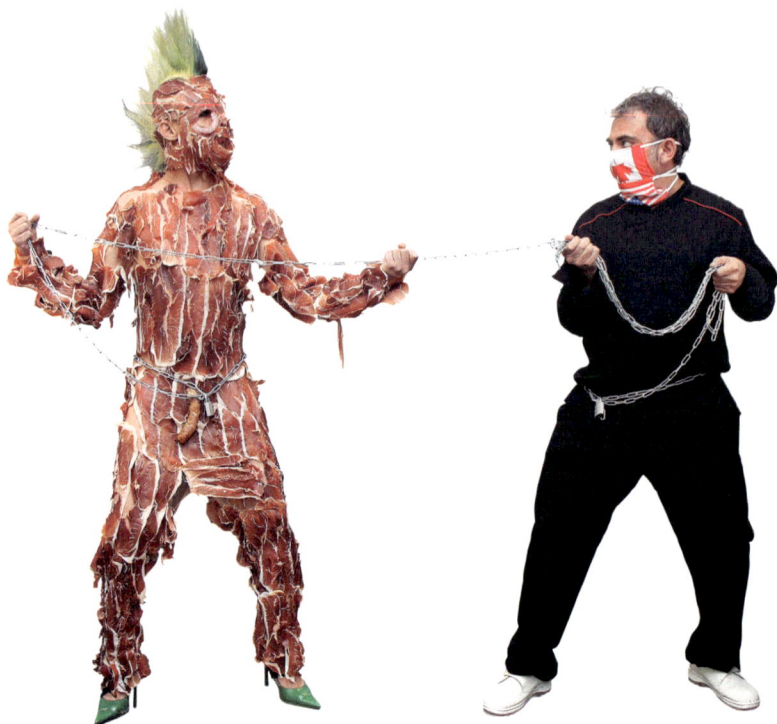

1a.1   *Xipe Totec Punk*, performance, *gastroeconómico*, César Martínez Silva (with Orgy punk), 2014.

"corpus delecti" (Fusco 1999) of many in which performance artists use their bodies to draw connections to the long historical arc of NAFTA time across the transnational borderlands of the United States, Canada, and Mexico.[2] *Xipe Totec Punk*'s enactment in Canada is crucial, not merely because of Canada's role in NAFTA but also because of Canada's long colonial history of regulating the gender and sexuality practices of First Nations peoples through policies such as the Indian Act of 1876 (Cannon 1998).

Xipe Totec is an Aztec deity, whose Nahuatl name means "Our Lord, the Flayed," he who took off his skin to feed the world. Calling his piece an "ofrenda gastroeconómica pos TLC" (a gastroeconomic offering after the free-trade agreement), Martínez projects text-heavy slides in the background to solidify the connection he wants to make between this pre-Hispanic figure and what he calls "el mundo PRI His-Pánico," a world in which the PRI political party, under President Miguel de la Madrid, Carlos Salinas de Gortari, and Enrique Peña Nieto, consolidates power through panic. One sentence repeats and remains visually present more than others. It reads: "Cuando México firmó el TLC con EUA y Canadá, México da la espalda a Latinoamérica" (When Mexico signed NAFTA with the United States and Canada, Mexico turned its back on Latin America). The performance pins NAFTA as the moment when Mexico took a detour from the rest of Latin America, which was in the throes of rejecting the Washington Consensus to experiment with a form of leftist socialist governmentality that has since been dubbed "the pink tide."[3] During a 2015 conversation with Martínez at his home in Mexico City, he explained to me:

> Xipe Totec, de esta deidad azteca que ofrece su piel para que la humanidad no muera de hambre. Entonces, lo relaciono con el TLCAN, porque México ofrece su piel, su dermis a un Tratado que nos deja como estamos. . . . Mi conexión con el NAFTA es lo que este tratado representa para muchos mexicanos: un gran sacrificio, una ofrenda contradictoria en pro de otros países como EUA y Canadá, a quienes más beneficia este TLCAN.

> (Xipe Totec, about this Aztec deity who offered his skin so that humanity wouldn't die of hunger. So then, I relate it to NAFTA, because Mexico offers its skin, its dermis to an agreement that leaves us how we are today. . . . My connection with NAFTA is what this agreement means for many Mexicans: a great sacrifice, a contradictory offering to other countries like the United States and Canada, who benefit more from NAFTA.)

As one performance of a larger gastroeconomic interdisciplinary project, *Xipe Totec Punk* portrays Mexico playing dueling roles: it is at once the eaten other (Xipe Totec), the sexualized bottom of the free-trade ménage à trois, and a free-trade colluder (Martínez's chef/priestlike persona). Mexico eats itself, trapping *los pueblos originarios*, draped in Sahagúnesque mythology, between the nationalistic fetishization of indigeneity as something to sell and its mortal attacks on the cultures and communities that fail to fit the celebratory frames and expectations of settler modernity. In this way, the performance presents the audience with a punk representation of a colonial, gendered, and highly racialized way of seeing that María

Josefina Saldaña-Portillo calls *el indio bárbaro* (the barbaric savage), a profit-generating and empire-consolidating binational construction that NAFTA and the War on Drugs reinvented through criminal representations of the undocumented immigrant and the *narco* (2016, 235–246). *Xipe Totec Punk* cannot be assimilated into what Kim TallBear (2018), Scott Lauria Morgensen (2011), Mark Rifkin (2011), and other queer, Two Spirit, and Indigenous scholars and artists term "settler sexuality," though it playfully flirts with the figure of *el indio bárbaro* as panic-inducing threat. In the performance's queer punk portrayal of an Indigenous deity, Xipe Totec is made palatable to normative bourgeois taste only insofar as he's installed in a gallery and draped in an iconic delicacy of haute Spanish gastronomy.

In performing as a delectable snack for art gallery-goers, Martínez's performance situates itself within the long and violent history of eating the other, wherein the Indigenous body serves as the literal body, the quintessence of that which cannot be digested by free-trade capitalism. Joseba Gabilondo succinctly characterizes the anthropophagic reach of free trade that *Xipe Totec Punk* enfleshes and eroticizes: "Nation-states in the situation of Mexico are striving to join global commercial ventures such as NAFTA by presenting themselves as desirable nations for foreign investment and consumption—ultimately regulated by the US economy. Conversely, the US imagination wants to consume kitsch representations of national Others in the specific form of feminine, working-class, heterosexual and desirable images and objects" (2002, 247). Recalling from the introduction the subjects of Daniela Rossell's photography, Mexican consumers too, especially NAFTA's political and economic "winners," eat up kitsch representations of indigeneity. To play on Helen Delpar's book title, the "enormous vogue" in all things Mexican (kitsch)—especially as they relate to race and, as Gabilondo mentions, the "working-class," "feminine," and "heterosexual"—travels through formal free-trade infrastructures connecting the transnational capitalist class to Blackness and indigeneity through sartorial choices of home decor and fashion. *Xipe Totec Punk* is thus unique in that, at the site of its enactment in Montréal and its Canada-located audience, it inscribes Canada into this circulatory logic of valorizing difference when it comfortingly matches the desires and fantasies of the domestic (nation/home). Here indigeneity as interior adornment, as another potential site of what Jodi Byrd calls "the transit of empire" (2011), uncovers a trajectory of movement in which colonialism is transferred through the curation of aesthetically pleasing objects within the bourgeois Mexican or Canadian home. The traffic in all things "Indian," traveling in related but distinct circuits from the racist and anti-Black antiques market, serves to expand empire through figuring Indigenous presence as past and pretty or, in the case of *Xipe Totec Punk*, yummy.[4]

Indeed, Martínez entices his audiences to ludically consume and, in the act thereof, exorcise some of their colonial demons. In line with other performances by queer hemispheric artists, such as Nao Bustamente and her performance art piece *Indigurrito* (1992), *Xipe Totec Punk* and Martínez's larger oeuvre on TLCAN manifest the intimate connection between performances of neoliberal pleasure-seeking and the erotic racializations of late capitalist consumption. Bustamante's *Indigurrito* invites white cis men to come onstage, get on their knees, and eat a burrito secured in her strap-on, a stand-in for her phallus/cock. She humorously frames this act as partial atonement for the sins of colonialism. In his performance with Orgy punk, Martínez invites us to become unwitting collaborators in the seductive force of free trade's fantasy. Performed in 2014, and thus bridging the 1990s version of free-trade capitalism with its twenty-first-century iterations, *Xipe Totec Punk*'s "view from the bottom" (Nguyen 2014) uncovers the lie. It shows how the erotic social performances of the gallery-goers, who eat Indigenous flesh represented in the form of expensive *jamón serrano*, became an irresistible form of participating in the performance's tantalizing prompt. Free trade, like the performance, could not proceed without this seduction of collective response.

The coloniality of race and its fetishes and repulsions structure cannibalistic fantasies of eating and eradicating the other through performances of pleasure. Looking to Aníbal Quijano's concept of the "coloniality of power" (2000) and María Lugones's "coloniality of gender" (2007) to analyze enactments of violence in the Americas today, Marcia Ochoa (2016) shows how European invaders used charges of sodomy and cannibalism as sexualized and racialized tools to authorize land claim and conquest. In choosing her artifacts of analysis, Ochoa purposefully time-travels between contemporary queer and trans spaces in twenty-first-century Caracas, Venezuela, and colonial representations of radical alterity by sixteenth-century engravers to unveil the savagery of the project of modernity in the Americas. *Xipe Totec Punk* is a time-traveling performance that juxtaposes pre-Hispanic ritual with NAFTA time to expose the brutality of the project of neoliberalism in the Americas, and, more specifically, the long and violent history of anti-Indigenous cultural and social performances through sexed and gendered disciplining. Like Ochoa, Martínez looks to sixteenth-century engravings, which for him connect NAFTA to the long history of European colonialism.

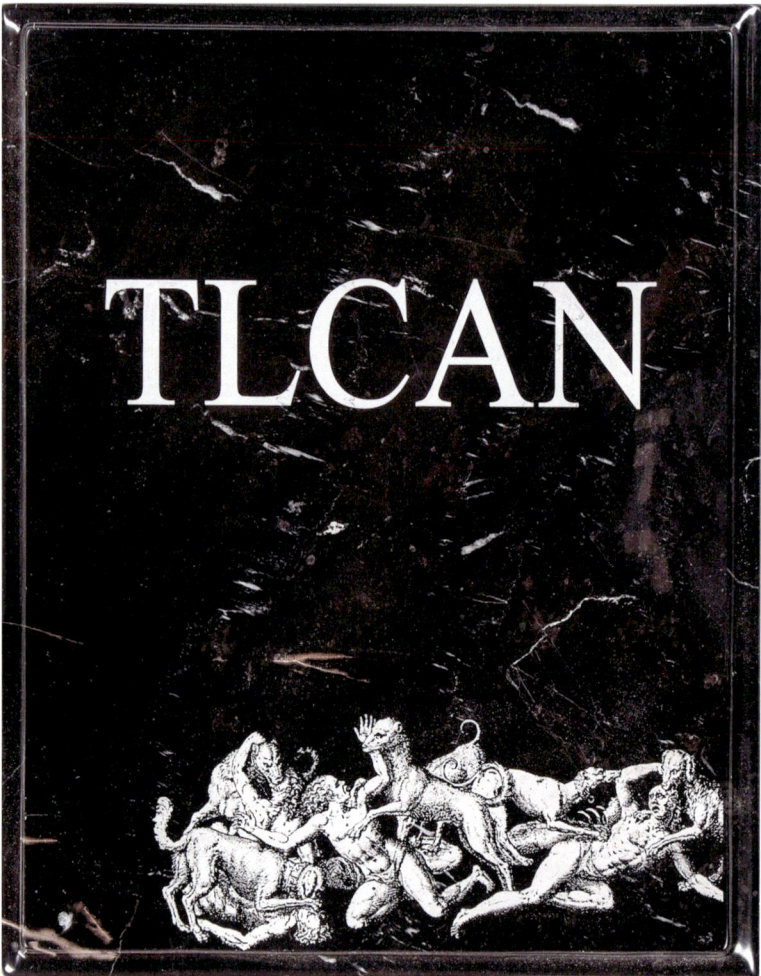

"Tratado de libre *comerse* en América del Norte, TLCAN," César Martínez Silva, black marble, Monterrey, 50 cm × 40 cm × 2cm, 2002.

What *Xipe Totec Punk* enfleshes in performance, Martínez carves into a small marble tombstonelike plaque in the work titled *Tratado de Libre Comerse en América del Norte* (the Free Eating Agreement, a play on *el Tratado de Libro Comercio*). Below the inscribed acronym "TLCAN" (NAFTA), he includes the lower portion of a sixteenth-century engraving by Theodor de Bry titled *The Dogs of Vasco Nunez de Balboa (1475–1571) Attacking the Indians* (fig. 1a.2). This segment of the marble plate depicts just what the title says, and it draws from engravings published in the 1598 book *Brevísima relación de la destrucción de las Indias* (A brief record of the destruction of the Indians) by Bartolomé de las Casas. The plaque and its image are meant to represent the many violent crimes the Spanish committed against Indigenous people. In de Bry's original engraving, a row of eight conquistador figures dressed regally in the colonial fashion of the time look down and, in some instances, point at the massacre in front of them with unaffected expressions. To look again, a queer twenty-first-century eye might notice the flip of a wrist, the popping of a hip, the flourish of a hat feather, and the extended leg of the Spanish colonialists to fit well within a lexicon of queer embodiments.[5] "They were half-man, half-hotpant!" Jesusa Rodríguez (2003, 231) exclaims con *relajo* in "La conquista según La Malinche" (The conquest according to Malinche).[6] This queering twist displays the distortions of ideological hierarchies of who gets to perform queerness, when, and to what ends. In this paradigm, nonnormative sex and gender dissidence are regarded as a form of embodiment that must be destroyed, because they failed to harmonize with the contemporary Euro-colonial norms of masculinity.

Like in *Xipe Totec Punk*, Martínez's marble tablet reveals the insatiably eroticized violence inherent in settler colonialism, and it positions free trade as one pivotal facet in that long history. Free trade is the logical extension of what Lisa Lowe describes as "the often obscured connections between the emergence of European liberalism, settler colonialism in the Americas, the transatlantic slave trade, and the East Indies and China trades in the late eighteenth and early nineteenth century" (2015, 1). Indeed, free trade emerged in the early nineteenth century in the crucible of debates between slave-holding southern states, which sought foreign markets to export cotton and tobacco, and northern manufacturing states where economic protectionism, a trend culminating in the Smoot-Hawley Tariff Act of 1930, was fostered as the means to insulate manufacturers from foreign competition.[7] The Treaty of Guadalupe Hidalgo was signed in 1848, and the resulting acquisition of more than half of Mexico's land reopened debates about slavery and played a role in provoking the Civil War in 1861. The two "treaties"— Guadalupe Hidalgo and NAFTA—are often viewed as the bookends to the tale of how the United States extracted the sovereignty of the Mexican people, continuing the land theft from the *pueblos originarios* that the Spanish had started five hundred years earlier. Of course, as Lowe has shown, "one does not observe a simple replacement of earlier colonialisms by liberal free trade, but rather an accommodation of both residual practices of enclosure and usurpation with new innovations of governed movement and expansion"

(15). On January 1, 1994, the EZLN/Zapatistas spectacularly reacted to the neoliberal version of these residual practices when they descended, armed for the battle, from the forests in Chiapas to protest NAFTA and its dependence on the extractive logic that "reduce[s], constrain[s], and convert[s] life into commodities" (Gómez-Barris 2017, xix). The Zapatista mantra *un mundo donde quepan muchos mundos* (a world where many worlds fit) speaks back to the smallness of a world that refuses to acknowledge Indigenous cultures and ways of life, including past and current Indigenous expressions of gender and sexuality.

The punk rendering of Xipe Totec boldly confronts these colonizing histories by grappling with his keeper in tableaus that leave Martínez with the chain entwined around his neck. In a kinky exchange of submission, Martínez gets down on his knees, lays down on the ground, and gets under Xipe Totec. When the chain is released (by whom it's not clear), Xipe Totec circumnavigates the space, inviting viewers to eat the *jamón* from his soon-to-be-naked body. At one point face-to-face with Martínez, he coquettishly offers Martínez two large piles of ham that he couldn't possibly fit into his mouth without gagging. In the end, Xipe Totec is indeed shredded and skinned, but not without choking his now-vanquished captor.

2

Importing Degradation

First, imagine that you are a book. You want to go to Canada. There are several points of entry, border crossings, including the post office, and you may stop at more than one of them. At some, you are pulled out of your shipment simply because of your title. *Strokes*, a book on rowing, was considered suspiciously suggestive, and detained. At other crossings, the entire shipment is held and everything is put aside for further examination. This is the introductory level of the detention process: the hunting expedition. The Customs officer, who opens the box and decides to detain the shipment for examination, and the "commodity specialist," who classifies obscenity, deciding whether to ban or release a book, will rule based on the guidelines suggested in the Customs Memorandum D9-1-1.

Janine Fuller, co-owner, Little Sister's Book and Art Emporium (1995, 27)

In 1994, the same year NAFTA went into effect, internationally acclaimed lesbian writer Sarah Schulman traveled to Vancouver, British Columbia, to testify to the Supreme Court of Canada and the "Crown" on behalf of gay author John Preston, who had recently died of AIDS. The Court and Crown argued and maintained that the books *I Once Had a Master* and *Entertainment for a Master* were "obscene" under the newly minted Butler Law of 1992, the Customs Tariff Act and its subsections on "prohibited imports," and NAFTA signer Prime Minister Bill Mulroney's Memorandum D9-1-1. In her book *The Gentrification of the Mind*, Schulman reprinted her testimony. With her signature wit, Schulman went on to say, "As we moved along [in the trial], I came to learn that Milord did not know what 'deconstruction' meant. And later he revealed a puzzlement over the meaning of the word 'enema.' *Oh no*, I thought. *If he has never heard of enemas or deconstruction, we are doomed*" (2012, 142). Ultimately, the judge ruled that Canada Customs (now the Canada Border Services Agency) possesses total discretion to decide what is and what is not "obscene," and thus a prohibited import. "Interestingly," Schulman stated, "they quickly ratified gay marriage [in 2005], while continuing to retain the right to insure that no married gay man will ever go looking for *Mister Benson* [another Preston novel]" (142). While countless gay, lesbian, and what we would now call nonbinary and trans masculine materials were seized, detained, and even destroyed by Canada Customs both before and after 1994, and despite Canada's global image as a progressive nation for 2SLGBTQ (Two Spirit, lesbian, gay, bisexual, trans, queer) rights, NAFTA time, when analyzed through the Canadian lens, is riddled with surveillance and repression. As the Fuller epigraph to this chapter attests, Memorandum D9-1-1 specifically offered instructions to Canada Customs to seize and detain any objects considered to be "suspiciously suggestive." Under the expanded reach of these administrative procedures, and in collaboration with criminal laws such as the Butler Law and police sting operations such as "Operation Soap" (bathhouse raids) and "Project P" (P for pornography), Mulroney's administration authorized Canada Customs officials to act as "commodity specialists" to label and destroy (mostly) US-imported "obscenity" that entered through Canada's southern border.

These repressive state and local activities of surveillance and destruction occurred not because of NAFTA but in the shadows of its negotiation and implementation. I return to the archives of this period in Canada's history of negotiating its trade relationship with the United States not to argue that the movement of sexual goods was invented under NAFTA nor to argue that trade and exchanges between the two countries arose in the 1990s. Rather, when free trade was formalized between Canada and the United States, first in 1989 under the CUSFTA and then in 1994 under NAFTA, it continued a long-standing relationship of anxiety over the exchange between two Anglo-dominant countries. What changed after the CUSFTA and NAFTA was frequency, volume, levels, and rates and not only of goods. The performativity of free trade, the repetitions of seeing certain goods endlessly restocked at retail locations, imposed an affective intensity of the presentness of culture, of language, of origin, and of the people who shepherded the precious imported cargo along the way. To understand the Canadian panic over the ubiquity of US cultural presence, I therefore cast a wider net. I examine the CUSFTA and NAFTA in the amendments to the 1867 Customs Act, and particularly Memorandum D9-1-1 (1985) and its ongoing updates, as historical artifacts for tracing the Canadian state's anxiety over popular culture from the United States. This anxiety inordinately came to bear on queer sexual life.

The archival records show how sexual panic intensified during NAFTA time. This state-sponsored panic over the importation of queer and trans sexual materials from the United States led to the creation of new lucrative infrastructures toward which massive amounts of private and state money flowed to fund surveillance, policing, and border security. The objective was to safeguard an affective nationalism based on Canadian "values" that reified the imaginary coordinates of the nation-state in allegiance to British colonial law on "sodomy" and other acts that Canada Customs frequently labeled as "degradation." "Degradation" was used on official customs documents, particularly Canada Customs' K27 forms, to target a broad category of queer traffic that ranged from sexually explicit words and images to contestations of white heteropatriarchy (examples of seized and monitored materials appear in figures 2.1 and 2.2). Alongside these documents and policies, the archive also tells a story of the undaunted desire for sexual culture and how the fight to consume it resulted in an activist coalition that forged queer alternative infrastructures and new forms of expertise to circulate a wide variety of pornographic and sexual education materials during the height of the AIDS pandemic in the United States and Canada.

To explore this moment in Canada's long history of sexual suppression, I had to approach the archive without a direct entry point, employing a multidirectional archival method that revels in traces, gossip, and "ephemera as evidence" (Muñoz 1996). As I meandered through the archives, I came across the names of people who faced off with Canada Customs, and I then sought out those people to chat, endeavoring to enrich what I found in the archive with the ongoing repertoire of lived experience and memory. Thus, interwoven with my extensive archival research in Toronto are the voices of various Canadian "queer traffickers." All these interlocutors were on the ground confronting the censorship and seizure of queer and trans cultural materials. Many of them employed a variety of different queer traffic tactics to reroute sexual culture productions through illicit practices, such as smuggling materials across the border or inventing fake addresses where queer materials were sent to evade Canada Customs' obscenity appraisers. I focus on how free-trade anxiety around cultural processes of exchange intertwined with

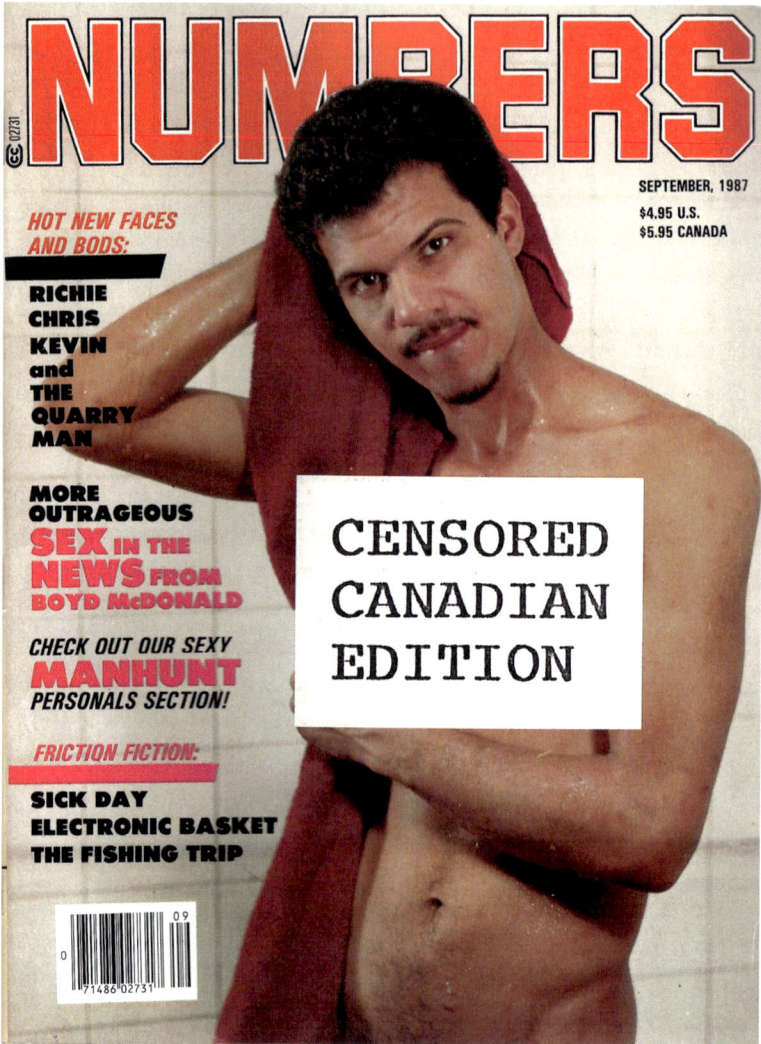

Censored *Numbers* magazine, September 1987. Sexual Representation Collection, Mark S. Bonham Centre for Sexual Diversity Studies, University of Toronto.

the fear of being replaced by the sexual culture of the United States. While the panic about what was then referred to as "homosexuality" and its embeddedness in imported objects most often appeared in the archive, the war waged on gay and lesbian culture extended to a variety of cultural productions that portrayed trans sexuality, sex work, indigeneity, and Black sexualities.

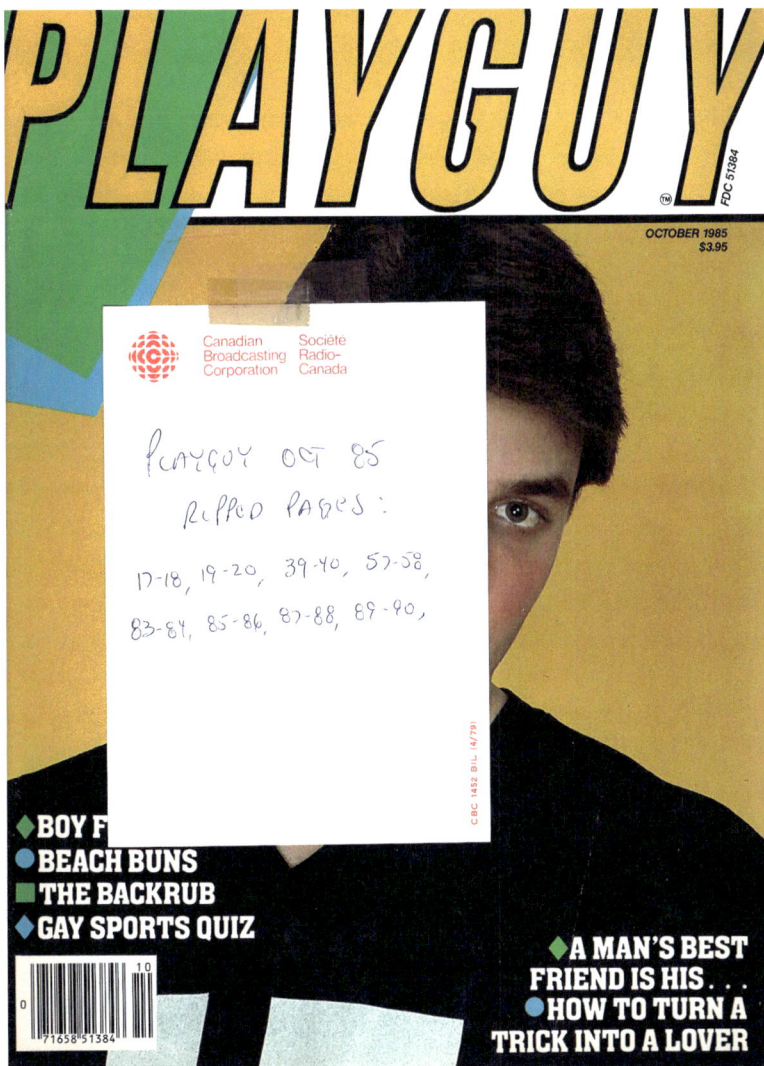

PLAYGUY

OCTOBER 1985
$3.95

Canadian Société
Broadcasting Radio-
Corporation Canada

PLAYGUY OCT 85
RIPPED PAGES:
17-18, 19-20, 39-40, 57-58,
83-84, 85-86, 87-88, 89-90,

CBC 1452 BIL (4/79)

FDC 51384

◆BOY F
●BEACH BUNS
■THE BACKRUB
◆GAY SPORTS QUIZ

◆A MAN'S BEST
FRIEND IS HIS. . .
●HOW TO TURN A
TRICK INTO A LOVER

2.2 *Playguy* magazine with pages ripped out, October 1985. Sexual Representation Collection, Mark S. Bonham Centre for Sexual Diversity Studies,
University of Toronto.

When viewed through the lens of queer traffic, the notion of a permeable
border between the United States and Canada in the lead-up to September 11, and in contrast to the US-Mexico border, is shown to be anything but.
NAFTA, I argue, further fueled the moral panic that the Canadian state waged
against the cultural imperialism of the United States and its long-standing

anxiety about becoming its southern neighbor's economic colony.[1] Indeed, it wasn't until the CUSFTA, then again with NAFTA, and yet again in 2020 with the Canada-US-Mexico Agreement (CUSMA for Canada, USMCA for the United States, T-MEC for Mexico, colloquially known as NAFTA 2.0) that Canada demanded an exclusion on cultural industries and "most-favored nation" (MFN) treatment, a free-trade method for nominally establishing the same trade terms for all participating countries. "This [cultural] exclusion," reported the Congressional Research Service after the ratification of the new CUSMA, "reflects the Canadian government's attempts to promote a distinctly Canadian culture and the fear that, without its support, American culture would come to dominate Canada" (December 28, 2021).[2] This long-standing fear inspired Mulroney to fight for and win cultural exemptions during the 1987 CUSFTA negotiations, such as the Canadian Radio-Television and Telecommunications Commission (CRTC) content quota requirements known as Canadian content rules, or CanCon (Canadian content).[3] While NAFTA experts I spoke to in Toronto largely view CanCon and Bill C-55 (split-run magazines) as the only direct cultural influence of NAFTA on Canadian content consumption, tracing the exchange of sexually explicit materials opens up other policy-related connections.[4]

The long history of Canada Customs' searches, seizures, and destructions of queer and trans print materials, while still ongoing, reached a crescendo in the years leading up to and immediately following NAFTA in 1994. I propose speculative connections between Canada's insistence on a cultural exemption clause in the 1987 CUSFTA and the 1994 NAFTA documents and the prime minister's guidelines to Canada Customs on "prohibited imports," or Memorandum D9-1-1. The cultural exemption clause, which was embattled during the 2018–2020 renegotiations, is an independent cultural policy that allows the Canadian state to treat cultural goods differently than other commercial products in crossborder trade with the United States. As I will show, queer sex and a wide range of sexual activities such as fisting, collectively gathered under the banner of "degradation" on Canada Customs forms, became the primary targets of the panic about the incursion of US popular culture and its perceived effects on Canadian values.

Canada's insistence on a cultural exemption to NAFTA signaled a regional fear about the importation of homosexuality during the HIV/AIDS crisis of the 1980s and 1990s. Mexico too feared the importation of materials from the United States that celebrated queer sex practices, safe sex, and gender queerness; resistance to cultural imperialism in Mexico, however, did not occur at the federal or governmental level. Writing in May 1994 about the "Nafta Generation" and only four months after NAFTA went into effect, *Mexico Insight* journalist Scott Morrison wrote, "Mainstream Mexican society is not yet ready to accept youths who disobey their parents, sport tattoos, use drugs, think independently, experiment with homosexuality or act promiscuously."[5] Despite Morrison's claims about an informal NAFTA panic in Mexico, this chapter inverts the well-worn stereotype of Catholic Mexico as repressed and liberal Canada as sexually free. It shows how the Canadian state instrumentalized Canada Customs to hire and train "obscenity appraisers," thereby creating an immense workforce to root out the queer traffic of US print culture. Unlike Mexico, Canada used the suppleness of administrative law at the border, and its unspoken collaborations with localized police sting operations and criminal law, to place an almost exclusive and inordinate pressure on queer sexuality and racial and gender difference as a form of US-based degradation that threatened the very core of Canadian society.

In 1992, Prime Minister Mulroney, who had formerly negotiated the CUSFTA with then-President George H. W. Bush, signed NAFTA. When Mulroney signed the CUSFTA with the United States in 1988, Canada reluctantly entered the agreement, owing to fear of US cultural imperialism and, for NAFTA, a strong ambivalence about formalizing free trade with Mexico. Although I take the Mulroney administration to task in this chapter, Pierre Elliot Trudeau and the Liberal party provided the initial motivation for free-trade agreements. Historian Tom Hooper makes clear that it was also Trudeau who only putatively decriminalized homosexuality in 1969. With the mere addition of an "exception clause" to the Criminal Law Amendment Act, certain sexual acts continued to be regarded as "gross indecency" and "buggery." Diverse forms of dissident sex only became permissible provided they happened under a strict set of circumstances. According to the exception clause—for me, a clear echo of the cultural exemption clause in the CUSFTA and NAFTA—one was entitled to be "grossly indecent" if the act occurred in private between consenting adults who were at least twenty-one years old and between "a husband and his wife" (Hooper 2014, 59–61). The Canadian Liberal Party, according to the research of Hooper and the Anti-69 Network, never decriminalized homosexuality in 1969 (Hooper 2019). This is the legal legacy that enabled Canada Customs to hunt and destroy gay and lesbian materials in the 1980s and 1990s. Both the fervor for free trade and the criminalization of queer and trans sex, therefore, span the political spectrum.

Under the auspices of the Crown and Memorandum D9-1-1, which will be the policy focus of what follows, Canada Customs created an expansive network of administrative practices to create an entire labor force of un-qualified "appraisers" who erratically adjudicated the presence or absence of obscenity across a broad swathe of objects entering the country. Schulman's testimony and the epigraph (quoting gay and lesbian bookstore owner Janine Fuller) that began this chapter are only two of countless moments in the queer Canadian archive that speak to the weaponization of administrative law at the border to enact such antisex homophobia. Queer sex, though, was only one of many targets. In a time before the internet and even before the advent of DVDs, most seized materials were in print form, including gay and lesbian magazines (e.g., *Honcho, Blue Boy, Bad Attitude, On Our Backs*); manifestos and zines (the OBZINE); newsletters, pamphlets, poetry, and novels, such as those written by John Preston, Patrick Califia, Dorothy Allison, Salman Rushdie, and Marguerite Duras; experimental books such as those by David Wojnarowicz; anthologies of Black queer experience by Joseph Beam; and even the Black feminist scholarship of bell hooks. This chapter returns to the archive—specifically The ArQuives: Canada's LGBTQ2+ Archives (hereafter The ArQuives) and the Sexual Representation Collection at the Bonham Centre for Sexual Diversity Studies at the University of Toronto—to argue that FTAs not only implicitly promote moral regulation but also profit from it. Moreover, this chapter aims to show how the affective economy of sexual panic influenced national and international trade policy. The archive tells a story about sexual culture on the move and the foment of a state-sponsored sex panic that led to the destruction of so many pathways and circuits for the flow of what the Canadian state deemed "degradation."

Drawing the Line

In 1990, a Vancouver-based three-woman lesbian collective by the name of Kiss & Tell mounted the exhibition *Drawing the Line*. It featured one hundred photographs taken by Susan Stewart that presented her collaborators, Persimmon Blackbridge and Lizard Jones, performing a wide array of sexual acts against backdrops that ranged from nature settings to bondage and discipline, domination and submission, and sadomasochism (BDSM) dungeons. Visitors were invited into the gallery, but only women were given markers to record their reactions to the photographs on the walls (men could do so in a notebook on the floor). Kiss & Tell displayed the photos based on their understanding of what would be viewed as an ever-increasing trajectory of sexual explicitness. Their goal was to take the temperature of lesbian feminist communities in cities such as Vancouver to see where these communities would "draw the line," meaning at what point along the axis of sexual explicitness these communities would declare "too much" for public display. Kiss & Tell's audiences surprised them, however, responding in multidirectional rather than linear ways. Passionate debates appeared on the walls and gave testimony to the arbitrariness of where the line should be drawn during a time when the Canadian state capitalized on the outrage of transnational antipornography feminism to expand the censorship of materials deemed "obscene" (see figs. 2.3 and 2.4). The wall inscriptions evidenced the diversity of lesbian communities' perspective on the question of "sex in public," to riff on a germinal 1998 article by Lauren Berlant and Michael Warner in which they unpack the "project of [racialized] normalization that has made heterosexuality hegemonic" (548) and how this project is insulated through antisex performances that they described at the time as "the spectacular demonization of any represented sex" (550).

One such spectacular performance of demonization was the bombing of the Red Hot Video store in Vancouver by a self-styled group of "urban guerrillas," who had, in 1982, changed their name from the Squamish Five to the Wimmin's Fire Brigade. Caught up in the radical feminist fury against pornography, further stoked by the influential visits of Catharine MacKinnon and Andrea Dworkin and encouraged by the regional circulation of feminist ire over Red Hot Video's alleged sale of snuff films, the Wimmin's Fire Brigade targeted its three franchises. In effect, the Wimmin's Fire Brigade did the surveillance and terrorism work of the state, insofar as they sought to interrupt and destroy the commercial trade in sexual materials. They viewed their actions as "self-defense" against a transnational pornography industry that peddled in sexist "hate propaganda" (Wimmin's Fire Brigade press release, 1982, as cited in Ellis 1983).

Drawing the Line, as comments from many female visitors attested, was a landmark museum exhibition that pushed back against conservative state forces and their demonization spectacles. Equally, Kiss & Tell provided a space where the lesbian feminist community and feminist communities broadly could use the white walls of the gallery to speak to each other about a politically intense and dangerous debate that mirrored, with important differences, what Lisa Duggan and Nan D. Hunter (2006) called the "sex wars" in the United States. For me, *Drawing the Line* acts as a metaphor for the ways in which state and citizen actors work together, often unwittingly, to drive sexual panics and draw inconsistent boundaries around acceptable sexual consumption and its circulation. Using available rhetorics of panic around HIV/AIDS and anal penetration, the state targeted queer, trans, and

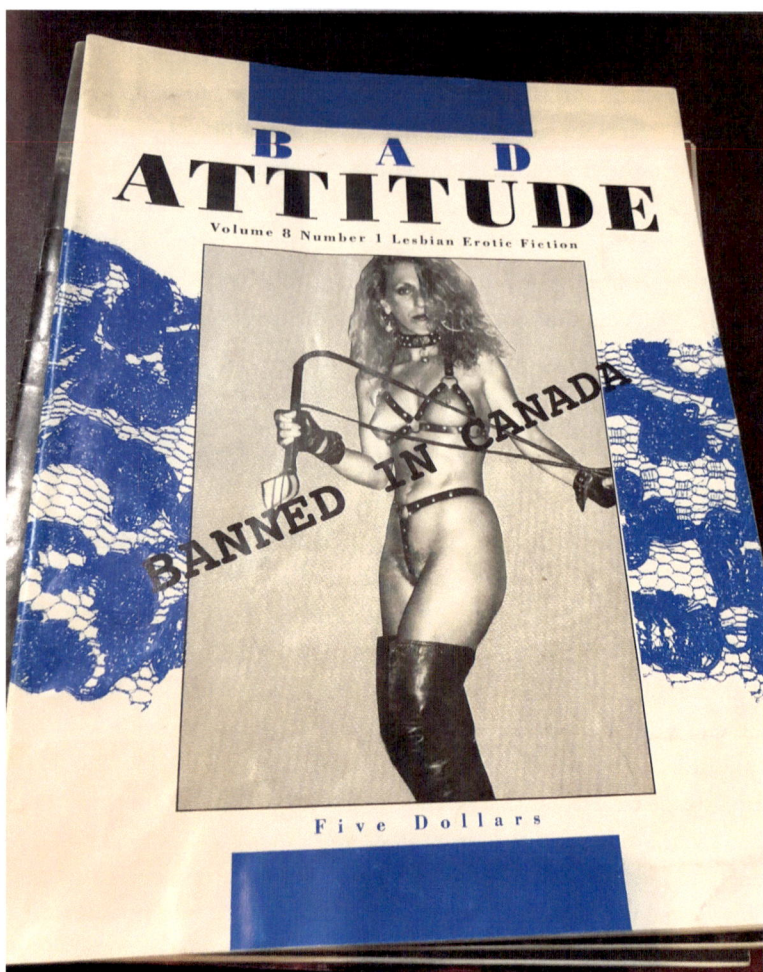

2.3   Banned *Bad Attitude* magazine, vol. 8, no. 1, January 1992. The ArQuives: Canada's LGBTQ2+ Archives, Toronto.

Black Canadian communities during what Sarah Schulman has called the "plague years" of the HIV/AIDS pandemic.

Groups such as the Wimmin's Fire Brigade informally aided the state in that project in the years leading up to the 1989 CUSFTA. However, certain feminist factions were not the only ones fueling the Canadian state's antisex and antiqueer policies. For example, Randy Shilts's 1987 book, *And the Band Played On*, places just as much responsibility for the HIV/AIDS epidemic on the "gay lifestyle" and "promiscuous sex" as it does the Reagan

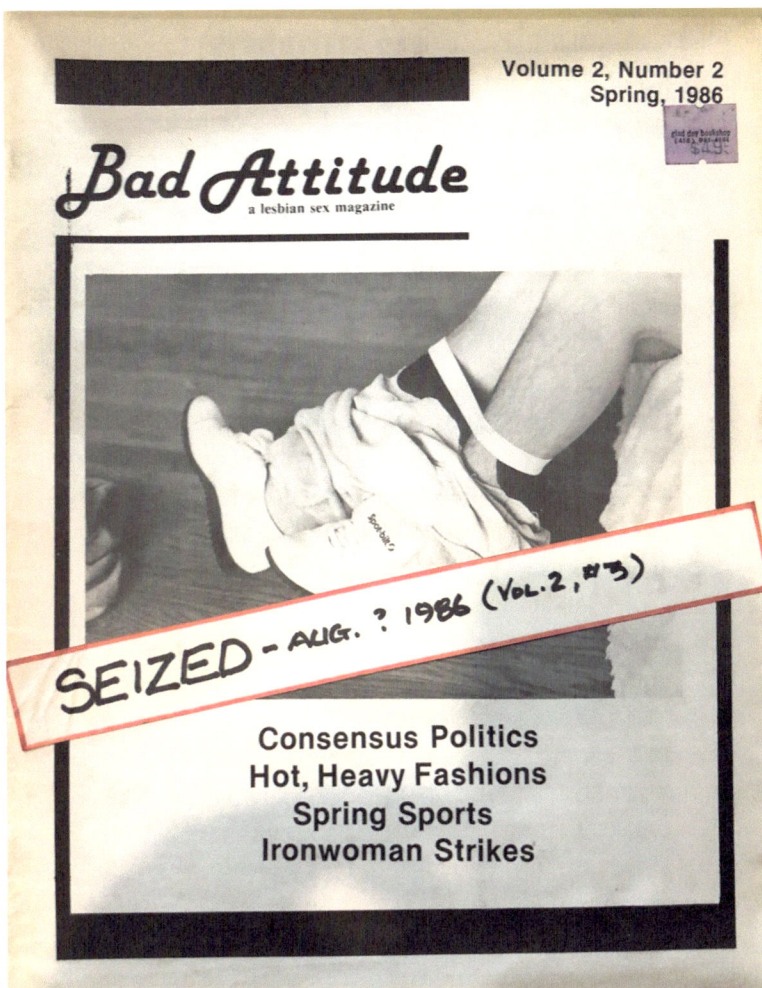

2.4   Seized *Bad Attitude* magazine, vol. 2, no. 2, Spring 1986. The ArQuives: Canada's LGBTQ2+ Archives, Toronto.

administration and the Centers for Disease Control and Prevention (CDC). As Douglas Crimp (1987) has argued, Shilts's book fed readers a lucrative version of Michel Foucault's repressive hypothesis, whereby antisex exposés masquerading as journalism seized on the profit-generating literary schemata of identifying villains and heroes, sexual monsters and sexual saviors. Shilts provided the straight mainstream media with the ultimate in transnational villains by creating the folk devil "Patient Zero," a French-Canadian airline steward named Gaëtan Dugas, who supposedly had lovers in every port where he would maliciously spread the virus to his lover-victims through his insatiable lust for promiscuous sex. Patient Zero is a literary stand-in, Crimp argued, "of the homosexual as imagined by heterosexuals—sexually voracious, murderously irresponsible. . . . Shilts therefore offers up the scapegoat for his heterosexual colleagues in order to prove that he, like them, is horrified by such creatures" (244). Books such as Shilts's were never seized at the Canadian border by Canada Customs; its indictment of a Québécois gay man fit within the long-standing conflicts between English and French Canada, the latter of which operated much more openly in relation to sexually explicit material. Shilts's book became a made-for-TV film in 1993 and was ultimately translated into seven languages, thus solidifying its status as a global authority on the origins of the virus to "ensure that the blame for AIDS would remain focused on gay men" (Crimp 1987, 242). In this way, the transnational circulation of books such as Shilts's should be seen as a crucial node in the history of the criminalization of HIV+ peoples, from the administrative violence of being denied passage across borders to the criminal law's surveillance and incarceration of peoples accused of willfully spreading the virus.[6] In the voluminous archive of attacking queer sex as the cause of contagion, *And the Band Played On* epitomizes what Richard Fung calls the "frame of gay male irresponsibility, that of a self-destructive and uncontrollable appetite for sex" (1995, 293).

Reading across circuits of sexual trade in Ontario, British Columbia, and Manitoba, I start from the premise that it is no coincidence that 1992, the year NAFTA was signed, also marked the year when the landmark Canadian Supreme Court decision of *R. v. Butler* was handed down. As Tom Hooper told me at the Glad Day bookstore in the fall of 2018, *Butler* transformed what were formerly charges of "obscenity" based on the vague notion of "community standards" to charges of "harm" against women and girls. Donald Butler had been the owner of a Manitoba video store that sold hardcore audiovisual and print materials, among other kinds of sexual accoutrement (in other words, a typical sex shop). A lower court had convicted him on charges of selling, possessing, distributing, and exposing "obscenity." Butler appealed, and in so doing he waged the first constitutional challenge to the British colonial obscenity law, section 163 of Canada's Criminal Code. Unlike in the United States, there are no First Amendment rights in Canada, and so the Supreme Court of Canada was instead charged with adjudicating whether section 163 violated the 1982 Canadian Charter of Rights and Freedoms, particularly subsection 2(b), the freedom of expression guarantee. Even though the Court ultimately found that section 163 violated the Charter, Brenda

Cossman and Shannon Bell explain that the Court justified this violation as a "reasonable limit prescribed by law" under section 1 of the Charter (1997, 3–4), thus ruling that obscenity, tout court, would always be considered an outlier to the freedoms designated in the 1982 Charter. "In its ruling," interpret Cossman and Bell, "the Supreme Court not only upheld the constitutionality of the obscenity laws but also set out a new test for determining whether representations are obscene," one "seen by many to signal the beginning of a new era of liberalization in the regulation of sexual representations" (4).

In the decision's wake, and despite the continued importation of straight and mainstream porn into Canada and the unrestrained disciplining and destruction of gay and lesbian materials, the Women's Legal Education and Action Fund (LEAF) and other radical feminist and antipornography activists hailed *R. v. Butler* as a huge victory. The scope of *Butler*'s influence on the circulation of queer materials in Canada extended to film festivals (Inside/Out Collective), to theaters (Buddies in Bad Times), and to galleries and museums (Mercer Union Gallery), including the display of another Kiss & Tell work, a videotape entitled *True Inversions*. In my book *Sex Museums* (2016a), I examined the synchronic attacks on museums and galleries in the United States, where First Amendment rights to freedom of speech exist but were too readily relied on as the sole defense for displaying sex in public. Without such an amendment, however, and with the Court having ruled that the violation of the Charter was admissible, administrative and criminal law could team up in what can only be called a frenzy for would-be homophobic, transphobic, and anti–sex work censors. While literary or visual depictions of "anal penetration" loom large in the Canadian state's definition of harm, the cultural productions of (leather)dykes and lesbians, particularly those featuring interracial, gender-nonconforming, and sadomasochistic sex acts, were especially hunted.

Preceding *Butler* and while negotiating the CUSFTA, Prime Minister Mulroney amended the existing Customs Tariff Act in 1986 (with its second supplement) and then again in 1987 (its third supplement) to embed within it Memorandum D9-1-1, the Interpretive Policy and Procedure for the Administration of Tariff Code 9956. While not a law per se, Memorandum D9-1-1 is a set of meticulously crafted guidelines for Canada Customs officials. This document was meant to be temporary, its interim status perhaps reflecting the aim of stemming the initial tide of "degrading" US cultural productions in the wake of the CUSFTA. The Memorandum, however, is no longer temporary, as it continues to be endlessly updated, with more recent updates aligning sexual materials with hate propaganda, among a bevy of

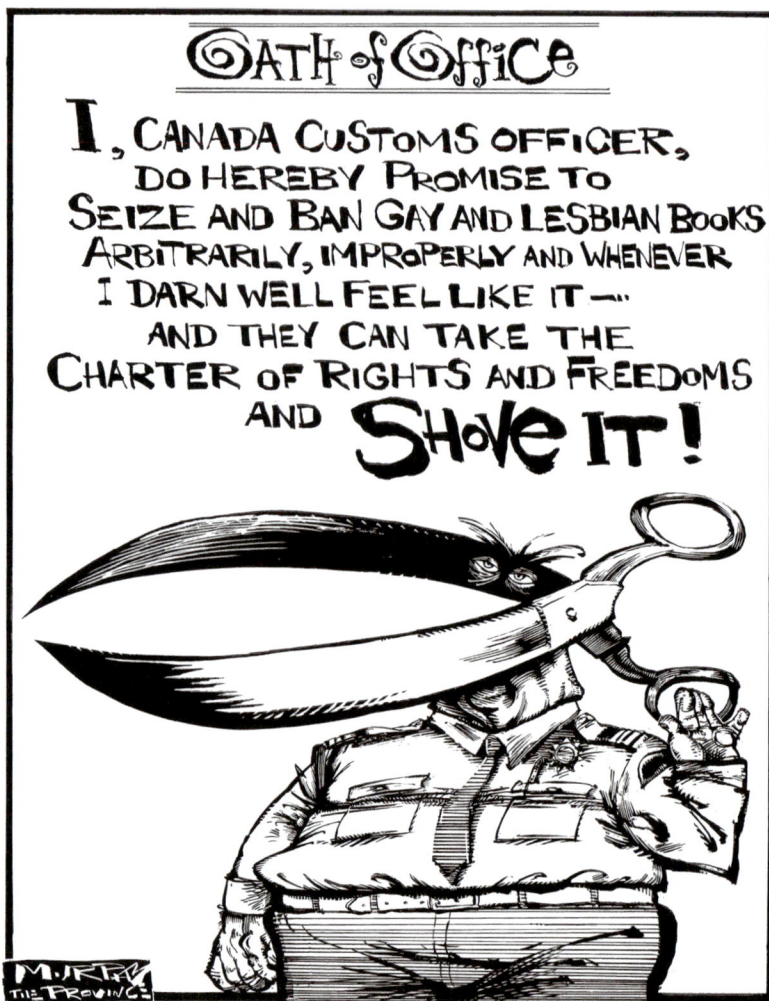

2.5 "Customs Appraiser" cartoon by Daniel Murphy, January 24, 1996. Courtesy of Daniel Murphy.

other so-called harm-inducing materials. Memorandum D9-1-1's administrative reach at the border allowed Canada Customs carte blanche to seize any sexually explicit materials that included descriptions or depictions of sexual acts they construed as obscene (see fig. 2.5).

The frenzy to seize can perhaps be best illustrated in the 1993 actions of one Customs "commodity specialist," who held back for inspection antipornography feminist Andrea Dworkin's book *Pornography: Men Possessing*

Women. In so doing, they exposed the absurd approach to appraising printed works for obscenity, as well as the apparent inability of Customs officials to read a subtitle. Indeed, guided by their training in explicit antisex, homophobic, and racist assessment strategies, Customs agents made swift and decisive seizures of materials. In the case of Dworkin's book, they declared the book obscene based on its pre-colon title alone. Even Dworkin—who along with Catharine MacKinnon had been so integral to the *Butler* decision and to the growing transnational and radical feminist alliance to eradicate heterosexual porn—spoke out against Canadian criminal obscenity laws, albeit belatedly and at times in contradiction to her earlier statements.[7] Dworkin, who once described pornography as "the new terrorism" (1978), contended that laws such as *Butler* ultimately "empower the state rather than the victims, with the result that little is done against the pornography industry."[8] A press release, "Statement by Catharine A. MacKinnon and Andrea Dworkin Regarding Canada Customs and Legal Approaches to Pornography," from which the previous quote is drawn, goes on to deny any connection made between *Butler* and Canada Customs' homophobic practices. It calls such claims "fabricated," owing to the technical disaggregation of the jurisprudence of administrative law at the border from the criminal law that is *Butler*. In the same press release, MacKinnon and Dworkin go on to say that they never supported a criminal law approach, and that Canada failed to adopt the civil rights law against pornography that they had intended. Furthermore, they asserted that under the administrative law at the border of the sovereign state of Canada, Canada Customs "has every right to control its borders—especially given widespread resentment against what is often viewed there as U.S. cultural imperialism," even as they admitted that "Canada Customs has a long record of homophobic seizures." I want to push back against the refusal to acknowledge the collaboration between the police and Canada Customs—not to propose some conspiracy theory between administrative law at the border and criminal law in Toronto and Vancouver but to argue that the co-constitution of these obscenity laws both reflected and created a holistic landscape of state homophobia.

At The ArQuives, I found one trace of interpersonal correspondence from the early days of email that conveyed the wide-reaching scope of Canada Customs' power over the crossborder flow of queer cultural materials, in this instance to Little Sister's Book and Art Emporium in Vancouver. "RUFFLE@cnc.bc.ca" forwarded a message from one "millera@ GOV-ON-CA@MHS@EPO" that offers an update on the 1995 *Little Sister's v. Canada Customs* case. "Basically LS [Little Sister's] wants Customs officials to not have the power to detain materials at the border." This email goes on to cite an anonymous but Little Sister's-issuing quote: "They (Canada Customs) can work with the police by reporting their findings to them. The Criminal Code allows plice [sic] to seize obscene materials." Through administrative and criminal law, the moral regulation of gay and lesbian materials became lucrative to the state and therefore, according to market logic, an acceptable facet of free-trade infrastructures. The email exchange about Little Sister's makes this claim about the criminal/administrative law connection and shows how some people were already aware of the potential for collaboration to discipline and control the importation of materials destined for bookstores such as Little Sister's.

Not ironically, the Canadian state, so obsessed with plugging the leak of what was construed as lowbrow US popular culture, welcomed with open arms the flow of US-based radical feminism that seemed to support its regulatory drive. While LEAF initially took up radical feminist ideas against pornography imported from the United States, after the Project P sting operation targeted Toronto's Glad Day bookstore to seize an issue of the lesbian sex magazine *Bad Attitude* and arrest store clerk Tom Ivison for trafficking in obscenity, the organization later rejected the influence of Dworkin and MacKinnon on Canada's Butler Law. Nevertheless, the Canadian state leveraged transnational radical feminist outrage, aligning it with Canadian values against "harming women." LEAF realized their error when the real targets of their ire, such as the magazine *Hustler*, entered the country freely while *Bad Attitude* and other lesbian sex literature was accused of "harming women" and "degrading" the Canadian state's purported gender freedom.[9]

In 1991 the Mulroney administration further refined Memorandum D9-1-1 to clarify and interpret the tariff code 9956 of Schedule VII of the Customs Tariff Act. The legislation covered

> Books, printed paper, drawings, paintings, prints, photographs or representations of any kind that
>
> > (a) are deemed to be obscene under subsection 163(8) of the Criminal Code.
> >
> > (b) constitute hate propaganda within the meaning of subsection 320(8) of the Criminal Code.
> >
> > (c) are of a treasonable character within the meaning of section 46 of the Criminal Code; or

(d) are of a seditious character within the meaning of sections 59 and 60 of the Criminal Code.

Under the Memorandum, national criminal law and administrative law at the Canada-US border targeted the importation and circulation of sexual materials. In contrast to a rhetorical nationalism in Mexico that informally regarded pornography as immoral, item number 6 was rigorously formal in its definitions. Item number 6 of the "Guidelines and General Information" defined "obscenity" and meticulously delineated for Canada Customs which cultural products should be considered "treasonous," "seditious," and "harmful":

6. The following goods, in so far as they are deemed to be obscene or hate propaganda within the meanings of the terms as set forth above, are to be classified under Tariff Code 9956 and their importation into Canada *prohibited*:

    (a) goods which depict or describe sexual acts that appear to degrade or dehumanize any of the participants, including:

        (1) depictions or descriptions of sex with violence, submission, coercion, ridicule, degradation, exploitation or humiliation of any human being, whether sexually explicit or not, and which appear to condone or otherwise endorse such behavior for the purposes of sexual stimulation or pleasure;

        (2) depictions or descriptions of sexual assault (previously rape). Any goods that depict or describe a sexual activity between male/female, male/male, or female/female which appears to be without his/her consent and which appears to be achieved chiefly by force or deception;

        (3) depictions or descriptions of bondage, involuntary servitude and the state of human beings subjected to external control, in a sexual context;

        (4) depictions or descriptions which appear to be associating sexual pleasure or gratification with pain and suffering, and with the mutilation of or letting of blood from any part of the human body, involving violence,

coercion and lack of basic dignity and respect for a human being;

(5) depictions or descriptions of sexual gratification gained through causing physical pain or humiliation, or the getting of sexual pleasure from dominating, mistreating or hurting a human being. This includes depictions and descriptions of physical force which appear to be used so as to injure, damage or destroy; of extreme roughness of action; of unjust or callous use of force or power; of spanking, beating or violent shoving in a sexual context;

(6) depictions or descriptions of mutilation or removal of any part of the human body or the taking of human life, real or implied, for the purpose of sexual arousal;

(7) depictions or descriptions of menstrual blood, fecal matter, urine or the inducement of feces through enemas as part of sexual arousal; and

[begin DELETED provision]

8) depictions or descriptions of anal penetration, including depictions or descriptions involving implements of all kinds;

[end DELETED provision].

Since the June 12, 1991 version, the deletion of subsection 6 (a)(8) has been the only change made to D9-1-1. Arguably, however, this deletion was never applied in practice, as Customs officials continue(d) to seize and destroy queer materials containing visual or textual descriptions of anal penetration well after 1991.

During my time in Toronto, I was able to speak to one former Customs official, a "commodity specialist" who in the late 1990s resigned the post in protest of Memorandum D9-1-1, section 163 of the criminal code, and the application of these laws through the K27 search and seizure customs form (an example of a K27 form is shown in figure 2.6). According to this former commodity specialist, customs officials were "trained in obscenity" at the Customs College in Rigaud, Québec, and were required to take refresher courses to keep up to date on revisions that newly defined a variety of mate-

2.6   Example of K27 form. Sexual Representation Collection, Mark S. Bonham
Centre for Sexual Diversity Studies, University of Toronto.

rials such as "hate propaganda." They told me that Customs treated gay and
lesbian materials "just like drugs," that customs officials took turns creating
spectacles of destroying materials at a gigantic warehouse, spectacles that commodity specialists were required to witness. They explained that these jobs
had a very high turnover rate fueled by what this person described as the
"every day, all day long" exposure to "heavy material," by which they were

referring to alleged "hate propaganda," the twin to sexual obscenity charges. They told me that two years was the saturation point for most of the workers employed in the massive labor force that D9-1-1 summoned into being.

This was not the first time Canada had assembled a labor force for protecting the nation against queer sex. The 2018 documentary *The Fruit Machine*, directed by Sarah Fodey, recounts Canada's Cold War stance toward queer people, when Canada viewed them as spies and threats to the nation.[10] Figuring homosexuality as a moral failing out of step with Canadian values, the "purge," as many of the film's interlocutors referred to it, became an indispensable business activity for the Royal Canadian Mounted Police (RCMP): 90 percent of the RCMP jobs depended on the continuance of the purge. Echoing the McCarthy era in the United States, "communist" and "homo" became somewhat interchangeable. In Canada, however, owing to the thinking that the Soviet Union's KGB (Committee for State Security, or CSS) would be looking to recruit people with secrets, "homosexuals" were their primary targets. In the film, sociologist Gary Kinsman explains that on that rationale the Canadian state could have targeted gamblers, adulterers, or people who performed other activities that were similarly viewed as morally failing to the affective nationalism of the nation. Instead, Canada leveraged the RCMP to single out homosexuality and created an elaborate series of assessments to adjudicate whether a suspected individual was "homosexual." How a person held their books (never to your breast bone; always to your side!), how they held their cigarette, whether or not they were considered butch and/or what we might call today trans masculine, whether they wore a pinky ring or drove a white convertible: all of these everyday performances would lead to an affirmative appraisal of the individual as a "homosexual" and therefore, during this Cold War context, a communist. The RCMP headquarters devoted an entire floor to looking for lesbian, gay, and genderqueer people, with maps created to track and trace the movement of queers, the maps' surfaces riddled with red dots that purportedly kept tabs on the "commie homos." Ironically, the red dots overtook the map, thus requiring that larger maps be made to accommodate the "growing homosexual menace." Invented by Carleton University professor F. R. Wake, the "fruit machine" of the film's title became the ultimate scientific test of homosexuality. Wake showed alleged homosexuals "dirty pictures" and measured their sweat and pupil responses to determine who was a "fruit." In the post–Cold War years, the legacy of the fruit machine continued, this time unleashing a huge labor force to root out and destroy gay and lesbian materials and by extension the successful gay and lesbian brick-and-mortar establishments for which they were bound. What labeled these objects as "suspicious" was usually not their obscured contents but rather their destinations. I turn my attention now to two sites that garnered particular attention: the gay and lesbian bookstores of Toronto (Glad Day) and Vancouver (Little Sister's Book and Art Emporium).

Gay and Lesbian Bookstores and the Fight to Save Them

The scale of the search, seizure, and censorship of pornographic materials at the border was so totalizing that it led to the closure of most gay and lesbian bookstores across Canada: they could no longer stock their shelves with the largely US-imported objects that constituted their primary retail items. Both The ArQuives and the Sexual Representation Collection contain K27 forms filled out by Canada Customs officers who were acting as appraisers of moral regulation. The most popular selection that Canada Customs officers made in these forms was "anal penetration," often accompanied by the empty signifier "other," within which officers would frequently inscribe the words "bondage" and/or "degradation." The archival materials I studied speak directly to the violent ways that Canada Customs officers dealt with these boxes as veritable vectors of contagion. Boxes were crudely opened, their contents were ripped and slashed with knives, and words were redacted, in addition to whole missing pages. In one circumstance, as related to me in an interview in 2018 with John Scythes, the second owner of Glad Day, cheap cooking oil was poured and slimed onto the materials. Of course, these objects weren't just censored and damaged. Untold numbers simply disappeared, were burned or thrown in the trash, or maybe even taken home by customs officials.

This penchant for destruction and disappearance coincided with a story that historian Tom Hooper told me about how the police destroyed one of the bathhouses in an area targeted for gentrification, designated by the police as Track 2.[11] They didn't just shut the place down; they destroyed the bathhouse beyond recognition, punching and kicking into the walls. This damage was condoned because the police participated in readying the establishment for its probable demolition. Thus, in the case of seizing and censoring and maiming gay and lesbian materials, Canada Customs destroyed in order to gentrify. They destroyed the objects destined for the gay and lesbian bookstores, and in so doing, they collaborated in clearing those sites—cleaning up "the gay ghettos" of Toronto and Vancouver for sanitized urban development.

Now the oldest gay bookstore in the world, Glad Day barely withstood the almost incessant obscenity charges. Jearld Moldenhauer, Glad Day's first owner, said this to me in an email in September 2018:

> Once Mulroney's Memorandum was handed over to Canada Customs' officers they proceeded to have a heyday, literally opening every parcel addressed to Glad Day from outside Canada. Probably 80% of these parcels came from the US, the remaining 20% from England, Germany, Italy, Spain and Australia. Canada itself produced very little in the way of gay or lesbian literature and even gay & lesbian writers in Canada had to get published in the US. Some days we would receive two, three or four seizure notices. The basic "plan" in the government's mindset was to put us out of business. If Customs detention went unchallenged they would destroy (burn or shred?) the books. Whatever happened, the bookstore still has to pay the bills within 30, 60, or 90 days. This assault went on for years—about a decade, only ending with the Supreme Court decision in the Little Sisters Case. For the first 4–5 years Glad Day was the main target.

Having promised his constituents "jobs, jobs, jobs" in the 1988 election, Mulroney commodified homophobia to invent an entire labor force. While Canada Customs provided an endless array of jobs to people with absolutely no training in print and film culture, bookstores with a small and modestly paid staff like Glad Day and Little Sister's now had to add a plethora of time-consuming activities to their everyday jobs. In a September 2018 interview with former Glad Day employee Kimberly Mistysyn, the only woman on staff at Glad Day at the time, she told me about incessant calls from cultural producers whose works were censored, complaints from angry customers who couldn't access the literature or films they wanted to consume, long and often fruitless phone calls with Canada Customs, and numerous interviews with the news media that overtaxed Glad Day's already-exhausted staff.[12] What the state did not consider, and what the archive clearly shows, is that this back-breaking labor of fighting the affective economy of moral panic produced collectives that developed expertise in the Customs Tariff Act, the *Butler* decision, the Theatres Act (which focused more on so-called obscene film and which was repealed in 2005), and the Ontario Film and Review Board (OFRB), which in 1993 came up with a set of instructions for what scenes to excise from what they called "adult sex films." In the face of this direct attack, Glad Day and Little Sister's were consistently tied up in expensive and laborious legal battles that were largely unsuccessful. Each was "a pyrrhic battle," as global and domestic business lawyer Gail Cohen explained to me during a September 2018 phone call. "Pyrrhic" because they resulted in little to no change to the Memorandum or the legal right of Canada Customs to seize the ever-increasing materials that the state found un-Canadian. Indeed, the financial costs may have outweighed the stress and labor that went into the activist struggle against Canada Customs. Yet Glad Day and Little Sister's would not have continued to exist if they and others around them had not joined the resistance.

While the fight against Canada Customs was never truly won, a loosely knit coalition of feminist, gay and lesbian, and leftist bookstores formed to contest *Butler*, the Customs Tariff Act, and Memorandum D9-1-1. As most of the sexually explicit material crossing the border was bound for these retail destinations, gay and lesbian bookstores became pivotal sites in the struggle for sexual culture. Glad Day employed a variety of queer traffic tactics to re-route sexual culture productions by smuggling materials across the border or inventing fake addresses, as in former Glad Day manager Tom Ivison's invention of the "St. Agnes Religious Society." Glad Day had queer sexual materials sent to this fake address, "and it worked, for at least two years," John Scythes told me at The ArQuives in 2018. "The government didn't grab any boxes of magazines. They were really pissed with us when they found that this had been a secret post office box at the subway station right close by. We would go over with the dolly and bring a hundred pounds of porn mags back." Scythes goes on to say that another "circuitous route" was through Benjamins, a huge distribution outlet for paper materials in Québec that was receiving porn magazines without them being censored or seized.[13] According to Scythes, the discovery of the St. Agnes tactic, after Canada Customs opened a particularly heavy box at the border destined for the phony religious society, directly led to the instantiation of Memorandum D9-1-1.[14]

First Amendment rights activist and former Canadian Broadcasting Corporation (CBC) personality Max Allen imbibes the queer traffic archive with another form of subterfuge to pervert what Allen calls the "moral entrepreneurship" (conversation with author, 2018) mobilized by Memorandum D9-1-1. In what can only be a facetious jab at the Butler Law, Allen and friends proposed a Canadian pornography company called Butler Films. The opening text of a pamphlet, titled *Sex Dreams*, found in the Max Allen Papers of the Sexual Representation Collection asked, "What about Canadian pornography?": "Everything we've seen (and defended in court) from *Vixen* to *Bad Attitude* has always been American porn. But what do Americans know about Canadian sex-dreams? Nobody in those California videos is ever shown doing it with a naked hockey player, or swatting blackflies, or talking about free trade, or freezing their ass off." Allen's text reveals a multiplicity of elements about Canadian queers: namely they have their own fantasies that depart from the United States porn industry's tastes and that certain conversations, such as free trade, circulate more widely among Canadian civil society. In a similar vein, Bruce Walsh, one of my interlocutors who was on the ground fighting Canada Customs, told me in an interview, "I didn't do this for the twinks in California." By proposing a Canadian pornography company, Allen threatened to fulfill the state's worst fear that all this censorship would propel the advent of Canadian-made porn. The queer activist response to the censors perverted the state's emphasis on "Canadian values" by proposing the emergence of a homegrown Canadian porn industry that would show that Canadians too are as obscene as queers in the United States (and Québec).[15]

Around 1993–1994, the resistance that arose to fight against the administrative abuse of power exacted by Mulroney, Canada Customs, and the OFRB, among other agencies that were invented and subsidized to censor, developed into a coalition of gay and lesbian and women's and feminist bookstores, American and Canadian book distributors and associations, sympathetic politicians (such as Svend Robinson), and the pioneers of sexual culture in Toronto and Vancouver that stood together to confront Canada Customs.[16] The struggle to repeal Customs Tariff Act policies that prohibited the importation of pornographic materials also brought together networks of feminist legal scholars, freedom-of-expression advocates who may not have cared a fig about queer issues previously, and PEN Canada. Additionally, it brought into being groups such as the Canadian Committee Against Customs Censorship (the CCACC, later Censorstop), which was established and largely run at the time by Bruce Walsh. The broader coalition against the censorship of gay and lesbian print materials that came about in the early 1990s was hard-won, according to Walsh. In an interview with him in the summer of 2018, he told me the activists who made up the CCACC were few, but they made themselves appear larger through the analog, pre-internet tactics of buttons and banners (fig. 2.7). Despite this small yet vocal coalition, most Canadians, Walsh told me, wanted to relegate censorship of queer culture as an "American" (US) problem. Canadians, he said, "didn't want to admit that it was happening in Canada." Instead, Walsh often heard Canadians citing the 1989 censorship and criminal prosecution of the curators who displayed Robert Mapplethorpe's *The Perfect Moment* and the 1990

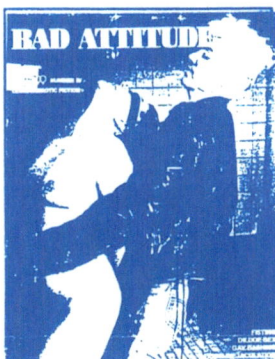

COPS HAVE BAD ATTITUDE!

OUTRAGE OVER RAID AT GLAD DAY!

Officers from Project Pornography raided the gay and lesbian Glad Day Bookstore on April 30. For selling Bad Attitude, a magazine by and for lesbians, Glad Day's manager has been charged with selling obscenity. The owner of Glad Day will also be charged on May 4.

Show the cops that we can't stand *their* bad attitude, and we want *ours* back!

DEMONSTRATE & MARCH!

SATURDAY MAY 2. CHURCH & WELLESLEY. 10 PM.

CCACC

Organized by Xtra! Magazine, Buddies in Bad Times Theatre, & the Canadian Committee Against Customs Censorship. Endorsed by Queer Nation & the Ontario Coalition Against Film & Video Censorship.

2.7 Canadian Committee Against Customs Censorship and *Xtra Magazine* protest poster after Project P sting at Glad Day Bookshop, 1992. The ArQuives: Canada's LGBTQ2+ Archives, Toronto.

National Endowment for the Arts (NEA) debacle, at which point John Fleck, Tim Miller, Karen Finley, and Holly Hughes were targeted by conservative lawmakers for creating "sick art by sick people."[17] Thus, queer communities, straight communities, and most damagingly, the national news (except the *Globe and Mail*, which did cover Canada Customs censorship early on) largely focused on instances of censorship occurring in the United States. In yet another tell of all-pervasive anxiety to distinguish itself from the United States, these publics sought to relegate censorship to a site "over there" on the other side of the border and not (ever!) in Canada.

Indeed, there was no queer circle of unity in effect where most gay and lesbian communities collectively stood against censorship. The affective economy of rooting out un-Canadian culture was both hetero- and homo-normative in scope and reach. The plot line for the 1999 film *Better Than Chocolate*, shot in Vancouver and directed by Anne Wheeler, parodies this fact. The film focuses on a lesbian-owned bookstore (viewed as a fairly direct reference to Vancouver's Little Sister's Book and Art Emporium) and its fight against Canada Customs.[18] The bookstore is thanked in the credits, and actor Ann-Marie MacDonald, who plays the bookstore's owner Frances Turner, is a well-known Canadian author. In one scene, Frances returns to the gay and lesbian bookstore she owns and upon receiving yet another customs seizure slip, she exclaims in exasperation, "Of course it's obscene! That's the point!" In a subsequent scene, Frances makes a trip to Canada Customs and interacts with a "commodity specialist" (Mr. Marcus) before unexpectedly running into an old lover (Bernice) who works security:

> Frances Seriously, Mr. Marcus, the Supreme Court has declared that anal sex is to gay male sex what Mozart is to classical music.
>
> Mr. Marcus Miss Turner, we are not here to discuss classical music. I myself am a huge Mozart fan, but . . .
>
> Frances Look, the fucking Supreme Court has declared this natural. It is not obscene.
>
> Mr. Marcus In case you haven't noticed this is not the Supreme Court. We're here in Customs, and I have a job to do.
>
> Frances We're just following orders, are we? Asshole!
>
> Mr. Marcus From your perspective, that must be a compliment of Mozartian proportions.

[*Frances lunges at the homophobic commodity specialist when Bernice, a brawny female security person, steps into the Customs office.*]

Bernice Do we have a problem in here?

Frances Bernice?! Oh my god, I haven't seen you since the women's music festival!

The Bernice character in *Better Than Chocolate* may refer to the real-life figure A. Lachance, the head of the Prohibited Importations Tariff Programs and suspected by some gay and lesbian activists of being a gay man. Certain members of the OFRB were also thought or known to be gay. If this is true, gays and lesbians also profited off Canada Customs as an arm of the administrative state to leverage homophobia to make a living, all the while contributing to a national homophobic project that destroyed the very pornography within which some of the only safe-sex material existed at this time. As Walsh told me, "Gays weren't getting their safe-sex info from a public health pamphlet. They were getting it from porn." The lesbian-owned bookstore in *Better Than Chocolate* was one such site targeted by Canada Customs where their clientele could access such life-giving information embedded in what the Canadian state regarded as "degradation."

Patrick Califia expands on the importance of pornography to lesbian communities in *Forbidden Passages*, an anthology that reprinted several texts that were seized by Canada Customs. "Despite the popularity of pornography, it is very difficult to get people angry about anti-smut campaigns," Califia wrote. "Even in the gay and lesbian community, where we have had to confront at least some of society's sex taboos before we could know ourselves and come out, too many of us remain hostile to sexually-explicit literature and ignorant about its role in the formation of modern gay and lesbian communities" (1995, 12). Here Califia points not only to those gays and lesbians who rhetorically collaborate (though don't legislate) within Canada's long history of sexual surveillance, but also to the difficulty of organizing the resistance to Canada Customs. In an echo of the questions art projects like Kiss & Tell's *Drawing the Line* exhibition put to feminist and lesbian feminist communities to think carefully about antipornography and anti-obscenity policies and laws, Califia goes on to say, "When I see lesbians picketing porn shops, it chills me to the bone. *We are pornographic*. Lesbians are indecent. We offend community standards" (12). The panic around pornography harming women thus assumes women as victims of the cross-border movement of so-called obscenity and very rarely as its consumers and never its producers. Free trade rather consumes and makes profitable those individuals who are left out of the ur-consumer status because they are too disenfranchised, too poor, too historically oppressed, too susceptible to corruption or abuse. Consumers of queer sex can't participate in the state's money-making designs as they are positioned as threats to the affective nationalism of the normative consumer. And so, while homophobia was used, and certainly the archive would tell us that this is a story largely about men, and white gay cis men at that, "harm against women" was also exploited for a wide array of capital gain. The state wittingly or unwittingly pitted feminism against gay activism to divide social movements, who have more in common than not, into combative silos.

It wasn't until he caught the attention of the *New Yorker*, Walsh told me, that Canadians and the Canadian news began to pay attention. The October 3, 1994, article "X-Rated," by former *New Yorker* columnist Jeffrey Toobin, focused on the surveillance and seizure of lesbian print material.[19] Most notably, Toobin wrote about Trish Thomas's story, "Wunna My Fantasies," from the *Bad Attitude* issue seized by Constable Patricia MacVicar at the Glad Day bookstore in Toronto in 1992 (fig. 2.8). While Canada Customs most frequently checked the box of "anal penetration" on the K27 forms, MacVicar's Glad Day sting operation, part of the larger Project P initiative, highlights the heightened surveillance of lesbian cultural production as well. MacVicar entered Glad Day already knowing what she wanted to purchase, and Tom Ivison was the unfortunate employee there that day to assist MacVicar in locating the magazine. Hidden under the cover of "harm against women" lurked the Canadian state's anxiety about lesbian, leatherdyke, and genderqueer sex acts, most notably fisting, which Canada Customs "appraised" as "sex with violence." The title of the article "No Porn for Lesbians . . . Because Bad Ole Het Men Will See It," published in *Xtra* on January 1, 2000, says it all. Sex-positive lesbian print materials that showed Black and Brown bodies, trans masculine bodies, genderqueer bodies, fat bodies, and crip bodies were the most frequently seized and destroyed by Canada Customs. For these reasons, the Canadian state's fear of being replaced by the United States shows itself for what it was: the anxiety of cis white straight men over homophobia's "moral failing," and more specifically the threat of the phallus being replaced by the dexterous fist of a hot, sex-hungry butch.

The seized issue of *Bad Attitude* (7, no. 4) serves as a case in point for how lesbian sex, particularly when it included dildos, fisting, interracial dyads, group sex, and BDSM, rattled the cages of Canadian values. Indeed, the issue's cover promises the reader "Fisting, Dildoe [*sic*] Sex, Gay Bashing,

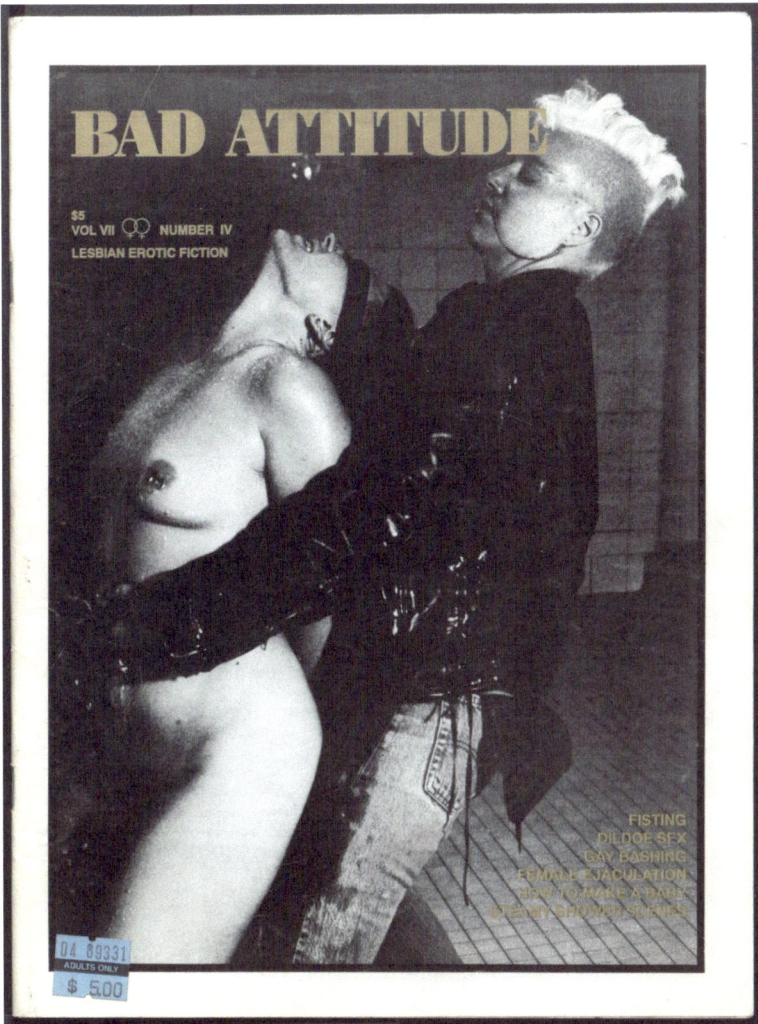

2.8   Cover of *Bad Attitude* magazine, vol. 7, no. 4, 1991. Photo by Schuyler Pes-
        cada. The ArQuives: Canada's LGBTQ2+ Archives, Toronto, LGBTQ Serials
        Collection, accession nos. 2009-038, 2016-053.

Female Ejaculation, How to Make a Baby, and Steamy Shower Scenes." The
steamy shower scene in question was the short story "Wunna My Fantasies,"
by Trish Thomas. The story features two models, Trashina, "a down and dirty
dancin' kind of girl" who "can usually be found sliming on slippery thighs
in some of SOMA's sleazier club's," and author Trish Thomas, "a fairly studly
white trash bar dyke who writes the way she talks" (25). In what is often

billed as a "one-handed read" intended to inspire the reader to masturbate, the story is punctuated with photographs by Schuyler Pescada that show a fully dressed (leather jacket, jeans with a chain) Thomas coming up behind a completely naked Trashina in the shower. Thomas blindfolds Trashina with a leather strap, binding her arms behind her back in handcuffs before fisting her on the wet tiles of the shower floor. Throughout this story of staged anonymous sex, Thomas revels in their ability to dominate Trashina, whom Thomas describes as a rich white bitch who can and needs to give up some power. The story ends with Thomas looking straight into Pescada's camera with Thomas's "hand still in her pussy up to my forearm" (29).

In terms of lesbian and gender-nonconforming materials, the presence of fisting and BDSM practices, read through the presence of whips, chains, leather, and nipple clamps, became the specific performance of lesbian and trans degradation most conspicuously on the radar of Canada Customs.[20] Unlike "anal penetration," however, there was no category for fisting on the K27 forms. Instead, BDSM and fisting were relegated to the category of "sex with violence," sex acts where women supposedly caused harm to other women. Throughout a series of spectacular performances put on by the state in litigating against the importation of print and visual representations of fisting, it showed itself to be ignorant not only on the topic of enemas and deconstruction but also on the topic of what inserting a fist into a vagina or anus actually entails. Like Sarah Schulman, Canadian scholar Becki L. Ross also took the stand, testifying in the December 15, 1992, case *Her Majesty the Queen Against Thomas Ivison and John Scythes of Glad Day Bookshop*, which happened in the wake of the MacVicar sting operation. At one point in the proceedings, Clare Barclay, the "counsel for the accused," questions Ross as to whether fisting is "normally accepted as an act of pleasure" in lesbian cultures, to which she responds, "This, yes . . . and in the next page you will see that there's a surgical glove that is being used that denotes the safe sex character of the practice. There's clearly a lot of lube which would be KY jelly or some water soluble product to facilitate penetration, but the vagina itself, of course, is an erogenous zone and has many nerve endings that stimulate pleasure" (*Her Majesty the Queen Against Thomas Ivison and John Scythes of Glad Day Bookshop*, 19). The Court ultimately disqualified Ross as an expert, claiming she spoke solely from "hearsay."[21] Two months later, on February 16, 1993, Scythes and Ivison were found guilty of the possession and sale of "obscene material." Judge C. H. Paris decided that the seized issue of *Bad Attitude*, and in particular the story "Wunna My Fantasies," constituted sex with violence and was therefore in violation of the Butler Law and section 163(8) of the Criminal Code.

The CCACC released a statement of purpose sometime in the late 1980s regarding Canada Customs' ongoing seizures of lesbian sex materials. In it, Walsh and his collaborators included a section on the "Implications for Lesbian Material" as follows:

> The release of *The Joy of Lesbian Sex* might lead one to conclude that these regulations are only being used against gay male material, but in fact, they are also being used to exclude books and magazines coming into Canada that are of particular interest to lesbians. The Boston-based lesbian magazine *Bad Attitude* has been stopped at the border in Ontario and British Columbia. Vancouver's Little Sister's Book and Art Emporium has had *Lesbian Sex* by Joulan Loulan and *Good Vibrations*, a women's vibrator manual by Joanie Blank, seized. And *The Body Politic* [the queer Canadian magazine] has declared its intention to defend *Private Pleasures* and *Shadows*, two lesbian-made sex videos that are now banned in Canada. While buggery/sodomy has long been associated with gay male sex practice, lesbian material is obviously not exempt from Customs' current campaign of harassment.[22]

In conversation with Carlyle Jansen outside her sex shop, Good for Her, we discussed how censors enacted a profound misunderstanding of lesbian sex acts, such as fisting and BDSM, when they labeled these materials as "sex with violence." "Certain things are considered normal when it comes to sex, but when women are in control," she said, "all of a sudden that's a bit much; it violates 'community standards.'" She went on to say that when one hears the word "fisting" she could understand that it sounds intimidating to the uninitiated. "You know whenever I teach workshops, I say 'fisting,' it sounds violent, but actually, generally, it's very slow, very gentle, very intimate." "It involves trust," I added. Indeed, "Dyke hands," wrote Black lesbian filmmaker and writer SDiane Bogus, "are the sexual organs of lesbian love" (1982, 72). Hidden in plain sight, they are the "etc." of body parts occluded, unseen, and unacknowledged as sexual instruments while amorously examined by a would-be lover. When used for pleasure, "dyke hands" move from the unremarkable "etc." to become weapons of mass destruction for Canadian values. They become in many ways the ultimate form of degradation. The lesbian fist, therefore, presents the most powerful competition to the free-trade fantasy of the big cis het dick, not a toy or dildo, but flesh itself.

Little Sister's *OBZINE* (1993) speaks directly to the gross misunderstanding of lesbian sex acts and the fear of the fist as sexual organ. This xeroxed black-and-white zine provides its own archive of lesbian sex materials labeled as "obscene," including Del LaGrace Volcano's *Love Bites* seized in 1991 and returned with pages ripped out and coffee stains on the centerfold ("Some customs agents must have been having quite a coffee break!" the zine facetiously chirps back) and photos from the January and February 1993 issue of *On Our Backs*, a lesbian sex magazine that Little Sister's never successfully got through Canada Customs. But perhaps the most telling example was a photo of a woman bound intricately with rope from Kiss & Tell's *Drawing the Line* exhibition. Because the photo was reprinted in the US lesbian magazine *Deneuve*, it was put in the category of un-Canadian obscenity even though it was produced by a Canadian performance troupe who had already exhibited the photograph in Vancouver. The point, again, was not over the photos or texts themselves, but rather where these "suspicious boxes" were headed and the white, cis, and heteromasculine values that Canada was so terrified to degrade. As one of *OBZINE*'s patchwork pages rightly declares, "Our Desires Threaten Your Dominance."

While fisting and BDSM were two grossly misunderstood practices, often regarded as "sex with violence" by Canada Customs, other lesbian materials such as the comix *Hothead Paisan: Homicidal Lesbian Terrorist* by Diane DiMassa were frequently seized at the border. While the "Wunna My Fantasies" story in the 1991 *Bad Attitude* demonstrated the reach of criminal law to block the consumption of materials that had made it past the border, the frequent seizure of *Hothead Paisan* more clearly uncovers the fear of female and trans masculinity instilled in the Canada Customs appraisers. According to Gabrielle Dean, the character of Hothead represents a "phallicized dyke" who is "at the mercy of her own rage against society, which she expresses by castrating men who are exaggerated stand-ins for the patriarchal order" (1997, 208). Focusing on the related yet more underground comic *Bitchy Butch* by Roberta Gregory, Y Howard further speaks to the ways in which the butch-identified lesbian designated the limit "of allowable and expressible forms of queerness in the late-twentieth century" (2018, 76). While DiMassa certainly represented Hothead as a sexual subject in her comix, giving her a lover, Daphne, whose gender is never specified, Canada Customs must have deemed these representations obscene owing to the cultural representations of anger and rage that this Italian-American comix figure acted out. While DiMassa jokingly called Hothead a "terrorist," Canada Customs took this literally, targeting its depictions of murderous tactics to rid the world of homophobia, racism, and sexism, one white straight cis man at a time.

In the minds of Canada Customs, anger was appraised as queer traffic, the expression of a negative and excessive feeling considered to be un-Canadian for exceeding the bounds of national affective belonging that constituted authentic Canadian values. In other words, anger directed against white patriarchal society was rendered obscene: it broke with the state's stereotypical estimation of itself as a nation that prioritizes speech acts of civility. It points, perhaps, to the reason why a book like bell hooks's *Black Looks* was briefly seized. With yet another use of the fist, Black Power and Black feminism were also on the surveillance menu of Canada Customs under Memorandum D9-1-1. Indeed, while many materials seized by Canada Customs pertained to white, gay, and male cultural production, archival traces show that this was anything but a white male issue.

In conversation with Black lesbian feminist Carol Thames at Glad Day in the fall of 2018, she reflected on the seizure of *Black Looks*.[23] Thames rhetorically asked,

> Why would you censor bell hooks? Because of bell hooks's analysis around feminism, right? Other than that, she was talking about strong Black women relationships and how we support each other through the struggles. Again, you're trying to amputate who I am and how I decide to move through the world whether I am queer, bisexual, or heterosexual. Yeah, no, I didn't see bell hooks as a queer writer, other than maybe the whole thing was racism. . . . From a political analysis, it doesn't make sense, but again, it does make sense if you're looking at it from a racialized lens, right? It does make sense. Because again, it's taking away knowledge, it's taking away power, and it's taking away the voice of revolution.

Thames speaks to the ways in which Black feminism threatened the Canadian state's sense of national identity and how the scholarship of bell hooks became a representative target of surveillance for Canada Customs at the same historical juncture that dissident sexual materials were also being seized. While I could not locate a K27 form and therefore the box that was checked to adjudicate the seizure of *Black Looks*, Black feminist literature also came to be viewed as a source of "US cultural imperialism" and a potential locus of what the state regarded as "degradation." This indeed was the primary motivation for the charges of "degradation"—the fear of revolution, sexual or otherwise.

In the lead-up to the 1989 CUSFTA, the queer-of-color group Zami (a reference to the Audre Lorde book of the same name) penned a letter in support of Glad Day to reject, as the letter phrases it, "arbitrary Customs laws" (fig. 2.9). Located at The ArQuives and dated September 22, 1986, a portion of the letter reads:

> "Glad Day"—almost everyone in the lesbian and gay community knows what those two words signify. We pass through almost every week just to see whats new, whats happening, check out new apartment listings, whats for sale, browse through, maybe buy something . . . but mainly to connect with our community . . . and yes the magazine section heightens a few pulses.
>
> We deplore this current attack on Glad Day, as it represents an attack on the rights and freedoms of all lesbians and gays: us.
>
> We support Glad Day and the Canadian Committee against Customs Censorship in challenging the arbitrary Customs law.
>
> We support the demand for the return of gay and lesbian materials seized under discriminatory internal customs guidelines.

The letter is signed "In solidarity, Douglas Stewart for ZAMI: Black and West-Indian gays and lesbians." Cofounded by Debbie Douglas, Sylmadel Coke, Derych Gordon, and Douglas Stewart in 1984, Zami was one of the first organizations in Toronto and all of Canada specifically by, for, and about gay and lesbian folks of color and particularly Black queer Canadians.[24] Mentions of the seizures of works by bell hooks and Joseph Beam sparingly dot the specific archival collections I studied while in Toronto. The Zami letter is the only trace of Black queer response to Canada Customs seizures that I could locate in these archives.

Black Canadian life and its relationship to these seizures constitute another form of queer traffic, a trace of the voices that may not have been front and center on the issue of Customs seizures, but as Thames so astutely stated in our interview, "we were always there." She remembered reading and loving *Bad Attitude* at the time and being angry at Canada Customs for "defining what is good, bad, or indifferent for me." "Even if you're not in the middle of it," she went on to say, "the sparks of those actions do affect your life as long as you're on the marginalized fringe of the mainstream of society."

While many of the lesbian and trans masculine magazines and zines thus far discussed largely included white models, there are notable examples of interracial sex, Black and Brown women, and trans masculine butches that

"GLAD DAY"- almost everyone in the lesbian and gay community knows what those two words signify. We pass through almost every week just to see whats new, whats happening, check out new apartment listings, whats for sale, browse through, maybe buy something.... but mainly to connect with our community....and yes the magazine section heightens a few pulses.

In a city that provides very few such safe havens, Glad Day bookshop holds a very special place in the lesbian and gay community. It is, was, and will be for many, a vital part of "coming out". It's volumes connect us to a history, culture, and community whose scope and diversity would otherwise be obscured to us. The power of this information, which helps to empower our own lives to deal with the overwhelmingly negative perceptions of the larger society would be and is diluted in any other bookstore. It's history (three former locations), easygoing atmosphere;you can browse until your eyes close, pleasant staff, support of community organizations in their social events and political struggles....makes Glad Day a treasured fixture in our community.

We deplore this current attack on Glad Day, as it represents an attack on the rights and freedoms of all lesbians and gays: us.

We support Glad Day and the Canadian Committee Against Customs Censorship in challenging the arbitrary Customs law.

We support the demand for the return of gay and lesbian material seized under discriminatory internal customs guidelines.

We also support the demand that these guidelines be immediately repealed.

It is in support of these demands that we will demonstrate on Wednesday September 24.

In solidarity

Douglas Stewart
for ZAMI: Black
and West-Indian
gays and lesbians

2.9   Zami letter. The ArQuives: Canada's LGBTQ2+ Archives, Toronto.

graced covers and pages. *Hothead Paisan* contains the character Sharquee, a Black queer sex worker and psychic card reader, whose mistreatment motivates Hothead Paisan's full frontal attack on white cis men. *On Our Backs* included various stories and images that focused on femme/butch, androgynous, and what we might now call nonbinary people of color. Examples abound of Black, Brown, and Asian cover models with features in the magazine: "Sarah & Marcy: butch on butch action," "Frankie and Dymond's Sexual Service Station," "Nigia and Brooks: Close Shave," "Siobhan and J.J.: Naked Desire," "Devra and J.J.: Mistress May I" (fig. 2.10). Collectively these

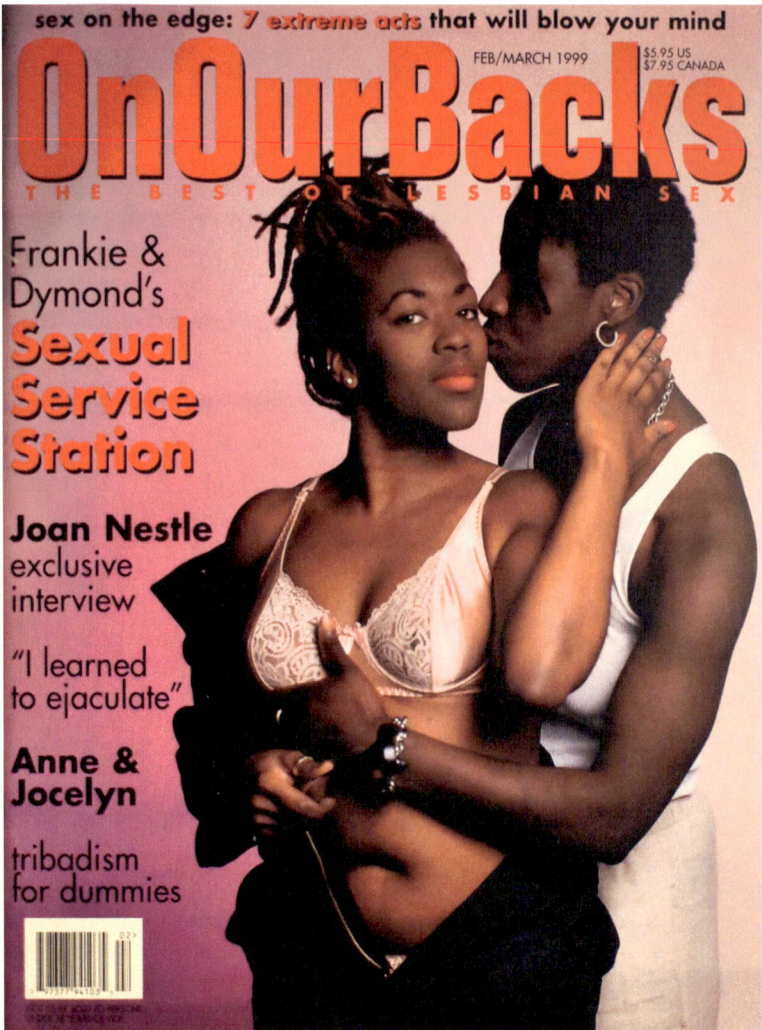

sex on the edge: *7 extreme acts* that will blow your mind

FEB/MARCH 1999
$5.95 US
$7.95 CANADA

OnOurBacks

THE BEST OF LESBIAN SEX

Frankie &
Dymond's
**Sexual
Service
Station**

Joan Nestle
exclusive
interview

"I learned
to ejaculate"

**Anne &
Jocelyn**

tribadism
for dummies

2.10   *On Our Backs*, February/March 1999. Personal collection of Y Howard.

lead magazine features combine images of hot sex in butch/femme, butch/ butch, or androgynous dyads nestled within articles about anal sex, fisting, female ejaculation, oral sex, public sex (e.g., on airplanes), tribadism, and various BDSM practices such as edge play, sexual servitude, and erotic piercings. While not expressly collected or named in the archives I consulted for this chapter, all of these magazine issues traveled in the same or similar circuitry as other forms of queer traffic and constitute an indispensable though often unspoken component in the history of prohibiting the importation of lesbian- and queer-of-color literature into Canada.

One K27 form sent to Glad Day on August 2, 1989, contains a note by Jearld Moldenhauer that comments on the seizure of twenty-five issues of *On Our Backs* (fig. 2.11). The note reads:

> <u>On Our Backs</u> is once [*sic*] of several new lesbian periodicals specifically dedicated to exploring issues of autonomous female sexuality. There are two matters worth noting. 1.) In 1986 & again in 1987, other issues of <u>OOB</u> were seized and prohibited. Why the change of attitude toward lesbian sexuality in 1989? 2.) Although Customs was unusually swift in releasing the magazines (12 days from seizure to release) they returned only 15 out of the 25 magazines seized. What happened to the other 10. Once again, we may "win" freedom for the book, but we loose [*sic*] financially because the bureaucracy has kept our goods.

Why indeed were these magazines not returned? While we may never know exactly which issues of *On Our Backs* were sent on to Glad Day and which were kept, destroyed, or returned to San Francisco, the "change of attitude" in 1989, I argue, resulted from a shift in the Canadian state's paranoia about the growing influence of US cultural production in Canada in the wake of the CUSFTA and in the lead-up to NAFTA. What changed was the mobilization of a tremendous labor infrastructure to root out individual magazines, later DVDs, and entire boxes that may have never been opened but that were bound for the few remaining gay and lesbian bookstores. Bureaucracy kept back the goods that pertained to white gay culture, but it was the combination of Black and Brown pleasure, sadomasochism, and fisting that piqued the turn in Canada Customs toward lesbian periodicals.

Canadian courts seemed only too happy to err on the side of censoring any material with a whiff of queer sex, genderqueerness, or queer of color critique. It became lucrative to the state to do so. "Hate," Sara Ahmed argues, "is economic; it circulates between signifiers in relationships of difference and displacement" (2004, 119). Throughout the 1980s and 1990s, countless Canadian jobs depended on the surveillance and censorship of sexual culture, especially when the productions in question depicted any form of embodied difference. Countless dollars were collected by the OFRB—$4.12 for every minute of suspicious sexual film that needed to be watched and bowdlerized or outright destroyed. Massive state funding went to the Toronto police department to resource Project P. And at the border, the suppleness of administrative law allowed the Canadian state to regulate what it saw as "obscenity," "degradation," and "hate propaganda" in the lead-up to September 11, 2001, and the global war on terror. The Canadian state interpreted the seized materials as a kind of terror, an affective affront to the political economy of respectability that the state aligned with proper Canadian values. While nominally about gay white men and their cultural productions, the queer traffic that this chapter explored goes well beyond the representation of anal sex. "Degradation" provided Canada Customs with the infrastructural net that they could cast, arbitrarily, over any representation, textual or visual. In declaring something degrading, "commodity specialists" in Canada Customs rendered queer sex and sexuality obscene to Canadian exceptionalism. Pornography, sex education materials, and erotic fiction constituted prohibited imports, and those who consumed, sold, or circulated them were enemies of the state and free trade.

Straight Trade

Fast forward to Toronto 2018. I'm listening to the CBC Radio podcast *The House* as I make my way to The ArQuives to conduct research on Canada Customs' targeting of the gay bookstores Glad Day and Little Sister's Book and Art Emporium. Jim Carr is on air, in his newly minted role as Minister of International Trade Diversification, amid the embattled trade war with the United States under Trump and the 2018 NAFTA renegotiation. He tells host Chris Hall about the "Canadian LGBTQ2+ Business Trade Mission" he convened in Philadelphia in partnership with the Canadian Gay and Lesbian Chamber of Commerce (CGLCC). Carr presided over the gathering, the first of its kind he proudly proclaimed, to address two perceptions of Canada, especially when we're talking about its national reputation on the world stage, which he presented as fact: (1) Canada is exceptional when it comes to the issue of LGBT rights; and (2) these markets are hugely untapped opportunities for binational economic growth between LGBTQ2+-owned Canadian businesses and US corporations. Only days later in an interview I conducted with leaders of the CGLCC, Bruce McDonald and Darrell Schuurman, I learned that none of the businesses represented at the trade mission summit pertained to sexual commerce and that few women and only one out trans person had attended. How can we begin to explain this movement, arguably only eight years after the last known queer materials were seized by Canada Customs, to the rhetorical assimilation of queerness into the Canadian vision for regional and binational capitalism under free trade?

Canada ▮◆▮

NOTICE OF DETENTION/DETERMINATION
AVIS DE RETENUE OU DE CLASSEMENT TARIFAIRE

9956

Importer / Importateur

Glad Day Bookshop
598A Yonge St.
Toronto, Ont.
M4Y 1Z3

Regional Control No. / N° de contrôle régional	
Point of Entry / Bureau d'entrée	
Point of Entry Control No. / N° de contrôle de bureau d'entrée	
Date	Aug 2, 1989

PART A — NOTICE OF DETENTION

The following goods have been detained for a determination of tariff classification. Once a determination has been made, you will be notified in writing.

Description of goods / Désignation des marchandises

PARTIE A — AVIS DE RETENUE

Les marchandises désignées ci-après ont été retenues aux fins du classement tarifaire. Nous vous aviserons par écrit du classement effectué.

25 Magazines- " On Our Backs July-Aug 1989 "

Exporter / Exportateur

526 Castro San Francisco Ca. 94114

PART B — NOTICE OF DETERMINATION

The following goods have been examined and their importation into Canada is prohibited under the provisions of s. 114 of the Customs Tariff and code 9956 of Schedule VII.

This represents a determination pursuant to section 58 of the Customs Act. Your rights respecting this determination are set out on the reverse of this form.

PARTIE B — AVIS DE CLASSEMENT TARIFAIRE

Après examen des marchandises désignées ci-après, il a été établi que leur importation au Canada est prohibée en vertu de l'article 114 du Tarif des douanes et du code 9956 de l'annexe VII.

Cette décision constitue un classement aux termes de l'article 58 de la Loi sur les douanes. Vos droits concernant ce classement sont énoncés au verso de la présente formule.

Customs Officer / Agent des douanes   Comm. Spec   Title / Titre   Aug. 15/89   Date of Determination / Date du classement

The following goods have been examined and their importation into Canada is admissible.

Après examen, il a été établi que les marchandises désignées ci-après sont admissibles au Canada.

15 magazines released and are being returned to the post office for delivery.

Please contact Canada Customs at the point of entry to make arrangements for the payment of duties on the admissible goods.

Veuillez communiquer avec les douanes canadiennes au bureau d'entrée afin de prendre des arrangements pour le paiement des droits.

		Type / Genre		Length / Longueur				Videotape / Ruben magnétoscopique	Format		Time / Durée
	Film				mm						

SECTION 1

9956
☐ Book / Livre
☒ Magazine / Magazine
☐ Comic / Bande dessinée

☐ Record / Disque
☐ Audi / Bande
☐ Play / Jeu

☐ Advertisement / Publicité
☐ Brochure / Dépliant

Mode of Transport / Mode de transport

Mail

If not declared, mode of concealment / Si non déclarées, mode

SECTION 2

Classification (Memorandum D9-1-1)
☐ a) Sex With Violence / Violence sexuelle
☐ b) Child Sex / Pornographie enfantine
☐ c) Ind
☐ Be

Title / Titre

Date of Appeal / Date d'appel   Date ser

Note: On Our Backs is once of several new lesbian periodicals specifically dedicated to exploring issues of autonomous female sexuality. There are two matters worth noting. 1.) In 1986 & again in 1987, other issues of OOB were seized and prohibited. Why the change of attitude toward lesbian sexuality in 1989? 2.) Although Customs was unusually swift in releasing the magazines (12 days from seizure to release) they returned only 15 out of the 25 magazines seized. What happened to the other 10. Once again, we may "win" freedom for the book, but we loose financially because the bureaucracy has kept the goods.

J. Moldenhauer

Continuation Sheet / Feuille supplémentaire

2.11   Example of K27 form. The ArQuives: Canada's LGBTQ2+ Archives, Toronto.

The state has followed the lead of corporations in incorporating gay men (mostly) and some wealthy lesbians into the fantasy of free trade. But sexuality is looked upon as a single issue, and not in connection or intersection with other categories of difference. Interestingly, the "LGBTQ2+ Business Trade Mission" to Philadelphia also invoked the Canadian state's rhetoric on First Nations rights, claiming that Canada is a model for how to think global capitalism in connection with First Nations issues. I could imagine First Nations, Métis, or Inuit radio listeners squirming in their chairs as Carr talked about Canada's progressive record on queer rights, and then quickly threw in First Nations rights as an afterthought. It's not coincidental that "2+" (for Two Spirit) is invoked in the letters for the trade mission but was hardly given any time or focus during the program in Philadelphia. To do so would reveal the discontents between gay and lesbian assimilation into the global capitalist marketplace and settler colonialism in Canada.[25] Like many others, Carr has thoroughly learned how to rhetorically incorporate a watered-down version of intersectionality theory (but not action) into the affective economy of Canadian nationalism and exceptionalism. His new title, Minister of International Trade Diversification, says it all. People only become important to free trade and its negotiations and the details that are at once everywhere and nowhere when they are assimilable into the free-trade construct of transnational investments and multinational corporate power. In the decades since the CUSFTA and NAFTA, "gay" and "lesbian"— as identities and not queer sex practices—have become capital-producing objects for the state.

Still, in the end, the finalized document for the new NAFTA in 2020 put the rights of even the most privileged members of the group called "LGBTQ2+" at risk when it weakened the protections for sexual and gender minorities included in its Article 23.9. Articulated in the October 2, 2018, draft as a commitment to "implement policies that protect workers against employment discrimination on the basis of sex, including . . . sexual orientation [and] gender identity," in the May 30, 2019, revision the language was changed to "implement policies that it considers appropriate to protect workers against employment discrimination on the basis of sex, . . . sexual orientation [and] gender identity" (Galbraight and Lu 2019). Similar to how environmental and labor concerns were ultimately scuttled into side agreements during the equally contentious NAFTA negotiations, protections against discrimination for sexual and gender minorities were also demoted in the final text of NAFTA 2.0. What's more, the final draft includes a footnote that many LGBTQ rights advocates argue completely nullifies the article.[26]

No doubt, this move resulted from pushback by conservative US congressional representatives who felt that the inclusion of "sexual orientation" and "gender identity" contradicted the anti-LGBTQ policies that Trump had otherwise instituted domestically. Colorado Representative Doug Lamborn explained in a letter to Trump, which was signed by thirty-seven other US House members, that "it is especially inappropriate and insulting to our sovereignty to needlessly submit to social policies which the United States Congress has so far explicitly refused to accept. One wonders at the contradictory policy coming through USTR when other Departments under your Administration are working to come into alignment on SOGI [sexual orientation and gender identity]."[27]

Canada was ready to holistically incorporate the pink dollar into its affective economy of capital circulation, but the United States under Trump returned to its 1990s-style homophobia, bolstered by the growing fascist outcry against trans people and their obvious rights to work, play sports, access health care, and use the bathroom. While the Canadian state under Justin Trudeau Jr. took a different tack toward SOGI and free trade, his desire for NAFTA won the day, thereby continuing the free-trade fervor begun by his father.

Given the transnational politics of pinkwashing, the inclusion of SOGI into NAFTA is not necessarily something to celebrate. Yet we should see the nullification of the sex- and gender-related policy in the new NAFTA as a tell of the return to the new/old sexual panics of the 1980s and 1990s and the inordinate surveillance placed on those most marginalized within global 2SLGBTQ communities. Studying the social life of what Canada Customs labeled "degradation" from the 1980s through the early 2000s offers archival lessons for understanding the digital and post–September 11 infrastructures of the surveillance state. The administrative laws that allowed Customs agents at the Canada-US border to search, seize, and in many cases destroy gay and lesbian sexual materials in macabre and often violent ways still exist on the legal books. Queers certainly helped to reshape laws in British Columbia and Ontario, to challenge the constitutionality of government censors, but most of the battles were lost and the laws that censored these materials still exist today. They await the next sexual dissidents, and their queer traffic, on which they can be used.

When the State Says "No One Likes Fat Girls"

The performance opens with an invocation by blue-haired Kat, the guitarist, as she strums her instrument. She is dressed in hot-pink platform stilettos, kitten ears, and a pale-pink corset with black-laced undies. Next, we hear Danna Paola's saccharine pop anthem "Mundo de caramelo" (World of caramel) as performance artist Erika Bülle Hernández enters. Completely naked, save for a silver-and-pink rhinestone princess crown on her head, Bülle wears makeup and her lips are locked around a large rainbow-swirled lollipop. Kat and Edgard Gamboa flank her on either side of the stage, really a gray stone echoey recess in the Ex-Teresa Arte Actual in downtown Mexico City. Gamboa stands motionless over a table of rubbing alcohol and medical needles. His black gloves suggest he will use these needles in some penetrative manner, that blood may be spilled. The gloves create an air of anticipation, even for those familiar with the BDSM practice of needle play. Needle play describes an alternative sexuality practice where the dominant pinches the submissive's flesh with needles. As with many durational BDSM practices, needle play can involve pain and fear, but it can also induce relaxation and connection, a kind of kinky acupuncture effect. Before Gamboa begins his work, however, we see Bülle dancing on the stage, continuing to lick her lollipop and playfully frolicking with other hanging lollipops strung with silver thread along a clothesline that spans the performance space. Comfortable in her skin, she looks ludically, enticingly, to the audience seated on the

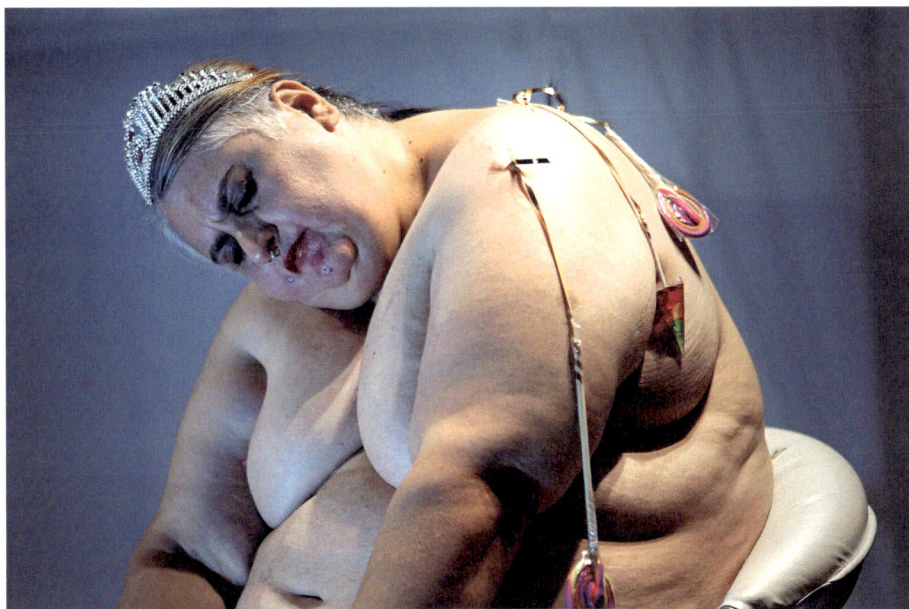

2a.1 Erika Bülle Hernández, *A las niñas gordas nadie las quiere*, 2017. Photo by Mario Patiño Sánchez.

ground in front of her. She seductively dances between Kat and Gamboa, a display of what Bülle calls "sexualidad no binaria," a nonbinary sexuality (Facebook message to author, August 23, 2021).

Suddenly, we hear a booming voice, recognizable to Mexican audiences as the right-wing governor of the Mexican state of Nuevo Léon, Jaime Rodríguez Calderón (who also goes by the hypermasculine nickname "El Bronco"). In 2016, in the run-up to his unsuccessful bid for the presidency, El Bronco made a public statement framed as parental advice to evade unwanted teenage pregnancies. Pregnant girls, he specified, will appear fat to their boyfriends and therefore, El Bronco rationalized, no longer be desirable. "Se van a buscar otras" (they'll go out looking for others), he said, thus targeting what he views as excessive sexual choices by taking down the bodies of all fat girls and women when he says "A las niñas gordas nadie las quiere" (No one likes fat girls).[1] Appropriating this comment in the title of her performance, Bülle performs a defiant response to Calderón's fatphobic rhetoric.

As the El Bronco track plays, Bülle pauses, aghast, the lollipop and its chewed-up contents falling out of her open mouth. Her face drops as she angrily throws the lollipop to the ground. Accompanied by Kat's ominously space-filling and discordant strumming pattern, Bülle moves to a chair to await Gamboa's piercings. With Kat helping Gamboa between her sets, Gamboa removes the lollipops, the same ones that Bülle lovingly and ecstatically played with earlier, from the clothesline. He ties a lollipop to each finished piercing that he has pinched into the flesh of her back, chest, face, and arms (fig. 2a.1). Collaboratively, they literally attach the sweets to her naked body, thus externalizing the criminal consumption that has led to her supposed abject state of fatness. Bülle, however, refuses the downtrodden affect that accompanies these displays: she arises from the chair and recaptures the performance's initial exuberance, twirling around and around with the now flesh-attached lollipops as the song "No controles" by the 1980s all-female Mexican pop group Flans plays. Gamboa hands her some scissors, which she irreverently puts to her mouth, miming the cutting out of her tongue, the instrument with which she swallows all these forbidden candies. With the help of Gamboa, she then circumnavigates the audience members, seated in a tight configuration, inviting them to cut the candies from her body—not to liberate or recuperate her body but to implicate the audience in eating more, not less, of the lollipops rendered into taboo objects through her performance. Bülle returns to the stage and ends the performance by throwing a huge bag of lollipops into the crowd. The consumption of these sugary delicacies, the performance suggests, should continue after the performance has ended. The lollipops become a form of queer traffic that Bülle circulates among the audience.[2]

A las niñas gordas nadie las quiere is a representative performance of Bülle's body of work, which consistently faces off against a phobic and pathological conception of the fat body. In using the term *fat*, I am referencing a field of scholarship and activism that celebrates the term as a defiant response to medical and societal models of standard body size. Bülle's performance simultaneously invokes the disgust and repulsion of *gordofobia* (fatphobia), the erotic and pathological fascination with the fat body, and the medicalization of the distance between the thin, able body (assumed to be the viewer) and the body prefigured to be out of control in its desire to consume. She employs what Caleb Luna calls "fat aesthetics as a technology for fat queer life and joy" (2022, xiv) to reroute the colonial and racializing agenda of fatphobia toward contexts of pleasure that revel in alternative sexuality practices such as BDSM.

By incorporating BDSM in her performance, Bülle participates in a long-standing hemispheric and transatlantic tradition that includes Ron

Athey, Sheree Rose, Congelada de Uva (Rocío Bolívar), Diana Torres, Nadia Granados (La Fulminante), Lechedevirgen Trimegisto, Guillermo Gómez-Peña, and other queer and dissident artists. Bülle's performance work likewise situates her within a body of hemispheric fat performance with deep connections to the aesthetic trajectory of Mark Aguhar, Laura Aguilar, and Yolanda Bonnell. In naming her performance after El Bronco's fatphobic statement, here standing in for normative viewpoints about sex and body weight, Bülle wages a direct counterdiscourse to it. However, it is not just conservative figures such as El Bronco whom she speaks to and against. Looking through the lens of NAFTA, the scope of her performance is broader: the transnational medicalization of the so-called obesity epidemic and the perception of obesity as a sign of social decay across the political spectrum (Paradis 2016; Schorb 2022). At the core of these phenomena is panic about body size and the sexual attractiveness of female and feminine bodies, which are assessed according to Anglo-specific and bourgeois beauty standards. These bodies are accused of sexual deviance, or else they are assumed to be so repugnant as to be undesirable and unfuckable.

The global panic surrounding obesity catches fire in Mexico after the signing of NAFTA. Fat feminine bodies served up the "evidence" of excessive consumption and the ruinous effects of consuming the colonizer's foodstuffs. These bodies become the ciphers for visualizing and policing the consumptive consequences of free trade's influence on food production and circulation. On the left, as Friedrich Schorb has shown, obesity is often figured as a "neoliberal epidemic," as a consequence of free trade that allegedly dupes fat people to unthinkingly heed the siren song of McDonald's and Carl's Jr. "NAFTA Largely Responsible for the Obesity Epidemic in Mexico" (Siegel 2016); "NAFTA, Free Trade and 'Exporting Obesity'"; "The Trade Deal That Triggered a Health Crisis in Mexico—in Pictures"; "El TLCAN y su papel en la obesidad en México" (NAFTA and its role in obesity in Mexico); "El TLCAN trajo obesidad a México" (NAFTA brought obesity to Mexico); "Obesidad, regalo del TLCAN a México" (Obesity, NAFTA's gift to Mexico): these are just a few of the headlines one readily encounters through an internet search, though these titles give only a taste of the breadth and volume of such argumentation.[3] Rhetorical connections made between obesity in Mexico and NAFTA took on global significance that only grew in the wake of September 11, 2001, when people such as Surgeon General Richard Cardona leveraged the looming specter of terrorism to name obesity as the "terror within" (Biltekoff 2007; Raila, Holmes, and Murray 2010). While the rhetoric that ties privatization and the opening of Mexico's markets to US foodstuffs and body size dates to the 1980s, it wasn't until NAFTA that we saw an explosion of news-related attention to this already-assumed-to-be-proven connection. The American Medical Association's decision to pass Article 420, which took "obesity" from a public health concern to a disease, no doubt encouraged this.[4] While countless studies have framed "obesity" as a global epidemic, NAFTA dominates the conversation as a major sticking point in the ongoing export of processed food and sugary sweets and thus, the argument goes, of obesity to Mexico from the United States. NAFTA was the first FTA to be directly blamed for causing obesity and thus innovated a conversation that has since gone global.

Of course, NAFTA has been shown to have a dramatic effect on diet, perhaps most notably through what free-trade parlance calls the "dumping" of cheaply grown and harvested US corn surplus to Mexico.[5] As I touched on in chapter 1, dumping describes a highly suspect yet available free-trade tool where a country (in this instance, the United States) exports products at prices lower than the importing market (in this situation, Mexico). Technically legal under WTO rules and often practiced by wealthy, powerful nations, dumping is nevertheless considered "unfair trade." The sheer volume of the export surplus can have devastating effects on the viability not only of certain markets in the importing nation but also for entire industries. During the 2018–2020 NAFTA 2.0 (USMCA) negotiations, for example, the renegotiation of the 1989 CUSFTA and 1994 NAFTA regarding the topic of "supply management," specifically in relation to Canada's dairy industry, threatened to flood the Canadian market with cheaper-priced dairy products. Ultimately the United States and Canada reached a compromise, with Canada agreeing to eliminate tariffs on dairy imports up to a set volume (3.6 percent of the Canadian market), though debates about whether Canada had adhered to the compromise began anew in 2022 but ended with the United States losing the trade dispute in 2023. The same cannot be said for the dumping of genetically engineered corn into Mexico since the 1990s and its destructive impact on what decolonial diet advocates such as Alyshia Gálvez refer to as the *milpa*-based diet.[6] Studies such as Gálvez's do indispensable work in showing how NAFTA influences everyday activities in Mexico and how it affects the body on a material level, what she calls "free trade in the body" (2018, 89–116). Indeed, one of the aims of *Queer Traffic* is to do for sex what Gálvez does for food in relationship to NAFTA.[7] While I align myself with activists and NAFTA critics who advance the concept of decolonizing foodways, for example, with those in opposition to the nonregulated incursion of the agrochemical corporation Monsanto in Mexico, I differ from some of these critics by rejecting a focus on the fat female body as the locus for understanding the colonizing force of NAFTA on the Mexican *milpa*-based diet. Like Gálvez, I look not to discourses about personal responsibility but to structural issues—such as NAFTA and Salinas's 1992 gutting of Article 27 of the Mexican Constitution—as primary motivators of change in diet in Mexico.

While Bülle's performance is only implicitly about NAFTA and sex, it demonstrates how easily panic about NAFTA's influences on the materiality of the body can be enticingly extrapolated across national and transnational borders and across the political spectrum. I challenge studies on the left that take for granted that fatness and what the transnational medical industry names "obesity" is a public health crisis and not a moral panic (Campos et al. 2006; LeBesco 2010). For as Bülle argues, "El primer problema que se encuentran al referirse al cuerpo gordo es la imperante necesidad de patolo-gizarlo y describirlo como algo atroz, sobre todo si corresponde al de una mujer" (The first problem we find in regards to the fat body is the overrid-ing need to pathologize it and describe it as something terrible, especially if it belongs to a woman) (2018, 57). Performances like Bülle's suggest that what is also exported to Mexico is an Anglo-dominated panic regarding the body normativity of thinness and whiteness. In the face of an ever-mounting fatphobia where NAFTA, catering to transnational corporations such as Monsanto, plays the sole villain in this binary-told tale, fat women and queers, especially women and queers of color who are poor, are cast as victims who can be rescued from their own uninformed and colonized con-sumption practices. Upon the bodies of these fat subjects rests the burden to reverse the totalizing force of multinational food corporations through individual responsibility. I focus on cisgender fat women here, because like the sex worker who is always already interpellated as sex trafficked by the anti-trafficking "rescue industry", she is always sexed female, gendered feminine, and assumed to be straight and cis by activists across the aisles of political critique as they pertain to NAFTA and its queer traffic. These charges provide the template for pathologizing all kinds of bodies and their food consumption practices.

Left critiques of free trade *could* line up with fat studies scholarship; how-ever, as Anna Mollow and Robert McRuer explain, "The Left uses fat bodies as signs for what's wrong with contemporary economic arrangements" and in so doing "it reinforces the same assumptions that provide justification for austerity politics" (2015, 25). When the fat bodies in question also hap-pen to be Black, Brown, and/or poor, they often become visual metaphors of overconsumption, metaphors meant to deny access to public services. Sabrina Strings has "show[n] how [beginning with the transatlantic slave trade] racial discourse was deployed by elite Europeans and white Americans to create social distinctions between themselves and so-called greedy and fat racial Others" (2019, 7). Thinness as a moral imperative then has a long history that was guided by white supremacy, anti-Blackness, and colonial desires to adjudicate the conquest and slavery of Black and Brown subjects who did not conform to a specific white body ideal. Charges of fatphobia, Strings argues, correlated overeating with a criminal practice, an "ungodly" pastime that distinguished citizens from savages. During NAFTA time in Mexico, as well as across the NAFTA borderlands, "obesity" comes to be regarded as an obscene disability with and through the rhetoric of "epidemic." While fatphobia is a transnational phenomenon, in Mexico it plays out alongside efforts on the left to "decolonize" diet, routing Mexicans, especially Mexican women, to return to a labor-intensive *milpa*-based menu that simultaneously keeps bodies smaller (and in the kitchen) while rejecting the colonizer's food. This unwitting obsession of the left aligns with twenty-first-century austerity politics to become a form of moral (trans)nationalism that separates legitimate and illegitimate bodies and incorporates the money-making enterprises of a colonial diet industry.

Normative purveyors of the obesity epidemic, Bülle states, "Miran el cuerpo gordo desde la óptica de la inmundicia del ser humano, como un cuerpo que se entregó a los burdos placeres ofrecidos por la industria chatarra de comida y la bebida" (They observe the fat body through a lens of human filthiness, like a body that indulged in the egregious pleasures offered by the junk food and beverage industry) (2018, 57). Fat women get caught between decolonial critiques of the *industria chatarra* (junk food industry) and neoliberal logics of personal responsibility. In this liminal space, they get cast as criminal overeaters. Like Bülle, I find a capitalist contradiction in this focus on the woman's body as the locus for tackling the "obesity epidemic." While efforts to decolonize diet, and therefore the influence of NAFTA on everyday foodways, nominally attack the logic of free-trade capitalism, they nevertheless compel other types of flows: "dietas de choque, fajas con varillas modeladoras, aparatos para ejercitar el cuerpo u objetos protésicos que aparentan adelgazar en tan sólo cinco minutos" (crash diets, girdles with shaping rods, body workout machines, or prosthetic objects that can be used to lose weight in just five minutes) (Bülle 2018, 57). In other words, a decolonial critique that focuses on the bodies of fat women as symbols of a public health crisis reinstantiates free-trade capitalism and its emphasis

2a.2   Erika Bülle Hernández, *Carnes disidentes*, 2017. Photo by Mario Patiño Sánchez.

on the patriarchal standards of the white-dominated diet, cosmetic, and fitness industries and the sexist assumption of women as failed economic actors. The body of the "obese" woman, full of US-imported junk food and its environmental toxicities, becomes its own kind of abject obscenity. She is an immoral affront to Mexican health and the norms of the Mexican state and a *malinchista* monster who publicly displays her traitorous acts of overconsumption. Bülle crips the obesity epidemic, however, when she tips the scales of the heterosexual, white-dominant, and bourgeois standards for body size that circulate in step with Cheetos and Coca-Cola.

In one photo from the series *Carnes disidentes* (Dissident flesh), Bülle and photographer Mario Patiño Sánchez extend the reach of the performance of *A las niñas gordas nadie las quiere*. Bülle is once again crowned, this time in an exquisitely rendered sculpture headdress made from silver kitchen cutlery (fig. 2a.2). Haloed, she becomes the patron saint of fatness as she once again puts her mouth on a multicolored lollipop. This time, however, the lollipop is studded with seven single-edge Dorco razor blades. From the blood dripping down her forehead, lips, and chest, the viewer can assume she's already cut herself. The photo captures her in a moment of defiantly returning to lick the lollipop. Like the performance previously described, Bülle uses her body, her dissident flesh, to act out a trenchant and irreverent disobedience to the dictates of fatphobia, here represented by the razor blades. According to Bülle,

> Siendo un movimiento que ha dado cabida a la desobediencia, considerándosele en ocasiones como grosero, resulta una de las mejores herramientas en México que puede tener un gordo para hablar sobre su disidencia corporal. Cabe señalar que cuando se muestra desnudo, el cuerpo gordo articula un sistema de confrontación para el espectador.

> (As it is a movement that has made room for disobedience and at times that movement has been considered rude, it is one of the best tools in Mexico that a fat person can have to talk about their bodily dissidence. It should be noted that when shown naked, the fat body articulates a system of confrontation for the viewer.) (2018, 60)

Bülle's work is part of a larger hemispheric movement that confronts *gordofobia* as a patriarchal, hetero- and homonormative, Anglo-based, able-bodied, and bourgeois ideal. Incapable of being closeted, the fat body requires alternative routes, "un *entre*" (a *betweenspace*), argues fat sex dissident and activist Constanzx Alvarez Castillo, "cuya arquitectura como pasadizo para una gorda tortillera anarkista feminista antiespecista es a veces túnel, a veces laberinto, a veces campo minado, a veces escenario, a veces callejeo ingobernable del deseo" (whose architecture acts as a passageway for a fat woman anarchist feminist antispeciesist tortillera [dyke] which is sometimes a tunnel, sometimes a labyrinth, sometimes a minefield, sometimes a stage, sometimes an ungovernable streetwalk of desire) (2014, 11). The explicit fat body in performance remains one potent form of queer traffic within a matrix of free trade, diet, and sexual panic. Bülle's body of work provides an alternative infrastructure to licit and legible free-trade, an oeuvre that incorporates the decolonial without placing the burden of undoing the colonial on her body and other fat people's bodies.

3

Sex, Drugs, and Intellectual Property Law

Crowned, cloaked, and surrounded by doves and angels, musical artist Luisa Almaguer appears as la Virgen del Sexo (the Sex Virgin) to teach us how to *putear responsablemente*, to be sexually promiscuous, responsibly. Redirecting the term *puta* in a move that Juana María Rodríguez also makes in her book *Puta Life* (2023), Almaguer taps into her ASCO Media–recurring character, la Virgen del Sexo, to encourage all of us to fuck "solo una misma, o con todo el mundo, como contigo, y con ella y él" (just yourself, or everybody, like you, or with her or him). She then pauses to slowly lift her thumb to her mouth to seductively suck it in admiration, "y ese wey [*sic*] de allá . . . [and with smoldering eroticism] *ese wey* [*sic*]" (And that guy over there . . . *that guy*) (fig. 3.1). Throughout the video, a twenty-first-century safe-sex PSA, la Virgen can be seen canoodling with other *putas responsables*, queer, nonbinary, and trans folks, who, like Almaguer, are important figures in Mexico City's underground music, art, activism, and nightlife cultures.[1] When encountered within the museum exhibition *El chivo expiatorio: SIDA + violencia + acción* (The scapegoat: AIDS + violence + action), the display of Almaguer's video provides one example within a vast hemispheric transfeminist performance genealogy that reinvigorates the normative oppositional binary of *la virgen* and *la puta* from "something spit rather than spoken" (Rodríguez 2023, 3) to a potent and still-needed message about sex and pleasure in the ongoing time of AIDS. What binds

3.1   Luisa Almaguer for ASCO, *La Virgen del Sexo: Putear responsablemente*, 2018. Digital HD, H264, MP4.

this genealogy is precisely its focus on the promiscuous subject (often cast as gay, trans, sex worker, poor, migrant, Indigenous, and/or Black) who is performatively situated in spectacles of sexual panic and positioned as a threat of contagion to national and international health and security.

Almaguer's trans camp send-up of *la virgen/puta* humorously confronts the ongoing sex panic around HIV (VIH, or Virus de la Inmunodeficiencia Humana) and AIDS (SIDA, or Síndrome de Inmunodeficiencia Adquirida). As Jih-Fei Cheng, Alexandra Juhasz, and Nishant Shahani argue in their introduction to AIDS *and the Distribution of Crises*, "precarity and the production of an underclass are integral to the seamless cycles of crisis" under capitalism (2020, 2). Indeed, they contend that it is the very rhetoric of crisis around HIV/AIDS that "occasions Global North nations to exercise power, exploit international asymmetries, and retrench individual rights at will" (3) in the Global South and within communities of color everywhere. This chapter takes the sex negativity of free-trade capitalism to task for its cultural consequences on sexual culture and sexual health. I focus on how the scapegoating of sex operates as one key tool in the making of a sexual panic about HIV/AIDS medicines. Sex as scapegoat, as the purported cause of sickness and death, abets the false narrative of scarcity of antiretrovirals and other HIV/AIDS treatments and how they move (or don't) transnationally.

Performances such as Almaguer's promote promiscuity in the aftermath of these deadly lies and foreground how eroticism, the body, and fluid exchange play indispensable roles in the struggle for sexual health. She, along with the other activists, artists, and writers I discuss in this chapter, revives "how to have promiscuity in an epidemic" (Crimp 1987) for the twenty-first century.

Free trade and living with HIV are intimately connected. Throughout the late 1980s, 1990s, and into the twenty-first century, free trade shaped the transnational scope of the AIDS crisis, making that connection most evident in the controlled distribution of HIV/AIDS medications, in particular anti-retrovirals. I start by giving a brief queer history of intellectual property (IP) and patent laws in NAFTA (chapter 17) and the fundamental continuation of these laws that cemented barriers to generic medication access in the 2020 USMCA, notwithstanding the ultimate removal of controversial provision additions on evergreening practices (the extension of patents that are about to expire) and lengthened data exclusivity time periods (Adekola 2020; La-bonté et al. 2019, 2020). I do so with an eye toward the global influence of NAFTA as the primary model for the 1995 WTO Agreement on Trade-Related Aspects of Intellectual Property Rights (TRIPS). I then shift to exploring two examples of queer traffic exchange to show how free trade distributes sexual health crises to poor, queer, trans, migrant, and Indigenous peoples living in Mexico. The first follows the drug Atripla as it moves through the informal networks of gay men in Tijuana and into the hands of a queer Honduran migrant. Once considered a game-changer in the 1990s for reducing the number of pills one had to consume daily, owing to its many side effects Atripla is now viewed as an outdated medication. Capital-accumulating IP patent laws in NAFTA often stymie the flow of newer drugs, some of which have lighter or fewer side effects, from widely circulating in Mexico. I re-visit the polygeographic connections forged in Tijuana in 2018 to explore how collectives of varying scales of formality and accessibility have come together precisely to counter the so-called scarcity of antiretroviral medi-cations directly related to free trade.

Next, I turn to the previously mentioned *El chivo expiatorio*, a 2018 multi-modal museum exhibition on AIDS activism and art in Mexico City that met with threats of censorship and a less-than-cooperative institutional reception at the Museo de la Ciudad de Mexico. Atripla reappears in the first gallery within the interactive display "El muro de los precios" (The wall of prices). This interactive medication price-comparison calculator forms one part of *The Big Pharma Project* put out by Ojo Público, a renegade reporting group that prides itself on uncovering conversations often buried or hidden under free-trade capitalism and other neocolonial projects.[2] The museum display serves as a didactic guide for visitors to bracket their museum experience with the knowledge of how global circuits of capital, trade, and drugs derive profit through the extraction of dissident life in Mexico and Latin America at large. I use that display to further unpack how NAFTA's IP and patent laws have been used to financially exploit Latin America, and particularly Mexico, a country that often pays the highest prices for various medications that include biologics, cancer drugs and therapies, and many antiretrovirals.

Like the exhibition, my analysis undulates up and over the macroeconomic and transnational elements by also focusing on the localized and subnational performances depicted in the artworks. To close the chapter, I discuss two videos displayed side-by-side in the exhibition's penultimate gallery to highlight the performances of Manuel Solano and the ways in which her intentionally juxtaposed artworks act as a kind of meditation on the sexual and embodied trajectory of an HIV+ trans and blind artist. Viewed together, and spanning the period over which Solano eventually became completely blind due to the local denial of antiretroviral treatment access, the videos *El cuerpo perdido* (The lost body, 2014) and *To Lose Yourself Is Eternal Happiness* (2017) mark two critical junctures for Solano as she navigates the circuitous transnational stopgaps orchestrated by the US-based pharmaceutical industry during NAFTA time. Even in Mexico City, here viewed as a polygeographic destination for the HIV+ in need of treatment throughout Mexico and increasingly throughout the Americas, Solano's *El cuerpo perdido* shows how HIV+ people in the Global South become pawns in the pharmaceutical industry's leveraging of free trade, even as the video is intended to actively confront a view of her body as "lost" to illness. For *To Lose Yourself Is Eternal Happiness*, Solano's collaboration with deceased artist Damien Moreau, I read it as a performance of defiance of the neoliberal necropolitics of NAFTA, one that portrays a pivotal juncture in Solano's journey to reclaim her sensuality, eroticism, and hot sex. *To Lose Yourself* offers another version of Almaguer's *putear responsablemente*, where Solano and fellow actor Jaime Chacon continue to experiment with their bodies, despite the deadly consequences of NAFTA on queer and trans sexual life. The scapegoating of sex and sexuality drives sex and scarcity panics alike and covers over the influence of NAFTA's IP laws on global sexual health. In the wreckage, certain sex acts become tantamount to death, a fallacious one-to-one causal relationship that places the onus of illness on the behavior of queer and trans people.

It is no coincidence that the invention of antiretrovirals in the 1990s coincided with the introduction of IP law. The multinational pharmaceutical industry vehemently fought to secure patents when the world was in dire need of affordable and accessible medications. In other words, the advent of the HIV/AIDS pandemic, much like we saw in the profit-seeking and infrastructural lack that plagued the initial COVID-19 vaccine rollout, was seized upon as a golden opportunity to establish a global IP and patent regime with profit, not patients, at its center. While NAFTA alone cannot explain why HIV/AIDS medicines are not widely available to vulnerable people across the Mexico-Canada-US borderlands, free trade offered a tool for multinational corporations to control the economics of HIV/AIDS treatments and impose an austerity logic on the politics and performance of sexual pleasure. Multinational corporations and rich CEOs fabricate a scarcity model to harness and exploit varied scales of risk for profit. In this model, sex practices become the *chivo expiatorio* (the scapegoat), the sacrificial animal meant to carry away the societal sin of promiscuity. The act of scapegoating sex covers over the ways in which free trade, among other national and transnational mechanisms, is leveraged by the largely US-dominated pharmaceutical industry to invent not only the medications but also the infrastructural gateways and roadblocks to circulation.

Direct action groups in the United States, particularly ACT UP (AIDS Coalition to Unleash Power), went to war against the power of this industry in the 1980s and early 1990s and used meticulously choreographed public performances of protest to garner nationwide attention, as in the storming of the Food and Drug Administration headquarters in 1988 (Schulman 2021, 99–135) and the National Institutes of Health in 1990 (535–561). With the splintering of ACT UP after 1992, as historian Jennifer Brier has shown, treatment activists almost exclusively focused on treatment development and not treatment access (2009, 184–189), particularly as it pertained to less wealthy nations in the Global South. This shifted in 1996 when the discovery of a protease inhibitor drug regimen and its projected cost of $20,000 a year per person was announced at the Eleventh International AIDS Conference in Vancouver (187). Previously, pharmaceutical companies took advantage of the activist focus on treatment development. They appeared to fight alongside treatment activists for expedited and less-regulated drug development during a time in which Ronald Reagan's 1986 deregulation and IPR pitch to the GATT assumed its full flowering under the Clinton administration and Clinton's obsession with neoliberal global competition (186). Clinton's simultaneous gutting of the Welfare Reform Act and his fetish for free trade from the perspective of multinational corporations ensured that poor folks in the United States would suffer from a whole host of public health inequalities, including the out-of-reach expenses of HIV/AIDS treatment. People abroad who were HIV+ would likewise die at alarming rates, owing to the exorbitant cost of drugs and, in many instances, a homophobic and transphobic national health care system. Before the internet, HIV/AIDS activists across the imaginary community of North America that NAFTA once summoned may have had a more difficult time joining forces and struggles across national borders. Even today, few groups see the work of HIV/AIDS activists in Canada, the United States, and Mexico as deeply connected by NAFTA and other domestic and foreign policies of sex-negative and white supremacist profiteering.

In the lead-up to the NAFTA renegotiations that began in 2018, policy activists in Canada warned against the strengthening of IP laws, the lengthening of patent and data exclusivity periods, and profit-seeking practices such as evergreening and "pipeline patents," or patents provided to drugs while still in clinical trials.[3] Organizations such as Canada's HIV Legal Network / Réseau Juridique VIH (formerly the Canadian HIV/AIDS Legal Network) lay out this history of how NAFTA's IP provision detrimentally influenced access to and the affordability of medications for marginalized populations within and beyond the three NAFTA-signing countries:

> Furthermore, history shows that the provisions in NAFTA have implications beyond Canada, the US and Mexico. Provisions on intellectual property first negotiated in the Canada-US Free Trade Agreement (in 1988), at the urging of the patented pharmaceutical industry, were then replicated and even tightened in NAFTA's intellectual property chapter (in 1993), reflecting a particular model of intellectual property privileges agreed among three countries (two high-income and one middle income) belonging to the OECD. However, these provisions on intellectual property were then further replicated, almost verbatim, in the WTO's Agreement on Trade-Related Aspects of Intellectual Property Rights (TRIPS) in 1994, thereby extending that model to the vast majority of the world's countries, despite vastly different levels of industrial development, income levels (including degrees of income inequality), disease burden and strength of health systems. The effects of this model have been felt

for nearly 25 years, and are still being felt, not least as the HIV epidemic ravages many countries needing rapid, sustainable access to affordable medicines.[4]

While NAFTA plays a huge role in the precarity of HIV+ folks in Mexico, so too does ongoing discrimination at health institutions, as well as Mexico's bizarre penchant for strengthening IP law even beyond what NAFTA's chapter 17 outlines. "Since the 1990s," Kenneth C. Shadlen explains, "Mexico has adopted a patent regime that goes far beyond its obligations as a member of the WTO, or even those that come from the North American Free Trade Agreement (NAFTA), and it has continued to strengthen patent protection over time" (2012, 301). What's more, Mexico has consistently advocated for the expansion of stronger IP protections globally. Thus, the Mexican state, on national and municipal scales, must also be held accountable both for its role in the severity of the ongoing AIDS pandemic and for supporting the export of these stringent IP and patent laws to the rest of the world. The United States' long imperialist role in protecting property for capital undoubtedly drives, at least partially, the fervor for free-trade IPR law in Mexico. Indeed, Mexico's adoption of "an exceptionally 'strong' patent system" in 1991 was "a precondition to initiating NAFTA negotiations" (Shadlen 2012, 301). The antisex and antipoor homophobia of the Mexican state, however, must not be overlooked when understanding Mexico's deadly approach to HIV+ peoples. Cumulatively these factors created a context in Mexico where "80% of the supply of antiretroviral medications consists of patented drugs" (Torres López, Herrera, and Ciriaco 2017).

The culture of gaming NAFTA and the sick investments of free trade are chronically global. As already mentioned, NAFTA's logic of investment and profit became the template for the TRIPS Agreement, thus guaranteeing that long-ranging and prohibitively expensive patents would be implemented everywhere. TRIPS became an effective global tool to pressure so-called developing nations to adopt strict IP law (Shadlen 2012, 300). Armed with the normativity of transnational IP law, and resonating with my discussion of "porn pirates" in chapter 1, Clinton's US trade representative Mickey Kantor called nations that failed to acquiesce, among them Brazil and Argentina, "patent pirates" (Brier 2009, 187). He put them on a watch list of "unfair" trading countries against which the US Congress could issue sanctions. Unlike Brazil, which avoided an FTA with the United States and enshrined the distribution of generic drugs under its 1999 Generic Drug Act, and unlike Argentina, which similarly avoided an FTA with the United States and, since 2014, largely imports pharmaceuticals from India, Mexico is bound by

NAFTA, and now the USMCA, to only buy patented HIV/AIDS medications from the United States. NAFTA, therefore, creates and imposes scarcity onto the circuits through which antiretroviral and other drugs, most notably biologics, travel. This scarcity is then exacerbated by various sectors of the Mexican government that apply antisex and phobic medical practices to HIV+ patients in Mexico. The point of rehearsing the history of NAFTA's influence on IP law is to emphasize how free trade operates as an infrastructure of death in which, under the banner of freedom, the state and multinational corporations collaborate to create scarcity. NAFTA marks a pivot point for understanding why HIV+ Mexicans lack access to antiretrovirals and what this scenario means for sexual culture in the ongoing time of AIDS.

Following the lead of the artists and curators in this chapter, I center sexual pleasure to counter how sex is harnessed as the scapegoat for illness and targeted within an infrastructure built by NAFTA's IP law. Evincive of this phenomenon, Michelle O'Brien's short, illustrated zine essay "Tracing This Body: Transsexuality, Pharmaceuticals, and Capitalism" explores how her use of medications such as Proscar bind her "within the international trade systems that allow those corporations to function, that bring the hormones to [her] door in a brown envelope" (2003, 11). O'Brien aims "to trace how [her] body fits within structures of transnational capital, the pharmaceutical industries and the state authority of the US empire" (1). In a hot sex scene with a flogger in another short zine piece "New Flesh, New Struggles" (2004), O'Brien describes the intensity of being recognized as femme in her sexual encounter with a butch queer woman to emphasize the crucial significance of hormones, as well as kinky sex practices, to her sexual-social life. Even so, she acknowledges the transnational routes through which these hormones travel and how "these corporations, quite simply, are making a profit off people dying" (2003, 7). O'Brien situates the global circulation of hormones alongside antiretrovirals to show how NAFTA, IP law, and international trade laws sacrifice the importance of sexual pleasure to our lives as queer and trans subjects and sexual and gender dissidents. "The issues of access to HIV medications are deeply interwoven with the rights of trans people to access hormones" (9), hormones that when consumed by O'Brien create "new flesh and new hope" that among many other embodied circumstances include a butch bottom who "wants me. She really wants me. And it has so little to do with what's between my legs" (2004, 18).

With the rise in criminalizing gender-affirming health care in the United States, it has become harder for trans people to access hormone therapies. Trans people and their allies who attempt to collect and distribute hormone therapies have come under increasing surveillance. They are harassed, threatened with incarceration, and accused of drug smuggling.[5] Yet these kinds of networks have a long and transnational history of circulating life-giving and life-affirming drugs, a history that reaches back to the 1980s and direct action organizations such as ACT UP, and as Jules Gill-Peterson has shown for synthetic hormone medication, as early as the 1960s.[6] These networks function outside free-trade infrastructures and forge alternative pathways for the queer traffic of pharmaceuticals in violation of the IP and patent laws of NAFTA and TRIPS.

Following Atripla

It was November 27, 2018, and the three of us gathered with our Styrofoam coffee cups around the plastic table at a local LGBT community center in Tijuana. The director of the center called to order the first meeting of what would later become the LGBTQ shelter Casa Arcoíris (Rainbow House). In the two months that followed, our group would grow, exponentially and diversely, gathering lesbians, bisexuals, trans, nonbinary, and genderqueer folks across the Tijuana–San Diego borderlands. But for now, it was just the three of us: an LGBTQ migrant activist, the director, and myself.[7] My appointed line on the typed agenda read, "Urban Mo's Donativo (Jenn)"; when we arrived at that agenda item, I shared the good news that the San Diego gay bar Urban Mo's had held a drag show fundraiser on behalf of LGBTQ migrants who had become binational news after the most organized and visible group arrived barely a month earlier. The bar's event had raised $2,000 for their cause, but with the money and no ready-made or known infrastructure for getting it to the people they sought to support, they had contacted me, out of the blue, when they happened to come across a successful GoFundMe site that I had started in late October.[8]

After the meeting, I privately approached the director to make what I thought at the time would be an impossible request. On a visit to one of the LGBTQ migrant shelters I'll discuss in the next chapter, a young gay Honduran man, I will call him Raúl, approached me to ask if he could have a word in private. Raúl told me with great worry in his eyes that he was running out of his HIV medication and that he was down to his last ten pills. At the time, I had no idea where I could find such medication, but I promised that I would ask around and that I would get back to him within a couple of days. A day later, the director handed over to me three bottles of thirty tablets, each 300 milligrams of Atripla, the brand name for the three drugs efavirenz, emtricitabine, and tenofovir. He told me that informal networks of gay men had been circulating HIV/AIDS medications across the Tijuana–San Diego border since the 1990s. People write emails or come into the center in need of medication. He then combs the city in search of the drugs. When he comes up empty-handed, he crosses the border and brings back whatever he can get his hands on. Even expired medications, he told me, have some efficacy, and so he reasons that they are better than nothing. The next time I was at the house where Raúl was currently staying we found a quiet corner where I took out the bottles I had in my backpack and handed them over. I told him whom he could ask for more and how to get in touch with the center directly.

When in the mid-1990s antiretrovirals became more widely (though belatedly) available in the United States, anyone with access anywhere had to take at least three drugs and follow a complicated and thus difficult-to-adhere-to antiretroviral therapy. Photographer Óscar Sánchez Gómez depicted this dilemma when he documented his own consumption of drugs in the late 1990s and early 2000s in Mexico City, often portraying the changes his body experienced with all the side effects of taking multiple antiretrovirals at once. When it became available in 2006 Atripla was viewed as a miracle drug, insofar as by combining three drugs into a single once-daily dose it reduced some of the pill burden that Sánchez Gómez had been commenting on in his work (fig. 3.2). In Mexico, by 2018, when Raúl approached me for medications and specifically asked me for Atripla, the drug had come to be viewed as prevalent but not ideal, owing to its many intense side effects.

While HIV+ folks in Tijuana could acquire Atripla and perhaps, though unreliably so, other more recently updated drugs, they would have to travel to el Centro Ambulatorio para la Prevención y Atención en SIDA e Infecciones de Transmisión Sexual (CAPASITS) in Morita, far from the city center and difficult and even dangerous to visit. The geographical location of CAPASITS marks the body that enters as *seropositiva/x/o* (HIV+); one outs oneself to onlookers in a far-flung location through the mere act of crossing its threshold. This architecture of stigma, fear, and blame is even more treacherous for trans women, for whom the journey to CAPASITS is nearly impossible, owing to the potential violence that awaits them en route, while there, and after leaving. The very stigma that attaches to the body that enters the clinic acts as a deterrent to folks in dire need of life-giving treatment. It has also encouraged the development of alternative infrastructures for accessing antiretrovirals. In addition to informal networks, organizations such as the University of California San Diego's Health Frontiers in Tijuana (HFiT) student-run

3.2   Óscar Sánchez Gómez, "Nudo bárbaro," from the series *Convihvencia-Adherencia*, 2003. Silver over gelatin, 20×16 inches.

free clinic have stepped in to valiantly confront the many barriers to trans women's access to antiretrovirals.[9] In December 2018 at their offices in the Zona Norte district of Tijuana, HFiT organizers told me that trans women can feel not welcome to participate in the informal networks of gay men who specialize in drug medication movement and exchange. Many trans women who live or lived in Tijuana, and who can cross the border, often opt to move to San Diego to access more up-to-date drugs, such as Biktarvy (bictegravi/ tenofoviral afenamide, or BIC/FTC/TAF), which was approved in the United States in February 2018. Some of the trans women I spoke to in Tijuana in the fall of 2018 told me that they had experienced fewer side effects with drugs like Biktarvy, side effects that artists such as Óscar Sánchez Gómez so clearly illustrated through his photography of the late 1990s and 2000s.

In an interview in February 2018, HIV activist and *Letra Ese* news supplement cofounder Alejandro Brito explained to me that from the mid-1990s to the early 2000s, the largest number of lives were lost, owing to the conservative backlash against reproductive rights and those bodies blamed for contagion: gay men, *travestis*, trans folk, sex workers, and migrating peoples. Brito reminded me that Carlos Salinas de Gortari's signing of NAFTA did not just accompany Operation Gatekeeper at the Tijuana–San Diego border and the abolishment of the *ejido* system, which stripped communal lands from Indigenous and rural farmers to make way for transnational investments; Salinas also reformed certain laws to allow the Catholic Church, and now the Evangelical Church, to engrain conservative Christian morality into public political life.[10] For example, Salinas appointed to the position of secretary of health the highly conservative Jesús Kumate Rodríguez, who in turn restricted access to medications until gay activist groups such as Colectivo Sol publicly began to demonstrate in the 1990s. But even then, and particularly between the years 1996 and 2003, only those with state health insurance could access antiretrovirals, thus precipitating a massive death toll.

At a time when the largest number of Mexicans were dying from AIDS, and despite the existence of the Mexican Council for AIDS Control and Prevention since 1986, "most of its operations continued to be carried out with international financing from various organizations, including the World Health Organization (WHO) Global Program on AIDS" (Torres-Ruiz 2011, 42). Similar to the ways in which Salinas's creation of the National Human Rights Commission (Comisión Nacional de Derechos Humanos, or CNDH) in 1990 acted as a façade, so too did the creation of the National Center for the Prevention and Control of HIV and AIDS (Centro Nacional para la Prevención y el Control del VIH y el Sida, or CONASIDA) during Miguel de la

Madrid's presidency. Founded in the early 1980s, CONASIDA, like CNDH, aimed to give Mexico's public health efforts a "First World" face in the lead-up to the NAFTA negotiations. As Antonio Torres-Ruiz has shown, the "increasing domestic and external pressures led the Mexican government to create the National Human Rights Commission . . . in 1990" (2011, 43). These sham public service centers were used to pad Mexico's petition to enter NAFTA. Entering economic and investor relationships with the United States spurred the formalization of human rights efforts and rhetorical performances of care and commitment that rarely or ever functioned for the vulnerable groups most in need of attention.

Until 2003, in Mexico if you did not have health insurance, you simply did not have access to HIV medications. People who were HIV+ and their allies formed subcultural networks such as the one that the LGBT center had been operating in Tijuana since the 1990s. Founded in 1938, the Clínica Condesa in Mexico City became a destination for HIV/AIDS treatments in 2000 and for gender-affirming care to trans people in 2009 (Pons Rabasa 2018, 223–224). This move fomented the creation of little clinics across the Mexican republic, and the government finally started purchasing medications in 2003. In the 1990s and early 2000s, the Mexican government argued that the prices of the drugs were simply too high to afford buying these expensive medications, what was cast, Brito told me, as a "*lujo*" (luxury). "Estaban totalmente amarradas de las manos por el tratado de libre comercio, y eso lo decían, además, abiertamente" (Their hands were completely tied by NAFTA, and they would say it openly), Brito explained. He continued:

> Es que el Tratado de Libre Comercio no nos permite declarar la emergencia sanitaria, caso el VIH, y, entonces, comprar medicamentos baratos. Y todavía hasta la fecha, de la América Latina, México es el país que compra más caro el tratamiento en comparación con todos los demás países, y es por el tratado de libre comercio.

> (It's that NAFTA blocks us from declaring a health emergency, as in the case of HIV, and thus from buying inexpensive medicines. And to this day, in all of Latin America, Mexico is the country that pays the most for treatment in comparison with all the other countries, and it's because of the free-trade agreement.)

Today, HIV/AIDS medications continue to be in short supply. Stockpiling and pill-dividing are common practices among HIV+ Mexicans, those without access to health care in the United States, and those who cannot afford the largely privatized pharmaceutical program in Canada. Furthermore, the unethical dealings of infamous CEOs and investors in the United States sent certain drug prices skyrocketing. Perhaps most infamously for HIV+ (and/or pregnant) communities, Martin Shkreli raised the price of a Daraprim pill from US$13.50 to more than US$750.

Thus, HIV+ people in the United States and Canada also engage in queer traffic tactics for circulating HIV/AIDS drugs. Until 1989 and the CUSFTA, Canadian drug manufacturers could produce a generic, even of a newly patented drug, under Canada's compulsory licensing law for patented pharmaceuticals (Harrison 2000). With NAFTA, as a condition of signing the agreement, the United States looped Mexico into its demand for stronger IP protections (460). The renegotiation of NAFTA under Trump in 2020 continued the duration of patents, thereby assuring that generic versions of these medications would be long in the coming. In many ways, the so-called new NAFTA resembles the old NAFTA, in this instance ensuring that HIV drugs and treatment would remain expensive and inaccessible for Canadians who have a universalized health care system but no straightforward universal coverage of pharmaceuticals.[11]

Tracing the movement of Atripla and other HIV/AIDS medications throughout the Americas shines a light on how the IP laws innovated by NAFTA mortally influenced COVID-19 vaccines and therapies. On May 6, 2021, the Biden administration decided to support the patent waiver in the WTO's NAFTA-inspired TRIPS Agreement.[12] That was a pleasant surprise, no doubt, but one that came six months after the initial proposal by South Africa and India in October 2020, amid an ongoing pandemic nightmare. Moreover, Biden's support of the waiver did not include therapeutics and diagnostics, because support for these components of COVID care would jeopardize profits globally. The EU, Brazil, and other nations never supported the waiver, and as the WTO works by consensus, the waiver could be (and was) sidelined by any one nation's disagreement. It wasn't until June 2022, after two years of activism by the vaccine alliance Gavi, that the WTO approved the vaccine patent waiver known as the "TRIPS waiver." Even upon approval, the waiver had been watered down from the initial October 2020 proposal and failed to include diagnostics and therapeutics. It also failed to anticipate and aid in pharmaceutical distribution, leading Gavi to abandon its former efforts. The United States International Trade Commission was given a deadline of October 2023 to decide whether to extend the waiver to diagnostics and therapeutics, while biopharmaceutical companies complained that simply entertaining the extension of the waiver had negatively impacted innovation.[13] On December 4, 2023, the WTO announced the decision to extend the waiver for the production and supply of COVID-19 therapeutics and diagnostics for five years from the date of the decision.[14]

While the WTO ultimately approved the waiver for COVID-19 vaccines in June 2022, support did not, at the time in 2020, result in passing the waiver for over two years. Negotiations took so long that the WTO's final deal had no impact on supply-side constraints, nor did it provide any pathways to establishing plants to manufacture the vaccine.[15] With fallacious, arcane, and neoimperialist arguments swirling across the political spectrum, authorities argued that vaccines needed to be produced in the West and that developing nations did not have the capacity to produce vaccines. While it is certainly true that a waiver of the global TRIPS IPR rules is/was not the only answer to supplying poorer countries with vaccines, the argument that non-Western countries do not have the manufacturing capacity is simply untrue. Pakistan, Bangladesh, and South Korea, among other nations, have factories that could have been easily adapted to produce vaccines. Moreover, sharing scientific information, as in the waiving of patents, is only one part of the equation. Pharmaceutical companies (e.g., Pfizer and Moderna) need to share manufacturing guidelines as well as therapeutic and diagnostic knowledge.

When it comes to HIV/AIDS or COVID-19, doing away with IP law is only one solution for undoing the necropolitical infrastructure that originated with the 1990s version of NAFTA. Unlike COVID vaccines, the available circuits through which HIV/AIDS medicines and treatments flow are predicated just as much on viral contagion as on an erotophobic stance toward sexual pleasure.[16] In this way, Almaguer's "putear responsablemente" PSA, and her recycling of Mexico's adulation of "virgin" saints in her *puta* persona la Virgen del Sexo, incisively cuts through the many rhetorical barriers on the road to comprehensive sexual health. Sexual health includes the choice to fuck, not just once, or with yourself, or with one person for life, but with everyone, anyone, promiscuously and responsibly, not in the service of the IP law and patents but in the service of sexual care, a kind of care learned from BDSM practitioners like Michelle O'Brien. As Almaguer reminds us in her performance, "Está bien sentir rico" (It's okay to feel good and sexy).

In the ongoing losses of HIV/AIDS, multinational corporations use FTAS to leverage death for profit and to scapegoat sex for the distribution of crises across borders. Almaguer's video, as well as the museum exhibition in which it appeared, disturbs these distribution pathways and provides another kind of queer traffic that shows how queer and trans sex always has been and always will be uncontainable. Collectivity in the face of free trade's increasing individualization may translate to polyamory and orgies but just as well might lead us to seeing sex as political, as historical, as transnational. The museum exhibition *El chivo expiatorio* is one such site for displaying this alternative to the capital fiction of scapegoating and scarcity and the denial of access and care to HIV+ people.

Desabasto/Desbordamiento (Scarcity and Excess)

During its run from June 7 to August 19, 2018, at the Museo de la Ciudad de México, the museum exhibition *El chivo expiatorio: SIDA + violencia + acción* (in which Almaguer's video appeared) performed a careful balance between critiquing the violence enacted against HIV+ people and promoting the sensuality and eroticism of queer sexual pleasure (fig. 3.3). El Museo de la Ciudad de México is housed in an eighteenth-century baroque building located just a few blocks south of the Zócalo, the site where conquistador Hernán Cortés and Moctezuma II allegedly met for the first time. Today millions of tourists from within and outside of Mexico take in the folklore and historic sites of Mexico City's downtown. Situated in the middle of tourists and the political elite, *El chivo expiatorio* serves up the archives, voices, and performances of HIV+ people amid publics who benefit from free trade's economies. The exhibition brackets sex, and in particular practices of pleasure, promiscuity, and sexual excess (*desbordimento*), to counter a context dominated by panic, scarcity (*desabasto*), and sex-shaming.

In Mexico City, exhibitions dedicated to gay, and less so lesbian, trans, and bisexual, cultures are nothing new. El Museo Universitario del Chopo has been a permanent home for an annual exhibition since the establishment of the Semana Cultural Lésbica-Gay (now el Festival Internacional por la Diversidad Sexual, or FIDS) in 1987, and since then, a plethora of display locations and groups such as Centro Cultural Border (closed; now Border Agencia de Activismo), Ex-Teresa Arte Actual, el Museo de la Mujer, Salón Silicón, Casa Gomorra, Biquini Wax (whom I collaborated with in 2018), and even certain underground metro stations have hosted exhibitions by, for, and about queer culture.[17] *El chivo expiatorio* stands out, however, as it revived the waning collective activism in and around AIDS during a time when the issues of marriage and adoption dominate gay rights politics hemispherically; it also displayed the long history and ongoing life of AIDS activism through an intersectional lens organized from the margins where

EL CHIVO
EXPIATORIO
SIDA • VIOLENCIA • ACCIÓN

7 DE JUNIO AL 19 DE AGOSTO
MUSEO DE LA CIUDAD DE MÉXICO
PINO SUÁREZ 30, CENTRO HISTÓRICO

www.cartelera.cdmx.gob.mx   @MuseoCDMX   museodelaciudadmx

Museo de la Ciudad de México   CC   border   ☀ FUNDACIÓN JUMEX
ARTE CONTEMPORÁNEO

Este programa es de carácter público, no es patrocinado ni promovido por partido político alguno y sus recursos provienen de los impuestos que pagan todos los contribuyentes. Está prohibido el uso de este Programa con fines políticos, electorales, de lucro y de otros distintos a los establecidos. Quien haga uso indebido de los recursos de este Programa, deberá ser denunciado y sancionado con la Ley aplicable y ante la autoridad competente.

3.3   Poster for the museum exhibition *El chivo expiatorio: SIDA + violencia + acción*. Courtesy of Eugenio Echeverría.

trans women, trans men, lesbians, nonbinary folks, migrants, sex workers, incarcerated people, rural populations, and the Indigenous/*pueblos originarios* share and dominate the exhibition space. Unlike other exhibitions mounted in underground and alternative display sites such as those mentioned above, this exhibition, curated by Eugenio Echeverría and his team of *El chivo* collaborators, took over display space in a mainstream museum located in the Centro Histórico (historic center) and managed by the city government.[18] This government, while left-leaning in some respects, still espouses an approach to sexual dissidence that pivots on tourism and tolerance—at times barely so, as the story of *El chivo expiatorio* demonstrates.

Upon entering the exhibition, I was immediately struck by the collective spirit that drove this exhibition, which was so obviously created by, for, and about sexual and gender dissidents in Mexico City. Also immediately apparent was the underresourced status of the project: its wall text lettering was askew, and in some places it threatened to become unglued from the dramatically painted red wall that opened the show. Five months later, I sat down with Echeverría at the day job he then held at the cultural center, Centro Cultural Border in Colonia Roma. When I asked Echeverría why he didn't mount the show at Border, he replied that he and his team wanted to take advantage of the cultural quotas that, according to Mexico City–specific rules, mainstream institutions such as Museo de la Ciudad de México must fill. *El chivo* sought to politicize the everyday museumgoer, who may or may not be queer or trans, to hail straight/*buga* and even nonallied visitors into participation by showing the intersectional scope of HIV/AIDS across and beyond different gendered, raced, classed, and sexed experiences. This queerly informed antineoliberal approach to forming and forging solidarity around the topic of HIV/AIDS was given a minuscule budget, no money for publicity, and no institutionally provided team to mount the exhibition.

In our interview, Echeverría told me that during the show's installation several of the institution's staff would pass by with *caras de asco* (faces of disgust) or meander through only to verbally criticize the exhibition. Performances of *asco* continued during the opening night and were enacted by such influential museum visitors as the secretary of health and even the museum director himself. And in the lead-up to the opening, one of these meandering museum officials paused long enough to view an excerpt of *El siglo de las luces* (The century of lights), audiovisual artist Jorge Bordello's 2017 epic five-part experimental video about one hundred years of homophobia and homoeroticism in Mexico.[19] After viewing Bordello's video segment, the museum official called for the removal of the video or else the entire exhibition, he threatened, would be canceled. Bordello's video was ultimately permitted to stay, but not without this threat first reinscribing the rhetorical structure of shame and stigma that the exhibition so deeply rejected.

The displayed video segment, "III. Atrapar un demonio," layers the sounds of wind, ocean waves, heartbeats, and breathing with the long gooey drips of viscous liquid that accompany an infrared cock being stroked. A hand jerks it off in slow motion until it cums in red, *mecos y sangre*, semen and blood, visually representing the eros and thanatos that circumscribe antisex AIDS/SIDA discourse. The words "La cáncer rosa" (pink or gay cancer) streak across the screen, followed by various PSAs warning cis women about the virus. The PSA is stylized as a *lotería* game in which all of the participants, regardless of class, age, race, or gender, lose their lives.[20] Expresidents Miguel de la Madrid, Salinas de Gortari, and Ernesto Zedillo, the architects of the neoliberal free-trade turn in Mexico, appear onscreen, strung together by the phrase "the State cannot, should not, acknowledge the existence of illnesses derived from perversions." Salinas with the Pope, Felipe Calderón, Vicente Fox, Andrés Manuel López Obrador, and Enrique Peña Nieto all appear so the video can indict them—and by implication their political parties, the PRI, the PAN, and the PRD—for distributing death. Simultaneously the screen flashes "1997," the year when the most lives were lost to HIV/AIDS in Mexico.

The video segment cuts to a kind of anti-eulogy for Lorenzo Servitje, CEO of Grupo Bimbo, a rags-to-riches tycoon who converted his father's family bakery into the multinational corporation Bimbo. The video shows Mexican celebrities, businesspeople, Enrique Peña Nieto, and then presidential candidate Margarita Ester Zavala Gómez del Campo (wife of former president Felipe Calderón) fawning over "Don Lorenzo," as they all refer to him. They attest to what a fine, brave, and dedicated defender of democracy and human rights he was. Meanwhile the video cuts between these testimonies on behalf of Don Lorenzo and images of the Ku Klux Klan burning crosses, thus aligning the images of former and would-be presidents in Mexico with the racialized terror and murder of Black and Brown people in the United States. Bordello superimposes lists of extreme religious right groups that "Don Lorenzo" founded, participated in, or funded, such as A Favor de lo Mejor, Opus Dei, Instituto Mexicano de Doctrina Social Cristiano, and Red Internacional de Empresarios Católicos. The video then lists the wide variety of sex, gender, and reproductive rights issues that he fought against: "Don Lorenzo trabajó exitosamente en contra de: La promoción de condón, la educación sexual en las escuelas, marchas gays, el aborto, las escenas eróticas en televisión, las expresiones artísticas inmorales, y los Talkshows" (Don Lorenzo successfully fought against the promotion of condom use, sex education in schools, gay pride parades, abortion, erotic scenes on television, immoral artistic expressions, and talk shows). Finally, Bordello takes on church and state by lampooning the 1988 visit of John Paul II with NAFTA signer Salinas greeting him as the Pope disembarks a plane in Mexico City. To render absurd this union of church and state, Bordello intersplices footage of the visit with a video of Timbiriche, a Mickey Mouse Club–like Mexican group, singing their sonic-saccharine ode to the nation-state, "México." Bordello's video proceeds to show each consecutive Mexican president accompanying church leaders, including Popes Benedict and Francis.

Paul II's declaration upon meeting Salinas in Mexico City for the first time in 1988 accurately sums up the phobic stance that Bordello's video contests: that AIDS is a *castigo de Díos* (God's punishment) and the fault lies with certain sex acts, such as anal penetration, and their practitioners, particularly those who take pleasure in receptivity and bottomhood. This moralizing of the bottom body, cast off as deserving of its suffering and punished for its sexual acts, becomes a subject of *asco*, much like what was written on the faces of the museum officials when they first experienced the exhibition. As Mexican scholar Siobhan Guerrero Mc Manus explains in a video on the exhibition's companion YouTube channel, the body of the HIV+ person becomes a cipher for the disgust that "se le pega a un cuerpo" (sticks to a body) that has been rendered undesirable and untouchable.[21] As I will soon discuss with the video work of HIV+ trans multidisciplinary artist Manuel Solano, the medical industry in Mexico is guilty of neglect and discrimination by denying or delaying medical treatment upon diagnosis and allowing HIV to progress. Doctors and other medical officials act as professional rationers for the state, covering over the decisions that led to such a scarcity and leveraging neoliberal and austerity arguments to wage their personal phobias. *El chivo expiatorio* directly speaks to the public about the irrationality of blaming the HIV+ person. It does so by bracketing artistic works with hard data, organized along the scalar axes of the subnational and the transnational, when it comes to the supposed *desabasto* of HIV medications and, just as significantly, the *desbordamiento* of potential pleasure experienced during sex.

In the same gallery as Bordello's excerpted video segment, an interactive display, "El muro de los precios" (The wall of prices), explicitly addresses the administrative violences of the transnational pharmaceutical industry. Based on the *Big Pharma Project*'s online "botiquín comparador" (a comparative medicine cabinet), this display showcases the terrain on which medical institutions and providers in Mexico capitalize on the scarcity of HIV medications, inclusive of pre-exposure prophylaxis (PreP), to distribute the crisis broadly.[22] Visitor interaction with the display reveals the relative cost of pharmaceuticals across Latin America, while an illuminated trade feed connects the visitor's act to the New York Stock Exchange (figs. 3.4 and 3.5). By offering an interactive, didactic experience directed by the museum visitor via the pushing of buttons, the display invites the viewer to meditate not just on statistics and numbers, as important as those are to understanding the breadth and scope of pharmaceutical necropolitics; it also prompts the museum visitor to question why the cost of pharmaceuticals is so high across Latin America, and particularly in Mexico. It's important that this display contains drug information across a range of conditions that include

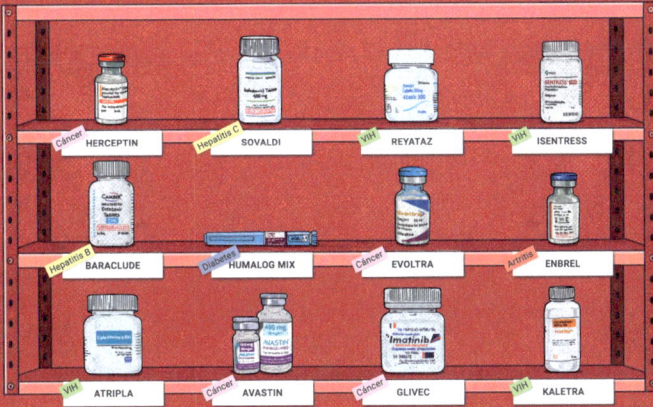

3.4   *Big Pharma Project* by Ojo Público, "El botiquín comparador," 2017.

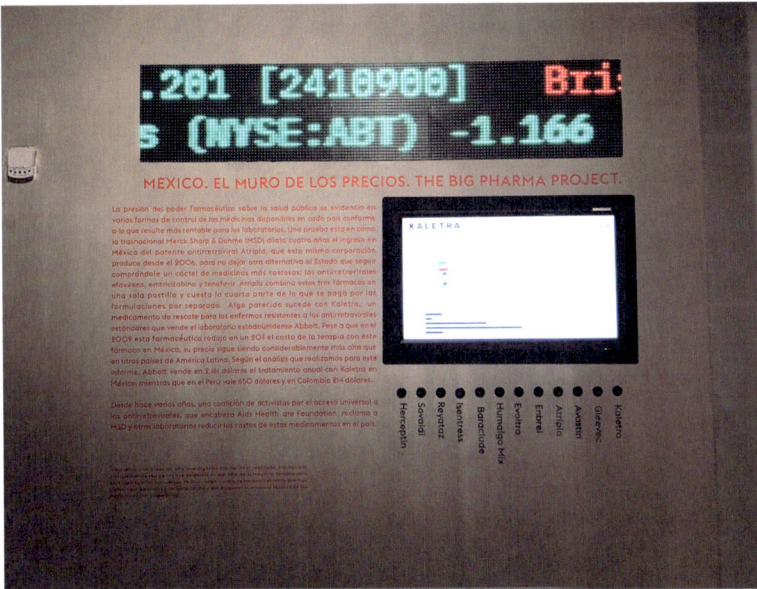

3.5   "El muro de los precios" interactive display. Photo by author.

HIV, cancer, arthritis, and Hepatitis B and C; providing this range encourages viewers who are not HIV+ or allies (yet) to grapple with the sky-high price of treatment through a collective public health lens that refuses to isolate HIV from other categories of illness.

El chivo's "wall of prices" cites some of the language from Ojo Público's *Big Pharma Project* website: "The pressure that the pharmaceutical companies' power has over public health is demonstrated in different ways by controlling the available medications according to whatever is the most profitable for the laboratories," the text begins (Torres López, Herrera, and Ciriaco 2017). Atripla reappears as an example of the ways in which multinational pharmaceutical companies, in this instance Merck Sharp & Dohme (MSD), delay the entry of certain drugs into Mexico. In the case of Atripla, MSD delayed the drug's entry into Mexico for four years. Their goal was to force the Mexican state to purchase instead "a cocktail of more expensive medications from them: the antiretroviral drugs efavirenz, emtricitabina and tenofovir" that Atripla combines into one pill at a quarter of the cost of the three-pill formula. According to the *Big Pharma Project*, "Currently, the cost of treatment with Atripla circles around 10,000 dollars per patient per year." For most HIV+ folks in Mexico, then, Sánchez Gómez's ludic depiction of the mountain of pills he and many others consumed in the late 1990s persists today as the cost of Atripla rose to become one of the most expensive and inaccessible in Mexico.

In the same YouTube video featuring Guerrero Mc Manus, Jorge Saavedra, executive director of the AIDS Healthcare Foundation (AHF), had this to say about the high prices for HIV pharmaceuticals and the connection to free trade:

> México es de los países en desarollo que más gastan o invierten en VIH. ¿Porque no se logra más? Porque se pagan precios muy altos por los nuevos medicamentos que en otros paises cuestan diez veces menos. Y esto es por el poco aceso a los medicamentos genéricos y esto es por el tratado de libre comercio de Norte América, dónde nos obliga como país a tener los mismos escqemas de patentes que Estados Unidos y Canadá.

> (Mexico is one of the developing countries that spends the most or invests the most in HIV. Why isn't more accomplished? Because new medicines are sold at exorbitantly high prices that cost ten times less in other countries. And this is due to the paltry access

to generic medicines, which in turn is due to NAFTA, which forces us as a country to have the same patent frameworks as the United States and Canada.)

Both the *Big Pharma Project* and Saavedra argue that the new face of successful HIV/AIDS activism depends on the circulation of expertise about free trade–related IP laws, which, as previously mentioned, developed precisely in the context of the fight against AIDS in the 1990s. By pivoting from marriage and adoption to the appropriation of knowledge about IP law and patent law, HIV activists and allies join a global movement for access to medicines.[23] While Saavedra and the *Big Pharma Project* identify this movement as "new," AIDS activists in Mexico had been organizing around medication access at least since 1997, when a major protest in Mexico City interrupted a conference of epidemiologists.[24] The 1997 protest, led by gay activist groups such as Colectivo Sol, belongs, then, in the long history of global AIDS protests. As in the 1992 formation of the previous HIV Legal Network in Montréal, or the many direct actions performed by ACT UP, Colectivo Sol's acquisition of expertise around IP law and patents is one of many subnational endeavors that link the three NAFTA countries through a shared, though differently scaled, polygeographic struggle.

On the smaller scale of a museum exhibition, by displaying a collective body of expertise made up of activist memory, activist archives, hard scientific data, and artwork, *El chivo* refuses the scapegoating of sex as a distraction from the many transnational blockages to treatment access. Indeed, the works of art displayed in the final galleries of the exhibition show how sexual practice mediates free trade to reject the pathologization of queer and trans sex. With this in mind, I now turn to two videos displayed toward the close of *El chivo*: *El cuerpo perdido* by trans artist Manuel Solano, and her collaboration with kink porn masochist and multidisciplinary artmaker Damien Moreau in *To Lose Yourself Is Eternal Happiness*. These two works, displayed in the same gallery to invite museum visitors to consider them in juxtaposition, are portals to understanding the relationship between free trade and trans sex during NAFTA time. As O'Brien wrote in reference to herself and other trans folk, "Other people's bodies are taken seriously as objects of biomedical research and health (2003, 4). "In the vast, proliferating world of consumer capitalism," she explains, "trans people just don't constitute a market niche when it comes to drugs" (2003, 3). Trans folks, unlike gay men, were not envisioned by free-trade architects or IP law policymakers as economic actors, and thus the objects that can pertain to their sexual lives, such as antiretrovirals and hormones, were never meant to flow to them in those brown envelopes that O'Brien described.

Upon entering the gallery, I first encountered *El cuerpo perdido*. While the video's title suggests loss, Solano told me in a 2021 phone conversation that the video actually commemorates one of the first times that she examines her new body, now a trans crip body, to "volver a querer este cuerpo y sentir bien" (to love this body and to feel good again). She recounted that she became blind in 2014 after being denied treatment in a private Mexico City hospital where she was diagnosed. Solano found her body and sex practice scapegoated at the crosshairs of a state-sanctioned trans- and homophobic medical environment, across public and private facilities and even in cosmopolitan Mexico City, where many in the Republic and throughout the Americas seek treatment. She was told that the medications she needed were too dangerous: the doctor fallaciously likened antiretrovirals to chemotherapies and claimed that HIV medications killed people four or five years down the road. Solano told me the doctor who failed to treat her said that "gente como yo . . . gente que actua como yo" (people like me . . . people who act like me) were intolerable. The doctor shamed Solano, scapegoating her feminine gender presentation and assumed bottomhood for her declining health. Even as she lost weight and became emaciated, her body covered with ulcers, her doctor told her to wait to start treatment, that her immune system was too vulnerable and that the life-giving drugs would kill her. At the time that Solano shot *El cuerpo perdido* in her room using her laptop computer, eighteen months had passed since her diagnosis, and she still hadn't received any treatment. *El cuerpo perdido* shows Solano as she is starting to feel better after making it through a harrowing year and only months before she would start to lose her eyesight and eventually become blind.

As *El cuerpo perdido* begins, Solano appears from the neck down in flowy androgynous black and gray attire, which contrasts with the white walls of her small room, and is accompanied by a Luis Nava mixtape that runs the video's 7:28 minutes. With a dark gray scarf draped over her head and cascading down her body, she stands upright and adjusts herself slightly, repositioning at her neck a simple silver pendant kept afloat by a leather string. The only skin visible is on her chin, front neck, lower forearms, and portions of her hands. Behind her, crumpled white sheets cover a mattress on the floor. A white plastic basket with an orange cloth slung over it and filled with scissors, lotion, and basic medical supplies rests on a small bedside table. She adjusts herself again, this time coughing into her fist before she sashays forward toward the camera as if modeling on a catwalk. She strikes a pose from every angle, her head out of the shot, giving the viewer time to see her clothing but obscuring her face. She moves closer to the camera, showing us now the silver pendant—is she selling us something luxurious from her humble bedroom?—before backing up again, face and head still out of shot. We get a glimpse of her face for a moment or two as she tries to arrange the folds in her crotch to make them lie more pleasingly. She comes closer again, this time without her hand in her pocket. At the precise moment when the viewer might first see the ulcer on her hand and wrist, she returns her hand to her pocket and backs up as if to begin again. *El cuerpo perdido* is therefore a literalization of all performance as re-performance, as twice-behaved behavior. At this point in the video, the viewer does not understand why Solano is rehearsing, again, and again, and again, this runway-model choreography, other than perhaps to show off her avant-garde, genderqueer attire using the well-known moves performed by fashion and jewelry models.

After about a minute, Solano finally reveals her face as she looks down at us, the camera now below her, and places us into the position of "bottom." The music seems to change as she sits in front of the laptop camera and obscures the other contents of the room and her body except for her head and shoulders. During this close-up confessional moment, we notice more wounds and scars on her neck and face, the redness and exhaustion in her eyes. Solano turns to the side to reveal a well-shorn, geometric take on the Caesar haircut, died in black. She swivels side-to-side in her office chair, performing as a model or influencer or starlet who will teach us how to apply the latest makeup trend. It becomes apparent that Solano is looking not at us but at herself, that she is examining her body just as we viewers are. She swallows. This is hard. This is new. This is scary for her. She is gifting us with the intimacy of viewing her body in detail, of witnessing her searching for herself in the ravages of the virus that has gone untreated for eighteen months.

In a gesture that communicates the summoning of a sexy, assured body, Solano next arises from the swivel chair and, like a diva, allows her shawl to fall to the ground; she then slowly folds and then lightly throws her jacket onto the mattress. Thus begins a slow, pained, yet insistent striptease. First the scarf. Then the necklace. Then the black shirt. Then the shoes. Then the black pants. All the while revealing more and more sores that cover nearly every inch of her body. Throughout, Solano repeats the aesthetics of runway modeling, but now she sniffles and coughs. About five minutes in, she is left wearing only her gray underwear and her gray socks, and once again, with her entire body and nearly every ulcer visible to the viewer, she repeats the runway choreography, striking a pose at every angle. She tries to maintain her composure, but the runway performance starts cracking as she again nears the camera and lifts it up so that we are again below her. This time, though, she starts to cry. As she sits down, she looks, really looks as if for the first time, at the intricacy of the ulcers that cover her face and neck. She brings a hand up to cover her mouth, overwhelmed. She licks her lips, sniffles, and swallows. She angles the camera down so she (and we) can look at what is perhaps the most open of the sores, the reddest and bloodiest on the upper right arm, and an equally large wound that has begun to clot itself into a scab, marking the spot where a scar will later appear. As she pivots in the chair again, we can see her chest heaving as she begins to sob. She lifts the camera and closes her eyes, breathing deeply to self-soothe. It isn't that long after she reopens her eyes and begins anew to rotate in the swivel chair, that her upper lip starts to quiver. She looks away defiantly for a moment, as if to reject what she sees, to reject what she feels in that moment. And yet she resignedly turns back and looks again.

I offer moment-by-moment details of *El cuerpo perdido* in part because Solano has decided to keep the video from public view. In conversation with Solano in 2021, she told me that she shot *El cuerpo perdido* at a moment of feeling better, whereas before she was so ill she was unable to get out of bed. When we spoke, she had already decided not to show the video in museum exhibitions. She explained to me that the exhibitionary frame of the exhibition invitations—trauma—fixed her body in a moment in time that preceded the video. In many ways, it's understandable that we, the viewers, might interpret the video as an enactment of the traumatized queer, trans, and crip body. However, the performance is not for a general "we": it is for Solano and others like her who are living amid a NAFTA-induced medical scarcity that scapegoats her and others' sexual practices as the cause of illness. While admittedly heartbreaking to watch, *El cuerpo perdido* is a performance of shedding skin and inhabiting a new body, a trans crip body, that is experiencing pleasure and looking forward to more.

At the time of *El chivo*, however, Solano pushed for the video to be included, while chief curator Eugenio Echeverría wanted to include one of her paintings, "What's Left of Me," from Solano's 2015 series *Blind Transgender with AIDS* (fig. 3.6). In the aftermath of the exhibition, Solano explained to me via personal email correspondence (April 6, 2021) that she had also decided to remove the video from her website due to the consistent impulse of viewers to fix her body as a static locus of loss. In contrast, Solano describes

3.6 Manuel Solano, *What's Left of Me*, from the series *Blind Transgender with AIDS*, 2014. Acrylic on paper, 87 × 47 cm.

the video as a celebration of what she recuperated from being denied access to treatment, namely her sovereign sensuality. Solano's crip response to the viewer's normalizing tendency to interpret the video as a portrayal of a body that lacks something, that irrevocably lost something, is to deny public access to the video. I include Solano's painting here, a painting completed after she became blind, instead of a video still from *El cuerpo perdido* out of respect for her choice for that video to remain unviewable.

For Solano, *El cuerpo perdido* is not isolated from other video work she created and participated in during these years. Through the exhibition *El chivo expiatorio*, and its side-by-side display of *El cuerpo perdido* and the 2017 video collaboration between Solano and Damien Moreau, *To Lose Yourself Is Eternal Happiness*, Solano accomplishes her intention for the viewer to grasp and understand that her trans crip body is whole, complete, and sensually alive. To further demonstrate this intention, and before I turn to *To Lose Yourself Is Eternal Happiness*, I want to briefly discuss another Solano/Moreau collaboration, the 2015 six-minute short-form video *Dreams*.[25] In it, Moreau films Solano, alone, on a bench at a Santa Monica, California, beach. The video depicts Solano as she approaches the shore, removes all her clothes except for her boxers, and enters the ocean, which laps up against her lower legs and knees. At this point, Solano has become completely blind in both eyes. You can see her trembling with fear and excitement at disrobing in a public place. She enters the water knowing that the watchful, tender, and loving eyes of Moreau are not only recording but also protecting her as she wobbles and puts her hands out, searching for footing as the waves enter the shore and lightly buffet her scar-covered body. Meanwhile, in a nondiegetic voice-over Solano relates the events that led her to come to the beach that day (Moreau invited her), that something "had happened" to her (the negligence of the national and transnational medical industry), and that she was scared to go to the United States and particularly to go to the beach. "And so I came here. I was with you. And suddenly I wasn't scared anymore," the voice-over says. Solano goes on to say that Moreau (the "you" invoked throughout) promised her that he would care for her as she learned to maneuver her trans crip body through space, thus enacting a queer ethics of care that reinvigorated Solano's sexual social life as a blind trans subject.

Dreams shows the ongoing process of coming back to a sense of embodied pleasure that culminates in *To Lose Yourself Is Eternal Happiness*, one of the last videos Moreau made before he died in 2019 by suicide at the age of thirty-five.[26] Shot in Taos, New Mexico, *To Lose Yourself* opens to the twang of the Sky White Tiger soundtrack, a psych-pop ballad that aurally envelops the half-naked bodies of actors Jaime Chacon and Solano throughout the nearly six-minute, otherwise soundless video.[27] Holistically, the video depicts a tender, loving, and repeated connection of flesh meeting flesh, a slow, dreamlike erotic meditation of soft caresses and open-mouthed kisses with ample tongue. Ruby-red pomegranate seeds fall to the ground during a time-lapsed moment where twigs twitch under the weight of the fallen juicy seed jewels. We then see Chacon nuzzling from behind the neck of an eye-patched Solano, his left hand in Solano's mouth as she lightly bites Chacon's pointer finger, baring her teeth. The video cuts to a hand breaking open a pomegranate, allowing the seeds and the deep-red juice to spill onto the ground and staining the fingernails that, because of the gold snake ring encircling her thumb that we see throughout the video, we know belong to Solano. The pomegranate, which signifies fertility, the body, and the land, but also blood and death, also reappears. In Mexican cuisine, pomegranates adorn the dish *chiles en nogada*, a green poblano chile bathed in a walnut cream sauce whose colors are meant to symbolize the Mexican flag, which is green, white, and red. *To Lose Yourself* eschews the pomegranate's association with patriotism. More akin to how the pomegranate figures in Greek mythology through the kidnapping of Persephone by Hades and her biannual descent into the world of the dead, *To Lose Yourself* uses the pomegranate, its seeds, its juice, and its flesh as a aphrodisiacal food item consumed to descend, a kind of desire for the journey into the underworld. In *To Lose Yourself*, the pomegranate is indeed a queer fruit, a lush and oozing talisman of exchange of the queer and trans pleasures acted out by Solano and Chacon.

These scenes of gushing pomegranates intermix with scenes of Chacon and Solano in a seeming backward movement through time. Solano is gradually redressed by Chacon, a reversed striptease that stands in stark contrast to the striptease Solano performed in *El cuerpo perdido*. In *To Lose Yourself*, each scene of eroticism is flanked by depictions of the land and the flora of Taos. Bathed in sunlight, these scenes involve the viewer in moments of synesthesia where what we see entices us to feel the light on our skin. Indeed, the intensity of this invitation was so much that on some viewings my body shivered as if drinking in the warmth of the hazy, dreamy light. Chacon continues caressing Solano from behind, his long brown hair draping over Solano's shoulders. In each interspliced scene of erotic tenderness, Chacon holds, even cradles, Solano's head, much like Moreau's cinematography enfolds Chacon's and Solano's half-naked, sun-drenched bodies (figs. 3.7 and 3.8). Chacon moves downward, unbuttoning Solano's pants; Chacon's hands caress Solano's torso while she makes inaudible sighs

3.7   Damien Moreau and Manuel Solano, *To Lose Yourself Is Eternal Happiness*,
      Música de Sky White Tiger, 2017. Digital video, 5:56.

of ecstasy. Around the second minute, they turn to face one another, Solano
enthralled by Chacon's ample chest hair and nipples. If the viewer has not
yet noticed Solano's scars, these shots make them unmistakable: Chacon
slides his hands down the right side of Solano's torso, and the camera, following this movement, reveals a trail of cicatrices. Chacon cups Solano's
crotch and opens her pants to begin sliding down her now-unbuttoned
slacks. Changing the positionality and directionality of the caressing, next
it is Chacon, his hair now tied up, who receives Solano's touch as her fin-
gers glide over his bare shoulder and ear. As Solano touches Chacon, more
and more of her scars appear clearly in the frame. Solano pulls Chacon's
hair down, which cascades onto his shoulders, and then they begin to kiss,
mouth to scar, mouth to chest. The sound of a rattle accompanies another
shot of a pomegranate dripping from the hands that opened it. Miming the
reverse directionality of the caress and leading the viewer to question who
initiated this erotic interlude, Chacon removes Solano's ripped black top,
which is partially held together by a safety pin and with yellow angel wings
printed on its back. One eye covered by a black eyepatch, Solano closes the

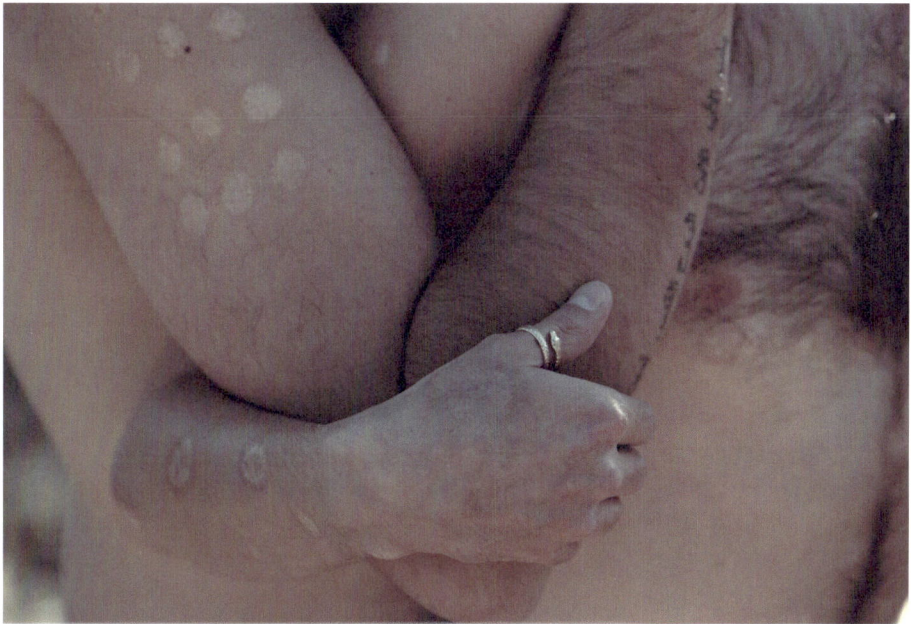

3.8   Damien Moreau and Manuel Solano, *To Lose Yourself Is Eternal Happiness*, Música de Sky White Tiger, 2017. Digital video, 5:56.

other eye. Through the holes of her shirt, now back on, we can now see her scars as we also see the tattoos that cover Chacon's body—tattoos that share a kinship with her scars, both of them a depiction of "performance remains" (Schneider 2014).

I view Moreau's and Solano's focus on the emerging scar and its reappearance in *To Lose Yourself Is Eternal Happiness* as, borrowing from Petra Kuppers, "a locus of memory, of bodily change" (2006, 1) and a palimpsestic site of rendering the body strange and pleasurable in new ways. When eroticized through Chacon's loving caresses and wet kisses, Solano's scars become a form of queer traffic, an unanticipated repurposing of the wound as erogenous zone. In the video, Solano reclaims the scar as a fount of joy and sexual pleasure. *To Lose Yourself* queerly repurposes Solano's eye patch and scars but not to deploy them as a fantasy of what Kuppers calls "wound culture, a term that refers to a view of identity politics that holds on to labels of victimhood and trauma in a negative, nonproductive manner, afraid to let go of that which has become the negative point of identification" (2006, 3). In this way, scars queer the body within the homonormative standards of able-bodied sexiness. *To Lose Yourself* models this move, harnessing scars for antineoliberal queer, crip, and trans pleasures.

In NAFTA's ongoing influence on queer sexual cultures in Mexico and beyond, Solano's performances stand out in relief against the global, transnational, and national dialogues of scarcity and scapegoating. Marked by these violences but not destroyed by them, Solano and her lovers embody a sensuality in excess of resistance, a way of navigating colonial atrocities through centering the body and the erotic collectives it gathers to it. Some modes of queer traffic are untouchable even by the capitalist state, and free-trade neoliberalism is indeed curable. In defiance of political slogans claiming that "there is no alternative" to neoliberal free trade, Solano, *El chivo expiatorio*, and the activists, artists, and scholars highlighted in this chapter declare that *there is an alternative*—an alternative performed and embodied in queer and trans sex dissidence.

Exhuming the Chupacabras

Performance artist Lechedevirgen Trimegisto stands alone, spotlit, on an otherwise darkened stage at the Centro Universitario de Teatro on the campus of the National Autonomous University of Mexico (UNAM) in Mexico City. They hover over a cardboard box and retrieve from it a spray can of CleanMex, a cleaner for PVC and other metal tubing. Miming a practice of cheap intoxication often employed to stave off hunger, they inhale the spray can's inebriating gas. For Lechedevirgen's performance, this inhalation signals the need to be anesthetized to get through what they are about to enact, to dull the pain of the encounter with what they will exhume.[1]

Lechedevirgen's *México exhumado* is performed to the backdrop of a nondiegetic narration that verbally unearths those lives, and bodies, that have been destroyed during NAFTA time. The narration includes in its list of such annihilations the 1994 assassination of Zapatista sympathizer and then-presidential candidate Luis Donaldo Colosio; the hangings of bodies from bridges as narco spectacles; the 2014 abduction and disappearance of forty-three male students of the Ayotzinapa Rural Teachers' College in Iguala, Guerrero; the violence and murderous impunity of US CBP; and the terrifying *feminicidios* (femicides) of cis and trans women. Next, speaking to the ways in which neoliberalism influences the politics of illness in Mexico, Lechedevirgen pulls from the cardboard box a medical-grade IV bag, referring explicitly to the public health atrocity committed by Javier

Duarte, the former governor of the state of Veracruz, when he organized to have distilled water, rather than chemotherapy, administered to children with cancer.

In pulling out the IV bag so early in the performance, Lechedevirgen frames the work as what Merri Lisa Johnson and Robert McRuer call a "cripistemology [that] further unwinds the spring between debility and capacity, not only by recognizing the ways one population's capacity depends on the debility of others, but also by recognizing the ways capacity depends on debility within a single individual's body or life" (2014, 135). By placing this symbol of state-induced debility in conversation with state-sanctioned murder, Lechedevirgen links illness and disability politics with the economic and social debility of Mexico wrought through the capacity of neoliberalism's beneficiaries. *México exhumado* is thus a work of solidarity art that, much like the texts Julie Avril Minich analyzes in *Accessible Citizenships*, reveals "potential political alliances between people with disabilities and racialized minority groups" (2014, 27). Inspired by Minich's scholarship, and illustrative of Lechedevirgen's reference to Duarte's denial of chemotherapy to children in Veracruz, Jina B. Kim's methodology of crip-of-color critique "urges us to consider the ways in which the state, rather than protecting disabled people, in fact operates as an apparatus of racialized disablement" and how this disablement spins on the axis of "resource deprivation" (2017).

Next, Lechedevirgen pulls from the box a *lele* doll, an *artesanía* (craft) from the Mexican state of Querétaro (Lechedevirgen's home state). Otomí and Mazahua women from Amealco traditionally make this type of doll, and in the Otomí dialect *lele* means "baby." In 2018, the state of Querétaro declared the *lele* doll as "Mexican Cultural Heritage," and in 2019, to attract foreign tourists to Querétaro, a giant *lele* doll toured Madrid, London, Sydney, and Shanghai. While these embroidered *lele* dolls almost always sport a friendly and welcoming smile on their faces, Lechedevirgen's *lele* doll is clearly frowning. Driving home the idea of staging Mexico as a fantasy for *gringo* tourists, the doll's frown constitutes a rejection of the imaginary of the Indigenous woman as compliant hostess and hospitable advertisement for tourism. *El jarabe tapatío* (the Mexican hat dance) begins to play in the background as Lechedevirgen starts dismembering the *lele* doll. They move to another spotlit part of the stage and sit on a chair, the silver scissors in their hands gleaming as they at first slowly and then violently take the doll apart. In an action reminiscent of Yoko Ono's *Cut Piece*, they first cut off the ribbons that bind her hair, then her *enredo* or poplin skirt, then

3a.1 Lechedevirgen Trimegisto, *México exhumado*. Photo by Herani Enríquez HacHe.

her high-neck blouse. But then they go a step further, ripping off each limb before roughly tearing off her head, decapitating her. They open her body, removing her stuffing.

In this and other performances, Lechedevirgen brings their body, a sexually dissident crip body with a history of chronic renal insufficiency, to close the gap between the 1990s and today (fig. 3a.1). While *México exhumado* focuses on the bodies that have become collateral damage during NAFTA time, it also calls out one of its most infamous perpetrators: Carlos Salinas de Gortari, the Mexican PRI president who negotiated and signed the NAFTA agreement. Then, Lechedevirgen begins their transformation. They undress themself from their beautifully crafted costume. First, they remove the elaborately decorated bright pink shirt with shimmery streamers flowing from their shoulders, then their vampire-bat imprinted boots, and finally their mariachi-style pants. Naked, they sit on a black box with a shallow peach-colored container and a small multicolored water gun filled with pink/red dye. In time with the voice-over that relates the atrocities previously discussed, they then use a large cotton pad to pat down their body before discharging the gun in the precise location of the murderous injury described. Each time the narratorial voice shifts, Lechedevirgen shoots their body with liquid, simulating bloodletting. The blood drips down their face and body as they pose seductively, looking out at the audience intensely as they assume an entire lexicon of positions often associated with pinup girls. About midway through the performance the voice-over ends, and the grating of steely synths serves as a sonic backdrop as Lechedevirgen engages in vigorous full body rubbing of the remaining contents of the plastic container. They nearly cover their body, head to toe, in Pepto Bismol pink, a visible critique of the (neo)liberal politics of pinkwashing.[2] They splash the remaining contents on their body, which creates the appearance of blood squirting from them. Turning their back to the audience and showing their buttocks, they dance seductively before putting around their neck a BDSM-style dog collar with a silver ring. Then, they don a widely known artifact of NAFTA time: the mask of Salinas with vampire teeth protruding from his mouth. This mask of Salinas as the *chupacabra* (the goat sucker) is meant to point toward how Salinas's collusion with the United States and his corrupt and murderous policies and practices slurped up the blood and lifeforce of Mexico and Mexicans.[3] Now both goat sucker and erotic dancer, Lechedevirgen adorns themself in a skin-tight crop top with long fluorescent green wings and nipple rings. They back into the dark unlit recesses of the stage before reemerging with wings unfurled, walking toward us and dancing menacingly, coming for our collective jugular (fig. 3a.2).

The audience might easily miss the illustration patched onto the bright pink boots that Lechedevirgen removes midperformance: a caricature of a pink-horned and winged Salinas, which clearly matches Lechedevirgen's costume. Bald with his signature mustache, this Salinas also has huge pink breasts, red-orange bat feet, and bloodshot green eyes (an obvious reference to his Anglophilia). His right hand carries a money bag, while his left holds a fluorescent green dildo that matches his eyes. Bringing together symbols of commercial sexual liberation as a form of cultural capital with those of the profit of the transnational capitalist class from which Salinas hails, the image is meant to satirize these twin attachments—in the first instance, the circulation of sex toys after NAFTA (Tyburczy 2016b); in the second, the wealth reaped by NAFTA's beneficiaries through opening the country to foreign investment. Apart from the color of the suit and his eye color, Lechedevirgen's Salinas directly and intentionally cites the poster of Vicente Razo's 1990s installation, the Museo Salinas (Salinas Museum). Installed in

3a.2 Lechedevirgen Trimegisto, *México exhumado*, 2019. Photo by the Hemispheric Institute of Performance and Politics at New York University.

his bathroom to evoke the scatological—the shit that Salinas and his cronies dished out—Razo's installation consisted of "juguetes de plástico, máscaras, calcomanías, títeres, objetos semi-porno, todo lo que llama 'bagatelas políticas'" (plastic toys, masks, stickers, puppets, and semipornographic objects—everything [Razo] calls "political trinkets") (Monsiváis 2002, 12).[4] Ironically, according to Federico Navarrete, the sheer volume, circulation, and diversity of these *objetos Salinizados* (Salinized objects) were made possible by an informal market of working-class artisans and street traders that arose in the ruins of Salinas's destructive economic policies and the prohibitive and privileged access to formal markets that followed NAFTA (2002, 18). The irreverent hope for the museum, as for Lechedevirgen's performance, was to depict Salinas as the quintessence of authoritarianism through ridicule, humor, and other satirical methods that even Salinas's free trade–frenzied policies could not touch (figs. 3a.3 and 3a.4). Indeed, one of the things *exhumado* (unearthed) by Lechedevirgen's performance is precisely this art genealogy of the 1990s, when in their work artists began to use tactics to

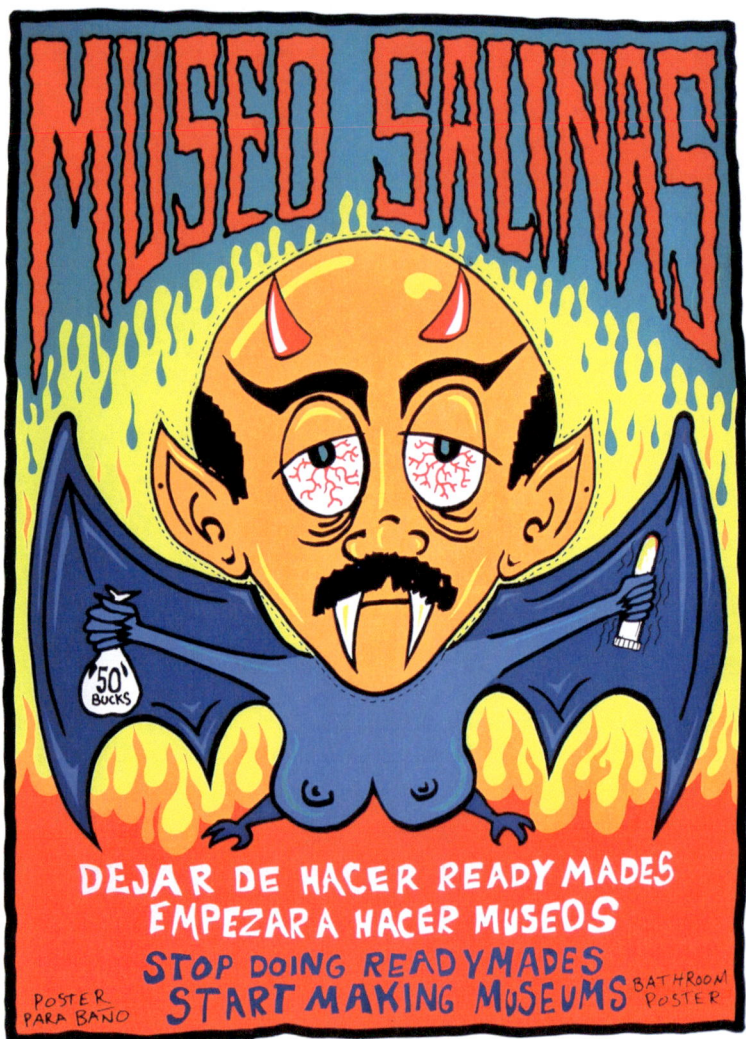

3a.3　Rolo Castillo and Vicente Razo, *Poster oficial del Museo Salinas*, serigrafía, 64×50 cm., 1996.

call out the Salinas and Ernesto Zedillo governments for 1994's economic collapse and the devaluation of the peso expedited by NAFTA's signing only two years earlier.[5]

As in Lechedevirgen's performance, prominent among these "political trinkets" in the Museo Salinas were Salinas masks. In 1993 Salinas masks started to appear everywhere, perhaps most memorably worn by children

3a.4   A view of Museo Salinas, 1997. Photo by Vicente Razo.

begging for money at the traffic lights of busy intersections. In a June 2015 interview Razo told me that, alongside the masks' signaling of a collective and irreverent rejection of Salinas and his policies, they also signaled a mass desire for a *sexual carnavalesca* (sexual carnivalesque), a Bakhtian mode for inverting the world, rendering it topsy-turvy. "Hasta en carnavales ya populares o de pueblo o así," Razo explained, "ponerte la máscara de Salinas para asustar a las mujeres, o bueno, a todo el mundo . . . entonces la máscara también tuvo, creo que tenía también por ahí poder sexual" (Even at popular or small town carnivals, you'd put on the Salinas mask like this to scare the women, or maybe, everybody. . . . And so, yes, the Salinas mask also had for a time, I think it had a sexual power). Razo juxtaposed Salinas masks to the *pasamontañas* (balaclavas) worn by Subcomandante Marco and the Zapatistas. In the same interview he told me that NAFTA served as a portal for the Mexican left to seize on "una energía vital o un eros" (a vital energy or an eros) that emanated from the seductive *mirada* (look) of Marcos's eyes and the then-erotic secrecy behind the *pasamontañas*. Indeed, the Museo Salinas contains one wooden figurine that stages a boxing match between Salinas and Marcos, thus satirizing the unequal fight by leveling the playing field and placing the two of them in arm-to-arm combat, the seductive left-ist hero versus the slimy ratlike Salinas. In both instances, though toward dramatically different ends, the *pasamontañas* worn by the Zapatistas and the Salinas masks worn by poor unhoused children and displayed in the Museo Salinas represent a centuries-long performance tradition of using masks, in both secular and religious rituals, to mime, mimic, and subvert power (fig. 3a.5).

Nearly thirty years after Salinas masks began to appear, Lechedevirgen's performance queerly resurrects these ritualistic uses of Salinas masks for the twenty-first-century NAFTA context. By wearing the mask, Lechedev-irgen simultaneously transforms the figure of Salinas into a genderqueer *chupacabra* and raises civic awareness about the interconnectedness of the NAFTA signer with the myriad state and narco atrocities that followed and continue to follow in its wake. "Traer puesta en la calle la máscara de Sa-linas," argued Carlos Monsiváis, "es afirmar la rebeldía, el desprecio a los malos gobiernos, la gana de relajo que no ahogan las precipitaciones de la economía, el gusto por los carnavales instantáneos, la ambición de satirizar a Los de Arriba y democratizar el caos urbano" (To wear a Salinas mask in the street is a badge of rebelliousness, of contempt toward bad government, of a desire to have fun which economic aftershocks cannot stamp out, of a

3a.5 "Niño de la calle como el chupacabras," México DF, 1996. Photo by Vicente Razo.

taste for instant carnivals, of the ambition to satirize the bigwigs and democratize the chaotic urban landscape) (2002, 10). *México exhumado* cites this long history of *Salinizando* popular culture to critique how NAFTA continues to extract from poor, Indigenous, female, and feminine subjects. Lechedevirgen exhumes the Salinas mask to explicitly traffic in the widely felt but rarely articulated connections among Salinas, NAFTA, and contexts of poverty and violence in Mexico today. Using their body—a queer crip nonbinarix, xenobinarix body—Lechedevirgen makes themself vulnerable through performance, riffing on yet exceeding the display of *objetos Salinizados* in Razo's private bathroom.⁶

"Efectivamente," Lechedevirgen told me in personal correspondence in 2019, "la reinterpretación del chupacabras con la estética bdsm y el color rosa es un ejercicio de 'cuirización' de esta figura mediática que funcionó para controlar a la población mexicana por medio del miedo y el shock. Al mismo tiempo buscaba resaltar sus cualidades monstruosas como una criatura de la criptozoología latinoamericana y un arquetipo de lo 'perverso' y lo 'desviado'" (Definitely, the reinterpretation of the goat sucker with BDSM aesthetics and the color pink is a "queering" of the media figure that worked to control the Mexican population by way of fear and shock. At the same time, I wanted to bring out his monstrous qualities, like a creature of Latin American cryptozoology and as an archetype of the "perverse" and the "twisted"). Indeed, in the act of performing with the Salinas mask, Lechedevirgen converts their body into an *objeto Salinizado*, aligning themself with the impoverished children who wore them to beg for money. In so doing, Lechedevirgen makes perverse and twisted that which has become flattened through the infrastructures of free-trade capitalism during NAFTA time.

4

Dancing *Punta* on NAFTA Time

At the LGBTQ migrant safe house, we lined up to fill our plates with food. There was enough for seconds and leftovers, so we indulged with teeming portions. After the feast, we danced *punta*, chatted, and smoked cigarettes on the patio. While parents and guardians continued the *fiesta* and paired off to dance, I hung out with the children, who dreamed up an elaborate game of hide and seek that they delighted in with squeals and excited emotion. They presented me with a plate of plastic fruit they had found in the house and "tricked" me into eating the green rubbery grapes, giddily laughing at what they perceived to be my silly gullibility, or at least my willingness to play along. With the grapes dangling from my mouth, they hung onto my neck, wanting to be picked up and held, wanting to play. I was overwhelmed with love for them and for the people who had invited me into their sanctuary these past two months. I would be leaving in just a few days, and knowing that I would never see many of them again we tried not to be overcome with emotion as we took photos together, embraced, and cried. We had these moments. We weren't outside of NAFTA time, as this unseen agent would always be the backdrop. But for a brief period, while still on it, we were not of it. We stole from NAFTA time.

Always a liminal site of passage and policing, though not historically characterized with the same dramatic performances of hypermilitarization as are on display today, the border is now a veritable war zone. In the space where Tijuana and San Diego kiss across what local *tijuanenses* (Tijuana residents) call in a belittling gesture *la línea* (the line), the United States under Trump had installed endless spiky swirls of barbed wire, floodlights that blind at night, *la migra* on horseback armed with guns and assault weapons, three or more helicopters illegally flying into Mexican airspace, and walls (walls upon walls, ever-growing, behind and in front of more and higher walls). The intention of these walls is to keep out those bodies rendered obscene across the polygeographies of NAFTA time: mestiza, Afro-Indigenous, and Afro-Latinx migrants from Central America's "Northern Triangle" (Guatemala, Honduras, and El Salvador); Mexican nationals from narco-run Mexican states such as Guerrero and Michoacán; Venezuelans and Cubans after President Joseph Biden ended the COVID-19 emergency border-security program; and Haitians arriving in multiple waves after Haiti's 2010 and 2020 earthquakes, Hurricane Matthew, the cholera outbreak in 2016, and the 2021 assassination of Haiti's President Jovenel Moïse. NAFTA, as Elaine Carey and Andrae M. Marak contend, "actually undermined the nation-state's control over borders (even as their policing of them has expanded)" (2011, 4). Indeed, the very tenuousness of the border, Ramón H. Rivera-Servera and Harvey Young argue, "fuels the compulsive, oftentimes violent, performance to uphold it" (2011, 1–2). There were 600 kilometers of wall, 800 barriers of all kinds, and an incremental increase of technological surveillance, specialized police, and migrant arrests, detentions, and deportations, and that was only the beginning.[1] NAFTA, much like those flying military helicopters meandering into Mexican airspace, uncovers the indeterminacy of where the border begins and ends.

At Tijuana's el Colegio de la Frontera Norte, I sat down with archivist Alfonso Caraveo Castro, awed by his collection of decades of photographic documentation of the Tijuana–San Diego border. Again and again, he pointed out the vast differences between *la línea* of 2018 and *la línea* of the 1980s, when Mexico had only just begun to be viewed as financially attractive to foreign investors (notwithstanding the Border Industrialization Program [the Maquiladora Program] initiated in 1964).[2] Caraveo Castro highlighted photographs that captured fleeting moments of conviviality between the border patrol and migrant populations, at the time largely, but not exclusively, Mexican. He did this not to romanticize these moments but to bring home the stark differences of what was possible at the border then and now. He showed me the games of *fútbol* in el Cañon Zapata on land now inaccessible to those outside the border-security regime; the Santa Claus

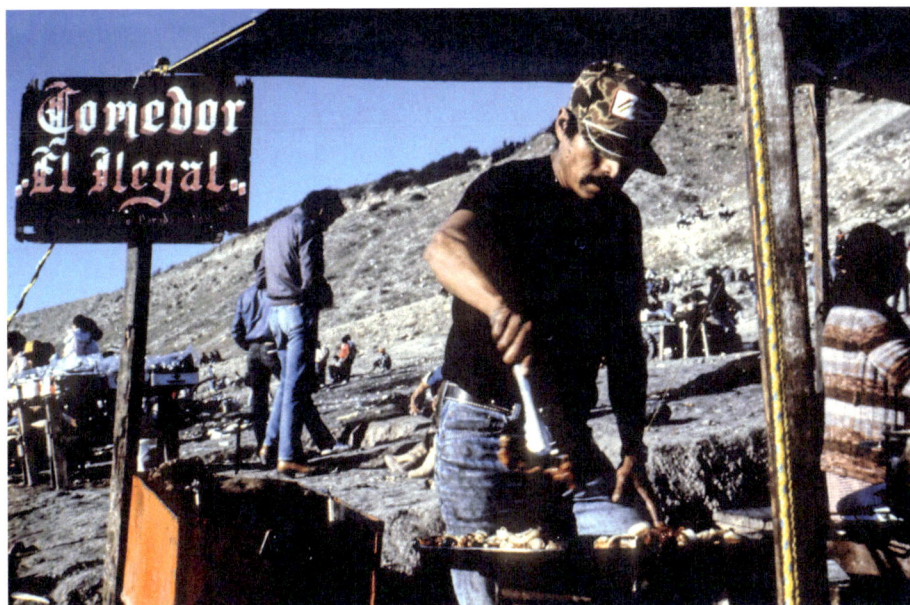

4.1   Comedor "El Ilegal." Photo by Roberto Córdova-Leyva, 1987. Archivo de el Colegio de la Frontera Norte.

visits with toys for the children; exchanges of laughter between the unlikely, such as *la migra* and migrants; and, perhaps most akin to this book's focus on queer traffic, a photo of the chicken vendor el Señor Roque cooking his delicious meats at his irreverently titled Comedor "El Ilegal" ("The Illegal" restaurant; see fig. 4.1). The photograph captures Roque as he turns over a chicken wing in a moment of silence when he would otherwise be hailing passersby with the *doble sentido* (double entendre) exclamation of "Pollos!," a play on the Spanish word for "chicken," literally referencing the barbecued meat on his grill and, cheekily, *los polleros*, otherwise known by the border security regime as "human traffickers." Through his archive, Caraveo Castro taught me in great detail how the changes in the infrastructure of *la línea* after 1987 transformed how people move toward, around, and through the borderlands.[3] Clearly depicted in the photos as we moved along in years was the dwindling array of nontourist, *obrero* (working-class) ludic practices that people could engage in and around *la línea* and the gradual but undeniable transformation of the Tijuana–San Diego border into a violent, militarized zone of surveillance, incarceration, and death.

But as Rihan Yeh so beautifully states in her ethnography *Passing: Two Publics in a Mexican Border City*, the term *la línea* simultaneously means many things: "the 'International Line,'" she explains, "is not the border per se. Rather *la Línea* is the area just south of San Ysidro, the city's main port of entry to the United States" (2017, 1), which is also the most traversed port of entry in the world. It is also the name of the street, Línea Internacional, where cars and pedestrians queue up to cross or be turned away, searched, and/or detained. *La línea*, therefore, is not just a spatial designation, "an east-west signifying prohibition and a north-south line signifying passage" (1); it is also a temporal configuration, as people wanting to cross will wait for hours or, in the case of the queer and trans migrants that I'll discuss in this chapter, interminably. One remnant of *la línea*'s more ludic past remains for those waiting in cars: the vendors of everything from Mexican antiquities, to *limonadas*, to ice cream, and a variety of Mexican *antojitos* (snacks) in these now tourist-designated zones of state-sanctioned waiting. Scenes of suffering, poor children and people missing limbs and asking for loose change, intermix with these touristy consumption practices. And in *el Bordo*, a waterless canal on the edge of *la línea*, the forgotten, the dying, and the almost dead accumulate in step with the deregulation of multinational corporations who dump toxins in the forbidden no-person's land that rubs up against *la línea*. It clearly marks a juxtaposition of the well-heeled and passported waiting to cross into the United States, possibly headed toward a "shopping without borders" experience at San Ysidro Plaza de las Americas, and the deported, the drug addict, the migrant who fell from the la Bestia train and lost his leg, the *maquila* worker who injured both her hands when a machine malfunctioned that bracket performances of waiting at the border. Indeed, as Josh Kun has shown for those crossing on foot across the San Ysidro land bridge, such as I have on numerous occasions, "the turnstile is the border's ticking clock," an emanating sound in a liminal zone that "is neither in nor out, but always both" (2011, 18). The "turnstile's clank" nominally means "perforation and passage" (18), but it's also an "aural architecture" (34) of regulation and militarism. It's a sound that most migrating peoples, queer, trans, or otherwise, will never hear because their asylum claims are denied or left unanswered, because they have decided to brave the harsh conditions of the desert to circumvent the inhumane asylum process, or because they have been transported to the United States in the suvs of *la migra* that drop them off at detention centers that rival the precarity, danger, and neglect of staying in Mexico.

In this chapter, I further develop the temporal concept I call "NAFTA time" to argue for the wide-spanning reach of NAFTA, in its lead-up and its ongoing aftermath. NAFTA time brackets the history of free trade as a formalization of exchange practices leveraged to install militarized displays of power unprecedented in their spectacular performances of grandiosity. In the case of the Tijuana–San Diego border, free trade set in motion a series of violent security operations to control and immobilize those perceived as threatening the temporal regime of NAFTA time: the traffic, contraband, and obscenity of "illegal personhood." NAFTA time is not only marked by normative, bourgeois, and Anglo-specific forms of morality and the fomentation of lucrative sex panics. It is also stained with the blood of First Nations Canadians fighting the Trans Mountain pipeline, of Black and Brown people hunted under the same War on Drugs that kills countless poor and marginalized Mexicans, the *feminicidios* of trans and cis women across the Americas, and, in the case of this chapter, the Central American migrants for whom the transit through Mexico, if not the desert borderlands or the *hieleras* of migrant detention centers, sadly matches the horror, violence, and death that they are running from in their US State Department–backed authoritarian nation-states. It is the time of the *retornadxs* (the returned) sent back to Mexico through Trump's "Migrant Protection Protocols" (MPP 1.0)—often referred to as the "Remain in Mexico" program, and the use of what was meant as a temporary COVID-19 policy, Title 42, under Biden's presidency.[4] It is the time in which Honduran trans woman Roxana Hernández was left to die, without her HIV medication, in her solitary cell at the Cibola County Correctional Center in New Mexico.[5] To endure NAFTA time is a deadly exercise.

Here, however, I want to focus on "how waiting is not just shaped by those who make others wait, but by those who wait" (Bandak and Janeja 2018, 8). Connecting the practice of endurance to durational performance art, performance studies scholar Sandra Ruiz proposes the concept "enduring time" to explain the colonial condition of being Puerto Rican: "To be Rican, then, means to ride out the inexhaustible constraints of one's life under limited self-control in a nonstop state of economic and political impotence" (2019, 9). I draw from Ruiz to theorize trans and queer migrants as particular publics in the migrant caravan who endure NAFTA time by shaping their conditions of waiting. Indeed, endurance is etymologically tied to duration, André Lepecki reminds us, and performances of endurance "are durational in that they subvert and subdue chrono-normative time" (2016, 3).

The durational aesthetics with which queer and trans migrants shape the practice of waiting are embodied through typically censored migrant performances, such as dancing, that "steal" time to derive pleasure, sensuality, eroticism, and joy from sexual and sexy play.[6]

As Rivera-Servera and Young have argued, "performance, as an optic that prioritizes the multi-sensorial experience of embodiment, is particularly attuned to the ways in which border spatializations and temporalities are formed in/as movement" (2011, 3). Migrant pleasures stolen back from NAFTA time break with the compulsory performances of the dutiful, deserving, and grateful migrant subject that must be enacted while waiting, as David A. B. Murray (2016), Elif Sari (2020), and other queer migration scholars have shown.[7] These acts of endurance consist of laughter and irreverence, sensuality and eroticism, often performed at great risk. In this way, migrant acts of sexual play "queer the regulatory synchronizations of time and history" (Mulhall 2014) as they relate to the border and the military industrial complex. They constitute a form of deep play, what the architect of the prison panopticon Jeremy Bentham described with distaste as a performance in which "the stakes are so high that . . . it is irrational for anyone to engage in it at all, since the marginal utility of what you stand to win is grossly outweighed by the disutility of what you stand to lose" (as cited in Ackerman 2000, 18). As the Pulse nightclub massacre in Orlando, Florida, in 2016 and the mass shooting at Club Q in Colorado Springs, Colorado, in 2022 reminded us, all queer pleasures, particularly those that belong to Black, Brown, trans, and gender-nonconforming experiences, constitute deep play. Migrant pleasures *in* NAFTA time, as Juana María Rodríguez argues for queer gesture *in* mambo time (2014, 99–138), change the tempo of the moves made, the rhythm of bodies in relation to one another in the space of a makeshift club, which here refers to the LGBTQ safe houses in Tijuana. Performing pleasure while migrating in/on NAFTA time, then, enacts a perverse aesthetics of irreverence toward the waiting and what one is supposed to embody as one passes the time.

I started visiting Tijuana in August 2017 and then again in the spring of 2018 to give a presentation on an artivism panel at the Jornada por la Diversidad Sexual alongside migrant activist and documentary filmmaker Gaba Cortes. There I first met a few migrating queer and trans folk. I returned in October–December of 2018 to meet up with some of these same people as the largest caravan to date arrived in Tijuana. While there, migrant leaders asked any less-surveilled person to perform quotidian acts (e.g., transport water jugs; wait outside the prison for folks to be released) and to support activities to cultivate migrant joy while waiting, a form of mutual aid outside the formal infrastructures of support provided by immigration lawyers and nongovernmental organizations. I became one of those people. What follows is an account of some of those moments.

In recounting these moments, I draw from Pavithra Prasad's method for writing memory wherein I position my "body as a souvenir of lived experiences of belonging, loss, and desire," a body that can only be accessed again through a performance approach to writing that reenacts/matches "a repertoire of embodied affects" (2015, 204). As one can imagine, as I remember this time, there were many painful moments of loss and sadness, of lives bound to and crushed on NAFTA time. So too were there moments of queer conviviality, posing for photos together, sharing an afternoon at the beach or a meal at a pizza parlor or at one of the LGBTQ houses. So, I decided to take a different tack in this chapter, highlighting LGBTQ migrants' ingenious tactics of cultivating pleasure on NAFTA time. Heeding the call of Tijuana-based scholar Sayak Valencia, I aim "to imagine new methods for the use of the body, power, and desire" (2018, 10), particularly along transfeminist lines, and even in the horrors of NAFTA time within which Valencia writes and within which my memories of Tijuana are ensconced.

Andrea and her current girlfriend, Cristina, sat quietly across from me at the breakfast table in my modest apartment at the very edge of Playas de Tijuana, right before one would reenter Highway 1D, Escénica Tijuana-Ensenada, toward the more respectable middle-class destination of Rosarito. They looked refreshed, saying they hadn't slept that well in months and enjoying, I was delighted to see, the scrambled eggs, hot corn tortillas, and homemade salsa I served them. The night earlier they had spent most of the time alone in the spare bedroom, and when I wasn't out on a walk or food shopping to give them some privacy, giggles and other joyful sounds filled the space. Today, we were to spend the day at the beach, and I had bought some Sabritas (potato chips), *cacahuates japones* (Japanese-style peanuts), and a six-pack of Tecate to enjoy with them.

Andrea, her girlfriend, and at least forty queer and trans migrants had taken up residence at a nearby home, closer to the main drag in Playas. This communal home rented via Airbnb by US-based organizations such as the Refugee and Immigrant Center for Education and Legal Services (RAICES) was always only intended as a temporary solution to address the urgent need for shelter apart from the caravan. Giving the movement biblical significance, caravans were frequently called *el éxodo* (the Exodus) by the migrating people I met in Tijuana. They describe a relatively new phenomenon in the Americas where people travel en masse to insulate themselves against the extreme narco and state violence that migrants endure as they travel through Mexico.

Colloquially known as a "city of migrants," Tijuana has always experienced migration as an everyday reality, but the phenomenon of the caravan, the choice to move together as a collective, rattled the infrastructure of the state. Most migrants who had come with the caravan were housed in squalid conditions at the Benito Juarez sports stadium near downtown Tijuana, and later moved to a far-flung gymnasium, el Barretal. There migrants lacking even the small amount of money for a bus ride could be kept out of sight of tourists who continued to come, albeit in smaller numbers, in the fall of 2018. This anxiety about the "crisis" at the border fomented antimigrant panics of racialized and sexualized threats to the public. Tijuana's mayor, Juan Manuel Gastélum, declared on the Univision TV program *Al Punto* "los derechos humanos son para los humanos derechos" (human rights are for upright humans). A "Make Tijuana Great Again" t-shirt popped up in a retail window display. A migrant Honduran woman who came to be known as "Lady Frijoles" was deemed *desagradecida* (ungrateful) after being "caught" on camera appearing to refuse a plate of beans. She subsequently received so many vicious death threats she had to leave Tijuana. Austerity narratives of scarcity emerged: the migrants were eating all the food, using all the medicine, and like Lady Frijoles, they were ungrateful, undeserving. I began to hear the phrase "nosotros pedimos; ellos exigen" (we ask, they demand). Passersby hurled epithets at them when they walked the streets, calling them "cochinos" (filthy) and saying "regresan a su país, no nos queremos aquí" (go back to your country; we don't want you here).

Prior to November 2018 migrating peoples across the polygeographies of the Americas had been traveling to and through Tijuana for decades. Over the course of 2015, a large yet staggered Haitian migrant population preceded the thousands from Central America who arrived, all at once, in the caravan. Upon arrival, they were met with already packed *albergues* (migrant shelters) filled with intranational migrants hailing from states such as Guerrero and Michoacán, two of the states experiencing some of the most intense narco and state violence. In November 2018 the arrival of migrant caravans became the primary collective means for making the journey to the Tijuana–San Diego border. After traveling through Mexico from Honduras, El Salvador, and Guatemala, queer and trans migrants were turned away from the few local *albergues* that would accept them. Upon arrival then, they found themselves at heightened risk of violence at times from within the caravan and always on the streets of Tijuana by those looking to take advantage of migrants on the caravan's margins. After having met some of the folks who emerged as guides of the rapidly forming LGBTQ migrant contingency in spring 2018, I learned that *tijuanense* migration activists, particularly from Espacio Migrante, the Comunidad Cultural de Tijuana LGBTI AC (COCUT), and the lesbian/bisexual group Lavanda Colectivo Lésbico Interdisciplinario de Tijuana (CLIT) were dreaming up new solutions. As word of new caravans forming arrived via WhatsApp and Facebook messages in the lead-up to October 2018, these activists came together, across their many differences and disagreements, to prepare for the sizable caravan and the more than eighty LGBTQ migrants that traveled with it. Their solution was to act as an intermediary between US-based nonprofit organizations, local queer solidarities, anarchist collectives such as Enclave Rabia Caracol, and certain migrant guides to find and prepare Airbnb rental homes, particularly in Playas de Tijuana, a twenty-minute car ride from downtown Tijuana where the state shelter was located. While the LGBTQ houses outside downtown Tijuana offered respite and a temporary solution to survive, they were crowded, with many people assigned to a limited number of rooms, and not enough beds to go around. Any modicum of privacy was elusive. It also brought together lesbians and bisexuals, some of whom traveled with children, and gay men, nonbinary folks, trans men, and trans women, some of whom were only just coming to a sense of their gender identity and sexual orientation, and some of whom could not manage the extreme stress of migrating and coming to terms with new gender expressions, identities, vocabularies, and experiences. Suffice it to say, quarrels were frequent.

Andrea was a leader of the LGBTQ caravan contingency who also acted as a guide for the larger caravan on several journeys. I met Andrea in the spring of 2018, when she arrived in Tijuana with a smaller group of LGBTQ migrants, most of whom, or at least the most visible of whom, were trans women, or, as they often prefer to be called, *chicas trans* (trans girls).[8] As a guide, Andrea dedicated her life, alongside others, to the safe passage of migrants to and through Tijuana. In an interview in 2018 in Playas de Tijuana, Andrea explained to me how she had already made several trips to Tijuana and other border towns. She had been arrested, detained for months to years, and deported various times. She vowed that she would never again try to cross and gave up the aspiration to live in the United States. While Andrea's life plan consisted of continuing the journeys through Guatemala, Mexico, and on to Tijuana to pursue either a life in Tijuana or a life in transit, she supported others' wishes to cross the border. She and her closest friend at the time, Lok'tavanej, a genderqueer activist and LGBTQ migrant guide, dreamed of an alternative route, a fantasy really about a boat that would shuttle her Central American queer *familia* out of the Northern Triangle and up to Canada, thus avoiding the violences that she knew awaited migrants in a NAFTA-decimated Mexico.[9] Of course, Andrea knew all too well that racist, anti-poor, and transphobic violence also awaited queer and trans migrants at the border and in the US carceral extension, the migrant detention system.

At Lok'tavanej's request, I invited Andrea to my place for the night where I and my lover at the time could cook a few meals for her and her girlfriend, give them some time alone for eroticism in the spare bedroom, and offer them a quiet place to sleep. In extending this act of friendship, I knew I was engaging in an activity that the Mexican state had recently made criminal. During the spring of 2018, I was invited by a local gay activist to Tijuana's Jornada por la Diversidad Sexual, an annual event of art, performance, and activism that increasingly took up the intersection of migration and queer and trans cultures.[10] Even as he was running the Jornada and working at his government job, he opened his home to seven *chicas trans* for whom shelter was not available, owing to the already overcrowded condition of most *albergues* and the lamentable trans- and homophobia of many of its directors. As one can imagine, hosting so many people in a small and humble home led to several heart-wrenching debacles. It also brought to his attention how the state had decided to criminalize this form of mutual aid. In the wake of the 2012 anti–sex trafficking laws, in which Mexico had only then changed the language from *trata de blancas* (white slave trade) to *trata de personas* (trafficking in persons), Mexican authorities interpreted the 2000 United Nations Protocol to Prevent, Suppress, and Punish Trafficking in Persons, Especially Women and Children (also known as the Palermo Protocol, or the UN TIP Protocol, which defines what constitutes "trafficking") according to their own terms and exigencies (Correa-Cabrera and Sanders Montandon 2018, 8–9). The protocol specifies that the "recruitment, transportation, transfer, harboring or receipt of persons" constitute the acts that must be present for an activity to be considered trafficking. It also specifies, however, that acts alone do not constitute human trafficking, and that the means (e.g., fraud, threat, force, abduction, deception) and the purpose of those acts and means (exploitation) must also be present (9).[11] In Mexico under the 2012 General Law to Prevent, Sanction and Eradicate

Crimes Related to Trafficking in Persons, and inspired by anti–sex work NGOS, the means were eliminated as a necessary component of the definition of trafficking (Correa-Cabrera and Sanders Montandon 2018, 13). Therefore, simply housing migrating people can open oneself to the charge of sex trafficker. It follows that in offering the home I shared with my lover to Andrea and her girlfriend, even for one night, I had become in the eyes of the Mexican state a potential sex trafficker. Anti–sex trafficking law, much like the criminalization of migration in Mexico, a gross infraction of the Mexican constitution that promises safe harbor and a resident visa to any migrant, is a cross-aisle issue, supported by those on the left and the right in all three NAFTA-signing countries. They act in similar ways, blocking the movement of peoples across national and transnational borders, to label legal acts in Mexico—sex work and migration—as criminal activities. It is from this recent phenomenon in Mexico of criminalizing migration that the activist cry "migrar no es un délito" (migration is not a crime) emerges.

At the breakfast table the next morning, Andrea and Cristina sat side-by-side looking at their phones, chatting away gregariously and stealing kisses. The corn tortillas from the farmer's market that lined the *paseo* every Tuesday were fluffy and hot off the *comal*. The salsa was fresh and extra *picante*. I'm sure it deliciously burnt their lips as they pressed them against each other, kissing. As they only had the clothes they came in the night before, I offered them some of mine: Andrea chose a blue-and-white striped dress, and Cristina picked out a purple t-shirt that read LESVY, created to commemorate the life of Lesvy Berlín Osorio, murdered by her boyfriend who strangled her with a telephone cord on the UNAM campus in Mexico City in 2017. The t-shirt was part of a performance by Mónica Mayer, one part of a larger performance installation project produced by Mexican performance artist Lorena Wolffer, Argentinian art historian María Laura Rosa, and me. *Estado de emergencia* (State of emergency) employed Wolffer's theatrical tactic of "public living rooms," where cis and trans women and their allies could gather to pause and rest in public (a revolutionary act for Mexican women, Wolffer argues) and in this instance to create art and conversations around the topic of *feminicidios* to confront the *estado de emergencia* of gender-based violence, torture, and death in Mexico and the Americas that the project was named for (López García, Antivilo, Rosa, and Wolffer 2019). For migrating peoples in the fall of 2018, pausing, resting, and enjoying the outdoors in Playas de Tijuana, especially downtown, became a similarly dangerous activity. In several instances, I was instructed by activists to serve as a chaperone, even for a short jaunt between a pizza parlor and a coffee shop, owing to the constant threat of kidnap, assault, and incarceration.

Dressed and showered, we went out for a morning cigarette. Andrea looked admiringly on as Cristina took a long drag off a yellow American Spirit, my cigarette of choice at the time—folks I shared them with always loved how long they burned. As she exhaled the long plume of smoke, the sound of crashing ocean waves reaching our ears, she sighed and said, "Qué tranquilidad se siente aquí" (It feels so calm here). After the morning smoke and some dawdling in the apartment, we walked a few blocks to the tall stone staircase that led down to the beach. At the edge of Playas, the beach was frequently unpopulated, save for a few locals (running, playing, swimming) and a gaggle of Amish drug tourists who often gathered at the top of the stairs to get a bit of sea air before commencing their search for affordable medicines. You could easily walk down the entire length of the beach, all the way to the wall that extended into the ocean and that seemed to grow higher and higher daily with more barbed wire and floodlights and fencing to sew up every crack and crevice. This part of Playas was more deserted and typically unwatched by police patrolling on ATVs and dressed in head-to-toe black to conceal their identities. We descended the stairs and looked out over the horizon, at the waves that kept rolling onto the shore and the vast stretch of beach that we largely had to ourselves. Along with the beer and snacks, I had brought a sunshade of sorts, one I had always struggled to assemble, especially on a windy day such as this. The four of us struggled to assemble the *pinche* thing, and I remember laughing so hard, telling a little joke that began *cuantas lesbianas necesitas para . . .* (how many lesbians do you need to . . .) in a version of the old light bulb joke that I'm still not sure translated so well into Spanish. But we had drunk a couple of beers, and the sun was shining, and we laughed, in *carcajadas*. We were happy. They were happy, having an uneventful day at the beach getting mildly intoxicated as we sat on the towels I brought and abandoned the ornery, disobedient sunshade. At their request, I took some photos of them looking admiringly at each other and smiling. Cristina posed with her Tecate in hand, her long light-brown hair blowing in the wind as Andrea put her arms around her, resting her head on her shoulder and squeezing her tightly to her.

This wasn't the first time Andrea and I had spent time at the beach. I had met her and Lok'tavanej the previous spring outside the offices of the COCUT where an outdoor concert to close the annual Jornada por la Diversidad Sexual was being held. As we walked together to a nearby bar known to be friendly to queer and trans folk, she told me she was from Honduras, that her lover was still there, that her cousins had been killed there, her brother threatened. This wasn't her first time making the long, arduous journey from Honduras to and through Mexico. In a December 2018 interview, she clarified: "He cruzado tres veces Estados Unidos y las tres veces no he estado libre. Siempre he estado presa" (I've crossed [the border into the] United States three times, and each of those times I was not free. I have always been a prisoner). The first time she was incarcerated in a migrant detention center in Houston. She fought for a month to be granted an asylum case, she said, but she didn't win. The second time she traveled a similar route, entering the United States at Piedras Negras and heading to Houston, just as she did the first time. When *la migra* picked her up, this time they had her photo on file. After a six-month incarceration in a detention center, they returned her to Mexico, and so she found herself in Monterey, Tamaulipas. She tried once again to return to Houston, but "me volvieron agarrar ahí mismo" (they grabbed/arrested me again there). They locked her up in a detention center for two years, and the judge's punishment included an order to not return to the United States for twenty years. May 2018, then, was her first trip as a guide and leader of the LGBTQ migrant contingency. "Entonces decidí cuando yo me vine ahorita de nuevo," she told me, "a de nuevo otra vez volver a cruzar ahorita. En marzo escuché de esta caravana y me gustó el movimiento de la caravana y me he quedado con la caravana y ayudar a las demás personas. Yo necesito ayudar a las demás personas para que las personas con aquel animo vengan en confianza con nosotros [y que] caminen todos juntos" (So I decided when I came up again now . . . to go ahead and cross again this time. In March, I heard about this caravan, and I liked the caravan movement, and I've stuck with the caravan and to help other people. I need to help other people so people with the same spirit put their trust in us and walk all together). Andrea went on to be a primary organizer of the fall 2018 caravan. She traveled in a small group of *chicas trans* the prior spring, and she returned in late October 2018 with a diverse set of queer and trans migrants guided by her migration philosophy, which was always aligned with the caravan and the idea of moving together through Mexico.

A few days after the Jornada, Andrea and I were in touch over WhatsApp. I was again staying in Playas de Tijuana, but this time near the beach wall. I invited her and Lok'tavanej to spend the day at the beach with me. We greeted each other with a kiss on both cheeks as they introduced me to a new friend, a Garifuna man named Brian. As we sunbathed, we discussed the relationship between free-trade capitalism and what Lok'tavanej called *transmigración*. In the lead-up to the arrival of the caravan in the fall, I crossed paths with Lok'tavanej and Andrea in Mexico City, a kind of halfway point in the route from Tapachula to Tijuana. In an interview at the now-closed lesbian transfeminist café and nightlife hub la Gozadera, Lok'tavanej defined *transmigración* as "un juego de palabras" (wordplay) that refers to "la marcha forzosa de un pueblo . . . por que las políticas neo-liberals te han despojado de tus tierras, que te han desalojado de tu casa" and the state's "militarización de esos territorios antes de la privatización" (the forced departure of a town and its people . . . because neoliberal poli-tics have stripped you of your lands, have evicted you from your home [and the state's] militarization of those territories under privatization). Equally, Lok'tavanej explained, *transmigración* refers to a phenomenon in which "la comunidad lgbti está transmigrando. Y las trans migrantes transmigran también" (the LGBTI [lesbian, gay, bisexual, trans, intersex] community is transmigrating. And trans migrants transmigrate too). In our interview, Lok'tavanej went on to say:

> Ahorita estamos en un momento que creó el neoliberalismo, antes el capitalismo creó la migración, pero, ahora, el neoliberalismo, que es la decadencia de todo eso, ha creado la transmigración. Es decir, con políticas neoliberales como estamos despojando ante [tus] tier-ras, tú ya tienes, este, que huir con toda tu comunidad, o con todo tu pueblo, con toda la comunidad LGBTI, por vehículos que hay. Se van juntando, se van portando, y se van migrando allí. Entonces, ese es el momento en que estamos viviendo. Esta marcha crea la transmi-gración, y están muchas comunidades, porque había gente que venía específicamente del Progreso (y todos se conocían, muy joven así), mirando. Otros venían desde la comunidad Garifuna, que se inte-graron, que eran de los que antes se solían pasar por aquí. Entonces, vienen pasando más gente, y más gente, y más familia y más meno-res y, como esta vez en la caravana que se dio en el tren, yo nunca había visto tanta gente. Pero de lo peor es que no están todas. Viene más. Hay muchísima más gente. Pero ¿por qué? Porque eso es lo que provoca la decadencia de, esta decadencia neoliberal, de que no haya para donde de urgencia y sobrevivir es tan grande que no se puede reflexionar en qué hacer. No se ve claramente qué hacer. Entonces, les tienes que hablar de esa posibilidad, porque sí. Y sí hay muchas comunidades, y es de esas comunidades que se viajaba en comuni-dad, y era toda la comunidad transmigrante, y ese momento que se

arropó, que se acuerpó para poder llegar a Estados Unidos ya que agarre conocimiento entre nosotros.

(Right now, we are in a moment neoliberalism created, before capitalism created migration, but now, neoliberalism, which is the decline of all that, has created transmigration. That is to say, with neoliberal policies that dispossess people from their land, you have to flee with your entire community, or with all your people, with the entire LGBTI community, by any means available. They get together, they carry everything with them, and they migrate there. So that's the moment we're living in. This march creates transmigration, and there are many communities, because there were people who came specifically from Progreso [a town in Honduras] (and they all knew each other, very young like that), watching. Others came from the Garifuna community, they joined up, who were among those who used to journey alone through here. Then, more people, and more people, and more families and more kids come and, since this time in the caravan they traveled by train, I had never seen so many people. But the worst thing is that's not all of them. More are coming. There are a lot more people. But why? Because that is what the decline of, this neoliberal decline, causes, that there is nowhere to go in an emergency and the risk to survival is so great that one cannot reflect on what to do. It is not clear what to do. So, you must talk to them about that possibility, because it exists. And yes, there are many communities, and it is from these communities that we all travel together in community, and it was the entire transmigrant community, and that moment that rallied us, that brought us together to be able to reach the United States once all of us learned together.)

Back at the beach, Andrea listened, enraptured by Lok'tavenej, her closest and dearest friend at the time. Sitting beside Lok'tavenej, Brian nodded his agreement as Lok'tavenej eloquently expounded on the relationship between neoliberalism and migration. What they all agreed on was that *transmigración* centered trans lives in a struggle to survive and migrate during NAFTA time. Equally though, *transmigración* referred to migrant collectivity, the desire to travel in the caravan together, in ways that intersected with all kinds of marginalized experiences.[12] Over the years that I was in Tijuana, migrants traveling on the periphery of the caravan, such as Brian, gravitated toward the queer and trans contingent for survival. Motivated by an acutely felt sense of shared precarity, they waited together for their numbers to be called, for the day to end, for the next meal, for the bathroom, for something, anything, that might let them feel free, even if but for a moment.

Brian stood up to remove his shirt, inviting us all to swim. Neither Andrea nor I had suits on, and not wanting to get wet in our underwear, we politely declined. I invited the group to a six-pack of beer, and while Brian and Lok'tavenej swam, Andrea and I took the short walk to the nearest Oxxo. Several mariachi bands competed for people's attention, and the sonic space teemed with Mexican folklore. Vendors sold bright balloons forming the shapes of young children's animated fantasies. Against this backdrop of merriment and festivity, there stood the wall, painted in a collision of collective and individual art projects and covered with so much hope and so much loss. Memorials and remembrances abounded, though painted in the colors of the rainbow, backdropped by a beautiful Baja sea where dolphins swam, at times breaching the waves as they so often did—vast schools of dolphins crossing *la línea*. We passed the Café Indocumentado (the Undocumented Café), a side project of artivist Gaba Cortes and her sisters Michelle and Lupita. The café provides a bird's-eye view of border agent shenanigans, a kind of countersurveillance of the uptick of state repression since the caravan arrived and in preparation for another one rumored to be forming in El Salvador; Café Indocumentado is also a place that gives free coffee to migrants, part-time work to *gente retornadx* (returned people), and the occasional place to sleep without being robbed by the police, kidnapped by narcos, or hurt by antimigrant locals.[13] We walked by the delicious *mariscos* (seafood) restaurants, ice cream shops, and an outdoor amphitheater for performances that lined the beach's main drag. At the Oxxo, we grabbed *chelas* and some Sabritas Limón. As we waited in the checkout line, I stupidly asked Andrea if she and Brian were an item. She stopped me in my tracks, looked straight into my eyes, and with one hand to her heart and another on my shoulder she said emphatically, with gusto and a little saucy offense for being misread as straight, "Yeni [as many like to call me in Mexico], yo soy *lesbiana*." We laughed and linked elbows before walking back with the beers and snacks. After snacking, we all walked along the perimeter of the wall, commenting on the art and memorialization of the dead and disappeared that covers its surface. Lok'tavanej took photos of us as we walked, at one point lying on the ground to take one of myself and Andrea as we looked into each other's eyes, a soft grin on both our mouths, and with the vast expanse of the ever-growing wall behind us. The painted sign behind us, adorned with rainbows and butterflies, read "La poesía es gente con sueños" (Poetry is people with dreams).

Samantha, Marlene, Teresa, and I went out to the parking lot to see what they thought of the donated clothing in the trunk of the car. Hanging back and on the lookout, Lok'tavanej was there too, carrying the six-year-old child Félix, who had made the journey with his guardians, a *chica trans* named Abril and her cis boyfriend, Juan. As I opened the trunk, Marlene, Teresa, and Samantha clasped their hands in front of their chests, waiting to see if any elusive treasures were discoverable within. Most likely, this was the first time in their long journey where they had a chance to choose which clothes they wanted to wear. *Chisme* (gossip) was that the gated and locked depository of donated clothing at the Benito Juarez stadium remained inaccessible to the thousands of people who had arrived in this wave of the caravan. Even when clothes such as those caged at Benito Juarez were given out, they would be apportioned according to the cisgender logic of sex-based distribution. Food and bathroom time were similarly meted out. For these and many other reasons genderqueer, trans, and nonbinary migrants were simply not part of the migrant activist's imaginary. Queer and trans activists who skipped the intermediary (in this case, the Tijuana municipality) sought to allow *las chicas trans* to choose their clothing according to their gender, yes, but also their *gusto* (taste). They wanted to create situations where *chicas trans* might feel a little like rummaging through a consignment store, a store not necessarily created with genderqueer and trans young adults in mind but where one might happen on a few articles of clothing that matched the sartorial style of a fashion-forward making do.

And so, when Samantha found the bra, she couldn't wait another second to put it on. She knew the cop might still be across from Lúmina Foto-Café, a local coffee shop and artists' space owned and operated by queer butch photographer Liliana Hueso. It was a common activity for police to hunt, arrest, and incarcerate all migrants for any perceived infraction, and walking while trans migrant would suffice in Tijuana in November 2018. But in that moment, it didn't matter. As her hands first touched the soft, beige, flesh-colored fabric, she drew it to her, rubbed her face on its silky surface and squealed delightfully. She took off the masculine and now dirt-caked t-shirt she had been wearing, likely for weeks. As she put the first bra strap over her shoulder, I saw her entire face and attitude change. Puckering her lips and breathing in self-assuredly, she went from shy and guarded to flirtatious and gregarious. She gracefully put the second strap over her other shoulder, its beige material contrasting with her medium-brown skin. With just a little wave of her hand, she silently gestured for me to clasp it around her back. "Gracias," she said in a beautiful sing-song voice as she shimmied the worn-down shirt over her now-clasped bra. She smiled as she slid her hands down her breasts, now encased in the bra, and sighed deeply, with relief and with joy.

They became deliciously discriminating as the process went on, a daring performance that breaks with the demanded script of the grateful and deserving migrant. There was just as much excitement as shade thrown, as some of the garments clearly did not meet their standards. Marlene displayed a flowered blouse against her chest to get Samantha's and Teresa's honest opinions. Samantha shook her head, pursing her lips again but for the purpose of saying "no, honey," while Teresa curled her lip in a sassy yet sincere attempt to steer Marlene away from said blouse. After about thirty minutes of play shopping, Lok'tavanej and I became a little nervous; we were being watched intently by people inside the hair salon that flanked the coffee shop in which they and about fifteen other LGBTQ migrants had been hiding in the back, smoking, chatting quietly, biding their time. With their clothing choices wrapped in their arms like precious cargo, Marlene, Samantha, and Teresa started to walk back inside the café, thus leaving me for a moment with Lok'tavanej, for whom I had put aside a flowy, multicolored boho-style skirt that I thought he would love. He handed Félix over to my arms as he slipped the long skirt over his threadbare leggings. He twirled around, his skirt billowing in the ocean breeze and the Baja sunlight. He smiled his thank you as we walked back to the café, to wait for the next move, for a call from someone who could tell them where they would sleep that night.

Many of them still wore the same clothes they had on when the caravan passed through their city or town. Some of them had had the luxury of a bit of advanced notice that the caravan was approaching; others had suddenly been alerted by social media and WhatsApp. Most had to make quick decisions, whether to stay or to go with the caravan. To stay meant ensnarement in the narco state run by US-backed authoritarian regimes. Like Andrea, many of them had family members who had already been threatened, killed, or disappeared.

For some LGBTQ migrants, however, deadly forms of discrimination, rape, and violence could also originate within their families. This reason for migrating is rarely discussed in the rhetoric of immigrant rights activism. As Karma R. Chávez and Hana Masri have shown, the normative rhetoric of the family "dominate[s] the campaigns and demands of the immigrant rights and justice movement" and its "deployment of familial, relational, and respectable norms harms all migrants, particularly those most vulnerable" (2020, 213). The LGBTQ migrant contingency often formed its own circles of kin and community. They depended on each other, not only for resources and protection but also for love, pleasure, touch, and joy. Even so, certain forms of normativity developed in that contingency, and not all LGBTQ migrants faced the same kinds or levels of danger.

"Confinement in motion" is how Martha Balaguera describes the migration experiences of *chicas trans*, even when they aren't physically traveling through space (2018, 643). For *chicas trans*, the pauses in time that make up waiting in Tijuana and along the journey are marked by discrimination, exclusion, misrecognition, and pervasive violence. In the lead-up to finding safe(r) housing for *chicas trans* in Tijuana, one shelter, Caritas, was burned by a transphobic and antimigrant neighbor who placed a bed mattress against the only entrance to the small house and set it ablaze while trans women, children, and a forty-five-day-old infant were trapped inside. The fire was put out by other neighbors who came to their aid and expressed support for the trans migrants who sheltered there. An act such as this, in support of migrants and their right to migrate, represents the norm rather than the aberration in Tijuana, LGBTQ migrant activists consistently stressed to me. Soon after the arson and attempted murder, I visited Caritas with one of these activists, Jorge Luis Villa. The charred door and its frame were still there. The shelter attendant told us that the act had been committed by one family on the block who owns several houses. Upon the arrival of the *chicas trans* to the shelter, the angry neighbors had hurled stones at them, menacingly warning "you are all going to die." This threat of death, however, follows trans women as they cross the border and enter the US detention system, as the death of Roxana Hernández makes clear. Hernández was a Honduran trans woman who arrived in Tijuana with the spring 2018 caravan. She ultimately died in the Cibola detention center in New Mexico, where she was placed in freezing conditions in solitary confinement without essential care such as her HIV medications. This carceral treatment by the US detention system, more an arm of the US prison industrial complex than a safe and humane space of waiting, is common for all *chicas trans* who are often placed in solitary cells, nominally to protect them. In other words, trans women who have undergone great danger and sacrifice to get to the US border meet similar abuse and violence at the intersection of the transphobic and antimigrant carceral system in the United States.

In one of my first group meetings with queer and trans migrants, I visited a pizza parlor with Villa to document what folks most needed now that

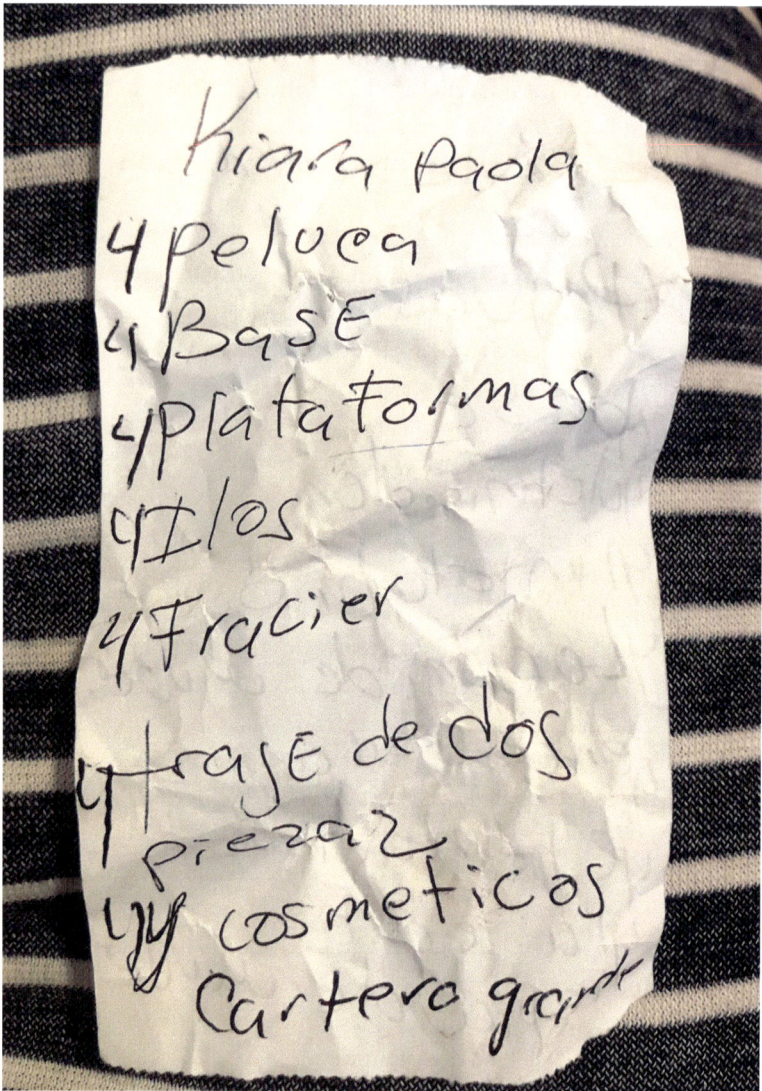

4.2   List of items requested by migrating LGBTQ folks. Photo by author.

they had arrived in Tijuana. Socks were frequently mentioned as were tennis shoes, soap, and shampoo. But so too were wigs and bras, makeup, and high heels, particularly for the *chicas trans* in the group (fig. 4.2). For the butch women, trans masculine, and nonbinary folks among them, tight-fitting sports bras and boxers were high on the list. As we left the pizza parlor, I was instructed to stay close to the group as we traveled back to the Enclave

Rabia Caracol, a coffee shop and community center that had recently become a sanctuary for migrating people to wait and rest. "Walking while migrant" in Tijuana had its own set of dangers. The wearing of *chanclas* (flip-flops) as winter approached constituted a tell-tale sign to the would-be extortionist (the police) and the would-be kidnapper (the narco) of someone's migrant status. Migrant peoples moving to and through Tijuana had become sources of human capital, a locus of global accumulation for a diverse array of state and nonstate entrepreneurs. Walking while trans and/or a visibly queer migrant, however, catapulted the migrant body into an adjacent array of everyday risks. *Chanclas* aside, the beautiful array of queer and gender-nonconforming movements and acts—hips swishing, wrists bending, hair flowing, voices lilting, lips popping, to name just a few—comprise an array of queer traffic gestures at odds with NAFTA time. Tennis shoes, therefore, were not just for comfort; they served to throw off the ocularcentric system of "clocking" trans and migrant bodies by an array of actors who sought to capitalize on their isolation within and outside the caravan.

With scribbled lists of items in hand, I crossed *la línea* in early November to collaborate with a friend in Chula Vista who had devoted her week to corresponding with me and gathering some monies, clothing, and toiletries from sympathetic friends. Collectively, we assumed a small role in the vast network of mutual aid across the Tijuana–San Diego borderlands that the caravan had given rise to. As we sat in her living room, organizing the items and loading them into my trunk, I thought about all of the people I had met thus far and their twin desires not only for basic hygienic goods and clothing that might allow them to circumnavigate the streets of Tijuana but also for the wigs, high heels, and makeup that would allow them to be themselves if and when they gained access to the house they were hoping to take up in Playas de Tijuana. I thought about the tension between the movement of the goods and materials needed to feed, house, clothe, and provide comfort and the immobility of those waiting for them. Administrative law and its tentacles at the Tijuana–San Diego border had not yet declared transporting goods in large volume inadmissible. In mere weeks, however, that situation would change. Soon after I made the crossing, another friend of mine crossed *la línea* at the San Ysidro–Puerta México point of entry with a car full of needed items. She recounted that she had been stopped by Mexican border control at the typically unoccupied checkpoint, where her car was x-rayed, part of an ongoing effort to control crossborder networks of care. Giving anything to migrants, of any sort, had become an illicit act, a form of queer traffic.

Owing to my timing, just a few weeks before armed Mexican border agents began to occupy a formerly crewless border crossing at San Ysidro, and always aided by my white skin, I cruised through the gates, unchecked, and rode into Playas de Tijuana, where Andrea and Lok'tavanej's group were to have occupied a home rented with monies partially coming in from RAICES. When I arrived in Playas, Andrea texted me that some neighbors who were opposed to living near a migrant shelter had prevented her group from entering the home. Unable to remain on the streets without being picked up by police, they traveled on foot to Lúmina Foto-Café, where I now briefly return in my story. As I parked my car, which was loaded up with supplies and clothing, I noticed the police car across the street. I entered the small café, a spot I had visited many times before. The baristas instructed me to go to the back where at least fifteen people were packed into the small open-air space where they could smoke and wait. After sharing the news about my cargo and seeing that the police car had since left, a small group of four or five people accompanied me to the car to see what might appeal to them.

Weeks later, and now installed into the LGBTQ migrant house in a quiet Playas neighborhood, I got to see the ingenious ways with which they transformed the hit-or-miss donated garments to create fierce and fabulous fashion ensembles. They held beauty contests, walked fantasy runways, and mimicked the interviews that awaited them once their numbers were called by humorously practicing the roles of both migrant and *migra*. Many of these games were recorded on phones and sent around among the group to parody the interminable waiting process. More so than any other practice of pleasure, however, it was the Garifuna song and dance form *punta* that held pride of place. *Punta*, the music and the moves, became one of the primary tools for creating queer and trans migrant nightlife at the LGBTQ safe houses.

One particular night stands out in my memory. In late December 2018, a few local activists and I arrived early to the safe house to prepare for a party celebrating the birthdays of four LGBTQ inhabitants; with a possible attendance of fifty people, that meant seventeen roasted chickens and four large birthday cakes. We delivered the chickens and all the fixings, the tortillas, the pasta salads, the chilis and onions to one of the main kitchens, and they set it up according to their liking. Andrea descended the spiral staircase, her hair beautifully braided by Héctor, another roommate in the LGBTQ house. Her excitement and happiness were palpable. It was her twenty-ninth birthday, and she had spent the large majority of 2018 guiding LGBTQ migrants through Mexico. Now she waited alongside them. And on this night, they worked that wait out on the dance floor.

"Yennifer! Ven pa'ca! Te enseño" (Jennifer, Come here! I'll teach you), said Andrea in seductive play as she grabbed my hands, leading me off the couch and onto the makeshift dance floor. With just a little bit of music, and the hard-won conviviality cultivated at the house, they had completely transformed the space into a *punta rock* club. "Que bélica bailes, Yeni" (How amazing you dance, Jenny), Auriel, another queer migrant friend, said with a wink and a little sarcasm in his tone as I was struggling to learn the fast-paced, double-meter ostinato, hip- and butt-centric moves of this highly sexualized version of *punta*. Andrea was lured away by the shuffling feet of another *punta*-dancing admirer, while Auriel took my hands, saying "Miráme" (Watch me). He moved his hips swiftly side-to-side, all the while keeping his upper body motionless and upright, thus enabling his hip and buttocks movements to be small and super tight, a kind of micro-twerk (Pérez 2016) that depended just as much on the subtle shuffle of the feet as it did on the stasis of the upper body. Feeling a little bit like *Dirty Dancing*'s Baby (but maybe I should have been left in a corner), Auriel, my fabulous queer Patrick Swayze, put his hands on my hips and rocked me, back and forth, up and down, until I started to get the rhythm and could move a bit faster. "Cheque!" (All right!), he exclaimed in approval, while everyone around us, even the wallflowers of the group, peeled away from their voyeuristic posts to enter the coquettish choreography. Everyone was dressed in their finest donated clothing in the most stylish and inventive outfit combinations. Hips swaying, eyes alluring, shoulders seducing, and lips puckering, sexual energy filled the space and invited all to partake in the overflow of deep play in this utterly queer and trans iteration of perhaps the most well-known and widely circulating diasporic cultural practice of the Afro-Indigenous, Afro-Latinx Garinagu, the Garifuna music genre and dance tradition *punta*.[14]

Dancing *punta* arose as the frequently enacted practice for summoning pleasure while waiting in the Mexico-US borderlands. Derived from the Bantu term *bunda* (Meléndez as cited in E. Pérez 2016, 8), and often translated to mean "buttocks," in Spanish *punta* literally means "point." The dance celebrates the movement of the buttocks, while the tips of the toes shift rapidly from place to place, a fitting metaphor for migration. The hips sway, emulating desire or, in the dance's more energetic forms, penetrative sex. Traditionally, the dance has an "opposite sex" logic and was meant to simulate a hen/cock mating ritual (Greene 2002, 190) based in choreographic skill and competition. *Punta* is a song and dance form that is both a symbol of the struggle felt by the Garinagu peoples and a performance of resistance and endurance. It has been and continues to be used as a festive mode for surviving and thriving amid the structural violences experienced by the Garinagu not only by way of tourism and colonialism but also by the racial prejudices of their fellow Hondurans.[15] Sex and desire, pleasure and intimacy, expressed through dance is a primary element of this antidote. It is not merely a mode for passing the time of struggle, but a way of wresting power from the temporality of domination. As Deborah R. Vargas argues, music's "rhythmic tempo, lyrical melody, and instrumental sound can speed up time" (2013, 57). Moving to it can also be a mode to slow down time, a way to savor the moments that reorganize the hustle of labor and life under neoliberal capitalism. "The practice of slowness," as Kemi Adeyemi calls it, places "pleasure as *the* currency" and values "microgestures of dissent and reformation that communities of color, and black communities in particular, have long practiced" (2019, 548).[16] The movements that make up dancing *punta* constitute a set of microgestures that LGBTQ migrants employ to simultaneously speed up and slow down the market tempos of free-trade capitalism during NAFTA time.

Dancing *punta* on NAFTA time is a durational performance enacted to derive pleasure, sensuality, and eroticism from collective movement amid great violence and precarity. Queer and trans subjects who dare to dance in/on NAFTA time bend that time, disordering it even as these playful practices make clear how normative and reproductive temporalities can govern the logic of migration and immigrant activism. While the party atmosphere describes one moment of queer nightlife performed at the LGBTQ migrant safe house, dancing *punta* occurred everywhere and at any time. I was *punta*-ed, if you will, several times while waiting in the queue at the grocery store, or on the beach when a certain song was heard or played on a cellphone. Nearly every time I ran into migrant acquaintances and friends in Playas, they would entice me to the LGBTQ house with the promise of teaching me how to dance *punta*. While several innovative games and pastimes were invented to pass NAFTA time, dancing *punta* most crystallized moments of solidarity. Expressions of desire, love, laughter, and playfulness on the makeshift dance floor could melt away some of the fights and disagreements that would inevitably occur in these crowded houses.

While most LGBTQ migrants were staying in separate homes, away from the state and city shelters, venturing outside was either strictly prohibited (depending on which house; different houses varied widely in their rules and regulations) or carefully choreographed and kept to a minimum. Migrating peoples, especially when their sexual and gender dissidence made them more visible, were frequently picked up by the cops, assaulted, robbed, and in some heartbreaking instances, disappeared. Inside, *las lesbianas, los gays, las chicas trans, la gente no binarix, y los hombres trans* hailed from across the polygeographies of Honduras, El Salvador, and Guatemala but came to be called in racist rhetoric as all "Hondureños." Inside the houses, then, LGBTQ migrants waged their own battles for space, for food, for water, for attention, for money, for aid of any kind from any of the many nonprofits, lawyers, and random activists who would show up and wander around the houses. Sometimes rules were attached to the aid, sometimes not. Still, being watched and judged as a deserving asylum petitioner was something they needed to perform, even in the queer/trans houses. Drinking, sexual activity, sex work, smoking weed, sometimes even leaving the house at all could be prohibited activities depending on the safe house in question. It is precisely in this context where *punta* arose to break the tedium and boredom, the surveillance, and the terror of NAFTA time. Dancing *punta* on NAFTA time became a site of respite and a way of letting off steam of an erotic variety that could lead to a sexual interlude or that could satiate, at least for a moment, the desire to be touched and the need for embodied connection and closeness.

Punta, the dance and the music, describes one form of Black diasporic cultural expression that is readily practiced, albeit sometimes subsumed, by mestiza Honduran migrants as their own. Paul Joseph López Oro calls for "Garifunizando" (or garifunizing) the politics of racial formation in the Americas and puts pressure on the concept of *mestizaje* for its violent erasure of what he names the "hemispheric entanglement of Blackness/Indigeneity/AfroLatinidad" (2020, 1). Garifuna cultural forms such as *punta* dislodge mestiza bodies from a category of knowledge about who and what belongs to Central American histories of transmigration. A largely mestiza LGBTQ migrant dancing *punta* while waiting on NAFTA time is, I propose, one context for imagining this hemispheric entanglement of Garinagu, Black, Indigenous, and Afro-Latinx belonging to the polygeographies of Central American and Caribbean people and cultures. Even as anti-Blackness can circulate readily among mestiza migrant populations, I want to open space for dancing *punta* as a performance of "ethnoracial intimacies in Blacktino performance" (Johnson and Rivera-Servera 2016, 1), one that keeps the cultural memory of the Garifuna culture present in and through embodied moments of queer migrant pleasures. Garinagu people, for example, Brian, gravitated for a short period of time toward the LGBTQ group, but to my knowledge no migrating Garifuna person ever stayed long in the largely mestiza Honduran, Guatemalan, and El Salvadoran LGBTQ houses. The presence of Garinagu people within migratory routes, therefore, was rarely inscribed in and through their bodies but rather through dancing *punta* in their absence—an erasure of the Garifuna migrant subject whose dance and music travel with greater ease than the bodies of those to whom it belongs. Following Rivera-Servera's scholarship on dancing *perreo* in Puerto Rico, *punta* not only reveals "the blackness of *Latinidad*" but also the potential (if not the promise) of a "serious engagement with black aesthetics, and potentially, the politics of the genre" (2016, 97). As a form of queer traffic, dancing *punta* on NAFTA time reorganizes that temporality to simultaneously bring close the plights of the Garinagu while also disidentifying with the heteronormative logic of the dance itself. *Punta* offers a portal into the ethnoracial intimacies that could emerge from the shared condition in Honduras that free-trade capitalism precipitated and across the varied scales of risk that people experience while migrating.

Less discussed are the migration tactics of the Garinagu, whose lands have been stolen through a process of deterritorialization that marks their land as "open for business," particularly to tourists and eco-pleasure seekers who, wittingly or unwittingly, participate in neoliberal environmental governance. In *Land Grab: Green Neoliberalism, Gender, and Garifuna Resistance*, Keri Vacanti Brondo focuses on two forms of green neoliberalism: "(1) neoliberal agrarian legislation and (2) neoliberal conservation policies—and their relationship to tourism development and power" (2013, 10). Brondo discusses how the World Bank, the Inter-American Development Bank, and the IMF seized on tourism as the primary mode for managing the country's debt. Afro-Indigenous, Black, and Afro-Latinx populations are also "on the front lines of vulnerability to climate change given that villages are particularly susceptible to land loss and tropical storm surges."[17] These storm surges, the loss of communal land to powerful interest groups that formed after the decline of the banana industry in the 1990s, restrictions on women's rights, murders and attacks against water and land protectors and Indigenous activists (e.g., Berta Cáceres), and the emphasis on new export products have given Afro-Indigenous and Afro-Latinx populations no choice but to join the caravans.

In these caravans, they are outsiders, and at home in Honduras, they have been largely excluded from Honduran national racial-ethnic identity. While the Garinagu organized themselves into an Afro-Honduran autochthonous people between the 1950s and 1980s, Honduras joined the free-trade capitalism bandwagon in the 1980s, further marginalizing this group from national recognition. From this wreckage, however, emerged the beginnings of what would become an Afro-Indigenous identity (Brondo 2013, 14), in a country where Blackness has been historically viewed as a threat to the country's racial purity. While Afro-Mexicans, Afro-descendants, and members of the Black population in Mexico were only included in the national census in 2020, the Garinagu became legible as a formally recognized ethnicity in the 1990s during the shift to neoliberalism and multiculturalism (Anderson 2009, 24).[18] It was also in the 1990s that *punta*, and its offshoot *punta rock*, rose to popularity and acted as a bridge, though admittedly not a sufficient one, between Honduran mestiza and Afro-Indigenous Hondurans. Garifuna language, dance, and music were officially recognized as a form of "Intangible Cultural Heritage of Humanity" in 2001, a mixed blessing that has further entrenched the vision of international finance institutions to draw ecotourism, culture tourism, and research tourism to Garifuna land.

The marginalization and erasure of the Garinagu people both at home in Honduras and in transit across the Mexican borderlands match the silence around *punta* as an Afro-Indigenous and Afro-Latinx dance form and choreography at the LGBTQ migrant safe houses. In the anthology *Queer Nightlife*, coeditors Kemi Adeyemi, Kareem Khubchandani, and Ramón H. Rivera-Servera make clear that queer nightlife is not necessarily a utopian space and can participate in alienation and exclusion, while they also acknowledge that "even paltry permissions for pleasure have expansive and long-lasting possibilities" (2021, 9). In one sense, then, the frequent *punta* dancing that set in motion the queer and trans nightlife experience at the LGBTQ migrant house connected the bodies of mestiza Hondurans to the Afro-Indigenous identity of the Garifuna and the Black aesthetics of *punta*. For most queer nightlife-goers, however, there is a "before" and an "after," an outside and "inside" to the club. Considering the relative absence of Garinagu peoples in these LGBTQ migrant houses and the fact that many LGBTQ migrants, for most of their interminable wait on NAFTA time, could not freely leave the house for fear of being harmed by a variety of actors, migrant queer nightlife demands a different kind of lens. The space of the "club" can double as a carceral site, a club with no "closing time" (Vogel 2009, 104–131). Dancing *punta* on NAFTA time certainly constitutes a "shudder out of time," as Diane Ackerman describes what deep play does (2000, 26), but it could also be read as reveling in the migration of Black aesthetics but not necessarily the desires and dreams of Black and Indigenous peoples. Yet, experiencing pleasure on NAFTA time recontextualizes the extreme forms of racism all migrants encountered when certain portions of *tijuanense* society charged the mestiza Honduran body with some of the same derogatory language used to demonize Blackness, particularly the previous influx of Haitian migrants to Tijuana in 2015. The presence of Hondurans, viewed as a different, darker, and more incalcitrant race, disrupts Mexican purity, much like Afro-Indigenous peoples disrupt the mestiza purity of the Honduran patrimony. "Honduras" thus became a racialized moniker spread over a vast number of mestiza migrant populations wherein the state applied an already honed language of anti-Blackness and anti-Indigenous rhetoric to prevent the movement of these bodies not only toward the border but also toward aid, care, compassion, recognition, safety, and, yes, sexual pleasure and gender freedom.

The migration of LGBTQ peoples to and through the Americas exceeds the bounds of what I've been calling NAFTA time. It wasn't until 2018, however, that queer and trans migrants were acknowledged as such, an accounting that converted them into a form of queer traffic that was regarded as too obscene, too excessive, too needy to coexist with the other migrating peoples at the already-overcrowded shelters. The queer traffic of sexual and gender dissidents is indeed a form of "sexilio" (Mogrovejo 2015), a "pathway of desire" (Carrillo 2017), but not always one infused with the hope or the goal of a "better life." Dancing *punta* on NAFTA time, like all forms of deep play, is not necessarily a heroic political act, but it is a dissident one that disorders the violent contexts of waiting. *Punta* served as an attainable vehicle for the enactment of queer nightlife and an act of deviance performed in irreverent mockery of NAFTA time. It is one of many in which migrants use dance and play to steal some modicum of control over the terms of their waiting. These tools disorganize the temporality of neoliberal formations that determine how (sexual) lives are structured and experienced.

It was my intention in this chapter to provide a radical recontextualization for what I call NAFTA time, a temporality that is specific to Mexico but that has reverberations throughout the polygeographies of the Americas and particularly in relation to Central America. Moments of play and pleasure may seem small, but they are practices of freedom that unsettle and disorganize NAFTA as a hegemonic framework for organizing the temporality of migrant experience. In so doing, NAFTA and its far-reaching influences, its seemingly quiet but all-pervasive ripples, get broken up, revealing the fissures that queer traffickers can use to uncover NAFTA as the precarious, unstable, and paranoid project it always was and always will be.

NAFTA's Funeral

Estamos celebrando la muerte de NAFTA. Porque NAFTA se murío. L'ALENA, el TLCAN, se murío. Y ahora nos quedamos con nuevos acuerdos. CUSMA. . . . No sé que. [We are celebrating the death of NAFTA. Because NAFTA has died. The ALENA (L'Accord de libre-échange nord-américain), the TLCAN (el Tratado de Libre Comercio) has died. And now we are left with new agreements. CUSMA. . . . I don't know what.]

So this is like a funeral/birthday party, and actually you can just get out of your seats and go to the bar right now, 'cause this show is over! There's nothing to see here. It's all the same shit.

So announced Montréal-based transdisciplinary artist Alexis O'Hara in *NAFTAlina: The Musical*, billed as "a chronicle of a 25-year-old love triangle," a one-off performance collaboration between O'Hara and Canadian performance duo 2boys.tv (Stephen Lawson and Aaron Pollard) and Mexico City–based artist Richard Moszka. *NAFTAlina* was performed at the Transnocheo cabaret performance of the 2019 Hemispheric Institute of Performance and Politics Encuentro in Mexico City. On the stage at el Vicio, a famous venue for cabaret theater and performance, their combined vocal improvisations, musical and sound interventions, theatrical actions, and video created a funeral/birthday party to memorialize what was presented to us as the death of NAFTA (ALENA in French; TLCAN in Spanish) and the birth of NAFTA 2.0. While the original NAFTA summoned the imaginary community of "North America" into being, the renaming of NAFTA 2.0 by each nation pried apart this always fictive communion into distinct yet related agreements: the USMCA, T-MEC (Tratado de México, Estados Unidos, y Canada), and for Canada, the CUSMA. The facade of liberal collectivity and transnational friendship fell away under the 2018 negotiations of the new NAFTA, and these new acronyms, with each nation-state putting its name first in the free-trade trio, signals the rhetorical abandonment of "North America" as an organizing economic bloc. O'Hara's address exposes this move and announces the zombielike return of the old NAFTA as the same old shit.[1]

Continuing the use of BDSM aesthetics that we've thus far seen in the previous three deviations, in *NAFTAlina* Moszka wears a full rubber fetish suit to stage the kink persona of the "gimp." (fig. 4a.1). Throughout the performance, he makes long phallic balloon sculptures to portray a kind of "nightmare children's birthday clown," Stephen Lawson told me in an email in 2020. Indeed, in the popular imaginary, gimps are often made to personify submissive yet threatening and inexplicable monsters. Widely depicted across a variety of media, perhaps most memorably in Quentin Tarantino's 1994 film *Pulp Fiction*, "the gimp's mediation in popular culture," writes Gary Needham about sadomasochistic (SM) fashion, "invokes a sinister and debasing spectacle . . . the total body coverage of an assumed sexual expression of terror and submission to torture" (2018, 151). That is, gimps come to stand for a literal interpretation of master/slave dynamics rather than a consensual relationship to dominance and submission. The fashion industry has taken up this tension between these two converging and diverging registers of non/consent to repurpose bondage suits as worn by gimps for haute couture. It often does so in ways that crisscross the goals of capital gain and subversive glamour. Celebrities such as Kim Kardashian and Cardi B. donned gimplike attire, doing so perhaps in refusal of paparazzi surveillance. The former creative director of the fashion house VETEMENTS, Demna Gvasalia, employed the gimp look in a runway show to represent his experience as a refugee who fled his native Georgia during the Russian invasion in 1993.[2] When Moszka appears in the head-to-toe bondage suit, he signals these fashion histories, their profitable success on the runway, and their queer possibilities even as the figure of the gimp, when attached to kink desires and sexuality, continues to be pathologized.

For those who identify or play as gimp, particularly from a queer and crip position in kink communities, "leather gimp" can be a playful identification

4a.1　*NAFTAlina: The Musical*, 2boys.tv with Alexis O'Hara and Richard Moszka, 2019. Photo by the Hemispheric Institute of Performance and Politics at New York University.

that, as I've argued elsewhere (2014), revalues and resignifies disability by employing an unfamiliar sense of leather-self that is nonetheless intelligible to the leather community's sexual interests in power exchange, role-play, and the inventive use of props. In *NAFTAlina*, which refers to the FTA but is also the Spanish word for mothballs, Moszka's gimp persona represents all these potential interpretations and acts as a kind of trickster who, alongside his performance collaborators, unveils the moldy stench of free-trade capitalism. The inclusion of the gimp in *NAFTAlina* thus performs the lack of mobility afforded to disreputable subjects under free-trade ideology, even as it holds space for the gimp to derive pleasure from subjection, abjection, sensory deprivation, and the concealment of identity.

As Moszka's gimp inflates balloons, Aaron Pollard, Lawson's performance partner in the Canadian duo 2boys.tv, plays ukulele in front of a video that opens with hands touching and caressing until it slowly pans out to reveal Donald Trump, Enrique Peña Nieto, and Justin Trudeau at a 2018 ceremony to sign the USMCA/CUSMA/T-MEC. The slow motion of the video reveals the expressions of disdain these leaders felt toward each other, reactions

NAFTAlina: The Musical, 2boys.tv with Alexis O'Hara and Richard Moszka, 2019. Photo by the Hemispheric Institute of Performance and Politics at New York University.

that could go undetected at normal viewing speed. Pollard plucks away, singing, "Tú pareces tanto a mí / Que no puedas engañarme" (You look so much like me / You can't deceive me). Exposing the ruse of the purported NAFTA love triangle, he sings, "Ya no quiero más problemas con tu amor" (I don't want any more problems with your love). Meanwhile O'Hara inflates a large white balloon already filled with *naftalinas* (mothballs) (fig. 4a.2). This balloon is launched into the audience, bouncing above the heads of the crowd until it eventually bursts and showers the audience with the acrid, opaque, and crystal-like balls. The final video portion of the performance screens the names of the thirteen richest billionaires in each of the NAFTA countries as a backdrop, a veritable list of what I called in the introduction "NAFTA's winners." "Why do you need so much money?" O'Hara languidly groans, evoking the synthetic eroticism of money and power that free trade secures for the already monied and powerful.

In the late 1980s and early 1990s, in the lead-up to the signing of NAFTA, free trade required a rhetoric of seduction to woo North American publics into the modern light of free trade. Normative sexual speak played a crucial role in this seduction. Beginning in 2018, media accounts touted the dangers of "pulling out" of NAFTA. These reports reassured us that the tariff battles occurred "all in the family," but also warned that the "honeymoon" between Trump and Mexico's president, Andres Manuel López Obrador, would not last. Media pundits suggested that "separate bedrooms" might be a better solution than a "NAFTA divorce." In describing the debates that ensued around free trade using heteronormative language, these rhetorical metaphors, like the performance *NAFTAlina*, reveal how the production of desire is at the very heart of free-trade capitalism.

Behind the scenes, and conspicuously leaving Canada out of the picture, the Mexico-US Business Committee (MEXUS) archives housed at the Benson Latin American Collection contain countless letters written between state and corporate leaders in the United States and Mexico that profess devotion in the lead-up to NAFTA. The goal was to attract one another back to the deal. These letters are laced with fond and affectionate memories of delicious meals shared and friendly jokes between men. These epistolary seductions of transnational friendship covered over the power inequalities of the nations who came to the table to signal a kind of gentleman's agreement between the state, multinational corporations, and the transnational capitalist class. "Although it has been years since you and I have sat down to talk about the United States and Mexico," Guy Feliz Erb, the former deputy director of the International Development Cooperation Agency, wrote to Councilman Richard Alatorre of Los Angeles in 1993, "I still remember our conversations and, in particular, our dinner in Los Angeles with pleasure." This letter is one example of many whose delivery verges on the romantic with the goal of enticing the recipient to vote in favor of NAFTA, a move that, Erb claims, "will determine the direction for the next decade or more of US trade and economic policy."[3] Also from the MEXUS collection, a cartoon embedded within an article celebrating the six-month "birthday" of NAFTA in an August 1, 1994, issue of the right-wing magazine *National Review* visualizes these capitalist bromances (fig. 4a.3). Alongside copy lampooning Ross Perot's opposition to NAFTA and his infamous phrase the "giant sucking sound" (his prediction that NAFTA would "suck" US jobs south), the cartoon depicts a group of five businessmen bearing gifts and a bouquet of flowers with a caption that reads, "Looks like an amicable takeover." In contrast, for the NAFTA 2.0 negotiations in 2018, the popular news

"Looks like an amicable takeover."

4a.3   "Looks Like an Amicable Takeover" cartoon, *National Review*, August 1, 1994. Mexico-US Business Committee Archives, Benson Latin American Collection, LLILAS Latin American Studies and Collections, University of Texas at Austin.

press concentrated on debates waged between USTR Robert E. Lighthizer and Canada's trade representative Chrystia Freeland, relegating Mexico's NAFTA 2.0 representative, Ildefonso Guajardo Villarreal, to the sidelines. Under the administration of López Obrador, who as a presidential candidate spoke out strongly against NAFTA, Mexico acquiesced to NAFTA 2.0 without struggle. By 2018, the Mexican state had come to regard free trade with the United States and Canada less as a "marriage of convenience" and more like a necessary and inescapable evil.[4]

On July 17, 2017, the Office of the USTR publicly released the document entitled "Summary of Objectives of the NAFTA Renegotiation."[5] Reading more like a rhetorical continuation of Trump's 2016 campaign trail speeches, especially in its preoccupation with the so-called unfair trade practices that have hurt "American workers" and its harnessing of antiglobalization speech as a vehicle to stoke white working-class rage, the seventeen-page document begins by applauding Trump for immediately addressing his campaign promise to "the American people." Namely, Trump will renegotiate NAFTA for the working-class American (meaning the white working class) or take the United States out of the agreement altogether.[6] In keeping with the rhetorical opacity of Trump's speech, Lighthizer hailed the summary as a historic and unprecedented first step "to ensure truly fair trade by seeking the highest standards covering the *broadest* possible range of goods and services" (2017, 3).

"The New NAFTA," as the document calls it, "will promote a market system that functions more efficiently, leading to reciprocal and balanced trade among the parties" through the lifting of what Lighthizer refers to as "expeditiously unwarranted barriers" such as "unfair subsidies, market-distorting practices by state owned enterprises, and burdensome restrictions of intellectual property."[7] This summary reveals the new NAFTA as no such thing: the new NAFTA differs from the old NAFTA only in the sense that the veil of trinational friendship falls away from the language of the document to uncover the plan to implement and enforce an agreement designed to benefit the United States, and by that I mean already wealthy and powerful stakeholders and foreign investors. Unlike the 1990s version, the new NAFTA rationalizes this benefit through the imposition of US legal principles on Canada and Mexico and removes important measures like the NAFTA global safeguard exclusion, which had previously protected Canada and Mexico from US-based decisions to impose broad barriers, as in tariffs or quotas, in the name of helping any US industry deemed to be "seriously injured." Near the close of the document, one line stood out, especially for this queer theorist's eye. Under "Maintain broad exceptions for government procurement regarding," the list includes "Protecting human, animal, or plant life or health" (a bogus inclusion as Trump rolled back more than one hundred environmental protections during his first term) alongside the more expected "National security" and "Protecting intellectual property," and finally the continuation of "Measures necessary to protect public morals, order, or safety."

There is a long history to what is called "the public morals exception," which appears in Article XX(a) of the General Agreement on Tariffs and Trade (GATT).[8] International law scholar Mark Wu explains that, in 1945 and during the early days of drafting the GATT, the United States first proposed "the idea of allowing countries to restrict trade on moral grounds"

(2008, 218). In every subsequent draft of the GATT, which served as a defining case for the WTO, NAFTA, and other trade-related policy documents, the exception clause remains. The US State Department argued that the retention of the moral exception was necessary "for moral or humanitarian reasons or to suppress improper traffic relate inter alia to intoxicating liquors, smoking opium and narcotic drugs, lottery tickets, obscene and immoral articles, counterfeits, pictorial representations of prize fights and the plumage of certain birds" (Charnovitz 1998, 9). The lack of a definite meaning assigned to "public morals" and the vagueness of the language of the article is not coincidental: This indeterminacy intentionally creates a highly portable and flexible means for adopting or enforcing trade restrictions on "improper traffic." Indeed, as Wu states, "Despite the fact that its scope and meaning remained unarticulated, both policymakers and activists continued to look to the exception to justify the legality of certain acts" (2008, 219). As I hope I have demonstrated throughout this book, a queer traffic perspective illuminates that "public morals" were used liberally during NAFTA time and across the polygeographies of the Mexico-Canada-US borderlands to stop, block, and criminalize flows that failed to harmonize with normative sexual values. Sex was/is a primary target for these activities earmarked to prohibit all kinds of people and things considered unassimilable and undesirable to the accumulation of capital while remaining ripe for the money-making ventures of the surveillance state and the policing infrastructures of free trade. The new NAFTA of 2020, as Alexis O'Hara so rightly phrased it, is "all the same shit."

Just like the social performances, visual art, film, direct action, archival materials, and community encounters I've shared throughout this book, *NAFTAlina: The Musical* communicates an unequivocal *desacuerdo* (disagreement) with NAFTA. Ending with a performance that incorporates the gimp seems an apt place to close *Queer Traffic*. A figure circulated for capital gain through the art market, the fashion industry, and the nightmares of the popular media imaginary, the gimp shows how sexual outlaws can be extracted from their nonnormative sex and fetish practices and funneled toward the fantasy of free trade. Despite the temporary market appeal, the gimp retains the status of inexplicable freak whose concealed identity in an age of hypersurveillance menaces the normativity of vanilla trade. He, she, they reconfigure the panic and disgust thrust upon their sexual persona to willingly engage this abject state for something else, an exchange of power, pleasure, and pain seemingly at the whim of the top in carefully choreographed scenes with a set beginning and a definite end. The gimp does so in a context of play that the bottom partially controls, either through previous negotiations or in the moment when the top deigns to unzip an earhole, a mouth hole, or an eyehole on the bondage suit to check in, to see if the limits of the bottom's capacity to take more have been met.

In playing with power, eroticizing the pain and the loss free trade dumps on the bodies of sexual outlaws, *NAFTAlina*'s gimp exemplifies what it means to enact bottomhood under free-trade capitalism. This is where the work of queer traffic lives, in a hiccup of unexpected yet intentionally sought pleasure that interrupts business as usual. It's more than just a fuck you to the state, to the peddlers of sex panics, to the subnational and crossborder censors, and the transnational capitalist class. Rather, it's an unsigned memo that reads: you've got it all wrong.

Epilogue

WHY QUEER TRAFFIC(K) NOW?

Using free trade, and in particular NAFTA as a pivot point, this book has sought to root out and refuse erotophobic modes of thought and the use of panic to target, demonize, and impede the movement of people and things that don't align with the normative values of late racial capitalism. Queer traffic is my humble offering for thinking sexual culture on the move and describes that which cannot (or refuses to) be harmonized within the fantasy of free trade. It points toward a set of objects, actions, and tactics that sensually communicate the texture, tone, and touch of sex as it transits across borders and the highly solidified ideological boundaries of hetero-, cis-, and homonormativities. Queer traffic is also a method for tracking how suspicion, surveillance, and violence disproportionately bear down on the embodied performances of minoritized sexual subjects considered dissident or deviant to the infrastructural logic of free-market flows.

Trafficking discourses and their legal and social applications mark a crucial arena in which we can see this logic play out. A theory on queer traffic pushes back against the ever-proliferating use of trafficking as a mode for describing labor exploitation, and it looks to the uses and abuses of the term "sex trafficking" as a quintessential example of this legal and social apparatus. My intention in proposing queer traffic as a pro-sex rejection of "trafficking" is to encourage the left to abandon this term. The social justice value of the word has been evacuated. Instead, it's now used to criminalize almost any form of movement across borders, as another weapon in the arsenal of the carceral surveillance state. I want the concept of queer traffic to inspire us to give pause in every invocation of "trafficking."

Since I started writing this book, the use of "trafficking" has only expanded as a carceral strategy. I write today from a post–*Roe v. Wade* world in which abortion, in medical and pharmaceutical forms, is increasingly criminalized. In March 2023, the Idaho State Legislature passed a bill that coined the term "abortion trafficking," in an attempt to punish adults helping those under eighteen who seek an abortion in another state or through medication. While a US District Court temporarily blocked Idaho's law, the phrase "abortion trafficking" has been copied in other such bills in states like Oklahoma, where "trafficking" in abortion pills now is a felony that can land someone ten years in prison and a potential fine of $100,000. Conservative lawmakers are quickly working on a copycat "abortion trafficking" bill in Tennessee, and in Texas, certain jurisdictions have used trafficking as a designation to criminalize anyone transporting a person seeking an abortion on certain local roads. Although how these new trafficking ordinances and laws will be enforced remains unclear, they still generate fear for those in need of medical care, effectively criminalizing the movement of people and goods.

These kinds of laws open a wide array of opportunities for politicians to experiment with new forms of surveillance to catch those violating what are now considered trafficking laws. The targeting of trans and trans-allied community networks equates the circulation of gender-affirming care across state lines with drug smuggling and creates contexts of dread, especially for the trans youth and their families living in one of the many US states that have passed laws or policies banning trans health care.[1] Abortion activist organizations in Mexico feel compelled to conceal their delivery and shipping methods as anti-abortion forces in the United States call for increased enforcement against sending Misoprostol through the international mail. Rerouting state monies away from long-funded issues, such as HIV, to focus instead on those claimed as human trafficking victims, as Tennessee Republican Governor Bill Lee announced in March 2023, demonstrates the political and policing reach of trafficking discourse and how its suppleness is used to siphon resources from, in this instance, sexual health.

In 2018, two laws, the Allow States and Victims to Fight Online Sex Trafficking Act (FOSTA) and the Stop Enabling Sex Traffickers Act (SESTA) amended Section 230 of the Communication Decency Act and made online platforms like Google, X, Craigslist, and WhatsApp civilly and legally liable for sexual content depicted by users. The laws rendered the online solicitation of sex, or any activity suspected of soliciting sex, as tantamount to sex trafficking. FOSTA-SESTA has had a profoundly deleterious impact on the ability of sex workers to use the internet to communicate with clients more safely. These laws have also generated algorithmic monitoring of sexual expression online and, in keeping with the argument I've made throughout this book, inordinately censor sexually dissident, queer, trans, and gender-nonconforming cultures and aesthetics.

The term "human traffickers" also often muddles understanding when it comes to the issue of migration. Focusing on traffickers as individual actors often distracts from the root causes of migration and legitimizes the militarization of the NAFTA borderlands, as was the case in Mexico's Programa Frontera Sur (Southern Border Program) in 2014.[2] Free trade, as I hope I have shown, plays a crucial role in these contexts of violence and control. While abuses of power, some of which take the form of sexual violence, certainly befall people as they migrate, anti-trafficking laws often do more to incarcerate and deport these same people than to "rescue," as they purport to do. As one arm in a larger arena of sex-trafficking talk, border gatekeepers make rhetorically and politically effective assumptions, oftentimes with absolutely no evidence, that migrating people assisted by *coyotes* and *polleros* are destined for lives of sexual slavery. In 2023, for example, those guiding a boat of migrants to the United States became not only "human traffickers" but potentially "sex traffickers." Captain James Spitler of the US Coast Guard's San Diego sector was quoted saying, "This is part of a transnational criminal organization effort. . . . These people are often labor trafficked and sex trafficked when they arrive."[3] Arguing that any migrating person who receives assistance from anyone along the arduous route to refuge is or will be sex trafficked plugs into a federal and transnational law apparatus that exceptionalizes sex trafficking over other forms of labor exploitation and provides an always easy and highly sellable argument against all migration. Dangling specious claims to safeguard the health, well-being, and safety of migrating people, the political application of this argument does more to enforce and militarize international borders. In making all migration guides into "human traffickers" and ultimately "sex traffickers," they create folk devils and scapegoats who are juxtaposed to supposed saviors liberating migrants from a life of sexual servitude.

The stakes for critically examining trafficking discourse and its instantiation in administrative, criminal, and transnational law have never been greater. With the renewed and legislatively fortified attempts at flattening sexual and gender difference under the weight of anti-abortion forces, trans-exclusionary feminisms, anti–sex work assemblages posing as "anti–sex trafficking" activist networks, and the fascist panic about "gender ideology," the power bottoms of free-trade capitalism take the risk and chisel out the time and space for sex on the move. A queer traffic analysis, which, above all, values sexual culture and those who make, circulate, and consume it, reveals the connections between trafficking talk and free trade as long-term and unrelenting tools aimed at stopping the flow of those materials and lives considered anathema to global capital. The queer traffic tactics enacted throughout the 1980s, 1990s, and into the twenty-first century forge alternative pathways for dissident sexual culture that circumvent the seemingly endless reach of free-trade capitalism and transform its rules of engagement toward other routes to pleasure.

ACKNOWLEDGMENTS

Writing these acknowledgments is an opportunity to remember and recognize all the people who gifted me their time, their voices, and their passions for sexual culture, art, feminism, queer and trans experience, and the belief that new forms of living can be invented within and beyond the brutalizing forces of late racial capitalism. Many of the people I include here have taken on more than one role in this research and in my life. Many have since become not only interlocutors but also friends, collaborators, and comrades. Many are talented across a range of arenas that include art, activism, and scholarship. They live within and across the NAFTA borderlands in Canada, Mexico, and the United States.

I begin in Mexico City where this book was born. Meeting the organizers and participants at the Seminario Histórico LGBTTTI Mexicano in 2012 led to so many fruitful connections and conversations. My gratitude goes to Natalia Anaya, Alonso Hernández, and especially Alexandra R. DeRuiz, whose writing and activism has deeply influenced my thinking and with whom I've formed a beautiful friendship over the last twelve years. Also in Mexico City, my thanks to all of the people who spoke with me about NAFTA and/or queer, trans, and sexual culture, including Alejandro Brito, Marco Antonio Bustos, Gloria Careaga, Laura Carlsen, Jorge Chang, Ingrid Colín, Kenya Cuevas, Zakhiel Cuirgarçon, El Diablo, Steven Diaz, Eugenio Echeverría, Gerardo Esquivel, Mildred García, Jorge Grajales, Siobhan

Guerrero Mc Manus, Itzayana Gutiérrez, Ana Paulina Gutiérrez Martínez, Carina Guzman, Gilda Alexandra Jara Saldaña, Francisco Lagunas, Natalia Lane, Alejandra Leal, Ramona Libertad, Paul Liffman, Fernando Macías, Jessica Marjane, Matlarock, Bertha de la Maza, Antonio Medina, Norma Mogrovejo, Oscar Montiel Torres, Ana Francis Mor, Gisela Helena Muciño, Luis Flores Perea, Luis Perelman, Alba Pons Rabasa, María Renée Prudencio, Héctor Reyes, Héctor Salinas, Mónica Solís Rendón, José Luis Valdés Ugalde, Uriel Valdez, Minerva Valenzuela, Jorge Yañez, Chavita Zavaleta, and Felipe Zúñiga. Special thanks go to Karine Tinat, who hosted me at el Colegio de México as part of my 2012–2013 Fulbright-García Robles fellowship. I extend my gratitude as well to the founders, organizers, and loving custodians of the following spaces: la Cañita, Casa Xochiquetzal, la Gozadera, Somos Voces, el Taller de los Martes, and, in Cuernavaca, Centro Tlahuica de Lenguas e Intercambio Cultural (CETLALIC), and Centro Internacional de Lenguas, Arte y Cultura Paulo Freire (CILAC Freire).

From my time in Tijuana, I express my gratitude to Jorge Luis Villa, who first introduced me to the ever-growing coalition of activists, artists, and scholars working for LGBTQ migrant justice. I send heartfelt thanks to Ilsa Aguilar Bautista, Paola Berber, Chris Chambers, Maya Chinchilla, Nicolasa Cordova Sire, Gaba Cortes, Andres Cruz, Liliana Falcón, Maxwell Franco, Michael Anthony Galvan, Andrea Gaspar, Yalila Grafikat, Owen Harris, Liliana Hueso, Ericka López, Jenny López, José Juan López Ramos, Miguel Lucero, Miguel Marshall, Paulina Olvera Cáñez, Betania Sabá (Beth Velvet), Lissana Sinatra, Ana Rosa Virgen López, Tita Viveros, Guillermo Yrizar Barbosa, and especially Irving Mondragon, founder of Casita de Luz. To the spaces and organizations that invited me in and that do so much for queer and trans folk migrating to and through Tijuana, I thank Espacio Migrante, Casa Arcoíris Albergue LGBTI, Enclave Rabia Caracol, Diversidad Migrante A.C., Centro Comunitario Caritas, Comunidad Cultural de Tijuana LGBTI AC, Lúmina Foto-Café, Lavanda Colectivo Lésbico Interdisciplinario de Tijuana (CLIT), and the University of California San Diego's Health Frontiers in Tijuana student-run free clinic. In Chula Vista, I thank Lynn D. for her generosity in helping me to gather supplies, clothing, and toiletries in the weeks before this kind of crossborder aid was criminalized. And in San Diego, many thanks to the eighteen fabulous drag queens, and especially Kickxy Vixen-Styles, for organizing a fundraising show on behalf of our migrating queer, trans, and gender-nonconforming *familia*. Special thanks to Sayak Valencia who hosted me at el Colegio de la Frontera Norte as part of the binational Fulbright Carlos Rico Fellowship, which I was awarded in 2018. Her scholarship, her friendship, and her collegial support have profoundly influenced this book and my life.

I spent the other portion of the 2018 Fulbright Carlos Rico in Toronto, and I send my gratitude particularly to John Paul Ricco for hosting me at the University of Toronto Mississauga. To Toronto and Vancouver, I also send my thanks to Max Allen, Joseph Arvay, Martha Balaguera, Robert Bothwell, Elspeth Brown, Charles Campbell, Gail Cohen, Brenda Cossman, Sujata Dey, Janine Fuller, Richard Fung, Bob Gallagher, Paul Halferty, Walid Hejazi, Tom Hooper, Jack Jackson, Carlyle Jansen, Patrick Keilty, John Kyper, Bruce MacDonald, Tim McCaskell, Kimberly Mistysyn, Jearld Moldenhauer, Darrell Schuurman, John Scythes, Dana Seitler, Carol Thames, Mariana Valverde, Bruce Walsh, and Don Wilson. I'll also take this opportunity to give thanks to a few of the queer, trans, and sexual spaces that, during my time there, became such an important part of this project: Good for Her, Glad Day Bookshop, Oasis Aqualounge, and Little Sister's Book and Art Emporium.

In my research travels, I spent a significant time in archives, and the research for this book would not have been possible without the guidance of archivists and archive directors. In Mexico City, I thank Bettina Gómez at the Centro de Documentación y Archivo Histórico Lésbico at the Universidad Autónoma de la Ciudad de México (Fondo I, CAMeNA/UACM). Also in Mexico City, my gratitude to the Centro de Investigaciones sobre América del Norte at the Universidad Nacional Autónoma de México and the Museo Salinas archives at the Museo Universitario Arte Contemporáneo. In Tijuana, many thanks to Alfonso Caraveo Castro at the Archivo de el Colegio de la Frontera Norte. In Toronto, special thanks to Patrick Keilty, who directed the Sexual Representation Collection at the Bonham Centre for Sexual Diversity Studies at the University of Toronto in 2018. Also in Toronto, many thanks to all the good folks at The ArQuives: Canada's LGBTQ2+ Archives and especially to Executive Director Raegan Swanson, archivist Lucie Handley-Girard, and reference archivist Daniel Payne. I also want to thank the Dolph Briscoe Center for American History and the Nettie Lee Benson Latin American Collection at the University of Texas at Austin, especially the former head of collection development, José Montelongo.

Art, aesthetics, and the work of artists across the United States, Canada, and Mexico were likewise pivotal to writing this book. Endless admiration goes to 2boys.tv, Julia Antivilo, Lino Arruda, Erika Bülle Hernández, Yecid Calderón, Cerrucha, Lia García, Nadia Granados, Xandra Ibarra, Invasorix, César Martínez Silva, Mónica Mayer, Orgy punk, Vicente Razo, Mirna

Roldán, Óscar Sánchez Gómez, Manuel Solano, Katia Tirado, Diana J. Torres, and Lechedevirgen Trimegisto. As part of my process in writing this book, I took two life-changing workshops with La Pocha Nostra: one in Mexico City where I met some of the artists listed above, and one weeklong intensive in Tijuana. Many thanks to Saúl García López, Guillermo Gómez-Peña, and Violeta Luna for their performance pedagogy. Artistic collaborations also played an important role in my research process. I send my thanks to Biquini Wax EPS for including my performance script "Avocado Toast" in their show on "NAFTAlgia," *Una obsesión peligrosa*, and to Mauricio Muñoz for performing it at Human Resources in Los Angeles. Deep gratitude as well goes to art historian María Laura Rosa and cultural artivist Lorena Wolffer for inviting me onboard to organize an urgent project, *Estado de emergencia: Puntos de dolor y resiliencia en la Ciudad de México*.

And to all the migrating queer, trans, and nonbinary folks, sex workers, porn actors, customs officials, and kinky practitioners who generously shared their experiences with me but who want (or need) to remain anonymous, I send infinite gratitude and admiration.

The opportunity to present portions of this research among scholars I admire invigorated this book project and, without a doubt, made it better. My gratitude goes to Paul Amar, Sérgio Andrade, Gabriela Arguedas-Ramírez, Raúl Arriaga Ortiz, Olivia Banner, Julio Capó Jr., María Célleri, Xiomara Verenice Cervantes-Gómez, Joshua Chambers-Letson, Manuel Cuellar, Jorge Díaz, Micaela Díaz-Sánchez, Kirstie A. Dorr, Faye Gleisser, Melissa González, Laura G. Gutiérrez, Jack Halberstam, Nell Haynes, Jillian Hernandez, Kimberly Kay Hoang, Y Howard, Tania Islas Weinstein, Kareem Khubchandani, Larry La Fountain-Stokes, Christina A. León, Juan Llamas-Rodriguez, Yolanda Martínez-San Miguel, Julie A. Minich, Gregory Mitchell, Cherríe Moraga, Ghassan Moussawi, Jennifer Musto, Marcia Ochoa, Dan Paz, Justin Perez, Joseph M. Pierce, Pavithra Prasad, Iván A. Ramos, Guillermo de los Reyes, Felipe Rivas San Martín, Leticia Robles, Christofer Rodelo, Judith Rodríguez, Anahi Russo Garrido, Montserrat Sagot, Gwyneth Shanks, Elena Shih, Marcos Steuernagel, Shelley Streeby, David Tenorio, Zeb Tortorici, Deb Vargas, María Amelia Viteri, Sarah Wilbur, Patricia A. Ybarra, and all the innovative thinkers at the Tepoztlán Institute for the Transnational History of the Americas. Tremendous thanks go to Macarena Gómez-Barris, Rosemary Hennessy, and Juana María Rodríguez who read the first full draft of the manuscript and provided indispensable feedback and support. Many thanks as well to the Center for Feminist Futures at the

University of California Santa Barbara (UCSB) for funding a game-changing manuscript workshop with these three brilliant scholars.

Also in Santa Barbara, I would have never made it through this process without the feedback and friendship of my fellow "salonistas," Felice Blake, Julie Carlson, Nadège T. Clitandre, Laila Shereen Sakr, and Sherene Seikaly. Thank you, dear friends, for the gift of our feedback group and for all your support over the years.

Since the beginning of the pandemic, Laura Horak has organized a binational online writing accountability group, and I thank her, Kester Dyer, Slava Greenberg, Katherine Morrow, Erica Rand, Dale Spencer, Chris Straayer, and Allison Whitney for being the best writing buddies a person could ask for.

I thank my amazing colleagues and coworkers in the Department of Feminist Studies at UCSB, especially Edwina Barvosa, Eileen Boris, Claudia Castaneda, Debanuj DasGupta, Jigna Desai, Caleb Luna, Mireille Miller-Young, Laury Oaks, Rosa Pinter, Matt Richardson, Leila Rupp, Anisha Thomas, and Jane Ward, as well as Dean Charles Hale, for all their support along the journey of researching and writing this book.

This research was generously supported by an American Council of Learned Societies Fellowship, two Fulbright fellowships, a "Queer Hemisphere; America Queer" residency at the University of California Humanities Research Institute, and, at UCSB, a grant from the Chicano Studies Institute, UC Mexus, and three Academic Senate Research Grants. I'm grateful to these grant and fellowship entities and to the committees who spent the time to assess my work.

Many thanks to series editor Macarena Gómez-Barris for her interest in the manuscript for the Dissident Acts series. For his embrace and confidence in the book, my deep gratitude goes to Senior Executive Editor Ken Wissoker. And to Assistant Editor Ryan Kendall, thank you for walking me step-by-step through the process that led to the book's publication. Special thanks as well go to Project Editor Ihsan Taylor and to the two anonymous readers for their excellent feedback.

I also want to thank Olivia Banner for expert copyediting; Dominique Amezcua, Allen Magaña, and Isabella Restrepo for interview transcriptions; Ka-Bang Lauron for research assistance; JD Pluecker for careful checks on my Spanish-to-English translations; Andrew Ascherl for indexing; and Kimberly Kay Hoang for generously reading the epilogue. Many thanks as well to all of the visual and performance artists who contributed images to the book.

To my neighbors on the Westside, your care and conversation kept me sane when the world was shut down. Special thanks to Yoko Fujita, Yogi Johnson, Eeva and Chris Moore, and Angela Watts for their friendship.

For their love and unwavering support of this book, I thank Y Howard.

To Olivia Banner, Alison Granito, Mario LaMothe, Tyler Mabry, Robin Mack, Jay Mays, Jeffrey Q. McCune Jr., Gregory Mitchell, Jessica Nakamura, Pavithra Prasad, Mónica Solís Rendón, Stalina Villareal, and Lorena Wolffer, anywhere and anytime we're together, it feels like home. Thank you, queer kin.

As always, I thank Liz, Ron, and Mike Tyburczy for believing in me.

As I finished the book, I lost my constant companion, in writing and in life, my beloved dog, Stevie. I'm grateful for the years we had together and for her continued presence in my dreams.

In 2023, and infused with decades of activism and scholarship, the collective Academics for Justice in Palestine formed at UCSB. I want to dedicate this book to all the academic workers across the country and around the world who tirelessly and bravely persist, refusing to stop until Palestine is free.

NOTES

Preface

1   By *switch*, I mean to refer to the versatility of a sexual subject who assumes and desires dominant and submissive (top/bottom) positions during sex. The term *vers* is sometimes used interchangeably with *switch*, though the latter emerges from BDSM cultures and practices, and for that reason I employ it here.

2   Here I draw from Michel Foucault's theory on the multidirectional flow of power in the second part of his first volume of *The History of Sexuality* (1978).

3   The saying is (in)famously attributed to the late nineteenth- and early twentieth-century Mexican dictator Porfirio Díaz, though the origins of this phrase cannot be officially traced.

4   For a museum exhibition that reconsiders how Malinche has been historically cast as a traitor, see *Traitor, Survivor, Icon: The Legacy of La Malinche* (Lyall and Romo 2022).

5   For a thorough history of the sex worker in political economy and Marxist discourse, see McClanahan and Settell 2021.

6   *Rasquache* is a Nahuatl word that means "leftover" or "of no value," and *rasquachismo* is a form of creative expression invented by Chicana/x/o artists and art theorists to describe something that has been recycled and repurposed, a kind of aesthetic politics from below. See Ybarra-Frausto 1989.

7　　"People smugglers" is the term used by Interpol (https://www.interpol
　　　.int/en/Crimes/People-smuggling). NAFTA is one of many international
　　　treaties that provide indirect platforms for transnational police coopera-
　　　tion, and Interpol is one such organization that coordinates those police
　　　activities.

Introduction

1　　See Babb 2001. Even though these businesspeople were all male, Mexico
　　　has a quota system wherein half of the representatives must be female.
　　　This binary quota system continues the occlusion of trans, nonbinary, and
　　　genderqueer subjects in government work.

2　　Free trade of sex toys between the United States and Colombia is technically
　　　listed under "Health and Beauty," but unlike the flow of these materials
　　　between the United States and Mexico they are also given a designated Har-
　　　monized System (HS) Code. The HS is a standardized numerical method
　　　of classifying traded products, thus rendering those objects with an HS
　　　code intelligible to free-trade infrastructures. For more on free trade and
　　　sexual commerce between the United States and Colombia with a focus
　　　on sex toys, see Alice Boyd, "US Trade Deal Brings Cut-Price Sex Toys to
　　　Colombia," *Colombia Reports*, November 22, 2011.

3　　For example, consider Kimberly Kay Hoang's book *Spiderweb Capitalism*
　　　(2022), where she shows how transnational capitalist elites participate in
　　　highly developed shadow economies that largely go unseen.

4　　For a germinal text that also grows out of and responds to the sex panics
　　　surrounding pornography, sadomasochism, and pedophilia, see Rubin
　　　2011a. Also see Halperin and Hoppe 2017.

5　　Orme and others argue that NAFTA was also about Japan, insofar as, at the
　　　time of the FTA frenzy in the 1980s and 1990s, Japan had dominated the
　　　discourse of the global economic battle to be the world's most powerful
　　　nation. Japan is no longer in that category, with some experts arguing that
　　　Japan's decline in birth rate, and the subsequent aging of its population,
　　　is the (sexual) reasoning for Japan's falling out of the vertical hierarchy of
　　　world power. NAFTA can also be viewed as a response to predictions of
　　　power consolidated under the then-burgeoning European Union.

6　　Abu-Lughod (1989) historicizes the beginning of world trading systems
　　　in the thirteenth century. For a historical perspective via China, see Rofel
　　　2007, 190–194.

7　　See Thornton 2021 for a Mexico-centric account of global economy gov-
　　　ernance and its history from the Mexican Revolution through the 1970s.

8　　The identities of the participants in *(Untitled) Ricas y famosas* were in-
　　　tended to be anonymous, but outrage grew when newspapers identified

some of Rossell's sitters as the children of PRI politicians. Some of the photographed reportedly threatened to sue the artist after seeing the work and book reviews that described their homes as "vast kitsch palaces." She received threatening messages and emails, was called a "traitor" and "self-loather," and has since kept a low profile. At one point she sent an actress to perform as her at book signings. See Ginger Thompson, "The Rich and Famous and Aghast: A Peep-Show Book," *New York Times*, September 25, 2002, http://www.nytimes.com/2002/09/25/international/americas /25MEXI.html.

9   SFMOMA (San Francisco Museum of Modern Art), "How Daniela Rossell's Photographs Came to Be Viewed as Images of Mexico's 'Poster Girls of Corruption,'" 2012, https://www.sfmoma.org/watch/how-daniela-rossells -photographs-came-to-be-viewed-as-images-of-mexicos-poster-girls-of -corruption/.

10   The study of the history of the term and figure of the *chacal* spans the twentieth and twenty-first centuries, and it includes work by notable writers such as Violeta L. de la Rosa, Carlos Monsiváis, Juan Carlos Bautista, Olivier Debroise, and Salvador Novo. See Hernández Victoria 2011.

11   For more on the documentation and archiving of sodomy as one of many "sins of nature," see Tortorici 2018.

12   See Rodolfo N. Morales S., "Chacales, príncipes de la fauna urbana," *Del Otro Lado* (Mexico City) no. 1, January/February 1992, 58–61, Centro de Documentación y Archivo Histórico Lésbico, Colectivo Sol Collection. For this article, Morales S. conducted "una investigación exhaustiva de los chacales en el Distrito Federal" (an exhaustive study of *chacales* in Mexico City) (58), where he engaged in "una investigación participante donde el autor ha convivido, con-bebido y compartido experiencias" (a participant study where he hung out with, drank with, and shared experiences) (58) with fifty men he labels as *chacales*. The answers to his questions, which he presents as statistical percentages, debunk the employment, class, and race assumptions that often circulate with the *chacal* stereotype. Indeed, *chacales* can be "choferos, soldados, taqueros, gaseros, y polícias" (drivers, soldiers, tacomakers, gasoline attendants, and police officers) (60), but they also work for private companies, for the government, and as students. Additionally, he reports that while *chacales* are often assumed to be "moreno" (dark-skinned), the men he hung out with "han demonstrado una amplia gama de tipos raciales y variedades" (have provided evidence of a wide range of racialized types and varieties) (59).

13   For an ethnographic study of gay sex tourism within the context of Brazil, see Mitchell 2015. On the relationship between the development of gay tourism in Mexico and Mexican sexualities, see Cantú 2009, 97–117.

14   "México, país de clase baja: Instituto Nacional de Estadística y Geografía (INEGI)" [Mexico, lower-class country: National Institute of Statistics and

Geography], *Animal Político*, June 12, 2013, https://animalpolitico.com /sociedad/mexico-pais-de-clase-baja-inegi.

15 Nathaniel Parish Flannery, "What's the Real Story with Modern Mexico's Middle Class?," *Forbes*, July 23, 2013, https://www.forbes.com/sites /nathanielparishflannery/2013/07/23/whats-the-real-story-with-modern -mexicos-middle-class/?sh=36d1659d1d42.

16 OECD, "Divided We Stand: Why Inequality Keeps Rising," 2011, 21–44, https:// www.oecd.org/en/publications/2011/12/divided-we-stand_g1g1483d.html.

17 Slim exhibited these photographs in at least two gallery exhibitions, one of which was titled *Rough Trade: Art and Sex Work in the Late 20th Century*, CLAMP, August 2–September 22.

18 Article 2205 of NAFTA allows the parties of the agreement to modify the agreement with the consent of the other members, or to withdraw after giving six months' notice.

19 As numerous studies have shown, most drugs and guns pass through official points of entry, and people migrating into the United States have significantly lower crime rates than the general US population. For example, see Light, He, and Robey 2020.

20 Trump's vigilantism and his use of racist stereotypes of Black and Brown men to foment sex panics reaches back at least to his involvement with the so-called "Central Park Five." See the miniseries *When They See Us* (2019).

21 For the original 1994 NAFTA preamble in its English version, see https:// www.italaw.com/sites/default/files/laws/italaw6187%2814%29.pdf.

For the 2020 NAFTA (USMCA) preamble in English, see the Office of the United States Trade Representative (USTR), https://ustr.gov /trade-agreements/free-trade-agreements/united-states-mexico-canada -agreement/agreement-between.

22 For the use of "queer traffic" as a way of reading US literary history of the late nineteenth and early twentieth centuries anthologically, see Hurley 2010.

23 For another use of the term *traffic*, see Gayle S. Rubin's germinal essay "The Traffic in Women: Notes on the 'Political Economy' of Sex" (1975). Rubin's main title is drawn from Emma Goldman's 1910 article of the same name, an article in which she critiqued the moral crusade of what we now call the White Slavery panic. Critical trafficking scholars trace the origins of the present-day "modern slavery" anti-prostitution movement to this period. For Rubin's pro–sex work reflection on her earlier essay's title, see Rubin 2011b.

24 For a critical stance on sex-trafficking discourse and representations in Mexico, see Jiménez Portilla 2022. For the ways in which global laws, transnational policies, and cultural flows play into sex-trafficking panics and carceral approaches to "rescue," see Agustín 2007; Bernstein 2018; Hoang and Salazar Parreñas 2014; Mitchell 2022; Shih 2023; and Vance

2012. In *Panics without Borders* (2022), Gregory Mitchell uniquely situates his book within the field of performance studies to examine the sex trafficking myths that surround global sporting events and the transnational discourse of sex trafficking as one rooted in white supremacy.

25 For a cultural study that situates media representations of the war on drugs within a long history of consolidating state power and marginalized resistance, see Marez 2004.

26 On the ways in which post-9/11 surveillance policies in the United States shape and regulate the category of transgender, see Beauchamp 2019. For a study of how state surveillance practices are structured on anti-Black racism, see Browne 2015. On the particularities of the surveillance state as it pertains to sex trafficking, see Musto 2016.

27 For the ways in which "queer time" disrupts normative conceptions of reproduction, family, and capital and labor flows, see also Halberstam 2005 (1–21) and Muñoz 2009 on "straight time."

28 Owing to the common usage by my interlocutors and to migrating people's identification with "migrant," I'm using this term throughout the book.

29 A hat tip goes to Gayle S. Rubin and her monumental reader, *Deviations* (2011).

Chapter 1. Porn Pirates

1 *Pambazos* are sandwiches filled with chorizo and potatoes and bathed in guajillo salsa.

2 *Güera* is a classed, raced, and gendered term, used in formal and informal retail spaces to address the potential buyer with the privilege of whiteness (fair haired and light skin, or even "blonde"). The term is specific to "women's" purchasing power, thereby recognizing a particular individual as being a potential buyer with money to spend rather than an interloper or a potential thief in the retail environment. In other words, women of any skin color may be called *güera* with the cultural assumption that any woman visually identified as having the means to buy what is on sale wants to be associated with lighter skin. For a reflection on the moniker *güera* in Chicana communities, see Moraga 1981, 27–34.

3 Aguiar's extensive ethnographic research on the criminalization of piracy in Mexico is largely focused on the San Juan de Dios market in the Mexican city of Guadalajara. His research (2010) has shown how President Vicente Fox's declaration of a "war on piracy" in 2003 further installed piracy as a top priority in Mexico's security agenda and led to more than six thousand raids and seizures in 2006 alone. His research (2012) also covers the 2008 Mérida Initiative signed under Felipe Calderón and George W. Bush,

wherein pirated goods were formally designated as an illegal flow and a threat to regional security.

4   For a 2003 statement that links piracy with terrorism, see "Statement of John G. Malcolm, Deputy Assistant Attorney General. Hearing on Copyright Piracy and Links to Crime and Terrorism, Subcommittee on the Courts, the Internet, and Intellectual Property, Committee on the Judiciary, US House of Representatives," as cited in Mcillwain 2005, 20.

5   Writing about Somali pirates, Cowen (2014, 129–161) argues that piracy be viewed as a political act that uses the ungovernability of maritime space to push back against the imperialism of nation-states.

6   Tortorici and his colleagues at the Mexico City–based grassroots archival initiative Archivo El Insulto collaborate on amassing and analyzing twentieth-century collections of Mexican sexual artifacts.

7   This section of the chapter is indebted to my conversations with Jorge Grajales and his extensive knowledge of underground film and its circulations in and through Mexico. I first learned of Grajales in 2013 when he organized a Mexican pornographic film conference in Mexico City. Later that same year, Grajales and I conducted an extensive interview about the history of certain sexual film genres and physical spaces for viewing pornography in Mexico City, with a focus on the NAFTA era. Grajales is one of only a few film experts with the cultural memory and expertise on the topic of Mexican pornography.

8   Nudie-cuties are an international genre of film that used advertising to evade the surveillance and censorship by playing up the humor of the films rather than their sexual components. This tactic emerged in response to the 1957 *Roth v. United States* case, when the Supreme Court ruled that obscene materials were not covered by the First Amendment. See Schaefer 2007, 23.

9   For more on the Bridge Project, wherein Bush mobilized a transnational evangelical task force to give teeth to the Clinton-initiated anti–sex trafficking agenda, see Tyburczy 2019, 100, 109, 113. For a study of the changing policies and rhetorics on sex trafficking over the course of the Clinton, Bush, and Obama presidencies, see O'Brien and Wilson 2015. In the article, the authors connect Bush's domestic policies on antitrafficking and his federal crackdown on sex work with his religiously informed foreign policy decisions on abortion vis-à-vis his reinstatement of the "Mexico City Policy" (also known by its critics as the Global Gag Rule). The Mexico City Policy, named so because it was announced by President Ronald Reagan during a 1984 conference in Mexico City, restricts funding for family planning, reproductive health, and USAID assistance to foreign NGOs if they fail to certify that they will neither promote nor perform abortions. Since 1984, the policy has been reinstated during every subsequent Republican presidency and rescinded during every Democratic presidency. See Behti

2019 for the ways in which the Trump presidency extended the policy in 2017 to restrict funding for HIV and all global health assistance, inclusive of maternal and child health. In this article Behti discusses the attempt to restrict domestic aid for NGOs fighting HIV/AIDS on a global scale unless they agreed to oppose "prostitution and sex trafficking" (11). In 2021, President Joe Biden rescinded the Mexico City Policy. The Trump administration reinstated his expanded version of the policy on January 24, 2025.

10   The only other functioning porn companies in 2012–2013 were the gay porn label Mecos, started by El Diablo (Gerardo Delgado), el Cártel del Paraíso, and Tierra Erótica, the latter started by El Maldoror (Marco Antonio Bustos) (El Diablo, interview, 2013).

11   This changed shortly after I spoke with them in 2013, though with only a short online run.

12   The word "mecos" has other connotations and valences in contemporary Mexico, such as gender-nonconforming significance as it relates to Indigenous performance in the state of Veracruz. See Cuellar 2023.

13   Matla used this term to describe what is now called *trata de personas* (traffic in persons). The year 2012 marked not only the turn to a more stringent anti–sex trafficking law in Mexico, but also a change in the terminology from *trata de blancas* (a racialized vestige of the White Slavery panic) to the nominally gender-inclusive and deracialized *trata de personas*.

14   On the need to reform Mexico's anti–sex trafficking laws, see Correa-Cabrera and Sanders Montandon 2018.

15   The three DVD copies Reyes and Matla gifted me were all cheaply encased in plastic, and only within the context of this film did I see their films packaged in the more expensive hardcase plastic.

16   Condoms are actively shown in use throughout Matlarock films. Sometimes, Reyes told me, they film couples who don't want to use condoms. In these instances, the film announces they are indeed a couple offscreen, thus, they hope, shielding them from any backlash against the absence of condoms in such a scene.

17   For more on body size and sexual public culture, see Hester and Walters 2016. For BBW, see Goddard 2007. For a pioneering study on the imbrication of fatphobia, anti-Blackness, and colonization of the Americas, see Strings 2019.

18   I would like to thank Iván Ramos for bringing this PSA to my attention. Consejo Nacional de la Publicidad, "Tratado de Libre Comercio 1992," 29 seconds, https://www.youtube.com/watch?v=fXkyQ_DP6Tc.

19   Mollow's crip theory of "disreputable disabilities" includes "fatness, alcoholism, addiction, HIV, AIDS, psychiatric disability, or chronic illness with no clearly defined medical cause" (2012, 304).

20 House Hearing, 108 Congress, "Alien Removals Under Operation Predator," Hearing Before the Subcommittee on Immigration, Border Security,
and Claims, March 4, 2004, Serial No. 73, https://www.govinfo.gov/content
/pkg/CHRG-108hhrg92347/html/CHRG-108hhrg92347.htm. Those in attendance ranged from Henry Hyde to Mike Pence, to Anthony D. Weiner,
and Maxine Waters. For an analysis of Bush's "child safety regime," including a conversation on Operation Predator, see Renfro 2020, 215–226.
For a brief conversation on the Operation Predator digital app, see Renfro 2018, 581. The Operation Predator app is yet another strategy used by
antitrafficking state actors that aim to recruit everyday people to surveil
potential "sex offenders." For an example of scholarship on how nonprofit
organizations recruit everyday people to monitor, track, and capture "sex-
trafficked victims" for the state, see Shih 2016. Of course, anyone traveling through US Customs can encounter posters with photos of cowering
women that charge travelers with the responsibility to "say something" if
they "see something," an obvious borrowing from war on terror rhetoric.

The Free Eating Agreement

1 To view *Xipe Totec Punk*, visit César Martínez's website at http://www
.martinezsilva.com/english/video_e.html.

2 Coco Fusco had intended to name her anthology (2000) *corpus delicti*
("the body of the offense or crime") but upon sending the title proposal
for a London-based performance showcase she accidentally misspelled
the term to read *corpus delecti* ("the body that derives or incarnates
pleasure"). I take up this felicitous misspelling to describe the queer aesthetics of *Xipe Totec Punk* and the friction it enacts between the criminal
and the edible.

3 On the failure of the pink tide to exact progressive change and for the
ways in which leftist leaders appropriated the language of decolonization to gain support for criminalizing grassroots social movements, see
Gómez-Barris 2018.

4 On the affective politics of racial kitsch objects, see Nyong'o 2002. See also
Tate 2019, 109–121.

5 For the full engraving image, see Ochoa 2016.

6 *Relajo* is an irreverent Mexican vernacular method that interrupts dominant
norms and painful colonial histories through playful language and joking.
See Rault 2017 for a discussion of *relajo* as a queer performance tactic.

7 The fallout from the Smoot-Hawley Tariff Act and the global trade war
that ensued led to the rerouting of power regarding trade decisions from
Congress to the executive branch. In 1934, President Franklin D. Roose-
velt signed the Reciprocal Trade Agreements Act, thereby liberalizing US

trade policy on a global scale. It gave the executive branch full power to unilaterally negotiate reciprocal trade agreements and tariffs with other countries.

Chapter 2. Importing Degradation

1   For scholarship on the complicated relationship between the United States and Canada, see Bothwell 1992, 2015; and J. Stewart 2017.

2   The May 29, 2024, update to the "Cultural Exemption" clause in the USMCA (CUSMA) goes on to read, "The U.S. entertainment industry, in particular, has long sought to have this provision eliminated. In the end, Canada prevailed and the exclusion remains in USMCA, although a provision was inserted allowing the United States and Mexico to take reciprocal action." Congressional Research Service, "The United States-Mexico-Canada Agreement (USMCA)," 1–35, 24, https://sgp.fas.org/crs/row/R44981.pdf.

3   CanCon requirements pertained and continue to pertain to radio and television, cable and satellite, audiovisual materials, film, and video, as well as some forms of print media. CanCon began in 1971, but it needed to be reified when CUSFTA was signed in 1988. Julijana Capone, "Stan Klees: The Man Behind Cancon and Why It Had to Happen," *National Music Centre Amplify*, December 6, 2014, https://amplify.nmc.ca/stan-klees-the-man -behind-cancon/.

4   Many thanks to Robert Bothwell (University of Toronto) and Walid Hejazi (Rotman School of Management), whom I spoke with separately, for sharing their perspectives with me.

5   Scott Morrison, "Generation NeXt," *MEXICO Insight*, May 15, 1994, 26–30, 28, Mexico-US Business Committee Collection, Benson Latin American Collection, LLILAS Latin American Studies and Collections, University of Texas at Austin.

6   While the United States became the first country to criminalize HIV+ nondisclosure, exposure, and transmission, now in a majority of states, Canada and Mexico also criminalize the nondisclosure of HIV to sexual partners. This phenomenon has gone global, and as of 2020, ninety-two countries had criminalized the nondisclosure of HIV. For an analysis of HIV criminalization and its deleterious effects on HIV+ people and public health, see Strub 2017, Tomso 2017, and Thrasher 2022, 21–42.

7   It's important to note that Dworkin never supported LEAF's approach to pornography, which largely focused on reforming the criminal code. See Califia 1995, 18, which cites Dworkin from Tim Kingston's 1993 article for the *San Francisco Bay Times*.

8   Catharine A. MacKinnon and Andrea Dworkin, "Statement by Catharine A. MacKinnon and Andrea Dworkin Regarding Canada Customs

and Legal Approaches to Pornography," August 26, 1994, http://www
.nostatusquo.com/ACLU/dworkin/OrdinanceCanada.html.

9   Madonna's book *Sex* was never seized at the border owing to the business
      deals cut between Canada Customs and Time Warner. In the archives,
      Sex was a frequently cited example of the arbitrariness of Canada Cus-
      toms' search-and-seizure policies and processes and how capital exchange
      dictated who had the privilege to circulate which sexual materials into
      Canada.

10   For a documentary account of the Canada Customs battles in the 1990s,
      see the film *Little Sister's vs. Big Brother*. I viewed this film while in Toronto
      at The ArQuives. It is not accessible for viewing outside queer archives in
      Toronto and Vancouver.

11   See Harry Sutherland's documentary, *Track 2: Enough Is Enough*.

12   Also see Mistysyn 1997.

13   Homegrown and foreign pornography has always been more widely avail-
      able in Québec. According to a letter I found in the Max Allen Collection
      at the Sexual Representation Collection, many gay men bought uncensored
      videos from Québec stores after viewing ads for them in the queer peri-
      odical *Xtra*. In the same letter, Allen, a former CBC Radio personality, a
      sometimes controversial proponent of free speech, and a gay man, wrote
      to *Xtra* informing them of WEGA Video's (Montréal) new requirement
      that all phone porn orders be accompanied with buyers' Social Identifica-
      tion Numbers. Allen argued that this new policy, apart from being illegal,
      rendered all porn buyers vulnerable to state surveillance. Max Allen, let-
      ter to *Xtra*, January 23, 1991, Sexual Representation Collection, Mark S.
      Bonham Centre for Sexual Diversity Studies, University of Toronto.

14   In 1998, the museum exhibition *Troubling Customs*, curated by Erica Rand,
      Harmony Hammond, Sallie McCorkle, Cyndra MacDowall, Mary Patten,
      and Robert Repinski, satirized the arbitrariness of administrative law at the
      Canada-US border. Displayed at the Ontario College of Art and Design,
      the show invited artists to "smuggle" queer materials across the border, a
      method inspired by the circulations and seizures I cover in this chapter.
      See Rand 1998.

15   Historically and rhetorically speaking, French Canada views itself as a
      colony of English Canada. In 1995, Québécois went to the polls in a second
      referendum that would decide whether to remain in Canada or proclaim
      sovereignty and become independent. They ultimately decided to remain
      in Canada, but only by a few percentage points.

16   The American Booksellers' Association was critiqued by the Canadian
      news for "the wording of a resolution [that] sounds as much like a defense
      of free trade as an objection to censorship." "Booksellers in US Condemn
      Customs," *Globe and Mail*, June 1, 1994.

17   See Meyer 2003. Also see Tyburczy 2016a, 101–103. The 1973 *Miller* court decision and its flexible definition of "obscenity" and the 1986 Report of the Attorney General's Commission on Pornography (the "Meese report") played pivotal and consistent roles in propagating panic about pornography and queer art in the United States.

18   This film is also notable because it depicts a romantic relationship between Frances, the cis lesbian store owner, and Judy, a trans lesbian and one of the store clerks. Unfortunately, however, the role of Judy was played by cis man Peter Outerbridge. See Drew Gregory, "'Better Than Chocolate' Turns 20, Remains the Only Movie Where a Trans Woman Has a Lesbian Friend Group," *Autostraddle*, August 13, 2019.

19   Jeffrey Toobin, "X-Rated," *New Yorker*, October 3, 1994, 70–78.

20   In a February 8, 2001, *Xtra* feature titled "Fucking Good, Fisting Bad, New Rules Crack Down on What Was Okay Before," the author explains, "Porn portrayals of both anal and vaginal fisting are now illegal to import (defined as 'insertion of a fist or a foot into an anal and vaginal orifice')."

21   Also see Ross 1997.

22   Max Allen Collection, Sexual Representation Collection, Mark S. Bonham Centre for Sexual Diversity Studies, University of Toronto.

23   Carol Thames, Carlyle Jansen, Chanelle Gallant, JP Hornick, Janet Rowe, and Loralee Gillis, at different times, made up the Toronto Women's Bathhouse Committee, which organized lesbian-inclusive sex party/bathhouse events known as "Pussy Palace." One of these events was raided by the police on September 14, 2000.

24   For more on Zami, see Catungal 2018, 48–52.

25   After NAFTA, Canadian mining companies moved into rural Mexico and have been known to violently push Indigenous and farming populations off their lands. See Hoogeveen 2015.

26   USMCA, Chapter 23 (Labor), Article 23.9, Footnote 13, reads: "The United States' existing federal agency policies regarding the hiring of federal workers are sufficient to fulfill the obligations set forth in this Article. The Article thus requires no additional action on the part of the United States, including any amendments to Title VII of the Civil Rights Act of 1964, in order for the United States to be in compliance with the obligations set forth in this Article." For a conversation about this footnote, see Tim Fitzsimons, "Footnote in New Trade Agreement Causes Confusion over LGBTQ Protections," NBC News, December 4, 2018, https://www.nbcnews .com/feature/nbc-out/footnote-new-trade-deal-causes-confusion-over -lgbtq-protections-n943591.

27   Letter from Doug Lamborn et al., Member of Congress, to Donald J. Trump, President of the United States (November 16, 2018). The letter was

previously found here but is no longer available: https://lamborn.house
.gov/uploadedfiles/letter_to_potus_re-_trade.pdf. The quotes I pulled
from the letter, however, can be found in Matthew Rozsa, "House Re-
publicans Take Issue with Trump's New Trade Plan—Because It Protects
LGBT People," *Salon*, November 19, 2018, https://www.salon.com/2018/11
/19/house-republicans-take-issue-with-trumps-new-trade-plan-because
-it-protects-lgbt-people/.

When the State Says "No One Likes Fat Girls"

1   See David Carrizales, "'El Bronco': A las niñas gordas nadie las quiere," *El
Universal*, June 14, 2016, https://www.eluniversal.com.mx/articulo/estados
/2016/06/14/el-bronco-las-ninas-gordas-nadie-las-quiere.

2   To view *A las niñas gordas nadie las quiere*, visit the Hemispheric Institute
of Performance and Politics website, https://hemisphericinstitute.org/en
/encuentro-2019-performances/item/2946-erika-bulle-hernandez.html.

3   Maryknoll Office for Global Concerns, "NAFTA, Free Trade and 'Exporting
Obesity,'" https://maryknollogc.org/article/nafta-free-trade-and-exporting
-obesity; James Whitlow Delano, "The Trade Deal That Triggered a Health
Crisis in Mexico—in Pictures," *Guardian*, January 1, 2018, https://www
.theguardian.com/global-development/gallery/2018/jan/01/free-trade
-deal-health-crisis-mexico-obesity-malnutrition-in-pictures; Andrew Jacobs and Matt Richtel, "El TLCAN y su papel en la obesidad en México,"
New York Times, December 11, 2017, https://www.nytimes.com/es/2017/12
/11/espanol/america-latina/tlcan-obesidad-mexico-estados-unidos-oxxo
-sams-femsa.html; Tania Casasola and Lorelei Sánchez, "El TLCAN trajo
obesidad a México," *El Universal*, November 18, 2017, https://alianzasalud
.org.mx/2017/11/el-tlcan-trajo-obesidad-a-mexico/; David Brooks, "Obesidad, regalo del TLCAN a México," *La Jornada*, April 6, 2012, https://www
.jornada.com.mx/2012/04/06/sociedad/036n1soc.

4   In 1998, the Body Mass Index (BMI), a metric that adjudicates who is
"normal" and "overweight" or "preobesity," was lowered from 27 to 25.
"Overnight," Harriet Brown said, citing the National Institutes of Health,
"millions of people became overweight" and were thus considered on
the path to obesity. Brown, "How Obesity Became a Disease," *Atlantic*,
March 24, 2015, https://www.theatlantic.com/health/archive/2015/03/how
-obesity-became-a-disease/388300/.

5   For a performance critique of the dumping of corn in Mexico, see the
theater piece by Jesusa Rodríguez and Liliana Felipe, *El maíz* (2006), as
described by Gutiérrez 2010, 179–187. For a performance studies analysis
of the Monsanto Corporation, see Taylor 2020, 226–244.

6   Gálvez defines the *milpa*-based diet as one that "relied heavily on products that are traditionally grown in a rural *milpa*, an intercropped field

that includes corn and also other plants such as squash, beans, tomatoes, tomatillos, and chiles. The core of *milpa*-based cuisine is corn that is grown locally" (2018, 2).

7   In her introduction, Gálvez includes a brief note inspired by fat studies scholarship and its refusal of the medicalized term *obesity*. The import of that note, however, remains in that short passage. Laudably, Gálvez writes about the debate she had with herself for even including the term *obesity* in her book. Ultimately though, she moved forward with the term so as "to be intelligible within these binational discussions" and "debates about obesity and overweight" (2018, 18).

Chapter 3. Sex, Drugs, and Intellectual Property Law

1   To view "Virgen del Sexo: Putear responsablemente," a production of ASCO media, visit https://www.youtube.com/watch?v=GoK-rwuiROs.

2   See Fabiola Torres López, Iván Herrera, and Mayté Ciriaco, 2017, "La vida tiene precio: Una investigación transnacional sobre los métodos de las farmacéuticas para prolongar sus monopolios en América Latina," https://bigpharma.ojo-publico.com/. An English-language version is also available.

3   For more on pipeline patents and how NAFTA exceeds TRIPS in gifting these patents to the pharmaceutical industry, see Shadlen 2009, 44–45.

4   Canadian HIV/AIDS Legal Network, "Towards a New NAFTA: Safeguarding Public Health and Access to Medicines," Submission to Global Affairs Canada: Consultations on the Renegotiation and Modernization of the North American Free Trade Agreement, July 18, 2017, 1–11, 2, https://www.ourcommons.ca/Content/Committee/421/CIIT/Brief/BR9174336/br-external/CanadianHIV-AIDS-LegalNetwork-e.pdf.

5   For example, consider the 2022 attacks made against a University of California graduate student who formed a network with other trans activists to pool unopened hormone therapies for trans people who can't access the care they need amid the national and subnational panics targeting trans bodies. Outside networks such as these, even those allied with trans access to health care, often reify the importance of formal trade channels and the authority of a medical doctor to access and prescribe hormone therapies. While these trans-allied voices often demand greater access to trans health care, they also tend to make the argument that unprescribed medications are more of a risk to trans people than not taking hormones at all. Unfortunately, even the sympathetic press refers to hormone distribution outside state-sanctioned and capital exchanges as "controversial" and potentially unethical, arguments we also see swirling when it comes to abortion pills in the aftermath of the overturning of *Roe v. Wade* in 2022. For example, see Colleen Flaherty, "Pressure over Trans Activist: U of California, Santa Cruz, Faces Online Mobbing over a Trans Student's Controversial Activ-

ism," *Inside Higher Ed*, August 19, 2022, https://www.insidehighered.com
/news/2022/08/19/uc-santa-cruz-grad-student-targeted-trans-activism.
On the history of the feminist organization Las Libres and their abortion-
pill outreach to the United States in the aftermath of the overturning of
Roe v. Wade, see Frédéric Saliba, "Mexican Feminists Take Action to Help
American Women Get Abortions," *Le Monde*, July 3, 2022, https://www
.lemonde.fr/en/international/article/2022/07/03/mexican-feminists-take
-action-to-help-american-women-get-abortions_5988894_4.html.

6   On the long history of DIY methods for circulating trans health care, see
Jules Gill-Peterson, "Doctors Who? Radical Lessons for the History of DIY
Transition," *Baffler*, no. 65, October 2022, https://thebaffler.com/salvos
/doctors-who-gill-peterson. In the article, Gill-Peterson remarks on how
trans women living in San Francisco would make trips to Tijuana to access synthetic hormones in the 1960s and 1970s.

   For a consideration of the difficulty of accessing trans health care outside the psychiatric approval of the transnational medical industry, see
Aizura 2018, 145–173; and Beauchamp 2015. On informal networks of hormone circulation and self-administration among transformistas in Venezuela, see Ochoa 2014, 162–164, 173. For an account of the self-administration
of testosterone, see Preciado 2013. For the state regulation of testosterone
as a controlled substance and the anxieties about the movement of hormones across borders, see Beauchamp 2013. On the relationship between
COVID-19 and HIV, particularly how anti-Black racism structures the lack
of access to health care in these simultaneous pandemics, see Gossett and
Hayward 2020.

7   I intentionally obscured the names of the center and those gathered around
the table (except for myself), because publicizing who is engaged in crossborder and intranational drug exchange can endanger those groups and
individuals, particularly during a time of heightened border security and
right-wing attacks on migrating peoples and the people who provide mutual aid.

8   For the story of the fundraiser and its aftermath, see Chantal Da Silva, "San
Diego Drag Queens Raise Thousands to Help LGBTQ Asylum Seekers in Tijuana," *Newsweek*, December 11, 2018, https://www.newsweek.com/san-diego
-drag-queens-raise-thousands-house-lgbtq-asylum-seekers-tijuana-1254073.

9   HFiT is the product of a binational partnership between the University of
California San Diego School of Medicine, the Universidad Autonoma de
Baja California School of Medicine, and Desayunador Salesiano "Padre
Chava," a community grassroots organization in Tijuana.

10 For more on the application of religious morality into Mexican political
life, particularly around the issue of abortion, see Morgan 2019. For the
ways in which Salinas made an agreement with the Catholic Church in
1992, the year NAFTA was signed, see page 545 of this same article.

11   Mental health services, including treatment for addiction, are similarly not universalized and often too expensive for working-class and poor Canadians.

12   Stephen J. Ubl, the president and CEO of Pharmaceutical Research and Manufacturers of America, put out a statement in objection to the Biden administration's support of the waiver on May 5, 2021. See https:// www.phrma.org/Press-Release/PhRMA-Statement-on-WTO-TRIPS -Intellectual-Property-Waiver.

13   For an account that sides with Big Pharma and its opposition to expanding the TRIPS waiver, see Marc L. Busch, "The Market's Response to the TRIPS Waiver," Wilson Center, July 14, 2023, https://www.wilsoncenter .org/article/markets-response-trips-waiver. For a piece that comes to a similar conclusion, see Chris Borges, "TRIPS Waivers and Pharmaceutical Innovation," Center for Strategic and International Studies, March 15, 2023, https://www.csis.org/blogs/perspectives-innovation/trips-waivers -and-pharmaceutical-innovation.

14   See World Trade Organization, "Decision Text on Extension of the 17 June 2022 Ministerial Decision to COVID-19 Therapeutics and Diagnostics," December 4, 2023, https://docs.wto.org/dol2fe/Pages/SS/directdoc .aspx?filename=q:/WT/GC/W913.pdf&Open=True.

15   See Bryce Baschuk, "WTO Approves Vaccine-Patent Waiver to Help Combat Covid Pandemic," *Bloomberg*, June 16, 2022, https://www.bloomberg .com/news/articles/2022-06-17/wto-approves-vaccine-patent-waiver-to -help-combat-covid-pandemic.

16   Erotophobic and anti-queer sex connections can surely be made between the state-imposed scarcity of HIV/AIDS medications and the lack of Mpox vaccines to vulnerable LGBTQ communities in 2022.

17   My piece for the event at Biquini Wax was titled "Avocado Toast," a messy, excessive, neoliberal romp with one of NAFTA's most quintessential objects of consumption: the avocado. It explored the *gringo* obsession with this fleshy green fruit as a humorous, at times raunchy, and always suspect performance of "eating the other." For the Biquini Wax lineup on "NAFTAlgia" (NAFTA nostalgia) titled *Una obsesión peligrosa* (A dangerous obsession), see https://www.h-r.la/event/biquini-wax-a-dangerous -obsession/.

18   Monumental queer and trans exhibitions have since appeared in other mainstream art museums such as *Imaginaciones radicales* at el Museo de Arte Moderno and *Positivo negativo: Adherencias culturales en la lucha contra el sida en México, 1978–2022*, at the Centro de la Imagen, both in 2023.

19   To view *El siglo de las luces*, visit Bordello's website, http://coarco.org/siglo -de-las-luces.html.

20   *Lotería* is a game of chance, yet the advertisement suggests that it is somehow the risk of playing at all that ensures your death. In other words, this is an abstinence-only PSA.

21   "El chivo expiatorio: Sida + violencia + acción—Entrevistas," https://www.youtube.com/watch?v=JjA1cBjVCcM.

22   To interact with the botiquín comparador, visit https://bigpharma.ojo-publico.com/apps/comparadordeprecios/.

23   For example, see Krikorian 2017 and Epstein 1996.

24   Torres-Ruiz (2011) identifies this event as the beginning of activist efforts on drug access in Mexico City.

25   To view *Dreams*, visit https://www.youtube.com/watch?v=qL6rqoweNDs&t=1s.

26   On Moreau's death, see Caitlin Donohue, "Before Life: Remembering the Pure Perversions of Damien Moreau," *Peep Show: News & Stories from the Sex Industry*, June 30, 2020.

27   To view *To Lose Yourself Is Eternal Happiness*, visit https://www.youtube.com/watch?v=5kwniILGVwQ.

Exhuming the Chupacabras

1   To view *México exhumado*, visit the Hemispheric Institute of Performance and Politics website, https://hemisphericinstitute.org/es/encuentro-2019-performances/item/2935-lechedevirgen.html.

2   The song playing in the background is "Tangiers" by Black Asteroid featuring Michèle Lamy.

3   For the ways in which the invention of the *chupacabra* as a folk monster figure speaks to the violent effects of neoliberal capitalism, particularly for communities of color, see Calvo-Quirós 2014. For the use of *vampiro* (vampire) as slang for male hustlers in the 1970s, see Cervantes-Gómez 2024, 75. Also see Prieto Stambaugh 2021, particularly 195–196, for a conversation on *murciélagos* (bats) in connection to (Zapotec) gods, the performance work of Lukas Avendaño, and Gloria Anzaldúa's concept of *nepantla* and the work of border artists.

4   All the essays in *The Official Museo Salinas Guide* are printed in both English and Spanish, a clear message that Razo meant for his book to circulate transnationally. Richard Moszka (who will reappear as the gimp character in the last deviation/*desviación*) translated the text into English. The translations from the essays included in this deviation are his.

5   Foreign economists came to call this moment of peso devaluation the "Tequila Effect," while those in Mexico referred to it as "el error de diciembre," or the December Error.

6   Lechedevirgen understands gender identity as a thing under constant mu-
tation. They've gravitated to the nomenclature of *xenobinary*, by which
they mean to refer to the inseparability of their body from the immuno-
suppressant medications they've taken for over a decade. Xenobinary also
refers to an experience of gender beyond the binaries imposed by and on
the human species. Lechedevirgen views themself as part machine, part
plant, and part hybrid organism, due in part to the transplant of a third
kidney in their body (Facebook post, October 7, 2020).

Chapter 4. Dancing *Punta* on NAFTA Time

1   While NAFTA contributed to blocking certain (im)migrants from crossing into the United States, it simultaneously started the "Trade NAFTA"
or TN visa for Canadian and Mexican professionals. See Goodman 2020
and Golash-Boza 2015 for two studies that describe the long and recent
histories of mass deportation practices.

2   The Bracero Program ended in 1964, just one year prior to when the Maquiladora Program began. Mexico viewed the latter as a replacement for
the former, which had allowed migrant men (mostly) to enter the United
States to fill seasonal employment needs. For a study of immigrant labor
history from the Bracero Program to NAFTA, see Mize and Swords 2011,
especially XXI-XLII, 175–192, and 193–214.

3   In 1994, the year NAFTA went into effect, California voted in favor of Proposition 187, which denied public services to undocumented immigrants. For
the ways in which Proposition 187 produced "illegal" identities to police
and regulate movement across the borderlands, see Cantú 2009, 441.

4   The MPP was terminated under Biden and then reinstated in 2021 after
a federal court in Texas ordered the Department of Homeland Security
to do so. Title 42 was a border policy that prevented migrating peoples
from petitioning for asylum in the United States. It used the flexibility of
administrative law at the southern border to expel asylum seekers on the
grounds of public health during the ongoing COVID-19 pandemic. The
Biden administration attempted to terminate Title 42 in May 2022 when
the federal COVID-19 Public Health Emergency ended, but a group of Re-
publicans convinced a federal court to block that termination on administrative grounds. Tellingly, in March 2022 Ukrainian refugees were granted
exemptions to Title 42. Over social media, the nonprofit Tijuana-based
law group El Otro Lado reported witnessing a change in behavior, with
Eastern Europeans now gathering at the ports of entry in Tijuana, which
they juxtaposed to the racist treatment of Black and Brown migrants from
Mexico, Central America, and Haiti. Title 42 finally expired on May 11, 2023,
but not without Biden instantiating "expedited removal" proceedings and
possible jail time for those who attempted to reenter after being deported

under the 1980 US asylum law, Title 8. On May 11, 2023, the United States also implemented the "Circumvention of Lawful Pathways" rule, which renders all those traveling through a third country before reaching Mexico and the US-Mexico border ineligible for asylum, with only limited exceptions. Under this rule, nearly all asylum seekers from Central America are rendered ineligible for asylum, as many pass on foot, train, and/or bus through Mexico. On May 25, 2023, Canada and the United States expanded the "Safe Third Country Agreement," wherein all those entering Canada anywhere across the land border, inclusive of internal waterways, are disqualified from making asylum claims. Furthermore, those who fail to use the infamously glitchy Department of Homeland Security scheduling system, the government phone app CBP One, are also considered ineligible to make an asylum petition.

5   For a description of the Cibola County Correctional Center and the conditions of trans detention there, see Balaguera 2023, 1802–1805.

6   For an elaboration on "stolen time" and performance, see Vogel 2018. For Vogel's study, "stolen time" refers to the ways in which midcentury African American performers stole time from the capitalist marketplace through Black fad styles and circuits, such as the Calypso Craze.

7   On the care with which queer migrants must curate their asylum documents in Toronto, Canada, see Autumn White 2014.

8   For an account of LGBTQ migration from Central America during the time of the 2018 caravan, see María Inés Taracena, "La caravana de la resistencia," NACLA, December 20, 2018, https://nacla.org/news/2018/12/20/la-caravana-de-la-resistencia.

9   In the Tzotzil language, Lok'tavanej means "image maker."

10   The name of this activist has been intentionally obscured, owing to the extreme and expansive use of sex-trafficking laws in Mexico after 2012. Because migration is increasingly criminalized throughout Mexico in flagrant violation of Article 11 in chapter 1 of the Mexican Constitution, the names of all migrating peoples discussed in this chapter are pseudonyms.

11   The Trafficking Victims Protection Act (TVPA), enacted in the United States in 2000, uses similar language to define sex trafficking as constituted by acts, means, and purposes (Correa-Cabrera and Sanders Montandon 2018, 9–10).

12   For an example of scholarship that focuses equally on these twin approaches to *transmigración*/transmigration, see Balaguera 2018.

13   Unlike in the United States where vocabulary around migration largely consists of in/out directional binary, Mexico has a richly diverse lexicon that speaks to the complexity of the country's history when it comes to the movements of its peoples across borders: *emigrantxs* (emigrants), *inmigrantxs* (immigrants), *deportadxs* (deported people), *retornadxs* (returned

people), *migración interna* (internal migration), *desplazadxs forazdxs* (forcibly displaced people), *solicitante de protección internaciónal* (applicant for international protection), and *refugiadxs* (refugees).

14   As Oliver N. Greene Jr. explains, "The Garinagu, commonly known as the Garifuna, are a people of West African and Amerindian descent who live along the Caribbean coast of Belize, Guatemala, Honduras, and Nicaragua and who share a common language, system of customs and beliefs, series of ancestor veneration rituals, and repertoire of music and dance. The word Garinagu refers to the people as a whole, whereas the term Garifuna refers to the language, the culture, and a person in the singular form" (2022, 189).

15   On the long history of anti-Black racism, the Garinagu, and the formation of *mestizaje*, see Euraque 2003. For a consideration of the politics of belonging in the Garinagu diaspora, see López Oro 2016. For an overview of scholarship that critiques the myth of *mestizaje* in Honduras through a critical race, gender, and sexuality lens, see Mendoza 2006.

16   Also see Adeyemi 2022, 39–61.

17   University Network for Human Rights, Harvard Law School's Immigration and Refugee Clinic, the Harvard Law School's Immigration Project, students from Yale Law School's Environmental Law Association, and the Yale Immigrant Justice Project, "Shelter from the Storm: Policy Options to Address Climate Induced Displacement from the Northern Triangle," April 2021, https://hls.harvard.edu/clinic-stories/legal-policy -work/shelter-from-the-storm-policy-options-to-address-climate-induced -displacement-from-the-northern-triangle/.

18   This hard-won success in Mexico was initiated in 2011 by el Colectivo para Eliminar el Racismo en México (COPERA).

NAFTA's Funeral

1   To view *NAFTAlina: The Musical*, go to the Hemispheric Institute of Performance and Politics at New York University website, https:// hemisphericinstitute.org/en/encuentro-2019-trasnocheo/item/3087 -trasnocheo-013.html.

2   For a brief history of the present and past appearances of the gimp in fashion, see Rodgers 2022.

3   Guy F. Erb Records of the Mexico-US Business Committee and Related Materials, US-Mexico Business collection, Benson Latin American Collection, LLILAS Latin American Studies and Collections, University of Texas at Austin.

4   In 1990 economist Sidney Weintraub coined the euphemistic phrase "marriage of convenience" to describe the relationship of Mexico and the United States as they developed the infrastructural basis for NAFTA.

5 "Summary of Objectives of the NAFTA Renegotiation," July 17, 2017, https:// ustr.gov/sites/default/files/files/Press/Releases/NAFTAObjectives.pdf.

6 As Bob Gallagher, the United Steelworkers communications director in Canada, told me in an interview in Toronto in 2018, "So we have a lot of membership who voted for Trump in these last elections. And it wasn't just our members, it was a whole lot of working class, particularly Midwest but also other working areas, voted for him . . . as long as they were white. Nobody fooled any Black workers that you should vote for Trump."

7 "Summary of Objectives," 2017, 3, 5.

8 GATT, Article XX General Exemptions, World Trade Organization, https:// www.wto.org/english/res_e/booksp_e/gatt_ai_e/art20_e.pdf.

Epilogue

1 In 2024, Maine Governor Janet Mills signed a shield law aimed at protecting Maine's health professionals who provide transgender and reproductive health care from out-of-state prosecution based on other states' bans or restrictions. Conservative politicians in Maine and anti-trans online influencers dubbed this law "transgender trafficking." Erin Reed, "Maine Governor Signs Transgender, Abortion Sanctuary Bill into Law: Bomb Threats Made Against Lawmakers Before Measure's Passage," *Washington Blade*, April 24, 2024, https://www.washingtonblade.com/2024/04/24 /maine-governor-signs-transgender-abortion-sanctuary-bill-into-law/.

2 For a critique of Programa Frontera Sur as "the most aggressive border control strategy of the Mexican state to date," see Balaguera 2018, 651.

3 Alex Riggins and Tammy Murga, "Smuggling Boat Tragedy Off San Diego Is Latest in Deadly Surge of Ocean Border Crossings," *Los Angeles Times*, March 13, 2023, https://www.latimes.com/california/story/2023-03-13 /smuggling-boat-crash-san-diego-deadly-maritime-border-crossings.

REFERENCES

Films and Recordings

Better Than Chocolate. Directed by Anne Wheeler. 1999. Motion International Trimark Pictures. 102 minutes.

Carmelita Tropicana: Your Kunst Is Your Waffen. Directed by Ela Troyano. 1994. 27 minutes.

Corrupción mexicana. Directed by El Diablo. 2010. Mecos Films. 87 minutes.

El cuerpo perdido. Created by Manuel Solano. 2014. Digital HD, H264, MP4. 7:28 minutes.

Cut Piece. Recording of live performance by Yoko Ono. March 21, 1965, at Carnegie Recital Hall, New York. https://vimeo.com/106706806/.

Dreams. Directed by Damien Moreau. 2016. Digital video. 6:04 minutes. https://www.youtube.com/watch?v=qL6rqoweNDs&t=1s.

The Fruit Machine. Directed by Sarah Fodey. 2018. SandBay Entertainment. 81 minutes.

Gente sw (*El vendedor*, Año 1, Vol. 3). Directed by Matla and Héctor Reyes. 2009. Editorial Matlarock. 38 minutes.

Hotel Garage, huilas mexicanas, cámaras escondidas, 100% reales, Abril, La Chacha, Brenda y Roxxana, mexicana caliente. Vol. 3, 2011.

Hotel Garage, huilas mexicanas, cámaras escondidas, Paulina, Paola, Gabriela. Vol. 4, 2012.

Hotel Garage, huilas mexicanas, cámaras escondidas Angelica 1 y 2, Valeria, and Camila. Vol. 5, 2012.

Hoteles de México: Putas en el hotel. Marvin Records. 2011.

Indigurrito. Recording of live performance by Nao Bustamante. Hemispheric Institute Digital Video Library. 1992. https://sites.dlib.nyu.edu/hidvl/mocfxpz3.

A las niñas gordas nadie las quiere. 2019. Recording of a live performance by Erika
Bülle Hernández. Ex-Teresa Arte Actual, Mexico City. Hemispheric Institute
of Performance and Politics. https://hemisphericinstitute.org/en/encuentro
-2019-performances/item/2946-erika-bulle-hernandez.html.

Little Sister's vs. Big Brother. Directed by Aerlyn Weissman. 2002. National Film
Board of Canada. 47 minutes.

México exhumado. Recording of live performance by Lechedevirgen Trimegisto.
Centro Universitario de Teatro, UNAM. 2019. Hemispheric Institute of
Performance and Politics. https://hemisphericinstitute.org/es/encuentro-2019
-performances/item/2935-lechedevirgen.html.

La putiza. Directed by Jorge Diestra. 2004. Mecos Films and WHAM Picture S.A.
de C.V. 2 hours and 10 minutes.

El siglo de las luces. Directed by Jorge Bordello. 2017. 53:47 minutes. http://coarco
.org/siglo-de-las-luces.html.

To Lose Yourself Is Eternal Happiness. Created by Damien Moreau and Manuel
Solano. 2017. Music by Sky White Tiger. Digital video. 5:56 minutes. https://
www.youtube.com/watch?v=5kwniILGVwQ.

Tongues Untied. Directed by Marlon Riggs. 1989. Frameline. 55 minutes.

Track 2: Enough Is Enough. Directed by Harry Sutherland. 1981. 1 hour and 28
minutes. https://www.youtube.com/watch?v=iN4_8eurids.

Untitled Fucking. Xandra Ibarra and Amber Hawk Swanson. 2013. 14:53 minutes.

La verganza. Directed by Jorge Diestra. 2005. Mecos Films and WHAM Picture S.A.
de C.V. 70 minutes.

Virgen del Sexo: Putear responsablemente. Cocreated by Luisa Almaguer. ASCO
Media, 2018. 1:55 minutes. https://www.youtube.com/watch?v=GoK-rwuiROs.

When They See Us. Directed by Ava DuVernay. 2019. Netflix. 4 hours and 56
minutes.

Xipe Totec Punk. Recording of live performance by César Martínez Silva and
Orgy punk. Phi Centre Montréal. June 24, 2014. http://www.martinezsilva
.com/english/video_e.html.

Interviews

Andrea. December 2018. Interview with author. Playas de Tijuana.

Brito, Alejandro. 2018. Interview with author. Mexico City.

Carlsen, Laura. 2013. Interview with author. Mexico City.

Echeverría, Eugenio. 2018. Interview with author. Mexico City.

El Diablo. 2013. Interview with author. Mexico City.

Gallagher, Bob. 2018. Interview with author. Toronto.

Grajales, Jorge. 2013. Interview with author. Mexico City.

Hernández Victoria, Miguel Alonso. 2013. Interview with author. Mexico City.

Hooper, Tom. 2018. Interview with author. Toronto.

Jansen, Carlyle. 2018. Interview with author. Toronto.

Lok'tavanej. 2018. Interview with author. Mexico City.

Macías, Fernando. 2013. Interview with author. Mexico City.

Martínez Silva, César. 2015. Interview with author. Mexico City.

McDonald, Bruce, and Darrell Schuurman. 2018. Interview with author. Toronto.

Mistysyn, Kimberly. 2018. Interview with author. Toronto.

Razo, Vicente. 2015. Interview with author. Mexico City.

Reyes, Héctor, and Matla. 2013. Interview with author. Mexico City.

Sandra. 2013. Interview with author. Mexico City.

Scythes, John. 2018. Interview with author. Toronto.

Thames, Carol. 2018. Interview with author. Toronto.

Walsh, Bruce. 2018. Interview with author. Toronto.

Zúñiga, Felipe. 2013. Interview with author. Mexico City.

Publications

Abu-Lughod, Janet. 1989. *Before European Hegemony: The World System A.D. 1250–1350*. Oxford: Oxford University Press.

Ackerman, Diane. 2000. *Deep Play*. New York: Vintage.

Adekola, Tolulope Anthony. 2020. "Revisiting the Public Health Implications of the United States-Mexico–Canada Agreement." *Globalization and Health* 16, no. 1: 1–2.

Adeyemi, Kemi. 2019. "The Practice of Slowness." *GLQ* 24, no. 4: 545–567.

Adeyemi, Kemi. 2022. *Feels Right: Black Queer Women and the Politics of Partying in Chicago*. Durham, NC: Duke University Press.

Adeyemi, Kemi, Kareem Khubchandani, and Ramón H. Rivera-Servera, eds. 2021. *Queer Nightlife*. Ann Arbor: University of Michigan Press.

Aguiar, José Carlos G. 2010. "Neoliberalismo, piratería y protección de los derechos de autor en México." *Renglones* 62: 1–23.

Aguiar, José Carlos G. 2012. "Policing New Illegalities: Piracy, Raids, and Madrinas." In *Violence, Coercion, and State-Making in Twentieth-Century Mexico*, edited by Wil G. Pansters, 159–184. Palo Alto, CA: Stanford University Press.

Aguiar, José Carlos G. 2013. "Smugglers, Fayuqueros, Piratas: Transitory Commodities and Illegality in the Trade of Pirated CDs in Mexico." *Political and Legal Anthropology Review* 6, no. 2: 249–265.

Agustín, Laura María. 2007. *Sex at the Margins: Migration, Labour Markets and the Rescue Industry*. London: Zed Books.

Ahmed, Sara. 2004. "Affective Economies." *Social Text* 22, no. 2: 117–139.

Aizura, Aren Z. 2018. *Mobile Subjects: Transnational Imaginaries of Gender Reassignment*. Durham, NC: Duke University Press.

Alarcón, Norma. 1983. "Chicana's Feminist Literature: A Re-vision through Malintzin/or Malintzin Putting Flesh Back on the Object." In *This Bridge Called My Back: Writings by Radical Women of Color*, edited by Cherríe Moraga and Gloria Anzaldúa, 182–190. New York: Kitchen Table/Women of Color Press.

Alarcón, Norma. 1989. "Traddutora, Traditora: A Paradigmatic Figure of Chicana Feminism." *Cultural Critique* 13: 57–87.

Alba, Carlos, and Marianne Braig. 2022. "'Good, Beautiful and Cheap': Sino-Mexican Trade Relations and Their Translocal Linkages." In *Latin America and Asia: Relations in the Context of Globalization from Colonial Times to the Present*, edited by Carlos Alba, Marianne Braig, and Stefan Rinke, 195–217. Darmstadt: WBG Academic.

Alcalá, Rita Cano. 2001. "From Chingada to Chingona: La Malinche Redefined or, A Long Line of Hermanas." *Aztlan: A Journal of Chicano Studies* 26, no. 2: 31–61.

Alilunas, Peter. 2021. "The King Is Dead, Long Live the Algorithm: MindGeek and the Digital Distribution of Adult Film." In *Digital Media Distribution: Portals, Platforms, Pipelines*, edited by Paul McDonald, Courtney Brannon Donoghue, and Timothy Havens, 317–341. New York: New York University Press.

Alvarez Castillo, Constanzx. 2014. *La Cerda Punk: Ensayos desde un feminismo gordo, lésbiko, antikapitalista, and antiespecista*. Valparaíso: Editado por Trío editorial.

Anderson, Mark. 2009. *Black and Indigenous: Garifuna Activism and Consumer Culture in Honduras*. Minneapolis: University of Minnesota Press.

Anti-69 Network. "Against the Mythologies of the 1969 Criminal Code Reform." https://anti-69.ca/.

Autumn White, Melissa. 2014. "Archives of Intimacy and Trauma: Queer Migration Documents as Technologies of Affect." *Radical History Review* 120: 75–93.

Babb, Sarah. 2001. *Managing Mexico: Economists from Nationalism to Neoliberalism*. Princeton, NJ: Princeton University Press.

Balaguera, Martha. 2018. "Trans-migrations: Agency and Confinement at the Limits of Sovereignty." *Signs* 43, no. 3: 641–664.

Balaguera, Martha. 2023. "Trans-asylum: Sanctioning Vulnerability and Gender Identity Across the Frontier." *Ethnic and Racial Studies* 46, no. 9: 1791–1811.

Bandak, Andreas, and Manpreet K. Janeja. 2018. "Introduction: Worth the Wait." In *Ethnographies of Waiting: Doubt, Hope, and Uncertainty*, edited by Andreas Bandak and Manpreet K. Janeja, 1–40. New York: Routledge.

Beauchamp, Toby. 2013. "The Substance of Borders: Transgender Politics, Mobility, and US State Regulation of Testosterone." *GLQ* 19, no. 1: 57–78.

Beauchamp, Toby. 2015. "Moving Violations: Synthetic Hormones, Sexual Deviance, and Gendered Mobilities." In *Mobile Desires: The Politics and Erotics of Mobility Justice*, edited by Liz Montgomery and Melissa Autumn White, 16–27. London: Palgrave Macmillan.

Beauchamp, Toby. 2019. *Going Stealth: Transgender Politics and US Surveillance Practices*. Durham, NC: Duke University Press.

Beckman, Ericka. 2012. *Capital Fictions: The Literature of Latin America's Export Age*. Minneapolis: University of Minnesota Press.

Behti, Anjalee. 2019. "Trump's Ruthless Expansion of the Mexico City Policy Threatens Reproductive Health Abroad." *University of San Francisco Law Review* 53, no. 1: 117–143.

Berlant, Lauren, and Michael Warner. 1998. "Sex in Public." *Critical Inquiry* 24, no. 2: 547–566.

Bernstein, Elizabeth. 2018. *Brokered Subjects: Sex, Trafficking, and the Politics of Freedom*. Chicago: University of Chicago Press.

Biltekoff, Charlotte. 2007. "The Terror Within: Obesity in Post 9/11 US Life." *American Studies* 48, no. 3: 29–48.

Bogus, SDiane. 1982. "Dyke Hands." *Common Lives/Lesbian Lives: A Lesbian Quarterly*, no. 5, 72–76.

Bothwell, Robert. 1992. *Canada and the US: The Politics of Partnership*. Toronto: University of Toronto Press.

Bothwell, Robert. 2015. *Your Country, My Country: A Unified History of the United States and Canada*. Oxford: Oxford University Press.

Brier, Jennifer. 2009. *Infectious Ideas: U.S. Political Responses to the AIDS Crisis*. Chapel Hill: University of North Carolina Press.

Brondo, Keri Vacanti. 2013. *Land Grab: Green Neoliberalism, Gender, and Garifuna Resistance*. Tucson: University of Arizona Press.

Brown, Wendy. 1995. *States of Injury: Power and Freedom in Late Modernity*. Princeton, NJ: Princeton University Press.

Browne, Simone. 2015. *Dark Matters: On the Surveillance of Blackness*. Durham, NC: Duke University Press.

Bülle Hernández, Erika. 2018. "Cuerpos gordos: Empoderamiento a través de las prácticas performaticas." *Revista Arbitrada de Artes Visuales*. Tercera Época: 56–63.

Bülle Hernández, Erika. 2020. *Cuerpa: Herramientas para una gorda rebelde*. Edición Independiente.

Byrd, Jodi. 2011. *The Transit of Empire: Indigenous Critiques of Colonialism*. Minneapolis: University of Minnesota Press.

Calderón, Yecid / Pinina Flandes. 2016. *Deviniendo loca: Textualidades de una marica sureada*. Santiago: Los Libros de la Mujer Rota.

Califia, Patrick. 1995. "Dangerous Tongues." In *Forbidden Passages: Writings Banned in Canada*, 9–24. Pittsburgh, PA: Cleis Press.

Calvo-Quirós, William A. 2014. "Sucking Vulnerability: Neoliberalism, the Chupacabras, and the Post–Cold War Years." In *The Un/Making of Latina/o Citizenship: Culture, Politics, and Aesthetics*, edited by Ellie D. Hernández and Eliza Rodriguez y Gibson, 212–233. New York: Palgrave Macmillan.

Campos, Paul, Abigail Saguy, Paul Ernsberger, Eric Oliver, and Glenn Gaesser. 2006. "The Epidemiology of Overweight and Obesity: Public Health Crisis or Moral Panic?" *International Journal of Epidemiology* 35, no. 1: 55–60.

Cannon, Martin. 1998. "The Regulation of First Nations Sexuality." *Canadian Journal of Native Studies* 17, no. 1: 1–18.

Cantú, Lionel, Jr. 2009. *The Sexuality of Migration: Border Crossings and Mexican Immigrant Men*, edited by Nancy A. Naples and Salvador Vidal-Ortiz. New York: New York University Press.

Carey, Elaine, and Andrae M. Marak, eds. 2011. *Smugglers, Brothels, and Twine: Historical Perspectives on Contraband and Vice in North America's Borderlands*. Tucson: University of Arizona Press.

Carrillo, Héctor. 2017. *Pathways of Desire: The Sexual Migration of Mexican Gay Men*. Chicago: University of Chicago Press.

Carroll, Amy Sara. 2017. *REMEX: Toward an Art History of the NAFTA Era*. Austin: University of Texas Press.

Catungal, John Paul. 2018. "'We Had to Take Up Space, We Had to Create Space': Locating Queer of Colour Politics in 1980s Toronto." In *Queering Urban Justice: Queer of Colour Formations in Toronto*, edited by Jin Haritaworn, Ghaida Moussa, and Syrus Marcus Ware, with Río Rodríguez, 45–61. Toronto: University of Toronto Press.

Centre for Contemporary Culture Strozzina. 2010. "Daniela Rossell." In *Portraits and Power: People, Politics and Structures*, 118–121. Milan: Silvana Editorale.

Cervantes-Gómez, Xiomara Verenice. 2020. "Paz's *Pasivo*: Thinking Mexicanness from the Bottom." *Journal of Latin American Cultural Studies* 29, no. 3: 333–347.

Cervantes-Gómez, Xiomara Verenice. 2024. *Bottoms Up: Queer Mexicanness and Latinx Performance*. New York: New York University Press.

Charnovitz, Steve. 1998. "The Moral Exception in Trade Policy." *Virginia Journal of International Law* 38, no. 4: 1–49.

Chauncey, George. 1995. *Gay New York: Gender, Urban Culture, and the Making of the Gay Male World, 1890–1940*. New York: Basic Books.

Chávez, Karma R., and Hana Masri. 2020. "The Rhetoric of Family in the US Immigration Movement: A Queer Migration Analysis of the 2014 Central American Child Migrant." In *Queer and Trans Migrations: Dynamics of Illegalization, Detention, and Deportation*, edited by Eithne Luibhéid and Karma R. Chávez, 209–225. Urbana: University of Illinois Press.

Cheng, Jih-Fei, Alexandra Juhasz, and Nishant Shahani. 2020. *AIDS and the Distribution of Crises*. Durham, NC: Duke University Press.

Cohen, Cathy. 2004. "Deviance as Resistance: A New Research Agenda for the Study of Black Politics." *Du Bois Review* 1, no. 1: 27–45.

Córdoba García, David, Javier Sáez, and Pedro Vidarte, eds. 2005. *Teoría queer: Políticas bolleras, maricas, trans, mestizas*. Barcelona: Editorial EGALES.

Correa-Cabrera, Guadalupe, and Arthur Sanders Montandon. 2018. "Reforming Mexico's Anti-Trafficking in Persons Legislation." *Mexican Law Review* 11, no. 1: 3–30.

Cossman, Brenda, and Shannon Bell. 1997. "Introduction." In *Bad Attitude on Trial: Pornography, Feminism, and the Butler Decision*, edited by Brenda Cossman, Shannon Bell, Lisa Gotell, and Becki L. Ross, 3–48. Toronto: University of Toronto Press.

Cowen, Deborah. 2014. *The Deadly Life of Logistics: Mapping Violence in Global Trade*. Minneapolis: University of Minnesota Press.

Crimp, Douglas. 1987. "How to Have Promiscuity in an Epidemic." *October* 43: 237–271.

Cross, John C. 1998. *Informal Politics: Street Vendors and the State in Mexico City*. Stanford, CA: Stanford University Press.

Cruz Hernández, Yutsil, and Alfonso Hernández. 2015. "The Obstinacy of Tepito." Translated by Irmgard Emmelhainz. *Scapegoat* 6: 167–173.

Cuellar, Manuel R. 2023. "Los Mecos de Veracruz: Queer Gestures and the Performance of Nahua Indigeneity." *Journal of Latin American Cultural Studies* 32, no. 1: 109–131.

Cvetkovich, Ann. 1995. "Recasting Receptivity: Femme Sexualities." In *Lesbian Erotics*, edited by Karla Jay, 125–146. New York: New York University Press.

Davis, Diane E. 2013. "Zero-Tolerance Policing, Stealth Real Estate Development, and the Transformation of Public Space: Evidence from Mexico City." *Latin American Perspectives* 40, no. 2: 53–76.

Dean, Gabrielle. 1997. "The 'Phallacies' of Dyke Comic Strips." In *The Gay '90s: Disciplinary and Interdisciplinary Formations in Queer Studies*, edited by Thomas Foster, Carol Siegel, and Ellen E. Berry, 199–223. New York: New York University Press.

Dean, Jodi. 2009. *Democracy and Other Neoliberal Fantasies: Communicative Capitalism and Left Politics*. Durham, NC: Duke University Press.

Debroise, Olivier. 1997. "Una tríada de géneros sin fronteras." In *De la calle al estudio: Fotografía Pedro Slim*. México: Museo Universitario del Chopo.

Delany, Samuel R. 2001. *Times Square Red, Times Square Blue*. New York: New York University Press.

Delpar, Helen. 1995. *The Enormous Vogue of Things Mexican: Cultural Relations Between the United States and Mexico, 1920–1935*. Tuscaloosa: University of Alabama Press.

DeRuiz, Alexandra R. 2023. *Crucé la frontera en tacones: Crónicas de una TRANSgresora*. Barcelona: Egales Editorial.

DiMassa, Diane. 1999. *Complete Hothead Paisan: Homicidal Lesbian Terrorist*. Pittsburgh, PA: Cleis Press.

Domínguez-Ruvalcaba, Héctor. 2016. *Translating the Queer: Body Politics and Transnational Conversations*. London: Zed Books.

Duggan, Lisa. 2004. *The Twilight of Equality: Neoliberalism, Cultural Politics, and the Attack on Democracy*. Boston: Beacon Press.

Duggan, Lisa, and Nan D. Hunter. 2006. *Sex Wars: Sexual Dissent and Political Culture*. New York: Routledge.

Duina, Francesco. 2006. *The Social Construction of Free Trade: The European Union, NAFTA, and MERCOSUR*. Princeton, NJ: Princeton University Press.

Dworkin, Andrea. 1978. "Pornography: The New Terrorism." *NYU Review of Law and Social Change* 8, no. 2: 215–218.

Dworkin, Andrea. 1981. *Pornography: Men Possessing Women*. New York: Putnam.

Ellis, Megan. 1983. "The Anti-Porn Movement in B.C." *Canadian Women's Studies / Les Cahiers de la Femme* 4, no. 4: 50–52.

Epps, Brad. 2008. "Retos, riesgos, pautas y promesas de la teoría queer." *Revista Iberoamericana* 74, no. 225: 897–920.

Epstein, Steven. 1996. *Impure Science: AIDS, Activism, and the Politics of Knowledge*. Berkeley: University of California Press.

Euraque, Darío A. 2003. "The Threat of Blackness to the Mestizo Nation: Race and Ethnicity in the Honduran Banana Economy, 1920s and 1930s." In *Banana Wars: Power, Production, and History in the Americas*, edited by Steve Striffler and Mark Moberg, 229–250. Durham, NC: Duke University Press.

Falconí Trávez, Diego. 2021. "La heteromaricageneidad contradictoria como herramienta crítica cuy(r) en las literaturas andinas." *Revista Interdisciplinaria de estudios de género de El Colegio de México* 7: 1–39.

Falconí Trávez, Diego, Santiago Castellanos, and María Amelia Viteri, eds. 2014. *Resentir lo "queer" en América Latina: Diálogos desde/con el sur*. Barcelona: Egales Editoriales.

Ferguson, Roderick. 2003. *Aberrations in Black: Toward a Queer of Color Critique*. Minneapolis: University of Minnesota Press.

Fiol-Matta, Licia. 2001. *A Queer Mother for the Nation: The State and Gabriela Mistral*. Minneapolis: University of Minnesota Press.

Foucault, Michel. 1978. *The History of Sexuality*. Vol. I. New York: Pantheon.

Freeman, Elizabeth. 2010. *Time Binds: Queer Temporalities, Queer Histories*. Durham, NC: Duke University Press.

Fuller, Janine. 1995. "The Case Against Canada Customs." In *Forbidden Passages: Writings Banned in Canada*, 25–43. Pittsburgh, PA: Cleis Press.

Fung, Richard. 1991. "Looking for My Penis: The Eroticized Asian in Gay Video Porn." In *How Do I Look? Queer Film and Video*, edited by Bad Object-choices, 145–168. Seattle: Bay Press.

Fung, Richard. 1995. "Burdens of Representation, Burdens of Responsibility." In *Constructing Masculinity*, edited by Maurice Berger, Brian Wallis, and Simon Watson, 291–298. New York: Routledge.

Fusco, Coco. 2000. *Corpus Delecti: Performance Art of the Americas*. New York: Routledge.

Gabilondo, Joseba. 2002. "Like Blood for Chocolate, Like Queers for Vampires: Border and Global Consumption in Rodríguez, Tarantino, Arau, Esquivel, and Troyano (Notes on Baroque, Camp, Kitsch, and Hybridization)." In *Queer Globalizations: Citizenship and the Afterlife of Colonialism*, edited by Arnaldo Cruz-Malavé and Martin F. Manalansan, 236–264. New York: New York University Press.

Galbraight, Jean, and Beatrix Lu. 2019. "Gender-Identity Protection, Trade, and the Trump Administration: A Tale of Reluctant Progressivism." *Yale Law Journal Forum* (October 7): 44–61.

Gálvez, Alyshia. 2018. *Eating NAFTA: Trade, Food Policies, and the Destruction of Mexico*. Berkeley: University of California Press.

García Canclini, Néstor. 2001. *Consumers and Citizens: Globalization and Multicultural Conflicts*. Translated by George Yúdice. Minneapolis: University of Minnesota Press.

García Manríquez, Hugo. 2014. *Anti-Humboldt: A Reading of the North American Free Trade Agreement / Anti-Humboldt: Una lectura del Tratado de Libre Comercio de América del Norte*. Crown Heights, NY: Editorial Aldus and Litmus Press.

Gaspar de Alba, Alicia, and Georgina Guzmán. 2010. "Feminicidio: The 'Black Legend' of the Border." In *Making a Killing: Femicide, Free Trade, and La Frontera*, edited by Alicia Gaspar de Alba with Georgina Guzmán, 1–24. Austin: University of Texas Press.

Gibson-Graham, J. K. 2006. *The End of Capitalism (as We Knew It): A Feminist Critique of Political Economy.* Minneapolis: University of Minnesota Press.

Gillespie, Kate, and J. Brad McBride. 2013. "Counterfeit Smuggling: Rethinking Paradigms of Diaspora Investment and Trade Facilitation." *Journal of International Management* 19, no. 1: 66–81.

Gill-Peterson, Jules. 2022. "Doctors Who? Radical Lessons for the History of DIY Transition." *Baffler*, no. 65. https://thebaffler.com/salvos/doctors-who-gill-peterson.

Goddard, Michael. 2007. "BBW: Techno-archaism, Excessive Corporeality and Network Sexuality." In *C'Lick Me: A Netporn Studies Reader*, edited by Katrien Jacobs, Marije Janssen, and Matteo Pasquinelli, 187–196. Amsterdam: Institute of Network Cultures.

Goffman, Erving. 1959. *The Presentation of Self in Everyday Life.* Garden City, NY: Doubleday.

Golash-Boza, Tanya Maria. 2015. *Deported: Immigrant Policing, Disposable Labor, and Global Capitalism.* New York: New York University Press.

Gómez-Barris, Macarena. 2017. *The Extractive Zone: Social Ecologies and Decolonial Perspectives.* Durham, NC: Duke University Press.

Gómez-Barris, Macarena. 2018. *Beyond the Pink Tide: Art and Political Undercurrents in the Americas.* Berkeley: University of California Press.

Goodman, Adam. 2020. *The Deportation Machine: America's Long History of Expelling Immigrants.* Princeton, NJ: Princeton University Press.

Gossett, Che, and Eva Hayward. 2020. "Trans in a Time of HIV/AIDS." *TSQ: Transgender Studies Quarterly* 7, no. 4: 527–553.

Greene, Oliver N., Jr. 2002. "Ethnicity, Modernity, and Retention in the Garifuna Punta." *Black Music Research Journal* 22, no. 2: 189–216.

Gruzinski, Serge. 1985. "Las cenizas del deseo: Homosexuales novohispanos a mediados del siglo XVII." In *De la Santidad a la Perversión o de porque no se cumplía la Ley de Dios en la Sociedad Novohispana*, edited by Sergio Ortega, 255–281. México: Editorial Grijalva.

Guillén Rauda, Héctor Daniel. 2016. "Performance e incertinumbre: La pornografía *amateur* en México." *Revista de Estudios de Antropología Sexual* 1, no. 7: 112–126.

Gutiérrez, Laura G. 2010. *Performing Mexicanidad: Vendidas y Cabareteras on the Transnational Stage.* Austin: University of Texas Press.

Halberstam, Jack. 2005. *In a Queer Time and Place: Transgender Bodies, Subcultural Lives.* New York: New York University Press.

Halperin, David M., and Trevor Hoppe, eds. 2017. *The War on Sex.* Durham, NC: Duke University Press.

Harrison, Christopher Scott. 2000. "Protection of Pharmaceuticals as Foreign Policy: The Canada-U.S. Trade Agreement and Bill C-22 Versus the North American Free Trade Agreement and Bill C-91." *North Carolina Journal of International Law* 26, no. 2: 457–528.

Hennessy, Rosemary. 2013. *Fires on the Border: The Passionate Politics of Labor Organizing on the Mexican Frontera.* Minneapolis: University of Minnesota Press.

Hernández Victoria, Miguel Alonso. 2011. "Chacal, los orígenes de un mito urbano." Encuentro sobre Disidencia Sexual en la UACM. Talk.

Herzog, Lawrence. 1992. "The Architecture of Tourism and Free Trade in Mexico." Paper delivered at the XVII International Congress, Latin American Studies Association, Los Angeles, CA.

Hester, Helen, and Caroline Walters. 2016. *Fat Sex: New Directions in Theory and Activism*. London: Routledge.

Hilderbrand, Lucas. 2009. *Inherent Vice: Bootleg Histories of Videotape and Copyright*. Durham, NC: Duke University Press.

Hoang, Kimberly Kay. 2016. "Perverse Humanitarianism and the Business of Rescue: What's Wrong with NGOs and What's Right About the 'Johns.'" *Political Power and Social Theory* 14, no. 1: 104–110.

Hoang, Kimberly Kay. 2022. *Spiderweb Capitalism: How Global Elites Exploit Frontier Markets*. Princeton, NJ: Princeton University Press.

Hoang, Kimberly Kay, and Rhacel Salazar Parreñas. 2014. *Human Trafficking Reconsidered: Rethinking the Problem, Envisioning New Solutions*. IDebate Press.

Hoogeveen, Dawn. 2015. "Intimate Geographies of NAFTA and Canadian Mining in Mexico." *Scapegoat* 6: 237–242.

Hooper, Tom. 2014. "'More Than Two Is a Crowd': Mononormativity and Gross Indecency in the Criminal Code, 1981–2." *Journal of Canadian Studies* 48, no. 1: 53–81.

Hooper, Tom. 2019. "Queering '69: The Recriminalization of Homosexuality in Canada." *Canadian Historical Review* 100, no. 2: 257–273.

Howard, Y. 2018. *Ugly Differences: Queer Female Sexuality in the Underground*. Urbana: University of Illinois Press.

Hurley, Nat. 2010. "The Queer Traffic in Literature; or, Reading Anthologically." ESC 36, no. 1: 81–108.

International Labour Organization. 2014. "Informal Employment in Mexico: Current Situation, Policies and Challenges." https://www.ilo.org/wcmsp5/groups /public/---americas/---ro-lima/documents/publication/wcms_245889.pdf.

Jiménez Portilla, Luz del Carmen. 2022. "Representaciones de la trata sexual de mujeres en contextos neoliberales: El papel de los productos culturales en la operación del dispositivo antitrata Mexicano." *Critical Reviews on Latin American Research* 10, no. 2: 85–98.

Johnson, E. Patrick, and Ramón H. Rivera-Servera, eds. 2016. *Blacktino Queer Performance*. Durham, NC: Duke University Press.

Johnson, Merri Lisa, and Robert McRuer. 2014. "Cripistemologies: Introduction." *Journal of Literary and Cultural Disability Studies* 8, no. 2: 127–147.

Jones, Steve. 1996. "Mass Communication, Intellectual Property Rights, International Trade, and the Popular Music Industry." In *Mass Media and Free Trade: NAFTA and the Cultural Industries*, edited by Emile G. McAnany and Kenton T. Wilkinson, 331–350. Austin: University of Texas Press.

Kay, Tamara, and R. L. Evans. 2018. *Trade Battles: Activism and the Politicization of International Trade Policy*. Oxford: Oxford University Press.

Kempadoo, Kamala. 1998. "Introduction: Globalizing Sex Workers' Rights." In *Global Sex Workers: Rights, Resistance, and Redefinition*, edited by Kamala Kempadoo and Jo Doezema, 1–28. New York: Routledge.

Kim, Jina B. 2017. "Toward a Crip-of-Color Critique: Thinking with Minich's 'Enabling Whom?'" *Lateral* 6, no. 1. https://csalateral.org/issue/6-1/forum-alt-humanities-critical-disability-studies-crip-of-color-critique-kim/.

Kim, Jodi. 2018. "Settler Modernity, Debt Imperialism, and the Necropolitics of Promise." *Social Text* 36, no. 2: 41–61.

Konove, Andrew. 2018. *Black Market Capital: Urban Politics and the Shadow Economy in Mexico City*. Berkeley: University of California Press.

Krikorian, Gaëlle Pascale. 2017. "From AIDS to Free Trade Agreements: Knowledge Activism in Thailand's Movement for Access to Medicines." *Engaging Science, Technology, and Society* 3: 154–179.

Kun, Josh. 2011. "Playing with the Fence, Listening to the Line: Sound, Sound Art, and Acoustic Politics at the Mexico-US Border." In *Performance in the Borderlands*, edited by Ramón H. Rivera-Servera and Harvey Young, 17–36. New York: Palgrave Macmillan.

Kuppers, Petra. 2006. *The Scar of Visibility: Medical Performances and Contemporary Art*. Minneapolis: University of Minnesota Press.

Labonté, Ronald, Eric Crosbie, Deborah Gleeson, and Courtney McNamara. 2019. "USMCA (NAFTA 2.0): Tightening the Constraints on the Right to Regulate for Public Health." *Globalization and Health* 15, no. 1: 1–15.

Labonté, Ronald, Deborah Gleeson, and Courtney McNamara. 2020. "USMCA 2.0: A Few Improvements but Far from a 'Healthy' Trade Treaty." *Globalization and Health* 16, no. 43: 2–4.

La Fountain-Stokes, Lawrence. 2021. *Translocas: The Politics of Puerto Rican Drag and Trans Performance*. Ann Arbor: University of Michigan Press.

Laite, Julia, and Philippa Hetherington. 2021. "Introduction: Trafficking, a Useless Category of Historical Analysis?" *Journal of Women's History* 33, no. 4: 7–39.

Lash, Scott, and John Urry. 1987. *The End of Organized Capitalism*. Madison: University of Wisconsin Press.

LeBesco, Kathleen. 2010. "Fat Panic and the New Morality." In *Against Health: How Health Became the New Morality*, edited by Jonathan M. Metzl and Anna Kirkland, 72–82. New York: New York University Press.

Leebron, David W. 1996. "Lying Down with Procrustes: An Analysis of Harmonization Claims." *Economic Analysis* 111: 41–117.

Lepecki, André. 2016. "Duration." In *In Terms of Performance*, edited by Shannon Jackson and Paula Marincola. Berkeley: Arts Research Center at University of California; Philadelphia: Pew Center for Arts and Heritage. http://intermsofperformance.site/keywords/duration/andre-lepecki.

Light, Michael T., Jingying He, and Jason P. Robey. 2020. "Comparing Crime Rates Between Undocumented Immigrants, Legal Immigrants, and Native-Born US Citizens in Texas." *Proceedings of the National Academy of Sciences (PNAS)* 117, no. 51: 32340–32347.

Lobato, Ramon. 2012. *Shadow Economies of Cinema: Mapping Informal Film Distribution*. London: BFI Publishing.

Lobato, Ramon, and Julian Thomas. 2012. "Transnational Piracy Research in Practice: A Roundtable Interview with Joe Karaganis, John Cross, Olga Sezneva, and Ravi Sundaram." *Television and New Media* 13, no. 5: 447–458.

López, Sergio Raúl. 2009. "'Uno es platillo y el otro la receta': Entrevista al Diablo, director de la productura Mecos Films." *Cine Toma* 5, no. 1: 32–34.

López García, Vanessa, Julia Antivilo, María Laura Rosa, and Lorena Wolffer, eds. 2019. *Estado de emergencia: Puntos de dolor y resiliencia en la Ciudad de México*. Mexico City: Secretaría de Cultura: Centro de Cultura/ E-Literatura Digital.

López Oro, Paul Joseph. 2016. "'Ni de aquí, ni de allá': Garífuna Subjectivities and the Politics of Diasporic Belonging." In *Afro-Latin@s in Movement*, edited by Petra R. Rivera-Rideau, Jennifer A. Jones, and Tianna S. Paschel, 61–83. New York: Palgrave Macmillan.

López Oro, Paul Joseph. 2020. "Garifunizando Ambas Américas: Hemispheric Entanglements of Blackness/Indigeneity/AfroLatinidad." *Postmodern Culture* 31, no. 1: 1–29.

Lowe, Lisa. 2015. *The Intimacies of Four Continents*. Durham, NC: Duke University Press.

Lugones, María. 2007. "Heterosexualism and the Colonial/Modern Gender System." *Hypatia* 22, no. 1: 186–209.

Luna, Caleb. 2022. "Undisciplined Bodies: Race, Size and Sexuality in U.S. Media and Culture." PhD diss., University of California, Berkeley.

Lyall, Victoria I., and Terezita Romo. 2022. *Traitor, Survivor, Icon: The Legacy of La Malinche*. New Haven, CT: Yale University Press. Exhibition catalog.

Mapplethorpe, Robert. 1986. *Black Book*. New York: St. Martin's Press.

Marez, Curtis. 2004. *Drug Wars: The Political Economy of Narcotics*. Minneapolis: University of Minnesota Press.

Marx, Karl, and Friedrich Engels. 1988. *The Economic and Philosophic Manuscripts of 1844 and the Communist Manifesto*. Buffalo, NY: Prometheus Books.

McClanahan, Annie, and Jon-David Settell. 2021. "Service Work, Sex Work, and the 'Prostitute Imaginary.'" *South Atlantic Quarterly* 120, no. 3: 493–514.

Mcillwain, Jeffrey Scott. 2005. "Intellectual Property Theft and Organized Crime: The Case of Film Piracy." *Trends in Organized Crime* 8, no. 4: 15–39.

McRuer, Robert. 2018. *Crip Times: Disability, Globalization, and Resistance*. New York: New York University Press.

Meléndez, Armando Cristano. 2002. *El enojo de las sonajas: Palabras del ancestor*. 2nd ed. Tegucigalpa: Editorial Cultura.

Mendoza, Breny. 2006. "De-mythologizing Mestizaje in Honduras: A Critique of Recent Contributions." *Latin American and Caribbean Ethnic Studies* 1, no. 2: 185–201.

Mercer, Kobena. 1994. *Welcome to the Jungle: New Positions in Black Cultural Studies*. New York: Routledge.

Meyer, Richard. 2003. "The Jesse Helms Theory of Art." *October* 104: 131–148.

Miller-Young, Mireille. 2014. *A Taste for Brown Sugar: Black Women in Pornography*. Durham, NC: Duke University Press.

Minich, Julie Avril. 2014. *Accessible Citizenships: Disability, Nation, and the Cultural Politics of Greater Mexico*. Philadelphia: Temple University Press.

Mistysyn, Kimberly. 1997. "Managing the Local Gay and Lesbian Bookshop." In *Liberating Minds: The Stories and Professional Lives of Gay, Lesbian, and Bisexual Librarians and Their Advocates*, edited by Norman G. Kester, 161–163. Jefferson, NC: McFarland and Company.

Mitchell, Gregory. 2015. *Tourist Attractions: Performing Race and Masculinity in Brazil's Sexual Economy*. Chicago: University of Chicago Press.

Mitchell, Gregory. 2022. *Panics without Borders: How Global Sporting Events Drive Myths About Sex Trafficking*. Berkeley: University of California Press.

Mize, Ronald L., and Alicia C. S. Swords. 2011. *Consuming Mexican Labor: From the Bracero Program to NAFTA*. Toronto: University of Toronto Press.

Mogrovejo, Norma. 2015. *Disidencia sexual y ciudadanía en la era del consumo neoliberal, migración y sexilio político*. Mexico City: UNAM.

Mollow, Anna. 2012. "Is Sex Disability? Queer Theory and the Disability Drive." In *Sex and Disability*, edited by Robert McRuer and Anna Mollow, 285–312. Durham, NC: Duke University Press.

Mollow, Anna, and Robert McRuer. 2015. "Fattening Austerity." *Body Politics* 5: 25–49.

Monsiváis, Carlos. 2002. "El Museo Salinas y las máscaras del Mexicano." In *The Official Museo Salinas Guide*, by Vicente Razo. Edited by Pilar Perez and translated by Richard Moszka, 7–13. Santa Monica, CA: Smart Art Press.

Montez, Ricardo. 2020. *Keith Haring's Line: Race and the Performance of Desire*: Durham, NC: Duke University Press.

Moraga, Cherríe. 1981. "La Güera." In *This Bridge Called My Back: Writings by Radical Women of Color*, edited by Cherríe Moraga and Gloria Anzaldúa, 27–34. New York: Kitchen Table Women of Color Press.

Moraga, Cherríe. 1983. *Loving in the War Years: Lo Que Nunca Paso por Sus Labios*. Boston: South End Press.

Moraga, Cherríe. 1993. "Queer Aztlán: The Re-formation of Chicano Tribe." In *The Last Generation: Prose and Poetry*, 224–238. Boston: South End Press.

Morgan, Lynn M. 2019. "Miss Mexico's Dress: The Struggle over Reproductive Governance in Jalisco, Mexico." *Journal of Latin American and Caribbean Anthropology* 24, no. 2: 526–554.

Morgan, Robin. 1980. "Theory and Practice: Pornography and Rape." In *Take Back the Night: Women on Pornography*, edited by Laura Lederer, 134–140. New York: William Morrow.

Morgensen, Scott Lauria. 2011. *Spaces Between Us: Queer Settler Colonialism and Indigenous Decolonization*. Minneapolis: University of Minnesota Press.

Mountz, Alison, and Winifred Curran. 2009. "Policing in Drag: Giuliani Goes Global with the Illusion of Control." *Geoforum* 40: 1033–1040.

Mulhall, Anne. 2014. "Dead Time: Queer Temporalities and the Deportation Regime." *Social Text Online*. https://socialtextjournal.org/periscope_article/dead-time-queer-temporalities-and-the-deportation-regime/.

Muñoz, José Esteban. 1996. "Ephemera as Evidence: Introductory Notes to Queer Acts." *Women and Performance* 8, no. 2: 5–16.

Muñoz, José Esteban. 2009. *Cruising Utopia: The Then and There of Queer Futurity*. New York: New York University Press.

Murray, David A. B. 2016. *Real Queer? Sexual Orientation and Gender Identity Refugees in the Canadian Refugee Apparatus*. London: Rowman and Littlefield.

Musser, Amber Jamilla. 2014. *Sensational Flesh: Race, Power, and Masochism*. New York: New York University Press.

Musto, Jennifer. 2016. *Control and Protect: Collaboration, Carceral Protection, and Domestic Sex Trafficking in the United States*. Berkeley: University of California Press.

Nakagawa, Junji J. 2011. *International Harmonization of Economic Regulation*. Oxford: Oxford University Press.

Navarrete, Federico. 2002. "El Museo Salinas o el gobernante como chivo expiatorio." In *The Official Museo Salinas Guide*, by Vicente Razo. Edited by Pilar Perez and translated by Richard Moszka, 15–24. Santa Monica, CA: Smart Art Press.

Needham, Gary. 2018. "Bringing Out the Gimp: Fashioning the SM Imaginary." *Fashion Theory* 18, no. 2: 149–168.

Nevins, Joseph. 2002. *Operation Gatekeeper: The Rise of the "Illegal Alien" and the Making of the US-Mexico Boundary*. New York: Routledge.

Nguyen, Hoàng Tân. 2014. *A View from the Bottom: Asian American Masculinity and Sexual Representation*. Durham, NC: Duke University Press.

Novak, David. 2013. *Japanoise: Music at the Edge of Circulation*. Durham, NC: Duke University Press.

Nyong'o, Tavia. 2002. "Racial Kitsch and Black Performance." *Yale Journal of Criticism* 15, no. 2: 371–391.

O'Brien, Erin, and Michael Wilson. 2015. "Clinton, Bush and Obama: Changing Policy and Rhetoric in the United States Annual Trafficking in Persons Report." In *Global Human Trafficking: Critical Issues and Contexts*, edited by Molly Dragiewicz, 123–139. New York: Routledge.

O'Brien, Michelle. 2003. "Tracing This Body: Transsexuality, Pharmaceuticals, and Capitalism," 1–12. Zine distributed by the Transgender Oral History Project. Lake Worth, FL: Downward Mobility Press.

O'Brien, Michelle. 2004. "New Flesh, New Struggles: Self-Discovery Thru Porn and Kink," 16–21. Zine distributed by the Transgender Oral History Project. Lake Worth, FL: Downward Mobility Press.

Ochoa, Marcia. 2014. *Queen for a Day: Transformistas, Beauty Queens, and the Performance of Femininity in Venezuela*. Durham, NC: Duke University Press.

Ochoa, Marcia. 2016. "Los Huecos Negros: Cannibalism, Sodomy and the Failure of Modernity in Tierra Firme." *Genders* 1, no. 1. https://www.colorado

.edu/genders/2016/05/19/los-huecos-negros-cannibalism-sodomy-and-failure-modernity-tierra-firme.

Office of the United States Trade Representative, Executive Office of the President. 2022. "2022 Review of Notorious Markets for Counterfeiting and Piracy." 1–53. https://ustr.gov/sites/default/files/2023-01/2022%20Notorious%20Markets%20List%20(final).pdf.

O'Hara, Claerwen. 2022. "Consensus and Diversity in the World Trade Organization: A Queer Perspective." Cambridge University Press on behalf of the American Society of International Law 116: 32–37.

Ojeda, Martha, and Rosemary Hennessy, eds. 2006. NAFTA from Below: Maquiladora Workers, Farmers, and Indigenous Communities Speak Out on the Impact of Free Trade in Mexico. Coalition for Justice in the Maquiladoras.

Orme, William. 1996. Understanding NAFTA: Mexico, Free Trade, and the New North America. Austin: University of Texas Press.

PachaQueer. 2016. ANO-SOBER-ANO. Arte Actual. May 30. http://arteactual.ec/ano-sober-ano/.

Paradis, Elise. 2016. "'Obesity' as Process: The Medicalization of Fatness by Canadian Researchers, 1971–2010." In Obesity in Canada: Critical Perspectives, edited by Jenny Ellison, Deborah McPhail, and Wendy Mitchison, 56–88. Toronto: University of Toronto Press.

Parrini, Rodrigo, and Ana Amuchástegui. 2012. "Normalised Transgressions: Consumption, the Market, and Sexuality in Mexico." In Understanding Global Sexualities, New Frontiers, edited by Peter Aggleton, Paul Boyce, Henrietta L. Moore, and Richard Parker, 21–33. New York: Routledge.

Parrini, Rodrigo, Siobhan Guerrero Mc Manus, and Alba Pons. 2021. "Incomodidad y desplazamiento." Revista Interdisciplinaria de estudios de género de El Colegio de México 7: 1–9.

Paz, Octavio. 1959. El laberinto de la soledad. México: Fondo de Cultura Económica.

Pelúcio, Larissa. 2014. "Possible Appropriations and Necessary Provocations for a Teoria Cu." In Queering Paradigms IV: South-North Dialogues on Queer Epistemologies, Embodiments and Activisms, edited by Elizabeth Sara Lewis, Rodrigo Borba, Branca Falabella Fabrício, and Diana de Souza Pinto, 31–52. Oxford: Peter Lang.

Pérez, Elizabeth. 2016. "The Ontology of the Twerk: From 'Sexy' Black Movement Style to Afro-Diasporic Sacred Dance." African and Black Diaspora: An International Journal 9, no. 1: 1–18.

Pérez, Hiram. 2015. A Taste for Brown Bodies: Gay Modernity and Cosmopolitan Desire. New York: New York University Press.

Pierce, Joseph M. 2018. "El ano dilatado: Un siglo de deseo pederasta en América Latina." In Inflexión marica: Narrativas del descalabro gay en América Latina, edited by Diego Falconí Trávez, 25–40. Barcelona: Egales.

Pierce, Joseph, María Amelia Viteri, Lourdes Martínez Echázabal, Diego Falconí Trávez, and Salvador Vidal-Ortiz. 2021. "Queer/Cuir de las Américas: Traducción, decolonidad, y lo inconmensurable." GLQ 3, no. 5: 321–327.

Pons Rabasa, Alba. 2018. "De la representación a la corposubjetivación: La configuración de lo transgénero en la Ciudad de México." In *Mujeres y VIH en México: Diálogos y tensiones entre perspectivas de atención a la salud*, edited by Ana Amuchástegui, 209–242. Mexico City: Universidad Autónoma Metropolitana.

Prasad, Pavithra. 2015. "Paradiso Lost: Writing Memory and Nostalgia in the Postethnographic Present." *Text and Performance Quarterly* 35, no. 2–3: 202–220.

Preciado, Paul B. 2013. *Testo Junkie: Sex, Drugs, and Biopolitics in the Pharmapornographic Era*. New York: Feminist Press.

Prieto Stambaugh, Antonio. 2021. "The Queer/Muxe Performance of Disappearance: Lukas Avendaño's Butterfly Utopia." In *Performances That Change the Americas*, edited by Stuart A. Day, 175–201. New York: Routledge.

Puar, Jasbir. 2007. *Terrorist Assemblages: Homonationalism in Queer Times*. Durham, NC: Duke University Press.

Puar, Jasbir. 2017. *The Right to Maim: Debility, Capacity, Disability*. Durham, NC: Duke University Press.

Quijano, Aníbal. 2000. "Coloniality of Power, Eurocentrism, and Latin America." *Nepantla* 1, no. 3: 533–580.

Raila, Geneviève, Dave Holmes, and Stuart J. Murray. 2010. "The Politics of Evidence on 'Domestic Terrorists': Obesity Discourses and Their Effects." *Social Theory and Health* 8, no. 3: 259–279.

Ramos, Iván A. 2022. "Pirates and Punks: Bootlegs, Archives, and Performance in Mexico City." In *Turning Archival: The Life of the Historical in Queer Studies*, edited by Daniel Marshall and Zeb Tortorici, 233–257. Durham, NC: Duke University Press.

Rand, Erica. 1998. "'Troubling Customs': The Issues, the Problems, the Process, the Result." *New Art Examiner* 25, no. 9: 11–13.

Rao, Rahul. 2015. "Global Homocapitalism." *Radical Philosophy* 194: 38–49.

Rault, Jasmine. 2017. "'Ridiculizing' Power: *Relajo* and the Affects of Queer Activism in Mexico." *Scholar and Feminist Online* 14, no. 2. https://sfonline.barnard.edu/ridiculizing-power-relajo-and-the-affects-of-queer-activism-in-mexico/2/.

Reguillo, Rossana. 2011. "The Narco-Machine and the Work of Violence: Notes toward Its Decodification." *Esmisférica* 8, no. 2. https://hemisphericinstitute.org/en/emisferica-82/reguillo5.html.

Renfro, Paul. 2018. "'Hunting These Predators': The Gender Politics of Child Protection in the Post-9/11 Years." *Feminist Studies* 44, no. 3: 567–599.

Renfro, Paul. 2020. *Stranger Danger: Family Values, Childhood, and the American Carceral State*. Oxford: Oxford University Press.

Rifkin, Mark. 2011. *When Did Indians Become Straight? Kinship, the History of Sexuality, and Native Sovereignty*. Oxford: Oxford University Press.

Rivera-Servera, Ramón H. 2016. "Reggaetón's Crossings: Black Aesthetics, Latina Nightlife, and Queer Choreography." In *No Tea, No Shade: New Writings in Black Queer Studies*, edited by E. Patrick Johnson, 95–112. Durham, NC: Duke University Press.

Rivera-Servera, Ramón H., and Harvey Young. 2011. "Introduction: Border Moves." In *Performance in the Borderlands*, edited by Ramón H. Rivera-Servera and Harvey Young, 1–16. New York: Palgrave Macmillan.

Rodgers, Daniel. 2022. "Bring Out the Gimp: Tracing Fashion's Obsession with Squeaky Bottoms." *Dazed*. May 23. https://www.dazeddigital.com/fashion /article/56154/1/gimp-mask-bdsm-latext-kink-fetish-gay-clothes-balenciaga -fashion-history-runway.

Rodríguez, Jesusa. 2003. "The Conquest According to La Malinche." In *Holy Terrors: Latin American Women Perform*, edited by Diana Taylor and Roselyn Constantino. Translated by Marléne Ramírez-Cancio, 231–234. Durham, NC: Duke University Press.

Rodríguez, Juana María. 2014. *Sexual Futures, Queer Gestures, Latina Longings*. New York: New York University Press.

Rodríguez, Juana María. 2023. *Puta Life: Seeing Latinas, Working Sex*. Durham, NC: Duke University Press.

Rofel, Lisa. 2007. *Desiring China: Experiments in Neoliberalism, Sexuality, and Public Culture*. Durham, NC: Duke University Press.

Román Pérez, Ernesto. 2006. *El cine pornográfico Mexicano de los '90*. Ciudad de México: Cineteca Nacional.

Ross, Becki L. 1997. "'It's Merely Designed for Sexual Arousal.'" In *Bad Attitude on Trial: Pornography, Feminism, and the Butler Decision*, edited by Brenda Cossman, Shannon Bell, Lisa Gotell, and Becki L. Ross, 152–198. Toronto: University of Toronto Press.

Rossell, Daniela. 2002. *Ricas y famosas: Mexico 1994–2001*. Turner Publicaciones.

Rubenstein, Anne. 2020. "A Sentimental and Sexual Education: Men, Sex, and Movie Theaters in Mexico City, 1920–2010." *Mexican Studies / Estudios Mexicanos* 36, no. 1–2: 216–242.

Rubin, Gayle S. 1975. "The Traffic in Women: Notes on the 'Political Economy' of Sex." In *Toward an Anthropology of Women*, edited by Rayna R. Reiter, 157–210. New York: Monthly View Press.

Rubin, Gayle S. 2011a. "Thinking Sex: Notes for a Radical Theory of the Politics of Sexuality." In *Deviations: A Gayle Rubin Reader*, 137–181. Durham, NC: Duke University Press.

Rubin, Gayle S. 2011b. "The Trouble with Trafficking: Afterthoughts on 'The Traffic in Women.'" In *Deviations: A Gayle Rubin Reader*, 66–86. Durham, NC: Duke University Press.

Ruiz, Sandra. 2019. *Ricanness: Enduring Time in Anticolonial Performance*. New York: New York University Press.

Russo Garrido, Anahi. 2020. *Tortilleras Negotiating Intimacy: Love, Friendship, and Sex in Queer Mexico City*. New Brunswick, NJ: Rutgers University Press.

Sáez, Javier, and Sejo Carrascosa. 2011. *Por el culo: Políticas anales*. Barcelona: Egales Editorial.

Saldaña-Portillo, María Josefina. 2016. *Indian Given: Racial Geographies Across Mexico and the United States*. Durham, NC: Duke University Press.

Salzinger, Leslie. 2003. *Genders in Production: Making Workers in Mexico's Global Factories*. Berkeley: University of California Press.

Sánchez Prado, Ignacio M. 2014. *Screening Neoliberalism: Transforming Mexican Cinema, 1988–2012*. Nashville, TN: Vanderbilt University Press.

Sari, Elif. 2020. "Lesbian Refugees in Transit: The Making of Authenticity and Legitimacy in Turkey." *Journal of Lesbian Studies* 24, no. 2: 140–158.

Sarkar, Bhaskar. 2016. "Media Piracy and the Terrorist Boogeyman: Speculative Potentiations." *positions* 24, no. 2: 343–368.

Schaefer, Eric. 2007. "Pandering to the 'Goon Trade': Framing the Sexploitation Audience from Advertising." In *Sleaze Artists: Cinema at the Margins of Taste, Style, and Politics*, edited by Jeffrey Sconce, 19–46. Durham, NC: Duke University Press.

Schneider, Rebecca. 2014. "Performance Remains." *Performance Research* 6, no. 2: 100–108.

Schorb, Friedrich. 2022. "Fat as a Neoliberal Epidemic: Analyzing Fat Bodies through the Lens of Political Epidemiology." *Fat Studies: An Interdisciplinary Journal of Body Weight and Society* 11, no. 2: 70–82.

Schulman, Sarah. 2012. *The Gentrification of the Mind: Witness to a Lost Imagination*. Berkeley: University of California Press.

Schulman, Sarah. 2021. *Let the Record Show: A Political History of ACT UP New York, 1987–1993*. New York: Farrar, Straus and Giroux.

Scott, Darieck. 2010. *Extravagant Abjection: Blackness, Power, and Sexuality in the African American Literary Imagination*. New York: New York University Press.

Shadlen, Kenneth C. 2009. "The Politics of Patents and Drugs in Brazil and Mexico: The Industrial Bases of Health Policies." *Comparative Politics* 42, no. 1: 41–58.

Shadlen, Kenneth C. 2012. "The Mexican Exception: Patents and Innovation Policy in a Non-conformist and Reluctant Middle Income Country." *European Journal of Development Research* 24: 300–318.

Shih, Elena. 2016. "Not in My 'Backyard Abolitionism': Vigilante Rescue Against American Sex Trafficking." *Sociological Perspectives* 59, no. 1: 66–90.

Shih, Elena. 2023. *Manufacturing Freedom: Sex Work, Anti-Trafficking Rehab, and the Racial Wages of Rescue*. Berkeley: University of California Press.

Shilts, Randy. 1987. *And the Band Played On: Politics, People, and the AIDS Epidemic*. New York: St. Martin's Press.

Siegel, Alana D. 2016. "NAFTA Largely Responsible for the Obesity Epidemic in Mexico." *Washington University Journal of Law and Policy* 50: 195–226.

Slim, Pedro. 1997. *De la calle al estudio: Fotografía Pedro Slim*. México: Museo Universitario del Chopo.

Smith, Paul Julian. 2017. *Queer Mexico: Cinema and Television Since 2000*. Detroit, MI: Wayne State University Press.

Star, Susan Leigh. 1999. "The Ethnography of Infrastructure." *American Behavioral Scientist* 43, no. 3: 377–391.

Stewart, John. 2017. *Strangers with Memories: The United States and Canada from Free Trade to Baghdad*. Montréal: McGill-Queen's University Press.

Stewart, Susan, in collaboration with Persimmon Blackbridge and Lizard Jones. 1991. *Drawing the Line: Lesbian Sexual Politics on the Wall.* Vancouver: Press Gang Publishers.

Stockton, Kathryn Bond. 2006. *Beautiful Bottom, Beautiful Shame: Where "Black" Meets "Queer."* Durham, NC: Duke University Press.

Strings, Sabrina. 2019. *Fearing the Black Body: The Racial Origins of Fat Phobia.* New York: New York University Press.

Strub, Sean. 2017. "HIV: Prosecution or Prevention? HIV is Not a Crime." In *The War on Sex*, edited by David M. Halperin and Trever Hoppe, 347–352. Durham, NC: Duke University Press.

Subero, Gustavo. 2010. "Gay Mexican Pornography at the Intersection of Ethnic and National Identity in Jorge Diestra's *La Putiza*." *Sexuality and Culture* 14: 217–233.

TallBear, Kim. 2018. "Making Love and Sex Beyond Settler Sex and Family." In *Making Kin, Not Population*, edited by Adele E. Clarke and Donna Haraway, 145–166. Chicago: Prickly Paradigm Press.

Tate, Shirley Anne. 2019. *Decolonising Sambo: Transculturation, Fungibility and Black and People of Colour Futurity.* Bingley, UK: Emerald Publishing.

Taylor, Diana. 2020. *¡Presente! The Politics of Presence.* Durham, NC: Duke University Press.

Terry, John, Lou Ederer, and Jennifer A. Orange. 2005. "Cross-Border NAFTA: The First Trade Treaty to Protect IP Rights." *IP Value.* https://www.mondaq.com /canada/corporatecommercial-law/30547/crossborder-nafta-the-first-trade -treaty-to-protect-ip-rights.

Thomas, Trish. 1991. "Wunna My Fantasies." *Bad Attitude* 7, no. 5: 25–32.

Thornton, Christy. 2021. *Revolution in Development: Mexico and the Governance of the Global Economy.* Berkeley: University of California Press.

Thrasher, Steven. 2022. *The Viral Underclass: The Human Toll When Inequality and Disease Collide.* New York: Celadon Books.

Tomso, Greg. 2017. "HIV Monsters: Gay Men, Criminal Law, and the New Political Economy of HIV." In *The War on Sex*, edited by David M. Halperin and Trever Hoppe, 353–377. Durham, NC: Duke University Press.

Torres López, Fabiola, Iván Herrera, and Mayté Ciriaco. 2017. "Multinational Pharmaceutical Companies Decide on Access to Health in Latin America." *OjoPúblico's Big Pharma Project.* Translated by Diego Meza Hernandez. https://bigpharma.ojo-publico.com/articulo/life-has-a-price-multinational -pharmaceutical-companies-decide-on-access-to-health-in-latin-america/.

Torres-Ruiz, Antonio. 2011. "HIV/AIDS and Sexual Minorities in Mexico: A Globalized Struggle for the Protection of Human Rights." *Latin American Research Review* 46, no. 1: 30–53.

Tortorici, Zeb. 2018. *Sins Against Nature: Sex and Archives in Colonial New Spain.* Durham, NC: Duke University Press.

Tortorici, Zeb. 2023. "Entangled Archives and Latin Americanist Histories of Sexuality." *Journal of the History of Sexuality* 32, no. 1: 66–78.

Tyburczy, Jennifer. 2014. "Leather Anatomy: Cripping Homonormativity at International Mr. Leather." *Journal of Literary and Cultural Disability Studies* 8, no. 2: 275–293.

Tyburczy, Jennifer. 2016a. *Sex Museums: The Politics and Performance of Display.* Chicago: University of Chicago Press.

Tyburczy, Jennifer. 2016b. "Sex Toys After NAFTA: Transnational Class Politics, Erotic Consumerism, and the Economy of Female Pleasure in Mexico City." *Signs* 42, no. 1: 123–152.

Tyburczy, Jennifer. 2019. "Sex Trafficking Talk: Rosi Orozco and the Neoliberal Narrative of Empathy in Post-NAFTA Mexico." *Feminist Formations* 31, no. 3: 95–117.

Urata, Shujiro. 2002. "Globalization and the Growth in Free Trade Agreements." *Asia-Pacific Review* 9, no. 1: 20–32.

US Customs and Border Protection. 2010, May 26. "Revocation of Two Ruling Letters and Revocation of Treatment Relating to the Tariff Classification of Vibrating Sex Toys." *Customs Bulletin and Decisions* 44, no. 22: 1–6. https://www.cbp.gov/bulletins/Vol_44_No_22_Title.pdf.

Valencia, Sayak. 2010. *Capitalismo Gore.* Santa Cruz de Tenerife: Editorial Melusina.

Valencia, Sayak. 2015. "NAFTA: Capitalismo Gore and the Femicide Machine." *Scapegoat* 6: 131–135.

Valencia, Sayak. 2018. *Gore Capitalism.* Translated by JD Pluecker. South Pasadena, CA: Semiotext(e).

Vance, Carol S. 2012. "Innocence and Experience: Melodramatic Narratives of Sex Trafficking and Their Consequences for Law and Policy." *History of the Present* 2, no. 2: 200–218.

Vargas, Deborah R. 2013. "Punk's Afterlife in Cantina Time." *Social Text* 31, no. 3: 57–73.

Vargas, Deborah R. 2014. "Ruminations on *Lo Sucio* as a Latino Queer Analytic." *American Quarterly* 66, no. 3: 715–726.

Vats, Anjali, and Deidré A. Keller. 2018. "Critical Race IP." *Cardozo Arts and Entertainment Law Journal* 36, no. 3: 735–795.

Vogel, Shane. 2009. *The Scene of Harlem Cabaret: Race, Sexuality, and Performance.* Chicago: University of Chicago Press.

Vogel, Shane. 2018. *Stolen Time: Black Fad Performance and the Calypso Craze.* Chicago: University of Chicago Press.

Weeks, Jeffrey. 1981. *Sex, Politics and Society: The Regulation of Sexuality since 1800.* New York: Longman.

Weintraub, Sidney. 1990. *A Marriage of Convenience: Relations Between Mexico and the United States (A Twentieth Century Fund Report).* Oxford: Oxford University Press.

Williams, Linda. 1991. "Film Bodies: Gender, Genre, and Excess." *Film Quarterly* 44, no. 2: 2–13.

Williams, Linda. 1999. *Hard Core: Power, Pleasure, and the "Frenzy of the Visible."* Berkeley: University of California Press.

Wilson, Ara. 2012. "Intimacy: A Useful Category for Transnational Analysis." In *The Global and the Intimate: Feminism in Our Time*, edited by Geraldine Pratt and Victoria Rosner, 31–56. New York: Columbia University Press.

Wilson, Ara. 2016. "The Infrastructure of Intimacy." *Signs* 41, no. 2: 248–280.

Wright, Melissa. 2006. *Disposable Women and Other Myths of Global Capitalism.* New York: Routledge.

Wu, Mark. 2008. "Free Trade and the Protection of Public Morals: An Analysis of the Newly Emerging Public Morals Clause Doctrine." *Yale Journal of International Law* 33: 215–251.

Ybarra, Patricia A. 2018. *Latinx Theater in the Times of Neoliberalism.* Evanston, IL: Northwestern University Press.

Ybarra-Frausto, Tomás. 1989. "Rasquachismo: A Chicano Sensibility." In *Chicano Aesthetics: Rasquachismo*, 5–8. Phoenix, AZ: Movimiento Artístico del Rio Salado. Exhibition catalog.

Yeh, Rihan. 2017. *Passing: Two Publics in a Mexican Border City.* Chicago: University of Chicago Press.

Zapata, Luis. 2022. *El vampiro de la colonia Roma.* Mexico City: Penguin Random House Grupo Editorial.

INDEX

Note: page numbers followed by *f* refer to figures.

Canadian drug manufacturers and, 142; CanCon and, 227n3; Memorandum D9-1-1 and, 91; supply management and, 124; Wimmin's Fire Brigade and, 88

capital, 11–13, 132, 135–136, 211; accumulation of, 3, 5, 206; administration of, 70; circulation of, 48, 119; cultural, 18, 20, 164; desire and, 22–23; erotic, 18; exchange, 228n9, 231n5; financial, 18, 20; gain, 106, 200, 206; gay, 20, 22, 26; human, 191; identity and, 118; ideology, 29; illicit forms of, 27; investment, 5; movement of, 36; queer time and, 223n27; racial, 7

capitalism, xviii, 8, 12–13, 116, 118, 184–185; consumer, 151; crisis and, 130; gore, 31; homocapitalism, 6; neoliberal, 15, 194, 234n3; racial, 5, 11, 29, 34, 40, 208; sex and, 18. *See also* free-trade capitalism

Caraveo Castro, Alfonso, 172–173

Carey, Elaine, 172

Carlsen, Laura, 68

Carmelita Tropicana, xxvi

Carr, Jim, 116, 118

Carroll, Amy Sara, 9

Catholic Church, 140, 232n10

censorship, 81, 87, 99, 102, 105, 115, 131, 224n8; free trade and, 228n16

Central America, 178, 198, 235n4; LGBTQ migration from, 236n8; Northern Triangle, 172, 180. *See also* El Salvador; Guatemala; Honduras

Cervantes-Gómez, Xiomara Verenice, xxvii, 60, 234n3

chacal, xxix, 19–22, 26–27, 60, 221n10

Chacon, Jaime, 132, 157–159

Chávez, Karma R., 188

Cheng, Jih-Fei, 130

chicas trans, 179–180, 183, 187, 189–190, 195

China, 49–50, 77, 220n6. *See also* BRICS

la chingada, xix, xxiv, xxix

el chingón, xxiv, xxvii

El chivo expiatorio: SIDA + violencia + acción, 129, 131, 144–148, 151, 154, 156, 160

Cibola County Correctional Center, xxix, 175, 189, 236n5

cines piojo, 45–46, 48–49

circulation, 8, 28, 33; of books, 90; of capital, 48, 119; of the *chacal*, 20; of cheap foodstuffs, 62; of cultural goods, 12; of dissident (sexual) acts, 36; of em-

bodied sexualities, 38; of food, 123; of gender-affirming care, 209; of hormones, 136, 232n6; of medications, 133; of *mestizaje*, xxiv; of *objetos Salinizados*, 165; of pornography, 42, 44, 46–48, 59; of queer materials in Canada, 91, 93; of sex toys, 164; sexual consumption and, 87; of sexual goods and labor, xxvii; of sexual materials, 95

class, xxviii, 14, 18–20, 146, 221n12; difference, 20, 25; identity, 35; justice, xxvii; power dynamics, 30; stratification, 46; violence, 32

Clinton, Bill, 3, 55, 69, 134, 224n9; administration of, 11, 133; Kantor and, 135

Cohen, Cathy, xxix

Colectivo Sol, 140, 151

Colombia, 1, 220n2

colonialism, 10–11, 74–75; European, 75; fantasies of, xxvi; free trade and, 77; Garinagu and, 194; settler, 6, 77, 118

coloniality of power, 10, 75

commerce, 29, 50; sexual, xxvi, 13, 19, 116, 232n2

commodities, xix, 23, 78; European expansion in, xv; transnational movement of, 11; transportation of, 29

commodity specialists, 80, 92, 96–97, 104–105, 116

consumption, 8, 30, 35, 49, 74, 110, 174; Canadian content, 84; cultural, 26; of dissident (sexual) acts, 36; of drugs, 138; of embodied sexualities, 38; excessive, 69, 123; of food 36, 123, 125; free trade and, 12, 42, 70; global narratives of, 14; localized, 18; in Mexico's informal market, 43; NAFTA and, 11, 233n17; of pornography, 44, 46–48; racializations of, 75, 126; sexual, 68–69, 87; of sexual artifacts, 45; of sexual material culture, 28; women and, 68

conviviality, 172, 193; queer, 177

copyright, 43, 51

corn, 230nn5–6; tortillas, 177, 181; US government–subsidized, xxvii, 56, 124. *See also* dumping; *milpas*; Monsanto

Cortés, Gaba, 176, 186, 214

Cortés, Hernán, xxiv, 144

Cossman, Brenda, 90–91

COVID-19, xxix, 71, 143, 172, 235n4; HIV and, 232n6; policy, 175; vaccines, 133, 142–143

exchange, 4, 8, 19, 29, 35, 175; capital, 228n9;
circuits of, 7, 22, 43, 49; cultural processes of, 82; drug, 140, 232n7; gift, xxvii;
non-NAFTA form of, 37; of pleasure, 157;
pornography and, 45; power, 201, 206;
queer traffic, 131; rate, 56; sexual, xxviii,
19; sexual economies of, 40; of sexually
explicit materials, 84; value, 9
exploitation, 35, 95, 180; capitalist, xxvi, 18;
labor, xxvi, 208, 210; sexual, 30
extractivism, 3, 7

fat studies, as field, 125, 230–231n7
fatphobia/*gordofobia*, 122, 125–126, 128,
225n17. *See also* obesity, as related to
panic
fayuca, 45, 49–50, 54
feminicidios, 31–32, 161, 175, 181
femininity, 15, 18
feminism, 106; antipornography, 87; Black,
111; radical, 68, 94; trans-exclusionary,
211; transfeminist, 130, 177, 184
femme people, xxvi, 28, 32–33, 68, 136
Ferguson, Roderick, xxvi
Fiol-Matta, Licia, xxiv
Foucault, Michel, 89, 219n2
Finger Vibrator, 2–3, 5, 11, 13, 36
Finley, Karen, 104
First Nations, 175; gender and sexuality
practices of, 72; rights of, 3, 118
fisting, 84, 106, 108–110, 113, 115, 229n20
Fleck, John, 104
flows: capital; criminalized, 28, 44, 206;
cultural, xix, xxv, xxviii, 27, 222n24;
diets and, 126; *fayuca*, 49; free-market,
208; free-trade, xxvii–xxviii, 36, 59,
128; of gay capital, 22–23; of gay desire,
22–23; global, 4, 6, 13, 19, 22, 34; illicit,
xxvii, xxix, 4, 27, 29; labor, 223n27;
merchandising, 19; NAFTA and, 12,
56; queer, 34; sexual, 4, 44; of sexual
goods, 1; trade, 44
foreign investment, xviii, 7–9, 27, 74, 164
FOSTA-SESTA (Allow States and Victims to
Fight Online Sex Trafficking Act and
the Stop Enabling Sex Traffickers Act),
209–210
Fox, Vicente, 147, 223n3
freedom, xxv, 12, 115, 136; of expression,
90, 102; gender, 94, 198; individual, 28;
maquiloca and, 33; NAFTA and, 10; sexual, 69; of speech, 91; women's, 32

Freeland, Chrystia, 204
free-trade agreements (FTAs), 8–11, 28,
85–86; IPR trade policies and, 43; sex
and, 6, 143
free-trade capitalism, xxviii, 13, 31–33, 132,
194, 201, 211; binaries of, 29, 33; the
body and, 74; bottomhood and, 207;
desire and, 203; diet and, 126; Honduras and, 196–197; infrastructures of,
170; limits of, 36; pornography and, 70;
queer desire and, 19–20; sex negativity of, 130; shadow economies and, 4;
transmigración and, 183; *Xipe Totec
Punk* (Martínez Silva) and, 75
free-trade flows, xxvii, 59, 128
free-trade policies, 5, 11, 34, 38–39
free-trade practices, 9, 67
friendship, xxviii, 12, 180; international,
xxvii; transnational, xxix, 200, 203; trinational, 205
The Fruit Machine (Fodey), 98
Fuller, Janine, 80, 86
Fung, Richard, 90
Fusco, Coco, 226n2

Gabilondo, Joseba, 74
Gallagher, Bob, 238n6
Gálvez, Alyshia, xxvi, 124–125, 230nn6–7
Gamboa, Edgard, 120, 122
García Canclini, Néstor, 69
García Manríquez, Hugo, xv–xix
Garinagu, 193–197, 236–237nn14–15.
See also *punta*
Gaspar de Alba, Alicia, 32
Gavi, 142
gay bars, 20, 137
gay men, 20, 59, 105, 112, 116, 140, 151, 179,
195, 228n13; AIDS and, 90, 131, 138
gender, xxviii, 35, 42, 110, 146–147, 187;
binary, 27; colonial conceptions of,
20; coloniality of, 75; constructs, xxix;
difference, 85, 210; dissidence, xxvii,
63, 195; dissidents, 136, 145, 198; feminine, 152; freedom, 94, 198; free trade
and, 30; FTAs and, 39; identity, 118–119,
179, 235n6; ideology, 211; inequalities,
10, 33; *mestizaje* and, 237n15; minorities, 118; NAFTA and, 10, 14; nonconformity, 91, 108, 176, 191, 210, 225n12;
nonnormative, 77; outlaws, 34; power
dynamics, 30; practices of First Nations
peoples, 72, 78; precarity and, 186;

gender (continued)
 queerness, 84; trade and, 19; *Untitled (Ricas y famosas)* (Rossell) and, 18; violence, 32, 181
gender-affirming care, xxix, 136, 141, 209
General Agreement on Tariffs and Trade (GATT), 43, 133, 205–206
gentrification, 21, 99
Gibson-Graham, J. K., xxv
Gill-Peterson, Jules, 137, 232n6
gimp, as related to BDSM, 39, 200–201, 206–207, 234n4, 237n2; in *Pulp Fiction*, 200
Giuliani, Rudolph, xxvi, 47
Glad Day bookstore, 90, 94, 99–101, 103f, 106, 111–112, 114–116
globalization, 10–11, 18; antiglobalization, xix, 205; neoliberal, 71; sexuality and, xxvii
global markets, 12, 29
Global South, 130, 132–133
Goffman, Erving, 15
Gómez-Barris, Macarena, 7, 226n3
goods, xxx, 3–4, 27–29, 36–37, 115, 191, 205, 209; from China, 50; cultural, 12, 84; foreign, xxiv, 45; illegal, 49 (*see also fayuca*); luxury, 14; NAFTA and, 13, 58, 80; pirated, 49, 223n3; sexual, xxvii, 1, 3, 80, 95; US, 11
Grajales, Jorge, 45–46, 48, 224n7
Greene, Oliver N., Jr., 237n14
Guajardo Villarreal, Ildefonso, 204
Guatemala, xviii, 8, 180, 195; migrants from, 172, 178
Guerrero Mc Manus, Siobhan, 7, 148, 150
Guillén Rauda, Héctor Daniel, 56
Gutiérrez, Laura G., 26, 230n5
Guzmán, Georgina, 32

Haiti, 172, 178, 198, 235n4
harmonization, 5, 7, 9; system, 3
Harmonized System (HS), 3, 220n2
hate propaganda, 87, 91, 94–95, 97–98, 115
Hennessy, Rosemary, 11, 30
Hernández, Roxana, xxix, 175, 189
Hernández Victoria, Miguel Alonso, 20–22
Hetherington, Philippa, 30
Hilderbrand, Lucas, 51
HIV+ people, 38, 134, 142, 144, 148; criminalization of, 90, 227n6; in Mexico, 132, 135–136, 138, 141, 150; sexual health of, 37

HIV/AIDS, 68, 79, 81, 87–88, 133, 135, 140, 146–148, 150, 209, 224n9; as *castigo de Díos*, 148; COVID-19 and, 232n6; criminalization of, 227n6; crisis, 84, 130–131; "disreputable disabilities" and, 225n19; drugs 36, 38, 134–138, 140–142, 150 (*see also* antiretrovirals); free trade and, 131; gay men and, 90; IP law and, 143; medicines/medications, 130–131, 133, 136–138, 141, 143, 148, 150, 152, 175, 189, 233n16 (*see also* antiretrovirals); ongoing time of, 129, 136; sex panic and, 130; treatments, 36, 130, 133–134, 141–143. *See also* activism: AIDS; activists: HIV/AIDS
Hoang, Kimberly Kay, 13, 220n3, 223n24
homophobia, 86, 93, 100, 105–106, 110, 119, 135, 146, 180
homosex, xxvii, 28
homosexuality, 82, 84–85; communism and, 98
Honduras, 8, 185, 195, 198; Garinagu in, 196–197, 237n14; *mestizaje* in, 237n15; migrants from, 172, 178, 182–183
hooks, bell, 86, 111–112
Hooper, Tom, 85, 90, 99
hormones, 39, 136, 152, 231–232nn5–6
Hotel Garage, huilas mexicanas, 51–57, 62, 70
Hothead Paisan: Homicidal Lesbian Terrorist (DiMassa), 110, 112
Howard, Y, 110
Hughes, Holly, 104

identity, 6, 35, 201, 206; Afro-Indigenous, 197; American, 26; female heterosexuality and, 14; feminine sexualized, 16; gender, 118–119, 179, 235n6; Honduran, 196; Indigenous cultures and, 15; *mestizaje* and, xxiv; Mexico's twentieth-century, xix; national, 111; normative categories of, 19; politics, 159
ideology: capital, 29; free-trade, 4–5, 7–8, 28, 40, 201; gender, 211; NAFTA as, 38; neoliberal, 14
illicit reproductions, 36, 44, 50, 70. *See also* piracy; *piratería*
immigration, 10, 177
imperialism: capitalist, 26; cultural, 84–85, 93, 111; debt, 11; of nation-states, 224n5; US, 19, 85, 93, 111
indigeneity, 18, 39, 73–74, 83, 195

Marak, Andrae M., 172
Martínez Silva, César, 39, 71–78, 226n1.
    See also Orgy punk
Marx, Karl, xxvi
masculinity, xxix, 20, 77; cis, 12; hypermasculinity, 19; toxic, 14; trans, 80, 98, 106, 110, 112, 190; working-class, 27
Masri, Hana, 188
materiality, 7; of the archives, 99; of the body, xxvii, 125; of experience, 13–14
Matla, 56–58, 60–61, 63, 225n13, 225n15
Matlarock Films, 56–67, 70, 225n16
McRuer, Robert, 23, 125, 162
Mecos Films, 59–60, 225n10
medications: abortion, 209; affordability of, 134; HIV/AIDS, 131, 133, 135–138, 140–142, 148, 150–152, 175, 189, 233n16 (*see also* antiretrovirals); hormone, 137; immunosuppressing, 235n6; life-giving, xxix; in Mexico, 132; for STIs, 28; trans people and, 231n5. *See also* antiretrovirals; biologics; hormones
Mercer, Kobena, 25–26
MERCOSUR, 8
mestizaje, xxiv–xxv, 15, 195, 237n15
mexicanidad, xxiv, 15, 56, 59
Mexico, 3, 8–9, 186, 225n12, 234n5, 237n18; abortion activist organizations in, 209; anti-sex trafficking laws, 64, 180–181, 225nn13–14, 236n10; Black population in, 197; Canada and, xxv, xxviii, 229n25; copyright infringement in, 43; corporate leaders in, 203; debility of, 162; elite of, 14, 18, 21, 144; fatphobia in, 128; foreign investors and, 172; foreign policy of, 22; gay tourism in, 221n13; Guatemala and, xviii, 8; Guerrero, 161, 172, 178; HIV/AIDS in, 84, 131–136, 138, 141, 147–148, 150–151, 227n6; homoeroticism in, 146; Indigenous peoples in, xxiv, 131; informal economy in, 42–43; IP protections and, 142; Ley General Para Prevenir, Sancionar y Erradicar los Delitos en Materia de Trata de Personas, 63, 181; Maquiladora Program, 235n2; medical industry in, 48; Michoacán, 172, 178; migrants from, 235n4; migrants in, 174–175, 178, 180, 183, 192; migration in, 181, 236n10, 236n13; NAFTA and, 5, 10–11, 26, 68–69, 72–74, 85, 123–126, 134–135, 141–142, 170, 180; NAFTA 2.0 and, 84, 200, 204–

205, 227n2; NAFTA time and, 198, 206; National Human Rights Commission (Comisión Nacional de Derechos Humanos, CNDH), 140–141; piracy in, 44, 49–50, 223n3; politics of illness in, 161; pornography in, 37, 42–51, 55–58, 60, 62, 66, 95, 224n7; pornways and, 43–44; Programa Frontera Sur, 210; queer sexual cultures in, 160; quota system in, 220n1; sex trafficking discourse in, 30, 222n24; sexual permissiveness and, 26; tariffs and, xxix; tourists and, 144, 162; underground film in, 224n7; United States and, xviii–xix, xxiv–xxv, xxviii, 1, 9, 11, 14, 18, 55–56, 77, 164, 204, 220n2, 237n3; US border, 1, 3, 30–31, 38, 83, 193, 235n4; US corn and, xxvii, 56, 124, 230n5; violence in, 31, 170, 181; women in, 14. *See also* chacal; *la chingada*; *fayuca*; *feminicidios*; Malinche; Treaty of Guadalupe Hidalgo; workers: *maquila*
Mexico City, xxvi, 1, 5, 23, 35, 38, 73, 138, 147, 152, 184; Archivo El Insulto, 224n6; businessmen, 11; *chacales* in, 221n12; Ex-Teresa Arte Actual, 120, 144; Garibaldi, 22, 46; gay bars in, 20; gay culture in, 21; Hemispheric Institute of Performance and Politics Encuentro, 199; HIV/AIDS in, 131–132, 141, 151, 234n24; La Lagunilla, 45; Mexico City Policy, 224n9; El Museo de la Ciudad de México, 131, 144, 146; National Autonomous University of Mexico (UNAM), 161, 181; pornography in, 45–47, 55–56, 58, 224n7; sex shops in, 56, 61; sexual culture in, 51; sexual and gender dissidents in, 145; Tepito (Baratillo), 37, 39, 41–42, 44–47, 49–51, 55, 60, 64, 70; UNAM, 161, 181; underground cultures of, 129; women in, 14, 18; Zona Rosa, 22
Mexico-US Business Committee (MEXUS), 35, 203
la migra, 172–174, 183, 192
migration, 11, 20, 176, 178, 180, 183, 193; activism, 194; activists, 179; of Black aesthetics, 197; capitalism and, 185; Central American, xviii, 236n8; *chicas trans* and, 189; criminalization of, 33, 181; Garinagu and, 196; of LGBTQ peoples, 198, 236n8; panics over, xxix; surveillance, 28

Orme, William, 9, 220n5
Orozco, Rosie, 55

Parrini, Rodrigo, 7, 69
Party of the Democratic Revolution (PRD), 9, 147
patent laws, 131–132, 135, 137, 151
patents, 43, 131, 133–135, 143, 151; duration of, 142; pipeline, 134, 231n3
Paz, Octavio, xxiv–xxv, xxvii, xixx; *El laberinto de la soledad*, xix
Peña Nieto, Enrique, 73, 147, 201
performance art, 38, 62, 67, 75; durational, 175. *See also* 2boys.tv; Bülle Hernández, Erika; Lechedevirgen Trimegisto; Martínez Silva, César
performance studies, as field, 4, 13, 145, 230n5; queer, xxvii–xxviii
Perot, Ross, 3, 203
Pfizer, 143
pharmaceutical industry, 132–134, 136, 148, 231n3
photography, 44; portraiture, 15, 18; Rossell's, 14, 74; Sánchez Gómez's, 140; Slim's, 23
pill dividing and stockpiling, xxix, 36, 141
pink tide, 73, 226n3
piracy, 4, 36, 43–44, 49–51, 223n3; as political act, 224n5; porn, 43, 70; terrorism and, 43, 224n4
piratería, 45, 50
pirates, 44; media, 43; porn, 37, 39, 44, 51, 60, 63, 70, 135; Somali, 224n5
pleasure, xxvii, xxix, 4, 6, 38–39, 109, 154, 189, 206–207; Black and Brown, 115; bottomhood and, 148; capitalism and, 5; eco-pleasure, 196; embodied, 156; everyday practices and, xxvi; female, 15, 18, 55; feminine sexual, 18; fisting and, 108; free-trade capitalism and, 36, 211; gimp, as related to BDSM, and, 201; intimate personal, 2–3; NAFTA time and, 176–177, 194, 197; neoliberalism and, 18, 75; *punta* and, 192–194; queer, 20, 176; sex and, 129, 148; sexual, 18, 95–96, 133, 136, 143–144, 159, 176, 198; trade and, 19
policing, 28, 81; borders and, 171–172; of fat feminine bodies, 123; of free trade, 206; of sex workers, 69; trafficking discourse and, 30, 209; zero-tolerance, 48. *See also* Interpol

Pollard, Aaron, 199, 201–202. *See also* 2boys.tv
polygeographies, 8, 34, 131–132, 151; of the Americas, 178, 198; of Central America, 195; of the marketplace, 20; of Mexico-Canada-US borderlands, 206
Pons, Alba, 7
porn/pornography, 36, 43–49, 51, 54–63, 67–70, 95; in the 1970s, 45; actors, 55, 61–64, 66, 70; BBW (Big Beautiful Women), 62, 67, 70, 225n17; booths, 44, 59; Canadian, 101–102, 228n13; companies, 59–60, 225n10; consumers, 67; *Deep Throat*, 45; Dworkin and MacKinnon on, 92–94, 227n7; feminism and, 87, 91; fisting and, 229n20; gay, 59, 225n10; heterosexual, 93; industry, 37, 43–44, 49, 56, 58–59, 87, 102; kink, 151; lesbian communities and, 105; magazines, 101; mainstream, 91; Mexican, 41–42, 46, 51, 55, 60, 224n7; panic and, 55, 63, 67–68, 105, 220n4, 229n17; piracy of, 43, 51, 55–56, 64, 70; pirates, 37, 39, 44, 51, 60, 63, 70, 135; postpornography, 63; smuggling, 4, 101; surveillance and, 28; US, 63, 70. *See also* Matlarock Films; Mecos Films
pornways, 42–44, 49, 51, 56–57, 62
power, xxix, 26–27, 40, 108, 111, 175, 177, 194; abuses of, xxviii, 102, 210; of aesthetics, 38; bottomhood and, xxiv, xxvii; of Canada Customs, 93–94, 96; coloniality of, 10, 75; corporate, 118; dynamics, xviii, 19, 30; eroticism of, 202, 207; exchange, 201, 206; Foucault on, 219n2; of the Global North, 130; green neoliberalism and, 196; hierarchies of, xix, 220n5; inequalities, 203; networks of, 7; panic and, 73; of the pharmaceutical industry, 133, 150; relations, xxvii; sex and, xxvi, xxviii; sexual, xxiv, 168; structures, 51; trade and, xxvi, 226n7; women's purchasing, 223n2
power bottoms, xxiv, 211
Prasad, Pavithra, 177
precarity, 3, 23, 30–31, 70, 130, 135, 174, 186, 194
Preston, John, 79–80, 86
pride, 6; flag, 22; parades, 147
production, 8, 11; colonial knowledge, xv; cultural, xxiv, 30, 34, 36–37; of desire,

tequila crisis (*el error de diciembre*), 21, 234n5

terrorism, 12, 36, 87, 123; pornography as, 93; piracy and, 43–44, 70, 224n4

Thames, Carol, 11–12, 229n23

thinness, 37, 125–126

Thomas, Trish, 106–108

Tijuana, 21, 35, 38, 172, 184; *el Bordo*, 174; Caritas, 189; Comunidad Cultural de Tijuana LGBTI AC (COCUT), 179, 182; Enclave Rabia Caracol, 179, 190–191; Espacio Migrante, 179; as free-trade zone, 31; gay bars in, 20; gay men in, 131; Health Frontiers in Tijuana (HFiT), 138, 140, 232n9; HIV/AIDS in, 138; hormones and, 232n6; Jornada por la Diversidad Sexual, 176, 180, 182–183; Lavanda CLIT, 179; LGBT community center in, 137, 141; LGBTQ safe houses in, 176; Lumina Foto-Café, 187, 192; *maquila* workers in, 31–32; migrants in, 176–181, 185, 187, 189–192, 198 (see also *chicas trans*); El Otro Lado, 235n4; Playas de Tijuana, 177, 179, 181–183, 191–192; trans women in, 140, 232n6

Tijuana-San Diego border, 11, 137–138, 140, 172–173, 175, 178, 191. *See also* Operation Gatekeeper

Title 42, 175, 235n4

TLCAN (Tratado de Libre Comercio de América del Norte), xv, xviii–xix, 68, 73, 75, 76f, 123, 199–200

Toronto, 35, 37, 81, 93, 96, 112, 116, 238n6; gay and lesbian bookstores of, 99 (*see also* Glad Day bookstore); NAFTA experts in, 84; police department, 115; queer migrants in, 236n7; sexual culture in, 102; Toronto Gay Film Festival, 60; Toronto Women's Bathhouse Committee, 229n23. *See also* The ArQuives; Zami

Torres-Ruiz, Antonio, 141, 234n24

Tortorici, Zeb, 44, 221n11, 224n6

tourism, 21, 162, 196; Garinagu and, 194, 197; gay, 221n13; sexual dissidence and, 145. *See also* sex tourism

trade liberalization, xvii, 11, 91

traffic, 27–29, 175, 222n23; criminal, 46; improper, 206; licit, 68; NAFTA's sexual, xxix

trafficking, 12, 30, 33, 180–181, 208–210, 222n23; abortion, xxix, 209; drug, xviii, xxix; human, xxix, 33, 180, 209; transgender, 238n1. *See also* sex trafficking

Trafficking in Persons (TIP) protocol, 64, 180

Trafficking Victims Protection Act (TVPA), 55, 236n11

translation, xv, xviii, xxvi

transmigración, 183–185, 236n12

trans migrants, 38–39, 174, 176–177, 180, 183–184, 189, 198; nightlife, 192; police and, 187

transnational corporations, 11, 125

trans people, 119, 129, 132, 151, 176, 182; gender-affirming health care and, 131, 141; HIV and, 140; hormone therapy and, 231n5; rights of, 136

Treaty of Guadalupe Hidalgo, xviii, 11, 77

Trudeau, Justin, 3, 119, 201

Trump, Donald, 3, 118, 172, 201, 204–205, 222n20, 238n6; homophobia and, 119; López Obrador and, 203; Mexico City Policy and, 224n9; Migrant Protection Protocols, 175; NAFTA and, xix, 26–27, 116, 142, 205

Two spirit, xxix, 74, 80, 118

United States, 5, 58, 68, 72–73, 156, 174, 179, 205; abortion pills and, 209, 231n5; anti-immigrant sentiment in, 11; asylum in, 235n4; bottomness and, xxix; Canada and, 9–10, 37, 80–85, 104, 106, 116, 119, 124, 226–227nn1–2; carceral system in, 189; censorship in, 104; Congress, 5, 119, 135, 226n7; corn from, 56; corporate leaders in, 203; *fayuca* from, 45; federal workers in, 229n26; First Amendment rights and, 90–91; free trade of sex toys and, 220n2; gender-affirming healthcare in, 136; Gini coefficient and, 21; grindhouse theaters in, 46; HIV/AIDS in, 133–136, 138, 140–142, 150–151, 227n6; McCarthy era in, 98; Mérida Initiative and, 223n3; Mexico and, xviii–xix, xxiv–xxv, xxviii, 1, 9, 11, 14, 18, 55–56, 77, 164, 204, 220n2, 237n3; migrants and, 27, 38, 174, 183–185, 210, 222n19, 235nn1–2; migration and, 236n13; murder of Black and Brown people in, 147; panic in, 229n17; porn from, 41, 51, 56, 61–62, 94, 102; Salinas and, 164; sexuality models from, 18; sex wars in, 87; Supreme Court, 224n8; surveillance policies in, 223n26; Trump and, 172